The Many Colors c

The Many Colors of Crime

Inequalities of Race, Ethnicity, and Crime in America

EDITED BY

Ruth D. Peterson, Lauren J. Krivo, and John Hagan

New York University Press

NEW YORK AND LONDON

NEW YORK UNIVERSITY PRESS
New York and London
www.nyupress.org

Library of Congress Cataloging-in-Publication Data
The many colors of crime : inequalities of race, ethnicity, and crime in
America / edited by Ruth D. Peterson, Lauren J. Krivo, and John Hagan.
p. cm. — (New perspectives in crime, deviance, and law series)
Includes bibliographical references and index.
ISBN-13: 978-0-8147-6719-1 (cloth : alk. paper)
ISBN-10: 0-8147-6719-2 (cloth : alk. paper)
ISBN-13: 978-0-8147-6720-7 (pbk. : alk. paper)
ISBN-10: 0-8147-6720-6 (pbk. : alk. paper)
1. Crime—United States. 2. Discrimination in criminal justice
administration—United States. 3. Minorities—United States.
I. Peterson, Ruth D. II. Krivo, Lauren Joy. III. Hagan, John, 1946–
IV. Series.
HV6789.M34 2006
364.973—dc22   2006003998

New York University Press books are printed on acid-free paper,
and their binding materials are chosen for strength and durability.

Manufactured in the United States of America
c 10 9 8 7 6 5 4 3 2 1
p 10 9 8 7 6 5 4 3 2 1

In Memory of
Dorothy Hagan and Charles Hagan
Marcia Krivo Weinberg and Albert Krivo
Lenora W. Peterson and Walter L. Peterson, Sr.

Contents

Acknowledgments

We are very grateful to the authors for their important contributions to this volume, and for their commitment to engaging in and facilitating work that will foster an understanding of what we collectively refer to as the "deeper meaning" of the interrelationships among race/ethnicity, crime, and criminal justice. We asked contributors to think in terms of "messing up" any simplistic understandings that we have of these relationships and to offer suggestions for "fixing" the field. They all took this task to heart and delivered just the kinds of papers that are needed. Moreover, they did so while conforming to our timetable (fast) and space (limited) demands. They have been the most wonderful of colleagues.

We are also grateful for contributors' participation in the activities that paved the way for this volume. Many of the authors spent long hours with us in workshops and other settings, engaging in thoughtful discussions about how best to foster quality research on the race/ethnicity–crime/criminal justice topic. This volume is the direct result of those meetings, and it represents the commitment of the contributors to laying the groundwork for the theoretical and empirical challenges ahead. We must also acknowledge workshop participants who did not develop chapters for the book. Their imprint is nonetheless on the volume through their contributions to the discussions that helped authors to refine their thinking. Thanks, Stacy Armour, Paul Bellair, Danice Brown, Khalilah Brown-Dean, Christopher Browning, Jorge Chavez, Dana Haynie, Donald Hutcherson, Kecia Johnson, Harwood McClerking, Joane Nagel, Mary Pattillo, Danielle Payne, Townsand Price-Spratlen, Sherod Thaxton, Harold Weiss, Patricia White, and Valerie Wright.

We are also very grateful to the National Science Foundation, especially its sociology and law and social sciences programs, for providing financial and institutional support for the workshops and meetings that allowed us to discuss and respond to one another's ideas about directions for the field. These stimulating discussions inspired us and facilitated our progress in developing the chapters. Importantly, too, they led us to recognize that important steps in moving the field can come from building on ongoing cutting-edge research and theorizing; focusing on the complexity and messiness of the relationships examined; integrating the ideas and perspectives of younger scholars with those of more seasoned colleagues; and drawing on the innovative ideas that stem from exchange among scholars of varied intellectual traditions and racial/ethnic backgrounds. As a whole, the volume is grounded in these dimensions, which were nurtured through our NSF-sponsored workshops.

We also received institutional support from a number of other entities. The Criminal Justice Research Center at Ohio State University provided the administrative home for the project. Ohio State University's Department of Sociology gave an intellectual boost to the project when it held a conference on "Inequality, Crime, and Justice" that featured a number of our contributors and gave us an additional forum for exchange of ideas about race/ethnicity–crime/criminal justice. We thank Robert F. Kaufman, chair of the sociology department, for giving us this opportunity. Ohio State University's College of Social and Behavioral Sciences provided support for a graduate research associate to assist with developing and finalizing the book. We are particularly grateful to Associate Dean Jan Weisenberger for her wisdom in seeing the value of supporting this work. Certainly we owe a debt of gratitude to the departments, schools, and organizations that are the intellectual homes of the authors: the American Bar Foundation; criminology/criminal justice/justice studies departments/schools at Arizona State University, Florida International University, the University of Florida, the University of Maryland, the University of Missouri–St. Louis, and Northeastern University; the College of Law at Columbia University; the human development and family studies department at Auburn University; the School of Social Work at the University of Houston; and the Departments of Sociology at George Washington University, Harvard University, Howard University, University of Iowa, University of Miami, Northwestern University, Ohio State University, University of Oregon, Stanford University, and the University of Washington.

We would like to thank several graduate and undergraduate students who worked diligently and very professionally to help bring the book to fruition. The team was led by Diana Karafin (who is also a coauthor of one of the chapters). Without a doubt, Diana's organizational skills kept our work on track, and her intellectual insights contributed to the creation of a better book. Susan Ortiz joined the project in its later phases and brought to the work the same kind of commitment and attention as Diana. We thank Kareema McCree-Wilson and Alyssa Bernhoffer, undergraduate students who worked hard on putting together an integrated bibliography. Graduate students Danice Brown and Valerie Wright lent a hand with the myriad of last-minute logistical details. We cannot adequately express our gratitude to all of these students. Finally, we dedicate this book to the memory of our parents, whose own approaches to "truth seeking" continue to inspire us.

Ruth D. Peterson
Lauren J. Krivo
John Hagan

Introduction

Inequalities of Race, Ethnicity, and Crime in America

Ruth D. Peterson, Lauren J. Krivo, and John Hagan

This book broadens and deepens our understanding of the way race, ethnicity, and crime are interrelated. It grew from discussions by a small working group who came together because of dissatisfaction with the way race and ethnicity are approached in criminological research. These constructs typically are treated as distinguishing features of the demographic distribution of crime while shaping its popular imagery. Much existing work focuses on etiological questions such as whether social disorganization, differential association, or strain apply in the same way to people and populations of different colors. Race and ethnicity are infrequently given serious consideration as structural influences creating criminogenic conditions; the responses of actors, groups, and institutions; and the consequences that flow from these. That is, current work often fails to consider how race and ethnicity are themselves central organizing principles within and across societies. Indeed, these dimensions of stratification condition the very laws that make certain behaviors criminal, the perception of crime and those who are criminalized, the distribution of criminogenic conditions and processes, the determination of who becomes a victim of crime under which circumstances, the responses to laws and crime that make some more likely to be defined as criminal, and the way individuals and communities are positioned and empowered to respond to crime. We believe that a fuller understanding of the inequitable sources and consequences of crime and violence can only come when race and ethnicity are taken seriously as organizing principles that explicitly and thoroughly permeate theoretical discussions and empirical analyses.

What are the concrete implications of such an approach? Overall, it will complicate our theory and research. Theoretically, race, ethnicity, and crime are social constructions that should be conceptualized in ways that take into account their broader and changing meaning. Empirical investigations should take these complex conceptualizations seriously while (1) moving beyond the black-white dichotomy to consider the *many colors* of crime and victimization, including among frequently neglected groups; (2) considering the often neglected intersections of race, ethnicity, gender, and class; (3) demythologizing both the stereotypes of the *criminalblackman*[1] and the innocence and integrity of whiteness; and (4) considering the diversity within *and* across groups along the many dimensions of societal stratification.

A fuller understanding also means taking steps to conceptualize, measure, and model the interconnections among race, ethnicity, crime, and criminal justice in ways that embed our work in relation to the multiple contexts and positionings of groups within society. This premise calls for analyses that (1) have a more structural, institutional, and historical focus; (2) capture the multiple dimensions and levels of interaction that undergird social relationships and impact outcomes for groups and individuals; (3) examine the interplay among different central constructs, e.g., structure and culture, race/ethnicity and agency, race/ethnicity and politics; (4) question the normalization of aspects of crime and criminal justice, e.g., violence against girls and criminality or incarceration by race/ethnicity; (5) have a broader comparative dimension, e.g., across multiple groups, societies, and time periods; and (6) examine the collateral consequences of criminal justice and societal policies.

This book provides a series of papers expressly designed to complicate the conceptual and empirical meaning of race and ethnicity as they relate to crime and criminal justice. Each chapter addresses an unanswered substantive question using one or more of the above foci. Authors were asked to begin from the premise set forth above that research and theory must incorporate race and ethnicity as fundamental orienting constructs in contemporary society. The papers are explicit about how this broad view shapes the particular aspect of crime and criminal justice being investigated. Contributors were also asked to focus on their topic of concern from a fresh and innovative perspective in order to set the stage for new directions in theory and research. Therefore, they each explicitly identify the types of investigations that should flow from the concepts introduced and/or the empirical findings. Although the topics are diverse, taken as a whole they seek to put a new and critical face on analyses of crime and criminal justice in which race and ethnicity take center stage.

The book is comprised of eighteen chapters, with several distinct types of papers. At the outset, Robert J. Sampson and Lydia Bean provide a discussion that orients the reader to the importance of moving the field toward a deeper understanding of the race/ethnicity–crime relationship. In their view, a deeper understanding of race and crime must come from incorporating spatial inequality into concepts of (dis)advantage by race, considering seriously the implications of immigration, and revising the view of culture that dominates current thinking. In developing their perspective, they anticipate a number of the concepts, empirical strategies, and interpretations of findings of the chapters that follow.

The remaining chapters take a variety of approaches. Some are conceptual, identifying constructs that must be incorporated and outlining issues that must be corrected to facilitate improved research. Others provide illustrative empirical work on populations or intersectionalities that have seldom, if ever, been examined. And still others address the social contexts for the racial and ethnic patterning of crime, or examine the mechanisms and processes by which race and ethnicity are connected to crime and criminal justice. Reflecting this variety, the book is divided into four topical areas: (1) Constructs and Conceptual Approaches; (2) Populations and Intersectionalities; (3) Contexts and Settings; and (4) Mechanisms and Processes.

Chapters on "Constructs and Conceptual Approaches" tackle issues of how race, ethnicity, and crime should be reconceptualized in order to motivate new thinking and analytic investigations. To date, most work has a limited view of race, of crime, and of the criminal justice workforce. For example, research often focuses on contrasts between Whites and Blacks. Doing so oversimplifies inequalities of race, ethnicity, and crime by viewing race/ethnicity as a dichotomy. And, it exaggerates differences by contrasting the most privileged group with the most long-term historically oppressed population. As a result, this limited view of race reinforces stereotypic understandings of group differentiation. Marjorie Zatz and Nancy Rodriguez place this oversimplification in perspective by admonishing researchers not to simply add other racial and ethnic groups and stir, but rather to problematize the way race, ethnicity, gender, class, and crime converge differentially across time and place.

Research on crime has also mainly analyzed the Federal Bureau of Investigation's (FBI) seven index offenses of homicide, forcible rape, robbery, aggravated assault, burglary, larceny, and motor vehicle theft. Emphasizing street crimes that constitute only a fraction of violations of criminal codes in the United States may reify the stereotype of the *criminalblackman* and direct attention away from the full range of criminal activities and the relative representation of participants with less colorful backgrounds. Vernetta Young's conceptual paper warns us of these possibilities and of the way they misconstrue the crime problem, thereby hindering the development of theories and policies that properly address the diverse nature of crime. Finally, racial representation in the occupations of criminal justice are presumed to affect disparities in crime and justice outcomes. Yet, little research explores theoretically or empirically the role of diversity among justice workers in crime and case processing. Geoff K. Ward takes up this issue, presenting an analytic framework concerning the hierarchical organization of the justice workforce to bring the array of occupations into systemic view. Application of the framework highlights the need to define justice workers, conceptualize the substantive representation of ethnoracial groups, evaluate the impact of diversity in the justice workforce on outcomes, and conduct cross-national comparisons.

The next set of chapters on "Populations and Intersectionalities" flows directly from recognition of the need for criminological research to expand the groups explored. For example, several of the chapters investigate understudied populations. María B. Vélez examines the racial invariance thesis as it applies to crime among Latinos in Chicago compared to their African American counterparts, arguing that lower Latino violence results from the distinct structural contexts of their communities. Ramiro Martinez, Jr., and Amie L. Nielsen attempt to elucidate the relative importance for crime of immigrant status versus Black race. They evaluate this by studying neighborhoods in Miami, Florida, and comparing Haitians (a Black and immigrant group) to Latinos (a heavily white and predominantly immigrant group in southern Florida) and to African Americans. Alexander T. Vazsonyi and Elizabeth Trejos-Castillo attempt to broaden our understanding of the role of race in crime and deviance by examining *rural* African American youth in the southern Black Belt. Doing so helps to correct the urban bias that is common in research on race and crime.

Additional chapters assess the consequences for offending and victimization of the intersectionality of race and ethnicity with other critical social statuses, particularly gender and class. De Coster and Heimer assess the literatures on masculinities, femininities, and violent offending and offer a structural interactionist perspective to guide future research. This perspective focuses on the way individuals make meaning of their social worlds within the context of cross-cutting social inequalities. Toya Z. Like and Jody Miller challenge race and crime researchers to incorporate gender into theoretical and empirical analyses in order to properly comprehend the impact of race and racism. They illustrate the benefits of doing so through their qualitative study of violence against African American girls in a distressed urban community.

Fundamental to the role of race and ethnicity in U.S. society is the fact that diverse populations are differentially situated with respect to a host of social and economic conditions that vary across group, time, and place. This is strikingly evident in terms of residential segregation, with large portions of Blacks and Whites living in distinct and racially homogeneous neighborhoods. To varying degrees, the experience of Latinos and different immigrant groups follows the same pattern. Racial and ethnic residential segregation is further interconnected with economic segregation, resulting in complex patterns of racial, ethnic, and class segregation. Along with residential differentiation, groups are often segregated in the types of schools attended, workplaces, social circles, and religious institutional memberships. Our third group of chapters considers the importance of these and other aspects of "Contexts and Settings" as sources of crime and its collateral consequences. Gary LaFree, Robert M. O'Brien, and Eric Baumer consider differential trends in arrest rates for Blacks and Whites in light of changing U.S. macrosocial and economic conditions. They mainly observe convergence in these trends consistent with racial assimilation views. Robert D. Crutchfield, Ross L. Matsueda, and Kevin Drakulich examine whether differences in social disorder and the local labor market context help to explain why African American, Latino, and Asian communities have high levels of violent crime.

Avelardo Valdez explores the interrelationships among drug markets, economic change, and involvement in the illegal economy among Mexican Americans in San Antonio. He highlights the devastating consequences of the spread of drug use and sales within this group, and the way they result from long-term social, economic, and policy changes that isolate select communities. Alex R. Piquero, Valerie West, Jeffrey Fagan, and Jan Holland consider the consequences of disproportionate incarceration of African Americans and Hispanics for the well-being of neighborhoods in New York City over a twelve-year period. The last paper exploring contexts and settings is by Lauren J. Krivo, Ruth D. Peterson, and Diana L. Karafin, who analyze perceptions of crime and safety in four racially and economically distinct neighborhoods. They emphasize the potential significance of internal and external conditions that differentiate unique race-by-class areas, particularly privileging the White middle-class community.

Chapters examining "Mechanisms and Processes" comprise the fourth section of the book. The papers take as a starting point that a deeper understanding of the meaning of the race-crime link involves not only assessing different patterns and contexts but also explicating the mechanisms by which the link occurs. This requires a focus on the way race and ethnicity are interconnected with structural conditions, cultural orientations, individual agency, and other factors that result in crime or different outcomes of criminal justice. Doris Marie Provine uses the crack cocaine saga to elucidate the way negative racial stereotypes animate policy thinking and influence policy choices to the disadvantage of subordinate populations. Doing so should encourage critical, race-sensitive thinking about the policy-making process. Wenona Rymond-Richmond explores how cognitive maps serve to organize the activities of neighborhood residents to maintain their safety and avoid conflict. She also highlights the significant harm that results when policymakers ignore these cognitive maps in their quest to improve communities.

Carla Shedd and John Hagan outline a comparative conflict theory that articulates the way the nature of police contact influences the development of differentiated youthful perceptions of criminal injustice across racial and ethnic groups. These adolescent perceptions are critical because they are enduring and may extend to perceptions of other types of injustice and to criminal behavior. Finally, Ross L. Matsueda, Kevin Drakulich, and Charis E. Kubrin explore a key mechanism that has been argued to link race/ethnic with violent crime—cultural codes of violence. They use data for Seattle to capture neighborhood codes, as distinct from individual codes, of violence, and investigate whether variation in these codes exist across African American, Latino, and Asian communities.

Taken together, the fine set of chapters in this volume offer keen and varied insights into the ways in which race and ethnicity permeate views and actions of crime and the criminal justice system in the United States. The meaning of race and ethnicity in crime and criminal justice is important but underinvestigated. Indeed, progress in expanding knowledge in this area has been hampered by a lack of a coherent approach and a failure to put forth race and ethnicity as core concerns in their own right rather than as simply dichotomous independent variables in analyses of aggregate and survey data. The papers in this volume offer correctives to these limited approaches. However, we acknowledge an important shortcoming of the chapters. They are almost entirely directed to the United States, though there obviously is much to be learned about race and crime beyond this nation's borders. As scholars continue to investigate the complex interrelationships among race/ethnicity, crime, and criminal justice, it will become increasingly important to situate the United States in the context of other diverse societies. In the meantime, the chapters herein offer starting places for a more holistic approach to the study of race/ethnicity, crime, and criminal justice that centers analyses in the positioning of groups within society. As such, these works should push forward a new agenda that accords race and ethnicity status as central orienting components of crime and criminal justice research and theorizing.

NOTE

1. Russell 1998; see also Young in this volume.

Chapter 1

Cultural Mechanisms and Killing Fields
A Revised Theory of Community-Level Racial Inequality

Robert J. Sampson and Lydia Bean

Ten years ago, Sampson and Wilson proposed a theory of race and urban inequality to explain the disproportionate representation of African Americans as victims and offenders in violent crime.[1] The basic idea put forth was that community-level patterns of racial inequality give rise to the social isolation and ecological concentration of the truly disadvantaged, which in turn leads to structural barriers and cultural adaptations that undermine social organization and ultimately the control of crime. According to this perspective, "race" holds no distinct scientific credibility as a cause of violence—rather, it is a marker for the constellation of social contexts that are differentially allocated by racial status in American society. Sampson and Wilson pursued this logic to argue that the community-level causes of violence are the same for both Whites and Blacks but that racial segregation by community differentially exposes members of minority groups to key violence-inducing and violence-protecting social mechanisms, thereby explaining Black-White disparities in violence.[2] Their thesis has come to be known as "racial invariance" in the fundamental causes of crime.

In this chapter, we revisit the central arguments of the racial invariance thesis. Our goal is to build on recent findings and articulate new theoretical directions for the study of race, ethnicity, and violence. The good news motivating this effort is that in a short ten-year span many research advances have been made and large-scale secular changes have dramatically reduced the crime problem in American society. Indeed, a veritable explosion of research on race and crime has taken place in recent years, including numerous direct tests of the thesis of relative invariance in the causes of crime by race. At the same time, society has changed in ways that are decidedly for the better, so much so that the United States is now witnessing one of the lowest rates of violence it has seen since the mid-1960s, which benefits Blacks and Whites alike.

Less noticed in some circles but equally relevant, American society has grown to be more diverse in interesting ways. We have witnessed an increasing representation of ethnic groups and increasing immigration from around the world, especially among Latinos. These changes have led to what some consider surprising paradoxes, such as the finding that Mexican immigrants, despite their economic disadvantage, experience disproportionately lower rates of violence compared to second- and third-generation Americans. Concentrated immigrant enclaves also appear to be comparatively safe. Increasing diversity and immigration have thus not meant increasing crime, as many imagine—if anything, the opposite is true.

The bad news is that the bleak picture of Black disadvantage relative to Whites (and Latinos) remains as durable as ever when it comes to violence and the criminal justice system. Sampson and Wilson wrote that "the evidence is clear that African Americans face dismal and worsening odds when it comes to crime in the streets and the risk of incarceration."[3] These dismal odds are still with us. African Americans are six times more likely to be murdered than Whites,[4] and homicide remains the leading cause of death among young African Americans.[5] Both police records and self-reported surveys continue to show disproportionate involvement in serious violence among Blacks,[6] and nearly one in three Black males will enter prison during his lifetime compared to less than 5 percent of White males.[7] Moreover, even as crime continues to decline, African Americans are at increasing risk of incarceration and subsequent weak attachment to the labor force, which in turn reinforces Black disadvantage and involvement in crime.[8]

The question of race and crime thus remains as salient as ever, but its parameters have changed. There is now more empirical evidence on which to assess theoretical claims, and the increasing diversification of society demands that we incorporate ethnicity and immigration more centrally into the theoretical picture along with an apparently robust decline in rates of violence. This chapter takes aim at these challenges by revisiting and expanding the theoretical grounds that were plowed by Sampson and Wilson.[9] One chapter cannot do justice to the complexity of the challenge, of course, so we must necessarily be selective in our points of emphasis. For example, it is beyond the scope of this chapter to engage in a detailed review of the literature, cover crimes other than violent ones, or review debates about the correct definition of "neighborhood."[10] Our strategy, then, is to summarize the literature produced after 1995 by highlighting key findings in a broad-brush format. We are fortunate in this effort to be able to rely on independent assessments of recent research that allow conclusions to be drawn about the racial invariance thesis.[11]

Once the basic patterns in recent research are laid out, we turn to promising new directions in conceptualizations of communities, race, and violence. Our argument highlights the implications of (1) "ecological dissimilarity" and spatial inequality by race, (2) ethnicity and immigration, and (3) a revised cultural perspective on violence. Our contention is that research on race and crime has been hampered by its persistent attempts to control for community-level conditions that are not comparable across racial groups. Moreover, prior research neglects extralocal processes of spatial inequality, gives little attention to the implications of increasing ethnic diversity, and takes an impoverished view of culture. On the latter, we present a critique of cultural modes of theorizing in criminology, followed by a theoretical formulation that draws on recent advances in the sociology of culture.

Communities, Race, and Crime

The dominant tradition in criminology seeks to distinguish offenders from nonoffenders, so it comes as no surprise that it is from this tradition that the race question has typically been addressed. Sampson and Wilson promoted instead a community-level explanation that examined the way community structures and cultures produced differential rates of crime.[12] Their unit of analysis was thus the community and not the individual. Using this strategy as a starting point, they posed two questions.[13] To what extent do rates of Black crime vary by type of ecological area? Is it possible to reproduce in White communities the structural circumstances under which many Blacks live? To the first question they responded that Blacks are not a homogeneous group any more than are Whites. It is racial stereotyping that assigns to Blacks a distinct or homogeneous character, allowing simplistic comparisons of Black-White group differences in crime. In fact, there is tremendous heterogeneity among Black neighborhoods that corresponds to variations in crime rates. Sampson and Wilson hypothesized that if the structural sources of variation in crime are not unique by race, then rates of crime by Blacks should vary with social-ecological conditions in a manner similar to the way they co-vary among Whites.[14]

The data are now in and confirm the wide variability in crime rates across White and Black communities along with robust similarity in their basic predictors at the community level—especially the concentration of socioeconomic disadvantage. This conclusion is confirmed in two rigorous assessments of the available literature from 1995 to the present by Peterson and Krivo and Pratt and Cullen.[15] It is unambiguously the case in meta-analysis, for example, that concentrated neighborhood disadvantage is the largest and most consistent predictor of violence across studies.[16]

More to the point in assessing the racial invariance thesis is the conclusion by Peterson and Krivo: "One consistent pattern emerges from race-specific studies irrespective of the outcomes, predictors and units under consideration: structural disadvantage contributes significantly to violence for both Blacks and Whites."[17] We would point out that what is important in the racial invariance thesis, in addition to the comparability of causal distributions (described below), is the invariance in the effect of an underlying concept or dimension (such as concentrated disadvantage), rather than a specific indicator or variable. This point has often been misunderstood in recent empirical research.[18] Even so, Peterson and Krivo further report that the invariance finding is "resilient to the exact configuration of factors representing disadvantage, e.g., differing combinations of poverty, income, family disruption, and joblessness/unemployment."[19] Hannon, Knapp, and DeFina also demonstrate that, when properly estimated, concentrated poverty's association with homicide is invariant across racial groups.[20]

Ecological Dissimilarity

We now address the second question raised by Sampson and Wilson.[21] Is it possible to reproduce in White communities the structural circumstances under which many Blacks live? Here again the data have been clear for a long time. Consider Shaw and McKay's observation in Chicago from over half a century ago:[22]

The important fact about rates of delinquents for Negro boys is that they too, vary by type of area. They are higher than the rates for white boys, but it cannot be said that they are higher than rates for white boys in comparable areas, since it is impossible to reproduce in white communities the circumstances under which Negro children live. Even if it were possible to parallel the low economic status and the inadequacy of institutions in the white community, it would not be possible to reproduce the effects of segregation and the barriers to upward mobility.[23]

We still cannot say that Blacks and Whites share a similar environment —especially with regard to concentrated urban poverty. Consistently over recent decades, the vast majority of poor non-Hispanic Whites have lived in nonpoverty areas compared to approximately less than a fifth of poor Blacks.[24] Moreover, whereas less than 10 percent of poor Whites typically live in extreme poverty areas, almost half of poor Blacks live in such areas. Sampson and Wilson attribute these patterns to macrostructural factors both historic and contemporary, including but not limited to racial segregation, economic transformation, Black male joblessness, class-linked outmigration from the inner city, and housing discrimination.[25] Segregation and concentrated poverty represent structural constraints embodied in public policy and historical patterns of racial subjugation.[26]

The combination of urban poverty and family disruption concentrated by race is so strong that the "worst" urban neighborhoods in which Whites reside are considerably better off than those of the average Black community.[27] The consequences of these differential ecological distributions were the basis of Sampson and Wilson's hypothesis that correlations of race and crime at the individual level may be systematically confounded with important differences in community contexts.[28] For example, regardless of whether or not a Black male juvenile is raised in an intact or single-parent family, or a rich or poor home, he will not grow up in a community context similar to that of Whites with regard to family structure and poverty. Yet poor Whites, even those from "broken homes," live in areas of relative family stability.[29] Reductionist interpretations of race and social class miss this key ecological mismatch. As recently pointed out by Peterson and Krivo, it is precisely because of ecological dissimilarity that the types of regression models typically estimated in criminology are counterfactual— they assume what does not exist.[30]

There have been two responses to this problem. One strategy has been to study community-level differences in crime in settings where Blacks and Whites can be directly and thus properly compared along the distribution of predictor variables. When this has been done, concentrated disadvantage is shown to have similar effects on Black and White crime rates.[31]

A second strategy has been to model directly the Black-White gap in violence in multilevel studies of individuals where Blacks and Whites were sampled from the same areas. Few studies have been able to follow this approach because to accurately satisfy critics of the ecological dissimilarity thesis, one must also account for correlated family and individual constitutional differences that might explain racial and ethnic disparities in violence. Restricted variation in disadvantage is another important challenge, as African Americans residing outside inner-city poverty areas tend to be underrepresented in criminological studies even though there is a thriving and growing middle-class Black population.[32]

To address these issues Sampson, Morenoff, and Raudenbush analyzed the Project on Human Development in Chicago Neighborhoods (PHDCN), a multilevel longitudinal cohort study that was conducted between 1995 and 2002.[33] The study drew samples that capture the three major race/ethnic groups in American society today—Whites, Blacks, and Latinos—and that vary across a diverse set of environments, from highly segregated to very integrated neighborhoods. The analysis focused on violent offending reported by almost three thousand males and females ages eight to twenty-five who were interviewed up to three times from 1995 to 2002. Data were also collected from police records, the census, and a separate survey where over eight thousand Chicagoans were asked about the characteristics of their neighborhoods.

The results cast doubt on theories that attribute racial disparities in violence to differences in IQ test scores, impulsivity (or hyperactivity), and even family poverty. "Constitutional" differences between individuals in impulsivity and IQ test scores accounted for only 6 percent of the disparities in violence between African American and White youth. Contrary to widespread belief, family poverty is also not a predictor of violence and explains none of the racial or ethnic gaps. Instead the findings showed that residential segregation exposes African American youth to neighborhoods with higher risk factors and fewer protective factors for violence than neighborhoods where youth from other groups live. Specifically, neighborhoods where more people have professional or managerial jobs are protective against violence, as are neighborhoods with higher concentrations of immigrants. Overall, more than 60 percent of the Black-White gap in violence was explained, with neighborhood (dis)advantage accounting for the largest portion of the gap. Further, Sampson et al. found no systematic evidence that neighborhood- or individual-level predictors of violence *interacted* with race, and there were no significant racial disparities in trajectories of change in violence.[34]

Using a national survey of adolescents but in a logically similar analysis, McNulty and Bellair showed that neighborhood disadvantage explains a significant portion of the Black-White disparity in propensity to violence.[35] In a study of Pittsburgh youth, Peeples and Loeber showed also that disadvantage at the ecological level accounts for a substantial portion of the race gap—although, as in most studies, they could not reproduce in White neighborhoods the disadvantaged environment that Blacks typically call home.[36]

Synthesizing the community-level and multilevel research findings, a reasonably consistent set of "neighborhood facts" relevant to crime has emerged:

- There is considerable social inequality between neighborhoods and clear evidence that concentrated disadvantage is linked with the geographic isolation of minority groups.
- Durable neighborhood predictors of violence include the concentration of poverty, the absence of professional workers, racial isolation, and single-parent families. Conceptually these indicators tap aspects of neighborhood disadvantage.
- The place stratification of local communities by concentrated disadvantage is a robust phenomenon that emerges for all recent decades and at multiple levels of geography, whether local community areas, census tracts, political wards, or other "neighborhood" units.
- Where studies have compared appropriate points in the ecological distribution, concentrated disadvantage predicts violence rates in a relatively invariant way for Blacks and Whites. There is no evidence, in other words, that the neighborhood causes of violence are distinct for different racial groups when properly compared.
- Although the empirical base is limited, neighborhood factors correlated with race explain a significant proportion of the Black-White racial gap in violence among individuals, and there is little if any evidence of an interaction between race and neighborhood factors.

Mechanisms: Social Organization and Culture

During the 1990s, scholars began to theorize the above set of facts by moving beyond the traditional focus on concentrated poverty and measuring directly the way neighborhood social processes bear on crime. Unlike the more static features of socio-demographic composition, like race or class position, social mechanisms provide more process-oriented accounts of *how* neighborhoods bring about a change in a given phenomenon of interest.[37] Although concern with neighborhood mechanisms goes back at least to the early Chicago school of sociology, recently we have witnessed a concerted attempt across studies to empirically measure the social-interactional and institutional dimensions that might explain how neighborhood effects are transmitted. Sampson, Morenoff, and Gannon-Rowley refer to this as the "process turn" in neighborhood effects research.[38]

Sampson and Wilson posited that the most important process-related factors explaining the relationship between concentrated disadvantage and crime were (a) structural social disorganization and (b) cultural social isolation.[39] Social disorganization was defined as the inability of a community structure to realize the common values of its residents and maintain effective social controls. The structural dimensions of community social disorganization refer to the prevalence and interdependence of social networks in a community—both informal (e.g., the density of acquaintanceship; intergenerational kinship ties; level of anonymity) and formal (e.g., organizational participation; institutional stability)—and in the span of collective supervision that the community directs toward local problems. In general, however, the main concept emphasized in social disorganization and also in collective efficacy theory is that of *social control*.[40] Concentrated disadvantage is hypothesized to weaken the activation of social control, which in turn predicts an increased risk of crime.

Although social disorganization theory is primarily structural in nature, Sampson and Wilson went on to argue that the ecological segregation of communities gives rise to what Kornhauser terms cultural disorganization—the attenuation of societal cultural values.[41] Poverty, heterogeneity, anonymity, mutual distrust, institutional instability, and other structural features of disadvantaged urban communities are hypothesized to impede communication and obstruct the quest for common values, thereby fostering cultural diversity with respect to nondelinquent values. Sampson and Wilson specifically argued that community contexts shape "cognitive landscapes" or ecologically structured norms regarding appropriate standards and expectations of conduct.[42] That is, in structurally disorganized slum communities a system of values emerges in which crime, disorder, and drug use is less than fervently condemned and hence expected as part of everyday life. These ecologically structured tolerances in turn appear to influence the probability of criminal outcomes.

This conceptionalization of the role of cultural adaptations is congruent with Wilson's notion of social isolation—lack of sustained interaction with individuals and institutions that represent mainstream society.[43] The social isolation fostered by the ecological concentration of urban poverty deprives residents not only of resources and conventional role models but also of cultural learning from mainstream social networks that facilitate social and economic advancement in modern industrial society. Social isolation is distinguished from the culture of poverty by virtue of its focus on *adaptations to constraints and opportunities* rather than *internalization of norms.* The concept of social isolation implies that contact between groups of different class and/or racial backgrounds is either lacking or has become increasingly intermittent, and that the nature of this contact enhances effects of living in a highly concentrated poverty area. Social isolation does not mean that ghetto-specific practices become internalized, take on a life of their own, and therefore continue to influence behavior no matter the contextual environment. Rather, reducing structural inequality should ultimately decrease the cultural role of social isolation and adaptation.

There is little research to date that directly tests the way social and cultural mechanisms at the community level explain the race gap in violence, especially in conjunction with concentrated disadvantage. The wheels are set in motion, however, because the measurement of social processes at the community level is no longer a rare phenomenon, offering the promise of an enriched and stronger set of tests of the main tenets of Sampson and Wilson and other macrolevel theories.[44] For example, there is some indication that social control, in the form of collective efficacy, does not explain the race gap in violence once concentrated disadvantage is controlled. On the other hand, cynicism about norms of law does explain a significant portion of the racial gap.[45]

We thus turn to an assessment of new directions that we believe should be pursued in the next generation of research on race and crime. Against the backdrop of a more concerted effort to understand social mechanisms at the community level, we advocate for (a) pushing the logic of ecological dissimilarity to its next logical step, (b) extending the focus of inquiry to the increasing ethnic diversification of the United States, and (c)) perhaps most challenging and important, reshaping the concept of *cultural* mechanisms in criminology.

Spatial Inequality and Ecological Dissimilarity

The reality of ecological dissimilarity by race means that to compare predominantly minority neighborhoods to White neighborhoods is to compare apples and oranges on key social predictors of violence. Krivo and Peterson get around this problem by limiting their analysis to a selection of Black and White neighborhoods that are comparable in their distribution of structural disadvantage.[46] They find that such neighborhoods exhibit comparable levels of crime. As a test of the racial invariance thesis, this strategy makes sense but it necessarily sets aside the majority of Black and White neighborhoods that have no racial counterpart and thus selects for comparison neighborhoods those that are in a real sense "outliers." Nor does this approach tell us *why* Black and White neighborhoods as a whole occupy such different places on the distribution of economic advantage and crime.

We therefore suggest that research needs to attend more directly to the sorting processes that create ecological dissimilarity in the first place. In essence we are calling for studying the way race organizes the spatial dynamics of communities in a larger entire metropolitan system. In one sense this is the age-old question of how racial segregation comes about, and we do know a lot,[47] but in a fundamental and surprising sense the question has never been satisfactorily answered because most research focuses on *intra*-neighborhood processes that are assumed to be independent of adjacent neighborhoods and larger processes of city change.

There are good reasons to revise this approach. Neighborhoods are interdependent and characterized by a functional relationship between what happens at one point in space and what happens elsewhere. Setting aside the problematic definition of neighborhoods in most studies, spatial dependence of the crime process is implicated by the fact that offenders are disproportionately involved in acts of violence near their homes, such that a neighborhood's exposure to homicide risk is heightened by geographical proximity to places where known offenders live. Moreover, to the extent that the risk of becoming an offender is influenced by contextual factors such as concentrated poverty, spatial proximity to these conditions influences the risk of violence in a focal neighborhood. Interpersonal crimes of violence are also based on social interaction and thus subject to diffusion processes. For example, a homicide in one neighborhood may provide the spark that eventually leads to a retaliatory killing in a nearby neighborhood. In addition, violence occurs among persons known to one another, usually involving networks of association that follow geographical vectors.

Unlike in traditional community studies, then, we argue that the characteristics of surrounding neighborhoods are crucial to understanding violence in any given neighborhood. Recent research supports this claim. If one controls for measured characteristics internal to a neighborhood, violence in a given neighborhood is significantly and positively linked to the violence rates of surrounding neighborhoods.[48] This suggests a diffusion or exposure like process, whereby violence is conditioned by the characteristics of spatially proximate neighborhoods, which in turn are conditioned by adjoining neighborhoods in a spatially linked process that ultimately characterizes the entire metropolitan system.

Perhaps more important, spatial dynamics are implicated in the sorting of neighborhood risk factors in the first place. The mechanisms of racial segregation manifest themselves in spatial inequality, explaining why it is that despite similar income profiles, Black middle-class neighborhoods are at greater risk of violence than White middle-class neighborhoods. To understand how spatial externalities are situated against a regime of racial and ethnic segregation, Sampson et al. examined Chicago neighborhoods divided into three categories: (1) at least 75 percent White, (2) at least 75 percent Black, and (3) other, consisting mainly of Latino immigrant and mixed areas.[49] White neighborhoods were 4.5 times more likely than Black neighborhoods and two times more likely than mixed neighborhoods to have high levels of child control. Although this finding is not so surprising, the spatial vulnerability of Black neighborhoods and Latino/mixed neighborhoods was much more pronounced and unexpected in magnitude. Among neighborhoods with high social control, Black neighborhoods were some *thirty-seven times more likely* and mixed neighborhoods *eleven times more likely* than White neighborhoods to face the spatial vulnerability of being in ecological proximity to neighborhoods with low levels of social control.

Seen from the opposite perspective of what might be called "free rider" spatial advantage, among neighborhoods with *low* child-centered social control, White neighborhoods were almost nine times more likely than Black neighborhoods and six times more likely than mixed neighborhoods to be near neighborhoods with high social control. The implication is sobering: *When* African American neighborhoods generate social control, their residents nonetheless face the added challenge of being situated in a wider spatial environment characterized by extreme disadvantage.[50] The situation of White neighborhoods is nearly the opposite—even when they are at high risk because of internal characteristics, their residents benefit from high levels of child control in nearby areas. In a real sense these White neighborhoods are benefiting from their neighbors despite low internal contribution to the collective good.

Ecological dissimilarity is thus apparently even more profound than previously thought, with the evidence suggesting that the differing spatial environments of Black neighborhoods and White neighborhoods play a role at least equal to that of internal structural characteristics (i.e., concentrated disadvantage) in generating racial inequalities. It behooves researchers to better understand how these inequalities are produced and socially reproduced as a way of understanding racial disparities in crime. The relevance of social-psychological mechanisms for understanding urban inequality may be a key to further advance in this area.[51] Neighborhoods with high concentrations of minority and poor residents are stigmatized by historically correlated and structurally induced problems of crime and disorder. These historically resilient and psychologically salient correlations have deep roots in American social stratification that help perpetuate a self-confirming structural prophecy whereby all actors are likely to disinvest in or move away from Black areas viewed as having high risk for disorder, but with Whites more sensitive in the first place and consequently more likely to move.[52] In this way, implicit bias in perceptions of crime and disorder may be one of the underappreciated causes of continued racial segregation and spatial disadvantage, and hence ecological dissimilarity in the United States.

Ethnicity and Immigration

The United States is becoming increasingly diverse ethnically, not just in our nation's cities but in suburban and rural areas as well.[53] Latino

Americans are now the largest minority group at almost 14 percent of the population, and immigration has neared peak levels historically. Some 12 percent of the current population is foreign born and over half is from Spanish-speaking Latin America. Yet the Sampson-Wilson story was mainly about race.[54] Can their "racial invariance" thesis be applied to ethnicity and crime?

The data are not sufficiently in but initial results are intriguing. Martinez and colleagues find that homicide among Latino Americans follows the same general pattern as among Blacks and Whites in terms of the predictive power of concentrated disadvantage, even though other predictors of Latino violence are somewhat unique.[55] In particular, the basic links among deprivation, disorganization, and homicide are similar for Blacks, Haitians, and Latinos.[56] Thus it appears that the racial invariance thesis may be extended to ethnic invariance in terms of community-level causes of violence, especially disadvantage.

Ethnicity, and its counterpart, immigration, bring in new issues that transcend race, however.[57] The main challenge is the so-called Latino paradox, whereby Latinos do much better on various social indicators, including violence, than Blacks and apparently even Whites given relatively high levels of disadvantage.[58] The concentration of immigrants also appears to tell a very different story with respect to violence than the concentration of African Americans. Martinez, for example, challenges the stereotype that increasing immigration is linked to increasing violence.[59] Overall, the weight of evidence suggests that concentrated immigration has little if any association with aggregate homicide, whereas the concentration of Blacks has long predicted homicide rates.

Using the Project on Human Development in Chicago Neighborhoods, Sampson et al. extend this line of inquiry through a simultaneous examination of individual and neighborhood immigration status, along with ethnicity.[60] They report that the lower rate of violence among Mexican Americans as compared to Whites was explained by a combination of having married parents, living in a neighborhood with a high concentration of immigrants, and having individual immigrant status. Interestingly, first-generation immigrants have lower violence rates than second-generation immigrants, who in turn have lower rates of violence than third-generation Americans. This is even true for Blacks. Living in a neighborhood of concentrated immigration is also associated with a reduced risk of violence even after a host of factors, including the immigrant status of the person, are taken into account. Thus immigration status exhibits individual *and* contextual effects, both protective in nature.

The emerging story is therefore complex but provocative. Although concentrated disadvantage and neighborhood characteristics associated with social organization appear to predict rates of violence in similar ways for all race and ethnic groups, the patterns for Latino Americans and immigration go against the grain of popular stereotypes. Following media stereotypes (and in line with the original Chicago school of thought), we would expect areas with large concentrations of recent immigrants to have higher homicide rates since these groups tend to settle in disorganized and economically disadvantaged communities. Immigration should also affect Latinos more than other groups since immigrants in recent decades largely originate in Spanish-speaking countries.[61] Yet immigrants and Latinos are less violent, even more so when they live in concentrated immigrant areas.[62]

A major task for future research is to solve the so-called Latino paradox and explain what about immigration makes it such a strong predictor of lower violence. This task is made more difficult by the radically different but textbook-familiar pattern that dominated early-twentieth-century America, where immigration was indeed linked with increasing crime and therefore became a founding motivator for the social disorganization theory of crime. By contrast, in today's world it is no longer tenable to assume that immigration and diversity automatically lead to social disorganization and consequently crime.[63] In fact, an implied thesis, perhaps the most intriguing of all, is that the broad reduction of violence in the United States over the last decade was due in part to increasing diversity and immigration. To our knowledge this possibility has never been included among the usual suspects in the crime drop, but the broad pattern of secular declines in violence at the same time that immigration skyrocketed suggests to us a plausible hypothesis to be added to the race/ethnic theory of invariance.

Traditional Approaches to Crime and Culture

We turn now to perhaps the biggest challenge in the study of race and crime—culture. Three contrasting views of culture have dominated the literature. One view relies on the notion that delinquent or criminal values are merely "pseudo" cultures—ad hoc rationalizations that have no causal import. A second position, derived mainly from social disorganization theory, posits culture as endogenous to structural constraints. Culture is an *adaptation,* in other words, and would erode or change under differing structural conditions. The third imbues enduring causal power and hence authenticity to subcultures. By this logic, even if subcultures may have stemmed from structural differences, they ultimately take on an independent life of their own. This section briefly reviews these traditional yet vying approaches to race and crime before introducing a revised framework that draws on recent advances in the sociology of culture.

1. *Culture doesn't matter.* In a blistering critique, Kornhauser argued that so-called deviant cultures are entirely epiphenomenal.[64] No one truly values crime, chaos, and misery. The cultural particularities of criminals are pseudocultures, the stories people tell to account for their disgrace after the fact. The real causes of petty crime, violence, and unemployment operate in the structural realm of networks, labor markets, and human capital. When hardened criminals glorify their choices and disavow the straight life, their words are only sour grapes. Obviously, the causal power of culture in this view is weak to nonexistent.

2. *Culture is endogenous to structure.* Researchers on race and violence more often theorize culture as an *adaptation* to structural circumstances.[65] The basic story runs something like this: In a violent, high-crime neighborhood, with few legitimate opportunities, people learn that it is expedient to be violent themselves. The social learning of violence is passed on to children through role modeling. Ultimately, however, crime is driven by the structural forces of high unemployment, concentrated poverty, and accompanying family disruption. Culture is an endogenous variable, a mediating mechanism that shapes people's subjective experiences and responses to these hard facts of life. Thus deviance is not positively valorized; rather, it is accepted as part of the "cognitive landscape" of everyday life.[66] Violent neighborhoods are also culturally heterogeneous, with residents who gravitate mainly towards the mainstream but switch between competing sets of cultural values depending upon the situation.

The key concept then is cultural attenuation—residents may share mainstream cultural values, but these values become existentially irrelevant in certain structural contexts.[67] Moreover, crime is caused primarily by the *absence* of "good," prosocial culture, not by the presence of "bad" culture. This last view is widely adopted by recent research on crime, and goes by a variety of names including "cultural social isolation" and "cultural disorganization." Ironically, this kind of explanation also gives little causal power to culture to explain violence, working as a softer version of "pseudocultures."

3. *"Culture" acquires causal force, independent of the structural circumstances that generated it.* This position holds that, once a culture is created, it takes on a life of its own. For example, White southerners from herding traditions[68] and nineteenth-century Corsicans[69] have been argued to perpetuate "honor cultures" that endorse the use of violence. Honor cultures were originally developed under contexts where reputations for toughness were deemed necessary to defend family and property from endemic threats. Wolfgang and Ferracuti famously argued that the harsh circumstances of slavery generated a "subculture of violence" among Black Americans, which persists to this day, long after changes in structural circumstances.[70] More recently, Anderson's "Code of the Street" argues that high-poverty neighborhoods generate an oppositional culture that inverts the values of mainstream (White) society.[71] Mainstream culture is said to value hard work, education, and civility, but the "code of the streets" valorizes violence, callousness, and anti-intellectualism. At points Anderson appears to stipulate that the street code would wither away if structural conditions improved, but this is neither emphasized nor necessarily implied by his argument.

Toward a Relational Theory of Culture

Since the late 1980s, sociologists have adopted less transcendent definitions that capture the role of "culture in action." Swidler opened the floodgates with her idea of the "cultural toolkit," a repertoire of evaluative schema, scripts, and cultural models that people use to construct and justify lines of action.[72] While crime researchers have experimented with this new vocabulary of culture,[73] there has not yet been a decisive theoretical reformulation of the old culture/structure debate. New definitions of culture are being poured into old paradigms, like new wine into old wineskins.

It is important to actively tease out the implications of new work in cultural sociology for research on crime and violence, especially given the strong influence of Kornhauser on this field.[74] As a step toward remedying this situation, it is helpful to review the differences between traditional cultural arguments in criminology and the post-1980s culture-in-action paradigm. Table 1.1 provides a conceptual scheme that organizes our effort.

TABLE 1.1

Conceptual Scheme of Cultural Perspectives

New: "Culture in Action"	Old: "Culture as Values"
Intersubjective	Personal
Performative	Authentic
Affective-Cognition	Value-Rationality
Relational	Consensual
World-Making	Worldview

Intersubjective, Not Personal

In the "culture as values" paradigm, culture is conceptualized as the switchman that directs the train of action toward ultimate goals.[75] Culture is *personal,* something embedded deep within each of us. The methodological challenge in past research was to extract this deeply personal culture from a complete stranger. In the "culture in action" paradigm, culture is *intersubjective.* Cultural repertoires provide resources for coordinating social action. Culture is not embedded *within* each of us—it is created *between* us in everyday social interaction.[76] For example, people use frames to reach a shared definition of the situation, account for their behavior, or interpret others' intentions.[77] People activate symbolic boundaries, or highlight intergroup distinctions, to mobilize people for collective action.[78]

Different methodologies can lend themselves to either old or new paradigms of culture. When researchers measure culture with a survey, they standardize the stimulus (situation) and tend to assume that culture operates primarily within the individual. If culture is personal, then it makes sense to ask people what their individual "culture" is. But if culture operates in interaction, than researchers need to measure culture using additional methods, such as ethnography, focus groups, and the coding of intersubjective social texts and performances.

Performative, Not Authentic

Erving Goffman introduced the idea of "facework," the presentations of self that we make for various audiences.[79] He even denied the existence of the "true self," the essential center of moral choice within each of us. Rather, each of us is a series of performances among which we scramble to maintain worthy, competent selves as we move from audience to audience. By implication, people do not behave morally because they are essentially moral. Rather, they stick to the straight-and-narrow to impress others and save face. By this logic, when people act morally alone, they are performing before the mirror, to "save face" in their own eyes. If we adopt such a performative notion of culture, then it makes no sense to ask if "decent" people are truly decent, and "street" people are truly street. It makes more sense to ask which audiences people are performing for, and in what venues. Every storefront preacher knows people who perform a "decent" identity at church on Sunday morning, and perform a "street" identity when they sell drugs on Monday night.

Unlike previous frameworks, then, identity in this view is performed and is thus more than a post-hoc rationalization of one's behavior. People elaborate their identities to make sense of their past actions and circumstances, but this identity also takes on a projective life of its own, as when someone experiences a social event that he or she makes sense of by elaborating a particular identity at a later time. When this identity is threatened, violence may erupt, suggesting that the performance of identity can play a role in precipitating contentious encounters.

Affective-Cognition, Not Value-Rationality

The culture-as-values paradigm assumes a fundamental split between ends and means. It was often implied that only one's ends were truly cultural, while the means were "noncultural," driven by rationality, habits, and other noncultural mechanisms. This means-ends split is exemplified by Merton's classic theory of deviance.[80] In Mertonian strain theory, deviants were actually directing themselves towards mainstream American values (in particular, the acquisition of wealth) through the only means that were available to them (theft and participation in the underground economy).

Swidler's "culture in action" paradigm breaks down the opposition of means and ends. People often adopt the course of action that uses the practical skills and cognitive tools they have at hand, without thinking of their preferred ends. For example, if students lack the "cultural capital" that they need to navigate the academic world, they may direct their efforts into the social games that they know how to play, e.g., street fighting and popularity contests. Ultimate ends are invented in retrospect, to justify their course of action after it has been completed. When people attempt rationality, culture guides the construction of both means and ends by providing heuristics, metaphors, and models for action. When behavior is driven by impulse or habit rather than calculation, people often construct legitimate post-hoc accounts of their behavior. Since the 1990s, this more nuanced view of culture and rationality has been influenced by developments in cognitive science that show how emotion and psychological mechanisms shape our decision making. The *affective-cognition* approach has become influential in the new Behavioral Economics as well as sociology but has barely penetrated criminology.[81]

Relational, Not Consensual

Older cultural perspectives often assumed that culture was consensual, where we might have different preferences and tastes but agree on a set of shared values. This consensual culture helps people achieve collective goals. While this culture may be personal, it is directed toward the common good. This consensual view of culture underlies most research in the "social disorganization" tradition and in the literature on social capital, trust, and informal social control.

The French sociologist Pierre Bourdieu debunked this rosy picture with the idea of culture as "symbolic violence." Culture is not the glue that holds society together; it is a weapon for reproducing social hierarchies and excluding social challengers. People use culture to define themselves and their friends as uniquely worthy, and to draw symbolic boundaries between worthy selves and unworthy others. These symbolic boundaries help groups defend their exclusive access to networks and resources against usurpers.[82] Culture is not consensual (a basis of social solidarity) but instead relational (the map that people use to position themselves in social space). The "culture wars" in the United States serve as a prime example.

This conceptualization implies that morality is not just a matter of adhering to abstract principles; it is about locating oneself in social space and defending one's position from challengers. For example, being a good person necessarily requires an invidious comparison to bad people. Instead of assuming that communities have common standards of morality, the empirical goal is to map the ways that people within a community divide themselves into moral categories and rank people by relative worthiness. Of course, different people and different groups may disagree about who among them is most moral of all. Each party might elaborate available cultural notions of worthiness in a way that places himself or herself on top.[83]

Wacquant draws our attention to the finely differentiated hierarchies elaborated at the very bottom of society, between people with slightly differing resources, network locations, and opportunities.[84] As an example, the "working poor" draw strong boundaries against the "nonworking poor" to emphasize their commitment to hard work and mainstream respectability.[85] Unemployed neighbors return the favor, defending their worthiness against the "chumps" who take "slave jobs." Even homeless men resist a low-status identity by drawing symbolic boundaries between themselves and the *real* bums.[86]

The insight we take away is that individuals draw symbolic boundaries not reducible to fixed categories of people. These moral labels become ammunition in ongoing cultural warfare between people trying to establish a worthy identity by drawing symbolic boundaries. Bourdieu claims that such symbolic violence defends people's exclusive access to valued social networks, jobs, and resources. The idea of symbolic violence further implies that culture does not *constrain* conflict so much as *structure* it. Battles over worthiness and rank are endemic to all societies, not just in the "honor cultures" of Appalachia, inner-city St. Louis, or nineteenth-century Corsica. Neither is conflict for honor limited to the private sphere; it clearly occurs in the workplace and even in so-called arms-length economic transactions.[87] Yet some social contexts produce higher rates of open, *physical* violence than others. The task for criminology, we argue, is to think harder about how culture plays out in these processes.

World-Making, Not Worldview

In early critiques of the culture-as-values paradigm, it was conceded that culture guided our understanding of "what is" as well as what "should be."[88] People always recognized a difference between their values and hopes and their mundane pursuits and expectations. Berger and Luckmann introduced an influential concept of culture as worldview, a deeply structuring mythology that people used to make sense of the mundane world.[89] In some times and places, people lived within a "sacred canopy," a coherent socially constructed world. In other times and places, they struggled to construct a meaningful existence, in a social environment torn between competing worldviews.[90] Unfortunately, crime researchers distilled these rich foundational statements of social constructionism into the narrower formulation of "culture as worldview." The idea of worldview is too static, cognitive, and unitary, reproducing a false dichotomy between social structure (the "hard facts" of life) and culture (the soft reflection of reality that informs our choices.)

In contrast, cultural sociologists conceive of culture as world-*making*. The hard facts of social structure—the economy, the state, violence—are themselves continually produced and enacted by our skillful and purposive social action.[91] Culture plays a structural role in the making of this world.

To understand the difference between culture as worldview and culture as world-making, it is helpful to consider Bourdieu's idea of the social field. A field is a distinct social space consisting of interrelated and vertically differentiated positions, a "network, or configuration of objective relations between positions."[92] Unlike a worldview, a social field doesn't exist in our heads. A field exists only in interactions with other people. A social field is practiced, not "believed." A field is therefore both a feature of one's social environment and continually reconstructed by agency—an essential point to which we will return. Relatedly, a *habitus* is the embodied set of dispositions and classificatory schemas that structure people's responses to social situations. In relation to a field, the habitus provides the "sense of the game": who the relevant players are, what's in play, and how the game is played. In this game, different players bring different amounts of capital to the field. Capital comes in many forms: economic, cultural, and social. *Cultural capital* consists in the mastery of performances, styles, language, and familiarity that can be used to gain access to status or resources. *Symbolic capital* consists in accumulated honor or prestige that resides in the person, analogous to charisma in positive forms and stigma in negative forms.

Importantly, there can be dominant and nondominant forms of cultural capital, defined in relationship to different social fields that are played out in different social spaces. Many ethnographers have noted that subordinate groups often develop nondominant cultural capital, which accrues to people who give masterful performances of an alternate cultural style.[93] However, marginalized people have little dominant capital with which to gain entrée to networks and resources. This is not to say that marginalized people lack competence or interpersonal skill—it takes a great deal of skill to navigate their worlds. The point is that not all cultural patterns in marginalized communities should be described as cultural capital, a concept distinct from *competence, script,* or *schema.* Capital can only be defined in relationship to a social field, in which the capital can actually be converted into status, resources, or access.

Implications for the Cultural Study of Race and Crime

We believe that criminology in general, and the racial invariance theory of communities and crime in particular, can benefit from the insights gained in recent advances in the sociology of culture. It is beyond the scope of this chapter to offer a full-blown cultural theory, but we can consider in abbreviated form how some of the general principles just reviewed call forth new directions in the study of race and crime.

For starters, the idea of "culture as adaptation to structure" is directly problematized. Consider the claim that people adapt rationally to a violent, desperate context by becoming violent themselves.[94] But how can culture be conceptualized as an adaptation to the context when participants are actively creating the violent context in the first place? Individual actions are part of creating violent neighborhoods; put differently, without the cultural agency of neighborhood residents expressed in ongoing engagements in violent altercations, the neighborhood context would not be violent. The relational approach understands culture not as a simple adaptation to structure in a one-way causal flow, but as an intersubjective *organizing mechanism* that shapes unfolding social processes and that is constitutive of social structure. From this perspective culture is simultaneously an emergent product and a producer of social organization, interaction, and hence structure.

Second, and relatedly, people do not exclusively use culture to accept their fate, or justify their failure.[95] They invent exciting and dangerous fates for themselves. Katz has vividly described how people actively create the macabre environment that is supposed to be their externally imposed "environment."[96] Youth gangs carve up their neighborhoods into imaginary territories and enact terrible performances of honor, conquest, and vengeance. "Taggers" literally inscribe these performances on their urban landscape with elaborate graffiti. Ethnographic accounts of high-crime neighborhoods force us to recognize that people are enacting elaborate dramas of violence, not just narrating their stories *in retrospect.*

Third, we believe that the idea of the social field offers particular promise for understanding high-crime, marginal communities. It is commonly argued that these neighborhoods are socially disorganized, but this raises interesting questions about how people acquire a stable habitus in such disorderly neighborhoods. What social games do neighborhood residents believe themselves to be playing, if any? Are there stable social fields in which residents compete for status and resources? Wacquant suggests that there are, in his ethnographic inquiries into the "social art" of the hustler.[97] More relevant for present purposes, Anderson describes a pattern of violence in a Philadelphia ghetto that we reinterpret as the characteristics of a social field: organized "staging grounds," common understandings about who the relevant players are, a sense of the rules, and a language that describes who has more or less capital in this field.[98] For example, in the code of the street, inner-city teenagers acquire "juice" by performing their fearlessness in combat. These youth believe that skillful displays of "heart" win them status in their local peer groups. However, this nondominant cultural capital can only be "cashed in" for resources and status within a certain social field. In other social fields, like middle-class education, the performance of heart is stigmatizing. But in neighborhoods with large numbers of individuals who cannot claim mainstream signals of social status, a social field of violence emerges where residents vigorously compete to construct an honorable sense of self.[99]

Fourth, it follows then that we should no longer speak of cultural deficits of individuals or groups, but rather about the *match* between the social fields around them and their endowments of various kinds of capital. Bourdieu's concept of the social field can help us understand why young people perpetuate dangerous games of violence, when everyone involved may stand to lose materially. The relevant cultural mechanism is not the worldviews of the people involved, but the logic of the social field in which they are embedded. Social fields are thus intersubjective processes, in which participants necessarily have varying levels of power and capital, regardless of their values and aspirations. The lack of cultural capital is not an individual attribute like the old "culture of poverty" or "cultural deficit" arguments in poverty research. And it's not enough to share the same values, preferences, or "repertoires of evaluation." As Kornhauser dryly commented in the 1970s, no one needs to be told that it is better to be middle-class than to be idle, that it is better to be safe than to be endangered. But one must have the right capital to play the middle-class (and of course, upper-class) game.

Finally, the newer conceptualization of culture helps us to better understand the role of law, or more accurately the lack thereof, in high-violence settings. More generally, we cannot fully understand the organization of violence apart from the state, which claims a monopoly on the legitimate use of violence. Research has found that high-violence neighborhoods are characterized by both state disinvestment in access to law and widespread "legal cynicism": the feeling among residents that legitimate channels of protection and redress are not viable options.[100] Residents in disadvantaged areas, who experience the highest rates of victimization, are less likely to report simple assaults to the police than residents of wealthier neighborhoods.[101] This occurs when neighborhoods experience a policing vacuum or police resources are dramatically insufficient to provide a basic level of safety. Even if one reports a neighbor to the police, the police cannot protect one from retaliation, especially if their investigation is unlikely to result in a conviction.

Minorities and residents of racially stigmatized neighborhoods feel especially alienated from police, who may be inclined to treat them like potential suspects rather than citizens in need of assistance.[102] Perceptions of injustice are a natural outgrowth, creating a "racial gradient" whereby Latino and Black youth are more similar to one another and distinct from Whites in their alienation from the legal system.[103] Under these circumstances, a common reaction is for minority residents to feel that they must resolve their conflicts themselves, obtaining the support of family and friends for doing so.

Legal cynicism fuels a distinct practice that Kubrin and Weitzer call "cultural retaliatory homicide."[104] Cultural retaliatory homicide differs from other forms of violence in its disproportionate emphasis on retaliation for "disrespect," or small slights to individual or female family members. Cultural retaliatory homicide also refers to the use of vigilante-style executions to punish infractions or resolve disputes that could be brought to the police. Perhaps most importantly, this kind of costly world-making consistently arises in certain structural contexts: Spatial inequality and residential sorting processes produce neighborhoods with high rates of poverty, unemployment, transience, and lack of access to formal law, which combine to produce legal cynicism and an emphasis on cultural retaliation in interpersonal disputes.[105]

Conclusion

Like Sampson and Wilson, our perspective views the race and crime linkage from a contextual lens that highlights the very different ecological contexts that Blacks and Whites reside in—regardless of individual characteristics.[106] We emphasize that crime rates among Blacks nonetheless vary by ecological characteristics just as they do for Whites and Latinos. Taken together, these facts suggest a powerful role for community context in explaining race and crime.

Time marches on, however, and increasing immigration is one secular change that cannot be ignored. We therefore offered revisions to the racial invariance theory that we hope will guide and be tested in future research. In particular, we believe that there is a rich set of hypotheses on the Latino paradox, diversity as a cause of the crime drop, the protective mechanisms of concentrated immigration, and other aspects of ethnicity as articulated above.

We also believe that extraneighborhood spatial processes deserve further scrutiny in the explanation of patterns of ecological dissimilarity by race and ethnicity, as do the social organizational and cultural processes that are correlated with but not redundant with structural features like concentrated disadvantage. To this end we have offered a "spatial externalities" perspective on racial (dis)advantage that moves beyond the traditional emphasis on internal neighborhood characteristics. In fact, our argument is that extraneighborhood and city-wide spatial dynamics create racial inequalities that are potentially more consequential than the ones already at play within neighborhoods. This revised view has direct implications for understanding the durability of violence in poor Black neighborhoods and the ever present threat of violence in what otherwise would be characterized as middle-class areas.

Finally, we have offered a preliminary cultural framework that revises Sampson and Wilson by drawing on the latest thinking in the new sociology of culture.[107] Our framework seeks to elide the unproductive culture versus social structure divide that has long hampered sociology in general[108] and the study of race and crime in particular. Although working at a fairly abstract level, our arguments, we believe, have import for concrete causal thinking. Kubrin and Weitzer's recent work exemplifies the relational approach to culture, structure, and violence that we advance here.[109] Put in present terms, their measures of culture operationalize the new paradigm: culture as *intersubjective, performative, cognitive, relational,* and *world-making.* For example, Kubrin and Weitzer code cases of cultural retaliatory homicide in terms of reports of family and community support for the action, an intersubjective measure of culture. They record embodied practices as played out on a public stage, not beliefs encased in the individual mind. They cite in-depth descriptions of murder reports that capture the relational aspects of killing, the perceived need to lash out in order to "save face" and establish a reputation. In their formulation, and consistent with the perspective proposed here, cultural retaliatory homicide is thus not caused by beliefs or values. Rather, the practice of violence exemplifies world-making at its most dramatic. We believe this type of approach to culture can help elucidate the mechanisms that link the production of social—and in this case killing—fields with durable macrolevel forces that find continued expression in concentrated disadvantage, the racial stigma of neighborhoods, and state disinvestment.

NOTES

1. Sampson and Wilson 1995.
2. Ibid.
3. Ibid.
4. Fox and Zawitz 2003.
5. Anderson 2002.
6. Thornberry and Krohn 2002.
7. U.S. Department of Justice 2005.
8. Pettit and Western 2004.
9. Sampson and Wilson 1995.
10. For discussion, see Sampson, Morenoff, and Gannon-Rowley 2002.
11. Krivo and Peterson 2000; Pratt and Cullen 2005.
12. Sampson and Wilson 1995.
13. Ibid.:39.
14. Ibid.
15. Peterson and Krivo 2005; Pratt and Cullen 2005.
16. Pratt and Cullen 2005.
17. Peterson and Krivo 2005:337.
18. For example, Ousey 1999.
19. Peterson and Krivo 2005:337.
20. Hannon, Knapp, and DeFina 2005.
21. Sampson and Wilson 1995.

22. Shaw and McKay 1969 [1942].

23. Shaw and McKay 1942:614.

24. Jargowsky 1997.

25. Sampson and Wilson 1995.

26. Massey and Denton 1993.

27. Sampson 1987:354.

28. Sampson and Wilson 1995.

29. Sampson 1987.

30. Peterson and Krivo 2005.

31. Krivo and Peterson 2000; McNulty 2001.

32. Farley 1996.

33. Sampson, Morenoff, and Raudenbush 2005.

34. Ibid.

35. McNulty and Bellair 2003a, 2003b.

36. Peeples and Loeber 1994.

37. Wikström and Sampson 2003.

38. Sampson et al. 2002.

39. Sampson and Wilson 1995.

40. Sampson, Raudenbush, and Earls 1997.

41. Kornhauser 1978; Sampson and Wilson 1995.

42. Sampson and Wilson 1995.

43. Wilson 1987.

44. Sampson and Wilson 1995.

45. Sampson et al. 2005.

46. Krivo and Peterson 2000. See also McNulty 2001.

47. Massey and Denton 1993.

48. Baumer 2002; Morenoff, Sampson, and Raudenbush 2001.

49. Sampson, Morenoff, and Earls 1999.

50. Pattillo-McCoy 1999.

51. Bobo and Massagli 2001.

52. Sampson and Raudenbush 2004.

53. Saenz 2004.

54. Sampson and Wilson 1995.

55. Martinez 2002; Nielsen, Martinez, and Lee 2005.

56. Martinez 2002; McNulty and Bellair 2003a, 2003b.

57. Hagan and Palloni 1999; Morenoff 2005.

58. Martinez 2002; Morenoff 2005.

59. Martinez 2002.

60. Sampson et al. 2005.

61. Martinez 2002.

62. Nielsen et al. 2005.

63. Hagan and Palloni 1999.

64. Kornhauser 1978.

65. For example, Massey 1995; Sampson and Wilson 1995; Wilson 1987.

66. Sampson and Wilson 1995.

67. Kornhauser 1978; Sampson and Wilson 1995.

68. Nisbett and Cohen 1996.

69. Gould 2000.

70. Wolfgang and Ferracuti 1967.

71. Anderson 1999.

72. Swidler 1986.

73. Heimer 1997; Morrill et al. 2000.

74. Kornhauser 1978.

75. Swidler 1986.

76. Matsueda and Heimer 1997.

77. Goffman 1956, 1974.

78. Lamont and Molnár 2002; Tilly 2004.

79. Goffman 1956.

80. Merton 1938, 1957.

81. Camerer 2003.

82. Bourdieu 1984.

83. Lamont 2000.

84. Wacquant 2002.

85. Newman 1999.

86. Snow and Anderson 1987.

87. Morrill 1995.

88. M. Gould 1999; Young 1999.

89. Berger and Luckmann 1967.

90. Berger 1967.

91. Emirbayer and Mische 1998; Hays 1994; Sewell 1992.

92. Bourdieu and Wacquant 1992:97.

93. Carter 2005.

94. Anderson 1999; Massey 1995.

95. Kornhauser 1978.

96. Katz 1988.

97. Wacquant 1998.

98. Anderson 1999.

99. Horowitz 1983.

100. Sampson and Bartusch 1998.

101. Baumer 2002.

102. Weitzer 1999, 2000a.

103. Hagan, Shedd, and Payne 2005.

104. Kubrin and Weitzer 2003.

105. See also R. Gould 2000.

106. Sampson and Wilson 1995.
107. Ibid.
108. Sewell 1992.
109. Kubrin and Weitzer 2003.

Part I

Constructs and Conceptual Approaches

Chapter 2

Conceptualizing Race and Ethnicity in Studies of Crime and Criminal Justice

Marjorie S. Zatz and Nancy Rodriguez

"Justice for all" is a central pillar of American society, yet thousands of books, academic journals, and legal cases raise questions about the extent to which the U.S. legal order truly provides equal justice for all. This book contributes to our understanding of the relevance of race and ethnicity to one of the most critical elements of our legal order: crime and the criminal justice system. In order to frame this discussion, this chapter reviews the recent literature addressing the relationship among race, ethnicity, and crime control policies and suggests potentially fruitful approaches to conceptualizing race and ethnicity in future criminological research.

We organize this discussion along three dimensions. First, we discuss race and ethnicity as social constructions and structural relations, focusing on the convergence of race, ethnicity, gender, culture, and class in U.S. society. Second, we draw attention to the importance of context in our conceptualizations of race and ethnicity, and particularly to regional and temporal variation. Third, we explicitly address public policy and institutional practices, examining the racialized and gendered perceptions and attributions that underlie many of our policies and practices, as well as their racialized and gendered ramifications.

Conceptualizing Race and Ethnicity: Social Constructions and Structural Relations

Race, ethnicity, gender, and class are critical elements in structuring social relations in U.S. society. Yet they do not have any inherent, absolute meaning outside of the way we as human beings construct them within particular social relations and institutional structures. That is, they are social constructions rather than fixed identities.[1]

The identification of race can be quite problematic, and a given individual may self-identify and be defined by others in very different ways. Often, miscues and misidentifications result from reliance by decision makers on indicators such as the individual's appearance, surname, and primary language. For example, a law enforcement or court official might assume that an individual is Latino/a based on the person's Spanish surname without being aware that many American Indians also carry the names of Spanish conquerors.

Increasingly in contemporary society, individuals do not wish to choose which of their multiple races and ethnicities is most salient in a given situation.[2] Consider, for example, an Afro-Caribbean person whose family moved to the United States from the Dominican Republic. On any given day, if forced to choose a racial/ethnic category, this person may self-identify as Black, Latino/a, or "other," depending on the context. Police officers, victims, and court officials (e.g., intake officers) might also use a variety of cues to determine this person's race/ethnicity. Thus, the same person may be identified and coded in at least three distinct ways by different actors (including the person him/herself) for the same offense, and also in disparate ways over time. Yet rarely are identity politics, let alone the problems of coding race in a multiracial society, raised in criminal justice and criminology research. This is particularly troubling in studies that rely on official data across multiple localities where the salience of distinct elements in one's racial and ethnic identity (e.g., skin hue, language, multigenerational ties to the land) may vary regionally.

Just as Meda Chesney-Lind has argued so forcefully that we cannot take theories that were developed and tested with males in mind and simply "add women and stir"[3] to come up with viable theories that explain female criminality and delinquency, neither is the Black-White paradigm that has long ruled criminological research adequate for explaining crime and crime policy. That is, we cannot take theories explaining Black-White relations and assume that we can simply add in other racial and ethnic groups and stir, or that like an elastic band the theoretical paradigms we have used to explain race and crime patterns and policies can stretch to include additional groups. Indeed, a large volume of scholarship now demonstrates the tremendous racial and ethnic variation that exists in crime and victimization patterns and in assumptions about who is scary and who is a "real" victim.[4] The result of this singular attention to Black-White patterns by most criminal justice and criminological researchers, even in the face of solid evidence of diversity within and across racial and ethnic groups, has resulted in the inability of criminal justice policy to adequately address the relationships among crime, victimization, race, and ethnicity.[5]

Further complicating matters, our conceptualizations of race and ethnicity are also intertwined with the meanings we attach to gender, culture, and class, at the structural level, and probably age and education at the individual level as well. We maintain that this *convergence* is central to our understanding of the relationship between race and crime. For instance, in a study of risk and protective factors, researchers found Native American women were more likely than Black women to be victimized.[6] Social class also conditioned the gendered racial and ethnic effects in this study in several ways. For example, the risk of victimization for Whites and Asians was mediated by employment status, and risk was increased for Hispanic women when they lived in public housing. More pointedly, Esther Madriz explicitly addressed fear of crime, and the social control functions served by this fear, in the lives of poor women and women of color. Madriz stated,

> Class and racial differences play a role in women's fear of crime, and these differences have been consistently overlooked. Most research on fear of crime has approached the issue as if it existed in a political, economic, and social vacuum, neglecting to relate it to the social disadvantage that most women, especially women of color, occupy in a predominantly white and male-centered society such as the United States.[7]

We need a wide lens when we look at race and ethnicity in the context of crime and the criminal justice system. Research, we suggest, must consider cultural differences, as well as the intertwining of race, ethnicity, culture, and class, when attempting to explain risks of violence among women.

The relevance of this convergence, or intersectionality, is now well established in the sociological,[8] criminological,[9] and critical race feminism[10] literatures. Nevertheless, criminologists too often focus on one variable at a time to assess the effect of race or gender, for example, on sentencing outcomes, or they may look at the interaction effect of two variables (e.g., race by gender). For instance, one of the central questions in recent court processing and sanctioning research concerns the interaction between gender and race/ethnicity, and specifically the conditions under which White women receive more or less lenient sentences than women of color, perhaps due to a chivalry effect.[11] It is easy to say that sometimes White women receive shorter sentences, sometimes Black women, and sometimes Latinas—and to conclude only that findings are mixed. Yet a failure to delve deeper harks back to Chesney-Lind's warning not to simply "add women and stir." That is, adding some new group to a database or existing theoretical frame is rather like adding another ingredient to a recipe. In neither case do we think critically about what we are doing and consider whether we need to fundamentally reconceptualize the task at hand.

Exactly how, we must ask, do race, ethnicity, gender, and class converge in their effects on the sentencing of different groups of women? In the context of what structural factors do we find distinct outcomes related to race and ethnicity, and why? How do our understandings of racial, ethnic, gender, and class relations color our sense of who and what is most threatening, and our selection of crime control policies? These are some of the more interesting theoretical and methodological questions we must ask if we hope to capture the nuances of how one's race, ethnicity, gender, class position, and culture come together to influence crime and victimization, as well as criminal justice policy and practice. In considering how these structural relations operate and are understood in specific situations, we turn next to regional and temporal context.

Conceptualizing Race and Ethnicity in Context: Regional and Temporal Variation

Recent sentencing research has substantiated the importance of court context in prosecution and sentencing decisions.[12] This research has tended to focus on factors such as the extent of urbanization, crime levels, percent of the population that is below the poverty line, percent of the population that is Black, and similar local characteristics. We concur that these factors are critical to understanding court decisions, but our focus here is on the very meaning of race and ethnicity, and on their relevance to criminal justice decision making, across space and time.

For example, the more punitive sentencing of Black female drug offenders in specific contexts highlights the critical role that race, class, and other structural dimensions play in the sentencing of women.[13] We must recognize that the conceptualization of race and ethnicity may also change over time, reflecting more a situational process than a fixed, constant process.

This consideration also draws our attention to the importance of culture. Inattention to culture is one of the major drawbacks of the dichotomized Black-White paradigm. When we look at the experiences of American Indians, Latinos, and the growing Asian populations in the United States, it quickly becomes apparent that cultures and customs are tightly interwoven with our conceptualizations of race and ethnicity. Cultural variation exists everywhere, but within the United States, it may be particularly noticeable to social scientists working in the southwestern and western states. Demographic patterns in this region are shifting rapidly, and theories based on the experiences of Whites and Blacks may have little relevance for American Indians, or for immigrants from Guatemala or Thailand. For instance, the very notion of an underclass, which was based on the experiences of Blacks in midwestern cities, has not been shown to be a very effective means of thinking about economic relations in southwestern barrios.[14]

In the southwestern and western parts of the United States, the immigration status of victims and offenders also has a relevance that may not be readily recognized by scholars living in eastern states. Victims are often fearful of reporting crime if they are undocumented immigrants or if their family members are undocumented because their fear of crime, in many instances, is secondary to fears that they, or a loved one, will be deported.[15]

Culture and language are also critical factors. Language presents a barrier to services and processing. The use of translators means resources must be made available for such services, and when they are not available, defendants and court officials must simply make do with the information available. This also creates a significant problem for family members and victims who may not be entitled to translators and thus may not fully understand court proceedings and instructions. For instance, if juvenile probation officers do not speak the same language as the parents of youths on their caseloads, they may not be able to communicate effectively with family members. Those parents, in turn, will be very frustrated and unable to help insure that their children are complying with court orders.

For American Indians and for many immigrants, language barriers may pale in comparison to cultural misunderstandings.[16] Silence in response to authority figures, for example, may be interpreted as indicative of sullen behavior or disrespect, when instead it is intended to indicate respect for a person in a higher-status position or fear of that person's power.

These cultural misunderstandings are too often further compounded by patriarchal assumptions. For instance, in a study of responses to wife battering among Native people in Canada, Razack suggests that White judges either downplayed the harm caused by Native men who battered their wives or concurred with the Native men that community forms of justice would be the most appropriate responses to wife battering, even when the women argued that they did not feel safe and wanted the offense to be treated more seriously.[17] Urban Indians and American Indians living on tribal land are also likely to have quite disparate experiences with the legal order given their different social and economic circumstances, as well as the substantial differences between traditional tribal means of dispute resolution and tribal courts compared with state and federal court structures and processes.

Past research on American Indians and crime and justice has typically been polarized in somewhat naïve and romanticized ways, focusing either on the ramifications of social problems such as alcoholism on Indian communities or the usefulness of indigenous values for restorative justice programs.[18] More than 560 American Indian and Alaska Native tribes and nations are recognized by the federal government today. While there are some similarities across them there are also a large number of differences. The customs and language of Plains tribes are quite distinct, for example, from those of members of the Pueblos in the Southwest. Yet generally researchers and policymakers have ignored American Indian populations. Growth in the political and economic clout of American Indians due to investments of casino profits in ways that enhance social capital (e.g., education, health care), shared revenue and tax payments to state and local governments from tribes with casinos,[19] and new water accords (which are central to southwestern and western economic ventures) may lead to greater awareness of the extent to which we rely on stereotypical images of American Indian cultures and political structures. With such awareness, hopefully, we will also see increased attention to the experiences of Indian peoples with respect to crime and criminal justice.

The political clout of Latinos/as as a result of their increasing numbers in many states means we will need to develop a greater responsiveness to an extremely diverse Latino population. Latinos/as are often regarded in criminal justice and criminology research as a relatively homogeneous population, but there are large differences in the experiences and options available to individuals as a result of immigration status, income and other measures of wealth, gender, education, and other structural and situational factors. Moreover, the role that immigration and difficulties with the English language play in the lives of Latinos (as well as persons whose families recently immigrated to the United States from Southeast Asia and other parts of the world) are central to their experiences and attitudes toward crime and the criminal justice system.

Finally, the meaning of racial and ethnic categories varies over time. For instance, what it means to be an African American today, including the form and virulence of the racial discrimination experienced, differs from the even more pervasive discrimination Blacks suffered under slavery, or before passage of the Civil Rights Act. As another example, the response of White Americans to the first wave of Cuban refugees following the success of the Cuban Revolution in 1959, most of whom were very wealthy and White, was quite distinct from the response to the Afro-Caribbean Marielitos who came to the United States from Cuba in 1980. We now turn to recent criminal justice policies that have impacted not only racial and ethnic groups in this country but also our conceptualizations of race and ethnicity.

Conceptualizing Race and Ethnicity in Public Policy and Institutional Practices

We cannot properly conceptualize race and ethnicity without careful attention to racialized policies and practices (e.g., racial profiling, targeting particular neighborhoods for crime reduction) and their interconnectedness with ethnicity, culture, gender, and class relations. This is quite problematic for criminologists because it means that our analyses of policies that directly affect particular racial and ethnic groups are suspect. We also must consider who is making the racial identification before we simply accept any data at face value. That is, victims and police officers may make incorrect assumptions when they report the race/ethnicity of offenders, court recorders may record race/ethnicity on the basis of appearance, surname, language, self-identification, and so forth. As a result, not only may the information recorded be incorrect (a validity problem), but it may also vary across coders and, for persons with lengthy police or court files, across court appearances (a reliability problem). Moreover, we do not have data on victimization rates for certain racial and ethnic groups.

This creates an interesting problem. On the one hand, we do not know if the quantitative data on race/ethnicity in criminal justice databases are valid or reliable, and yet we do know that criminal justice agents (police officers, probation officers, prosecutors, judges, etc.) make decisions based on presumed attributes of the racial/ethnic group to which they assume the victim and/or offender belongs. These racialized and gendered attributions are, we suggest, theoretically quite compelling. In addition to our own work on this subject,[20] a number of other scholars are looking closely at social constructions and attributions by legislators, police, and court officials.[21]

Images, we suggest, are important—perhaps even more important than the realities of crime since our crime control efforts are closely tied to those images. Many of our policies are clearly linked to constructions of race, including the war on drugs and the war on gangs.[22] New theoretical discussions of "racialized space"[23] can help us to better understand how fears of dangerous places are closely tied to the social structures of racism and to economic restructuring, and how these fears are manifested in policing practices. For instance, the "broken windows" model of policing[24] makes certain assumptions about criminality based on the appearance of neighborhoods. Unkempt communities characterized by broken windows and litter have been directly linked to the social stability of that community and the political and economic clout (or lack thereof) of its residents. The broken-windows approach regarded disorder within a community as synonymous with crime and led to massive support for punitive and harsh control policies by police. At the same time, minimal attention was paid to the effects of economic restructuring and other causes of crime.

This also raises some intriguing questions about how constructs developed for one group may or may not fit another. For instance, the police practice of racial profiling has received a good deal of attention in recent years.[25] "Driving While Black" has become almost a generic term used to reference the targeting of Black drivers by police who use minor traffic offenses, such as a broken tail light, as excuses to stop and search African American drivers.[26]

Attention to racial targeting brings us back once again to the concept of racialized space. It is not the case that people of color are more apt to be arrested everywhere. Where the offense occurs and who is victimized or feels threatened are critical elements in determining the response by police and other law enforcement officers. In racially segregated neighborhoods, White offenders (who are probably preying on White victims) are arrested disproportionately.[27] A growing body of research is relying on data from the National Incident-Based Reporting System (NIBRS) to examine the likelihood of arrest by race. Interestingly, researchers have found that White juvenile offenders who commit violent crimes are significantly more likely to be arrested than non-White juvenile offenders.[28] Studies have also shown that the likelihood of arrest is higher for Whites than Blacks in robbery, aggravated assault, and simple assault offenses.[29] While on the surface these findings are not indicative of racial targeting, they do not consider the racial composition of the victim-offender dyad and changing demographics of the community. Further, the current nonrepresentative nature of NIBRS data makes such findings suspect at best.

Studies of police behavior must recognize that such behavior varies by ecological and/or neighborhood context, where, for example, enhanced surveillance of Black drivers increases as Blacks drive farther from Black communities and into wealthier White communities.[30] Black and Latino/a citizens continue to perceive police stops as unwarranted and unjustifiable actions guided by the driver's race.[31] Experiences of Blacks and Latinos/as with police officers indicate that police-minority relations are far more complex than previously thought. For example, Latinos/as report less abuse by police than do Blacks and are less likely than Blacks to believe that verbal abuse and corruption by police occur frequently.[32] In contrast, when compared with Whites, Latinos/as are more likely to report that they have seen police brutality in their communities, even when they live in affluent neighborhoods.[33]

The racial profiling of offenders has also been regularly reported by African American women targeted by department store security who assume they are shoplifting, Latino/a men and women in Mexican border states who are stopped for potentially being undocumented or bringing undocumented persons or drugs over the border illegally, and persons who appear to be of Middle Eastern or Arab descent who are stopped by police and immigration officials as potential terrorists. We must ask whether our analyses of racial profiling, which have been primarily restricted to Blacks, fit such situations, both theoretically and empirically, or whether we dilute the concept when we "add and stir" another racial/ethnic group into the mix. In addition, criminal justice research must now address crime control policies that directly apply to transnational crime, such as drug and human trafficking and terrorism.[34]

While zero tolerance arrest policies are sold as effective crime control strategies, studies must examine the long-term impact of such policies on marginalized populations, especially in perpetuating a "dangerous class."[35] Current initiatives, such as Project Safe Neighborhood, designed to curb firearms violence are expected to decrease crime within communities, but they are also likely to continue to marginalize racial and ethnic minorities.

Research that incorporates community and neighborhood measures may be better able to identify the structural components that lead to increased levels of violence among certain racial and ethnic groups in particular communities.[36] For example, research shows that juveniles who live in single-parent homes are more likely to be victimized within their neighborhoods. Further, Whites are less likely to be victims of stranger violence than Black and Latino/a youth.[37] However, these racial and ethnic differences disappear once family and community factors are included into the analyses, emphasizing the importance of context, including risk and protective factors that are unique to each racial and ethnic group.

We must be attentive to the devastating ramifications of our social constructions of young Black and Latino men, and increasingly, women, as criminal. The war on drugs (especially, but also the war on gangs and other racial typifications) has had tremendously disruptive impacts on family and neighborhood structures. For example, we see grandparents and aunts raising children whose parents are incarcerated, and the loss of social buffers in the form of Black and Latino/a professionals and other "bridge people" alters community dynamics, often dramatically.[38] While sentencing research has established how racial/ethnic stereotypes play a role in the more severe treatment of Blacks relative to Whites,[39] recent criminal court studies call attention to the attributions that link Latinos/as to crime and result in more punitive treatment relative to other racial/ethnic groups.[40] Researchers attribute the severe treatment of Latinos to particular stereotypes that serve to disadvantage Hispanics in ways that are distinct from the disadvantage experienced by Blacks.[41] The role of citizenship status, language barriers, and possible unfamiliarity with the criminal justice system can lead to ethnic stereotypes that present Hispanics as lazy, irresponsible, and involved in drug trafficking.[42]

Language and cultural barriers may also lead to stereotypes that serve to disadvantage American Indians.[43] Stereotypes that depict American Indians as "outsiders" and heavily involved in drug and alcohol abuse may lead to more severe treatment of American Indians, given the limited resources that exist to serve Native people.[44]

For members of some racial and ethnic groups, the problem is not so much stereotypes that identify them as more prone to violence but rather stereotypes that present them as unlikely participants of crime. For example, although the number of at-risk Asian Pacific Islander youth has increased, their unique needs remain unidentified and unaddressed in light of their "model minority" status.[45] In fact, the "model minority" status is inappropriate once the various differences (e.g., class, education, circumstances and time period of immigration, and language skills) that exist among Asian Pacific Islander communities are examined.

The massive incarceration of Blacks and Latinos/as due to the war on drugs has also severely impacted democratic processes and electoral politics. A generation after Blacks won the right to vote, large numbers of Blacks (and Latinos/as) are disenfranchised due to laws that restrict voting rights of felons, sometimes for life.[46]

Massive increases in incarceration have led to more than two million prisoners. As offenders complete their prison terms, record numbers of offenders are being released, with more than half a million ex-prisoners (six hundred thousand) each year returning to their communities.[47] At the same time, fewer resources are being allocated to fund programs that appropriately prepare inmates for release (e.g., job training) and address problems that increase parole revocations (e.g., substance abuse).

Reentry programs have recently been created to address prisoners' transition into the community. Such programs combine correctional services with community efforts to develop multi-agency strategies designed to facilitate prisoners' reintegration back into the community. However, early findings from studies show reentry programs were unable to address the challenges offenders face in finding affordable housing and employment.[48] As crime policy increasingly focuses on the successful reintegration of offenders back into the community, programs must be sensitive to the factors that are most effective for offenders from specific racial and ethnic groups. For example, White males report that college courses in prison are especially beneficial in making the transition from prison to the community (e.g., in continuing their education after release and experiencing few barriers to finding employment). However, Black males indicate that vocational training is crucial to gaining employment following release from prison.[49] Studies that examine the impact of reentry efforts must be able to appropriately document the role of structural dimensions that can serve to challenge the reentry process.

As with the study of reentry programs, research on community justice/restorative justice programs must recognize that community dimensions can facilitate *or* hinder offenders' reintegration. Community characteristics such as crime, racial/ethnic composition, and economic resources can directly influence the reintegration process.[50] A fundamental component of community justice and reentry programs is the community's capacity to successfully reintegrate offenders. Such programs must ensure that communities are characterized by culturally and gender-appropriate programs and services that develop well-defined skills and meet basic needs, including, for example, child care. Criminologists must recognize that this capacity is likely to vary across various regions and communities. Further, the opportunity to take part in reintegration programs is not the same for all offenders.

A recent study of a restorative justice program showed that race and ethnicity play a significant role in court officials' decisions of which juveniles to select for participation in the program.[51] Both Black and Hispanic/Latino juveniles were *less* likely than were White juveniles to be selected for placement in the restorative justice program. Findings from this study also indicate that juveniles from communities characterized by higher levels of unemployment were more likely to be selected for restorative justice participation, yet juveniles from communities characterized by higher levels of Spanish-speaking households and racial/ethnic heterogeneity were *less* likely to be selected for the restorative justice program.

Conclusions

The relationships among race, ethnicity, crime, and criminal justice policy are complex and multifaceted. We suggest that research in this area must attend to the convergence of race, ethnicity, culture, gender, and class if we are to make sense of people's experiences as offenders, victims, and agents of the criminal justice system. These are structural relations that are extremely powerful in U.S. society, and they are evidenced daily in our images and social constructions of who is scary and threatening and in our responses to such fears.

We have attempted in this chapter to move our thinking about these relationships forward, recognizing that whenever we incorporate new dimensions into our theories we risk simply "adding and stirring." As Meda Chesney-Lind argues so forcefully in speaking about gendered theorizing, we must be careful not to simply add Latinos and Latinas, or American Indians, or Asian Pacific Islanders, or any other group, to our existing Black-White paradigms and assume that so doing is sufficient.

Our theoretical constructions and our criminal justice policies and practices must be reflective of the everyday experiences and structural realities of the groups we are discussing. And, we must recognize that within each racial/ethnic group there is tremendous variation related to gender, culture, language, class position, education, employment status, and age, among other factors.

We need to be attentive to the potential of qualitative data that provide richness and a more complete understanding of how social constructions of race, ethnicity, gender, culture, and class develop in criminal justice organizations. While capturing the development and presence of such constructions may be difficult, if not impossible, to obtain through quantitative data, such information can be gathered through qualitative methods. Efforts to obtain such data require that researchers work alongside justice officials rather than act as passive recipients of such data. They also require researchers to assume a heightened sense of responsibility given the possible sensitive nature of these data.

With regard to quantitative data, we must improve our measures of race and ethnicity in criminal justice research to extend beyond simple "White and non-White" or even White-Black-Hispanic categories. The U.S. census has now enabled disaggregation of race and ethnicity data based on respondents' self-identification; criminal justice researchers should do the same. When working with criminal justice officials, researchers may suggest more appropriate measures of race and ethnicity than are currently found in official records. Also, whenever possible, researchers should attempt to capture cultural differences from quantitative data, whether from secondary data sources or from self-report accounts. It is important that we measure race, ethnicity, *and* culture regardless of context and recognize that such measures may vary across different regions of the United States.

Multidisciplinary, culturally competent models of crime prevention and intervention that address these dimensions must be developed if we are to create effective crime control strategies. There are now studies proposing the value of cultural and gender-specific strategies. For example, the Arizona Integrated Girls' Initiative has explicitly outlined the critical need of the juvenile justice system to provide gender-specific treatment and promote cultural awareness and sensitivity among communities to best address both their prior victimization and their delinquency. Our strategies for addressing crime and victimization, including models of policing and of reintegrating prisoners into the community, must be gender and culturally appropriate. Effective policies for eliminating racial, ethnic, and class disparities in crime must attend to levels of economic, political, and social inequality. Finally, we must supplement quantitative data on crime and victimization with qualitative studies if we hope to understand the multiple dimensions and nuances of current policies and their ramifications.

NOTES

1. Lopez 1996; Oboler 1995; Omi and Winant 1994; West and Fenstermaker 1995; West and Zimmerman 1987.

2. Grieco and Cassidy 2001; U.S. Bureau of the Census 2000d.

3. Chesney-Lind 1988.

4. See, for example, Madriz 1997; Mann and Zatz 2002; Martinez 2002.

5. Myers, Cintron, and Scarborough 2000; Zatz 2000.

6. Dugan and Apel 2003.

7. Madriz 1997:14.

8. Anderson and Collins 2001; Bobo, Hudley, and Michel 2004; Ferrante and Browne 2001; West and Zimmerman 1987.

9. Gaarder, Rodriguez, and Zatz 2004; Mann and Zatz 2002; Messerschmidt 1997, 1993; Miller 1998; Russell-Brown 2004; Zatz 2000.

10. Crenshaw 1989a; Harris 1990; Matsuda 1992; Montoya 1994; Morrison 1992; Williams 1991; Wing 1997.

11. Belknap 2001.

12. Britt 2000; Ulmer and Johnson 2004; Wooldredge and Thistlethwaite 2004; see also Myers and Talarico 1987 for examples of earlier work in this area.

13. Crawford 2000.

14. Moore and Pinderhughes 1993; Portillos 2004.

15. Escobar 1999; Martinez 2002.

16. Melton 2002; Zatz, Lujan, and Snyder-Joy 1991.

17. Razack 1994; see also McGillivray and Comaskey 1999.

18. Lujan 1995.

19. For example, Arizona tribes provided the state of Arizona with $9.9 million for the October–December 2004 quarter, for a total of $86 million in shared revenue from casino gaming since 2002 (Associated Press 2005).

20. Gaarder et al. 2004; Mann and Zatz 2002; Zatz 2000.

21. Bridges and Steen 1998; Russell 1998; Walker, Spohn, and DeLone 2004.

22. See, for example, Hawkins, Myers, and Stone 2003; Mann and Zatz 2002; Mauer 1999; Miller 1996.

23. Bass 2001; Herbert 1997; Portillos 2004.

24. Bayley 1994.

25. Russell-Brown 2004; Weitzer and Tuch 2002.

26. Russell-Brown 2004.

27. Stolzenberg, D'Alessio, and Eitle 2004.

28. Pope and Snyder 2003.

29. D'Alessio and Stolzenberg 2003.

30. Meehan and Ponder 2002.

31. Lundman and Kaufman 2003.

32. Weitzer and Tuch 2004.

33. Holmes 1998.

34. Stenson and Edwards 2004.

35. Karmen 2004.

36. Sabol, Coulton, and Korbin 2004.

37. Lauritsen 2003.

38. Austin 1992.

39. Albonetti 1997; Bridges and Steen 1998; Chiricos and Crawford 1995; Steffensmeier and Demuth 2000; Steffensmeier, Ulmer, and Kramer 1998.

40. Spohn and Holleran 2000; Steffensmeier and Demuth 2000.

41. Demuth 2003.

42. Brown and Warner 1992; Demuth 2002, 2003; Musto 1987; Portillos 2002.

43. Bachman, Alvarez, and Perkins 1996; Bynum and Paternoster 1984; Leiber 1994; Young 1990; Zatz et al. 1991.

44. Levy, Kunitz, and Everett 1969; Robbins 1984; Zatz et al. 1991.

45. Laidler 2002; Tang, Um, and Umemoto 2001.

46. Feliner and Mauer 1998; Uggen and Manza 2002.

47. Travis and Lawrence 2002.

48. Lindquist, Hardison, and Lattimore 2004.

49. Case and Fasenfest 2004.

50. Clear and Karp 1999.

51. Rodriguez 2005.

Chapter 3

Demythologizing the "Criminalblackman"

The Carnival Mirror

Vernetta Young

Newsflash! The police report that they have received numerous calls from citizens who indicate that they have been accosted in the mall parking lot after sunset by an armed gunman. The lone gunman approaches from behind, demands money and jewelry, hits the victim on the head with the butt of the gun, forces the victim to the ground, threatens to shoot if the victim calls out, and disappears into the night. Victims describe the offender as male and at least five feet six inches tall.

Who is this dangerous offender? Our victims cannot identify him. He came at them from behind. Still, it is probably the case that many mall goers have an image of just how this offender looks. One primary identifier will be his race. How will this offender look in the minds of those who have not seen him? How will he be presented in printed news stories and on television news? Will he be American Indian or Alaska Native, Asian, Black or African American, Native Hawaiian or Other Pacific Islander, or White?[1] Or will he be of some other race? Will the offender be presented as Hispanic or Latino or Not Hispanic or Latino? Who will mall goers look at with suspicion? On whom will mall security focus its attention?

In this hypothetical example, just as in crime stories reported daily in U.S. local newspapers and on television, the image of crime, the *real* danger, is that of the criminalblackman.[2] Reiman suggests that the criminal justice system *mirrors* what the media presents as the *real* dangers in society.[3] This characterization of the "criminalblackman" is based, in part, upon regular reports that Blacks are overrepresented in crime statistics relative to their proportion in the population (i.e., disproportionate involvement) and that Blacks have higher rates of criminal involvement (i.e., arrest). These ways of counting crime present Blacks as the most dangerous of criminals. Both the disproportionality and arrest rate statistics are determined by examining offenses relative to the size of the population. This is done because we are often told how important it is to look at the base when comparing statistics. Yet doing so can focus attention away from dominant groups and onto smaller groups who become defined as "the problem." For example, if we start with a small group that has just one crime and add one more, this group's offending has increased by 100 percent. If instead we start with another larger population with ten offenses and add one more, this group's involvement has gone up by only 10 percent. Yet this latter group comprises the vast majority of all criminal events before and after the change. The question is which should concern us most and when should it concern us. This issue of perspective is critical when we talk about race, which usually means Black, and crime in the United States.

To be more specific, consider the types of crimes that tend to receive most of the attention from the criminal justice system, legislators, and the media. These include the eight index offenses (murder, rape, robbery, aggravated assault, burglary, motor vehicle theft, larceny-theft, and arson) along with the more general part 2 nonindex crimes. According to the 2003 Uniform Crime Reports, Whites accounted for 70.6 percent of all arrests; 60.5 percent of all arrests for violent index offenses; 68.2 percent of all property index offenses; and 71.4 percent of arrests for part 2 offenses.[4] One would think that the fact that more than 60 percent of the participants are classified as being from one group would lead to an emphasis on that group and on the nature of their participation. However, this is not the case for crime. The above numbers have been pretty consistent over time but this has led *not* to a consideration of the participation of Whites in crime *but rather* to a focus on the approximately 27 percent participation of Blacks who make up about 13 percent of the total population.

Reiman reviews this depiction of crime and the criminal in America; however, he contends that we must question the accuracy of this mirror presentation because "the American criminal justice system is a mirror that shows a distorted image of the dangers that threaten us—an image created more by the shape of the mirror than by the reality reflected."[5] The purpose of this chapter is to explore the impact that this distorted (carnival) image of crime and the criminal has had on the development of the discipline of criminology/criminal justice. I contend that the fixation with the "criminalblackman" has cast Blacks as the source of all sorts of societal ills associated with crime and has caricatured the Black male as the boogey man. This fixation has also hindered the development of theoretical explanations of crime; prevented the development of programs and policies to fight crime problems other than street crime; and contributed to the misconstruction of criminal events like those perpetrated by the "trench coat mafia."

In contrast, we see numerous examples of non-Black crime portrayed as aberrational and less dangerous. As "The Apocalypse of Adolescence" reports,

> This spring one of two Vermont teenagers charged with the knifing murder of two Dartmouth College Professors will go on trial. The case offers entry to a disturbing subject—acts of lethal violence committed by "ordinary" teenagers from "ordinary" communities, teenagers who have become detached from civic life, saturated by the mythic violent imagery of popular culture, and consumed by the dictates of some private murderous fantasy.[6]

What seems to be "ordinary" about these teenagers and their communities is that they are not Black and not urban. The report provides a teacher's description of the inmates of a correctional facility as ". . . the young, the male, the white, the angry, the ignored, the overstimulated, the intelligent if not well educated. The dangerous dreamers."[7]

More intriguing is that in this same report the author notes that these murders were not unique in Vermont but rather were a continuation of a cluster of assaults (and murders) that began in 1997. As a result, there were three deaths and one aggravated assault perpetrated by sons and daughters, foster children, and neighbors. Although we were not told the race of the offenders, and in fact because we were not told, it is a surprise that the victims and the offenders are all White. The violence of these "bewildered, depraved children" was attributed to the influx of Hispanic urban youth gangs to the community. More specifically, the author contended that these gangs were able to gain a foothold because the youth of Vermont felt "lost, disenfranchised," and alienated.

In addition to stories like this one are lists that chronicle school shootings of the 1990s: 1995—Jamie Rouse in Lynnville, Tennessee; 1996—Barry Loukaitis in Moses Lake, Washington; 1996—David Dubose, Jr., in Atlanta, Georgia; 1997—Evan Ramsey in Bethel, Alaska; 1997—Luke Woodham in Pearl, Mississippi; 1997—Michael Carneal in West Paducah, Kentucky; 1998—Andrew Golder and Mitchell Johnson in Jonesboro, Arkansas; 1998—Andrew Wurst in Edinboro, Pennsylvania; and 1998—Kipland Kinkel in Springfield, Oregon.[8] Twenty-three people were killed and numerous others were injured. These shootings occurred after earlier shootings in California and Missouri and before the shootings in Colorado (Columbine) and at other schools across the country. And still supposedly there is no pattern; there is no rhyme or reason.

The list of school shootings continued into the 2000s: 2000—Darrell Ingram in Savannah, Georgia; 2000—Nate Brazill in Lake Worth, Florida; 2001—Charles Williams in Santee, California; 2001—Jason Hoffman in Granite Hills, California; 2001—Donald Burt in Gary, Indiana; 2003—James Sheets in Red Lion, Pennsylvania; and 2003—John Jason McLaughlin in Cold Spring, Minnesota. Nine people were killed and numerous others injured in these incidents. An editorial by McLaughlin in the *Minnesota Daily* in response to the shooting suggests that, although there is a reluctance to identify a pattern, there is an attempt to understand and explain:

> The small community is shocked, and everyone is wondering how he obtained his handgun and why he chose to use it . . . something in society is out of whack. Kids killing kids is not natural, especially at the disturbing rate we see today. The culture that helps make the John Jason McLaughlins of our day possible must be addressed. . . . Teen anger, depression . . . are pervasive problems legislators cannot fix. Neither is this just a matter of "family values." These are issues society must solve.[9]

These examples all involve juveniles but we could easily present a listing of other crimes that are described in ways that depart from, or question whether they fit, the dangerous man image. For example, serial killers and mass murderers have been catalogued by the Federal Bureau of Investigation (FBI) and others. Included among these offenders are mass murderers Timothy McVeigh (1995), Terry Nichols (1995), James Huberty (1984), and Charles Whitman (1966), as well as, serial killers Donald Harvey, Ted Bundy, and John Wayne Gacy. The general description is of a White male between twenty-five and thirty-five. The more detailed descriptions include a string of adjectives such as "cunning," "handsome," and "intense," all geared toward the view of the given individual as an unlikely suspect. Surely, he is not like the more dangerous "criminalblackman."

The same can be said for white collar crime and criminals. These offenders are seldom considered as dangerous or harmful and most certainly are not Black. Only on rare occasions do white collar criminals become the subject of substantial media attention. For example, many have heard of Enron and Kenneth Lay, WorldCom and Bernie Ebbers, and Martha Stewart.

In brief, then, the contention here is that there are some types of crimes and criminals that we tend to fold into our theories and programming, and there are others that we exclude. When the offenders and crimes are "typical" (racial/ethnic minorities and street crime), we apply such theories as strain, social control, and deterrence, and offer solutions stemming from these theories to address the problem. When offenders are other than Black or Hispanic and the crimes are not street crimes, we tend to be puzzled about how to explain the behavior or the involvement of the individuals. We do not know who or what to blame. We are not satisfied to attribute cause to inept parenting, lack of social control, weak social bonds, limited economic opportunity, a violent subculture, the family, the schools, or any of the other factors that we use to account for the criminal behavior of Blacks or Hispanics.[10] The crime and offenders do not fit the scheme, the pattern, or the picture of the dangerous criminal so we presume that there is insufficient knowledge for interpreting and dealing with the behavior. If we were to admit that the scheme, the pattern, or the picture is based upon a "colored" presentation of reality that stems from our proclivity to see only those who are other than White as dangerous or crime prone, it might be easier to address questions of crime control. As indicated earlier, this state of the field has had an impact on the development of the discipline of criminology, the advancement of theory in criminology, the substance of programs and policies proposed in criminal justice, and the social construction of the criminal.

The Discipline of Criminology

The history of criminology has been the subject of ongoing interest and debate. In his presidential address to the American Society of Criminology, Laub argued that "the field of criminology lacks a sense of its own history."[11] Even so, Rafter identifies a number of historians of criminology who have examined the origins of the field.[12] This history begins in the late eighteenth century and extends to the early nineteenth century, with important milestones in the twentieth century. It crosses traditional disciplines (e.g., sociology, psychology, law) as well as geographic areas (e.g.,

Europe, the United States). As we reconstruct this history, it is important to look objectively at our warts.

Rafter points out that "biological explanations shaped criminology at its inception."[13] These early explanations were based on kinds-of-people paradigms whereby criminals were viewed as different from noncriminals. They were viewed as innately inferior to noncriminals. They were paupers, the insane, and immigrants. Most importantly, criminals were "others."

Cesare Lombroso, often regarded as a father of criminology, argued that criminals were a throwback to primitive peoples. These primitive people were identified as born criminals who could be recognized by a number of physical traits and characteristics.[14] The descriptions seemed to some to be inherent to certain races, and pictures of criminals presented by Lombroso, especially those in *The Female Offender,* supported this characterization. Not only were criminals "others" but they were race and class specific. Others following in this tradition portrayed the criminal as the criminalotherman, soon to become the "criminalblackman."

Biological explanations eventually gave way to sociological explanations as we moved into the twentieth century. Sociological explanations tended to be based on kinds-of-place paradigms.[15] However, such explanations placed an undue emphasis on certain locations or places as sources of crime to the exclusion of other locations or places, signifying that the focus is still indirectly on kinds-of-people. Thus, the move to sociological explanations has not broadened the types of crimes of most interest. For the most part, the spotlight remains on limited crime categories, namely, the types of crimes that are perpetrated more frequently by the kinds of people who have been the focus of biological explanations. These are defined in terms of class, race, and location.

This kinds-of-people paradigm, which has remained a central part of criminology, to some extent dictates the substance of our studies. It circumscribes who we define as criminal and what we define as crime. Through acculturation, ethnic immigrant Whites, the kinds of people who early on were associated with the types of street crime of interest, have assimilated. This has left the kinds-of-place explanations and associated targets of interest, who because of race and class have not assimilated, namely, racial and ethnic minorities, and more specifically African Americans, especially Black males.

Consequently, the discipline of criminology has been hampered by the inability of scholars to throw off the blinders that protect the self-defined image of crime. It is past time that we look more closely at the full picture of crime without limits on the spectrum of colors that we use to fill in our picture. There were some earlier attempts to redefine the terrain. Sutherland's introduction of the phrase "white collar crime" in 1933 and his articulation of differential association, a theory to explain both white collar and common street crime, was a masterful stroke. The efforts of conflict, Marxist, radical, and critical criminologists have also added to the canvas. However, we have made limited headway.

Theory in Criminology

In 1942, Sutherland applied his theory of differential association to white collar crime. Sutherland was dissatisfied with conventional explanations of crime; did not accept the emphasis on poverty and other conditions concentrated in the lower socioeconomic classes; and argued that this emphasis obstructed the development of a theory sufficiently general to cover the whole range of crime.[16] Almost six decades later Tatum argues that class bias continues to prevail in theories of crime.[17] In presenting the colonial model as a theoretical explanation of minority crime, she suggests that there are a number of similarities and differences between the theoretical arguments of mainstream and minority perspectives. More specifically, like the minority perspectives, the mainstream theories of social disorganization and strain focus on class stratification, positing that "individuals in the lower social strata experience blocked structural opportunities that, in turn, lead to frustration that leads to a behavioral response."[18] But, one of the major limitations of mainstream explanations centers on their class-based bias. Thus, Tatum's critique suggests that Sutherland's caution about the emphasis on class obstructing "the development of a theory sufficiently general to cover the whole range of crime" and *criminals* continues to have merit.

In a critique of the state of knowledge on race and crime, Sampson and Wilson charged that there was a near absence of research seeking to explain differential rates across racial and ethnic groups.[19] The silence that they lamented has resulted in intensified efforts to understand "why black levels of street violence exceed by such a large margin levels for whites."[20] This research has advanced knowledge about what characteristics affect rates of crime for racial/ethnic groups. Yet, it continues the focus on the disproportionality of Blacks in crime statistics and the practice of looking to explain the behavior of the "criminalblackman."

Researchers, having defined (or accepted) the "criminalblackman" as the really dangerous criminal, have been preoccupied with disproportionality but have failed to concede that Whites are overrepresented in crime, even street crime, when the overall numbers are considered. What does overrepresentation mean? Does it mean more than one-half? Or more than the contribution of others? Is it necessarily related to population size? And if so, why is it or must it be? Existing criminological theory has not yet provided a clear explanation of crime differences that simultaneously captures why Whites are responsible for the bulk of crimes even when Blacks contribute more than their population share would lead us to expect. If Whites are overrepresented in crime, meaning that their contribution is disproportionate to that of other groups, is this also because of inept parenting, the lack of social control, weak social bonds, limited economic opportunity, a violent subculture, the family, and/or the schools? This must be the case because Whites comprise most of the respondents in samples on which conclusions about the causes of crime are based. Unfortunately, our focus on disproportionality by population size leads us to assume that Whites *do not* suffer from and are *not* impacted by these negatively characterized social conditions.

Moreover, the key may be not how disproportionately different the races are, *but* the ways in which they are similar. Two recent studies have reported that irrespective of race there are certain variables, like disadvantage, that explain levels of violence.[21] What are the resources and crime-producing conditions within different racial/ethnic groups? Which of these tend to be related to criminal behavior within various groups? The factors that explain the criminal behavior of Whites may be similar or different from those that explain the criminal behavior of Blacks, of Hispanics, or of others. But how will we know if we do not focus on the behavior and characteristics of all groups?

Even more germane is the recognition that, regardless of race/ethnicity, criminals and delinquents make up a small proportion of the total population. Thus, even when we find a factor that is related to criminal behavior, most of those with this characteristic are not criminals or delinquents. How do we explain this and what prevents so many from becoming criminal/delinquent? For example, if we find that single parenthood is related to crime, we need to go one step further and look at those from single-parent families who are not criminal. How do single-parent house-holds with nondelinquent/noncriminal persons differ from those with criminals? Finding the answer to this question should get us closer to understanding the more direct sources of crime for all groups.

The attention to the "criminalblackman" also means that women and girls are often ignored in analyses of crime.[22] In fact, one critic argued that women are ignored or stereotyped in the major criminological approaches —anomie, labeling, differential association, subcultural theory, and Marx-ism.[23] Others noted that criminological theory is often presented as gen-der neutral and race specific.[24] While some advances have been made in the study of gender and crime, our theoretical progress is hampered by the failure to recognize the diversity among females. Instead, theories pur-porting to explain female crime treat women as a single group (generally White), ignoring Sojourner Truth's refrain, "ain't I a woman?"[25]

Some scholars assert that our theories are constructed to explain the behavior of male criminality to the exclusion of female criminality, and this is true to an extent.[26] However, I suggest that the more accurate state-ment is that our theories have been constructed to explain the behavior of the "criminalblackman." Thus, theoretical explanations of criminality do not account well for the criminal involvement of either White males or females of any color. They exclude explanations of street crimes that are committed by Whites and females; and they exclude explanations of white collar crime. Of course, this means that we are unable to explain most of what we call crime and most of those who would satisfy our legal defini-tions of criminals.

Programs and Policies

The emphasis on the "criminalblackman" and theories purporting to explain his behavior has limited programs aimed at addressing the crime problem. If the cause of crime is somehow related to the deficiencies of the Black or Hispanic communities, or some of their members, then efforts to reduce crime are directed at controlling these communities. During the 1980s and 1990s, efforts at containment focused mainly on punishment and its administration as reflected in sentencing guidelines, mandatory sentences, three strikes and you're out, and truth in sentencing.

Although there is knowledge of structural contributors to the "crime problem," this discussion has not been well integrated into the broader discourse for solving crime. Any existing discussion on the impact of these structural contributors has focused on the Black population to the exclusion of other groups. It may be important to keep in mind that not all Whites have the benefits of adequate parenting, presence of social control, strong social bonds, and unlimited economic opportunity. And even those who do may be involved in criminal behavior because of some other factors that have not been included in our discourse, in part because of the kaleidoscopic focus. It is another part of the refrain that we hear so often: How could it happen here or there? How could it happen to them; they were the all-American family? Perhaps something is amiss in our consideration of what is important in the development of stable units and whole human beings.

If our programs and policies are based on theories that misdefine or misspecify the components of our explanatory model, then what are we really explaining? Moreover, of what benefit are the explanations that bring forth the programs and policies? And, what harms stem from such misspecification? I suggest that focusing so narrowly on the "criminalblackman" has numerous consequences:

1. Those who are Black and involved in crime may see the disparity in their treatment and define the situation as unjust and not worthy of corrective action on their part.[27] This means that they are likely to continue or even escalate their involvement in crime. Given the intraracial nature of most crime, this also means additional victimization of other Blacks, increased fear of crime among those in the targeted communities, and a further decline in the quality of life of community members.

2. Those who are Black and not involved in crime may see the greater punitiveness toward Blacks as unjust and seek to reduce the impact by taking steps such as jury nullification, failure to report, and the like, knowing, at some level, that these actions are harmful to the community. In a system that is viewed more as "just us" than justice, steps taken to "protect" those who are unjustly accused by a discriminatory system of criminal justice may be viewed as the only tool available to right the wrongs. This approach to "taking the law in your own hands" further undermines the viability of the criminal justice system.

3. Those who are White and involved in crime see the focus on Blacks as a cover for them to engage in and get away with crime. In many

instances, they may fail to define their violations of the law as real crimes and rather define them as pranks, mistakes, or aberrations. Furthermore, those who feel the need for assistance and help with whatever may be the causal factor contributing to their behavior may act out because of neglect, etc.

4. Those who are White and not involved in crime may see the source of the crime problem as other than them—bluntly, as "those other people," namely, Black people. When others are defined as problematic, different, unworthy, and outsiders, and members of one's own group are viewed as non-troublesome individuals, there is little incentive to tackle the more popularly defined crime problem.

5. Those who view the "criminalblackman" as the scourge of the "war on crime" and the "war on drugs" probably see racial disparities in the imposition of the death penalty and the one hundred to one crack cocaine sentencing differential as justified.[28] However, the penalties and their application broaden the punishment gap between Blacks and Whites and perpetuate the stereotypes of Blacks, especially Black males, as criminals. Moreover, they contribute to the destabilization of the community through the disruption of families, the loss of labor force participants, and the weakening of the community.

Misconstruction of Criminal Events

As indicated above, numerous violent acts are perpetrated by young White males against family, neighbors, and schoolmates. These events are often attributed to the influence of foreign elements over individual young people who exhibit such individual characteristics as anger and isolation, or who have been victims of bullying and teasing. The depiction of real crime as that perpetrated by the "criminalblackman" has contributed to the misconstruction of criminal events like those perpetrated by the "trench coat mafia" as less culpable. These events have been viewed as "one of a kind" happenings, as individualistic, although there have been a number of similar events almost always involving, at some level, at least one coconspirator. Similarly, serial killers and mass murderers are looked upon as actors who are troubled, psychologically damaged, or overcome by personal trials.

In addition, we pretty much ignore the involvement of Whites in run-of-the-mill crimes and in white collar crimes. It is almost as though White offenders are homogenized. Their behavior is viewed less as crime and more as unfortunate deviance, something that everyone engages in from time to time. This is behavior that is not really worthy of vilification. The harm and costs are downplayed. Thus, the criminality of Whites is either ignored or associated with behaviors that are barely criminal whereas the criminality of Blacks and Black criminals become the crime problem. If this is not misspecification, it is definitely misconstruction of the crime problem. At some point, we should ask how much crime there is and who is actually committing it. The assessment of crime should be concerned with how many people are harmed and how much loss is incurred.

Conclusion

The picture of crime in America is in large part a reflection of what and who is defined as the crime problem. The mirror of crime that is projected for or to the larger society is based upon what is included in the picture. If the picture that is presented is skewed or misrepresented, the image will also be skewed or misrepresented. By changing the lighting or the focus or the angles of the glass, we get a distorted image of the real picture. So, like the carnival mirror that we pay to view for entertainment, the carnival mirror of crime is like a caricature that takes the features of crime and magnifies the easily identifiable characteristics until they become the standouts. They become the major characteristics.

Crime in the United States is committed by members of all racial groups: Blacks, Hispanics, Asian Americans, Native Americas, Whites, and others. Crime in America is committed by members of all class groups: lower class, middle class, and upper class. There are also differences in crime in America by race/ethnicity and class. Some groups commit more, and some commit less. Some commit more serious and others less serious crimes. Some crimes cause physical injury, some cause loss and damage to property, and still others inflict psychological harm. The more we learn about who does what and why, the more able we will be to develop plans for stemming involvement in crime. If we continue to narrowly define the danger as having a Black face, we will fail to provide safety and security for all members of our population, and we will continue to alienate those we unfairly disparage.

NOTES

1. These are the racial categories commonly used by government agencies, including the U.S. Bureau of the Census and police departments.

2. Russell 1998.

3. Reiman 2001.

4. Federal Bureau of Investigation 2004.

5. Reiman 2001:60.

6. Powers 2002:58.

7. Ibid.:65.

8. Ramsland 2004.

9. *The Minnesota Daily*, September 26, 2003.

10. Simons et al. 2003.

11. Laub 2004:1.

12. Rafter 2004b.

13. Rafter 2004a:1.

14. Lombroso and Ferrero 2004.

15. For example, Shaw and McKay 1969.

16. Moyer 2001.

17. Tatum 2000.

18. Ibid.:9.

19. Sampson and Wilson 1995.

20. Peterson and Krivo 2005; also see this paper for a review of literature.

21. McNulty 2001; Krivo and Peterson 1996.

22. See DeCoster and Heimer, as well as Like and Miller in this volume.

23. Leonard 1982.

24. Klein and Kress 1976; Smart 1984.

25. "Sojourner Truth's Speech to the Akron Convention, 1851."

26. Daly and Chesney-Lind 1988.

27. Cloward and Ohlin 1960.

28. See Provine in this volume.

Chapter 4

Race and the Justice Workforce
Toward a System Perspective

Geoff K. Ward

> That Justice is a blind goddess is a thing to which we
> blacks are wise. Her bandage hides two festering sores,
> that once perhaps were eyes.
>
> —Langston Hughes[1]

Racially and otherwise stratified societies are challenged with reconciling diverse group interests in prevailing ideas and practices of justice. This problem marks not only the pages of political philosophy but also the living histories of justice systems themselves, through contests over representation in processes of social control. While oppressed groups have historically sought representation to gain equal protection under the law, dominant groups have moved to limit such influence, thus maintaining dominion *in* and *through* law. This context provides an analytic frame for the study of race and the contemporary "justice workforce," the vast and insufficiently charted field of service workers and professionals employed in the definition and administration of justice.

The scope and significance of ethnoracial group representation in justice administration has escaped close and sustained scrutiny in race, crime, and justice research. The volume and depth of research on justice workers pales in comparison to studies of race, crime, and punishment, where ethnoracial minorities are cast as criminal problem populations, as victims of crime and as targets of direct and indirect discrimination. In each case, race is operationalized as a status affecting passive subjects of justice processes. Research has been less attentive to ethnoracial group agency in justice processes, including the ways race and ethnicity relate to policy interests, organizational cultures, levels of influence, and eventual distributions of services and sanctions within justice systems themselves. Imbalanced attention to the subjectivity of marginalized groups in justice processes and neglect of actual and potential group agency not only limits appreciation of the complex dynamics of racialized social control but may also reinforce stereotypes about crime and its racial dimensions.

This chapter encourages more systemic engagement with justice workers in future race, crime, and justice research. To this end, it proposes an analytic framework for bringing multiple justice-related occupations into systemic view, a perspective essential to determining the scope and significance of diversity in the justice workforce. While several studies examine representation within isolated contexts of justice administration—such as policing in select cities, correctional officers in specific prisons, or judges in certain courts—few consider the nature of racial stratification across sectors of the justice workforce. Defined as a hierarchy of service occupations and professions involved in the definition and administration of justice processes—a division of justice-related labor—the justice workforce offers a unit of analysis amenable to systematic theoretical and empirical research across social-historical contexts.

On Justice of Color: Background of the Research Agenda

In a classic social history of American criminal justice, Samuel Walker identifies the high degree of popular influence as a defining feature of these systems.[2] Segments of the public have influenced justice administration directly through participation in formal and informal justice processes and indirectly through electoral processes, mass protest, and other means. Democratic appearances notwithstanding, this participation has not been essentially progressive. Popular justice has often furnished or endorsed repressive practices of criminal social control, as ideas and practices of justice become tailored by the sympathies and interests of those social groups most able to establish and exploit direct and indirect channels of influence. Walker thus points to the mid- to late-twentieth-century growth of a vast criminal justice bureaucracy as a progressive development in American criminal justice, especially for its effectiveness in regulating the passions of popular justice.[3]

Surprising in light of its thesis, this work largely overlooks the ethnoracial diversification of the justice workforce, and the relevance of diversification for shifting the scales of popular justice and affecting the homogenizing impact of bureaucratization. The original edition of *Popular Justice* in 1980 barely mentions dramatic nineteenth- and twentieth-century changes in levels of direct and indirect influence in justice administration for long excluded constituencies, including ethnoracial minorities and women. In theory, increased participation would redistribute the range of interests served by justice systems, extending the horizons of popular justice.

A second edition incorporates occasional and still brief considerations of diversity in justice-related occupations, ultimately suggesting that the entry of women and non-Whites into positions of authority has made no difference in the operation of justice systems.[4] But research on race and the justice workforce is not so clear. Indeed, such research lacks the depth and refinement necessary to establish such firm conclusions.

This chapter does not attempt to settle the diversity debate but rather to draw out its dimensions and complicate its terms, to encourage and hopefully benefit future research on race and the justice workforce. I begin by outlining several prevailing assertions regarding the significance of ethnoracial group representation in the justice workforce, and major tendencies and limitations of the existing research.

On the Presumed Relevance of a Diverse Workforce

Decades of popular, official, and academic discourse yield insight into the assumed relevance of ethnoracial diversity in justice-related occupations. A continuum of assertions with two extremes characterizes these claims. One extreme holds that diversity *substantively* improves justice administration (i.e., promoting fairness and multiculturalism). An alternate position emphasizes that diversity is *symbolically* significant to the appearance of system legitimacy.[5]

Many have suggested that racial and ethnic groups bring unique skills and perspectives to the administration of justice and that diversity may, thereby, affect processes and outputs of justice systems. According to this view, the burden or threat of discrimination sensitizes ethnoracial minorities to demands for equal protection under the law, socializing a class of justice workers attuned to issues of system fairness, or as the opening poem by Langston Hughes puts it, "wise" to the existence of injustice. The

Honorable Thurgood Marshall, a pioneering civil rights lawyer and the first non-White Supreme Court justice, credited Black lawyers with playing "a unique role in American history" as determined advocates of equal rights. "Imbued with respect for the rule of law and the responsibility that such belief engenders," he wrote, "[black] lawyers have used their legal training not only to become masterful technicians but to force the legal system to live up to its creed: the promise of 'equal protection under the law.'"[6] A leading historian of race in the legal professions also claims that, at least in early generations, "the black lawyer, always mindful of his slave ancestry, 'humble parentage,' and race, viewed himself as an emancipator of his people."[7] The bylaws of the Judicial Council, a national organization of Black judges established in 1971, began with the objective of "eradicat[ing] racial and class bias from every aspect of the judicial and law enforcement process."[8]

Few still assert that African-Americans or other ethnoracial minorities, as a rule, bring emancipatory agendas to the justice workforce. Contemporary claims of substantive distinction more often emphasize ecological and cultural differences. For example, a recent report on racial profiling suggests that law enforcement agencies should promote diversity in the police ranks because "officers who know the community and are familiar with different cultures can assist their Departments to avoid the biases and mistrust that are at the heart of racial profiling."[9] Such arguments stress the lack of social distance between minority justice workers and disproportionately minority charges, and the benefits of their shared experience, language, and other cultural characteristics to effective policing, court processing, and prison administration.[10]

A third position emphasizes the symbolic value of a diverse workforce irrespective of whether actual differences in orientation or impact obtain. This premise holds that ethnoracial diversity in justice-related occupations bolsters the perceived legitimacy of justice systems. Such arguments have been especially common in discussions of policing, a primary target of twentieth-century protests against minority underrepresentation in justice-related occupations, especially in the wake of U.S. urban rebellions. In 1968 and 1973, national advisory commissions attributed urban rebellions to tensions between minority communities and White police, recommending recruitment of minority officers at rates equal to their proportion in the population. Combining an instrumental premise with assumptions of substantive distinction, these reforms were based partly on the unproven theory that minority police "would more evenhandedly enforce the law and thus gain greater acceptance in the minority community" but also on the expectation that simply seeing non-White police officers patrolling in these communities would cool the flames of racial conflict.[11]

More recent U.S. government proposals to increase diversity among justice workers similarly combine elements of the symbolic and substantive rationales. Without much elaboration or evidence, official discourse in the past decade has suggested that promoting ethnoracial diversity among decision makers has the potential to bolster actual justice system performance and improve perceived legitimacy. A recent announcement of a U.S. Justice Department initiative to increase diversity among federal attorneys illustrates this prevailing logic:

> Our pursuit of justice is stronger, and fulfillment of our national mission more effective, when we bring to bear the *experience, judgment,* and *energy* of colleagues from a wide spectrum of racial, ethnic, economic, and geographic backgrounds. . . . To succeed fully in our mission, we must earn and retain the *trust* and *confidence* of all Americans in how we fulfill our responsibility as custodians of justice. And that . . . is a function of the American people's understanding that [the Department] draws on the finest legal talent from every quarter of this great nation (emphasis added).[12]

This effort began with a study of diversity in the ranks of U.S. attorneys, which was withheld until the Congressional Black Caucus and others forced its release. The Justice Department later distributed a report with heavy redactions in sections detailing underrepresentation in positions of influence, hostile work environments, and other indications of racial inequality, drawing criticism from minority legislators about the department's commitment to addressing these conditions.[13]

State courts have also advanced diversification agendas premised on substantive and symbolic benefits. Between 1990 and 1997, at least twenty-two states and the District of Columbia initiated or expanded efforts to increase ethnoracial diversity among court workers. A 2002 report by the National Center for State Courts suggests that concerns about "customer relations more than promoting racial justice" may guide some of these efforts. The report's introduction notes how

> businesses have realized that hiring a diverse staff helps them respond with more insight and sensitivity to a variety of markets, both foreign and

domestic. . . . [E]ffort to keep up with the increasing diversity of our population has become a great challenge for the courts also. Many courts are
realizing that they can *better serve* their customers as well as *enhance credibility* of the justice system if their staff more closely represents the diversity
of the customers they serve (emphasis added).[14]

Demands for greater ethnoracial representation in justice administration are neither new nor confined to the United States. Racially and ethnically stratified societies worldwide—ranging from South Africa and
Australia to Western Europe and the Middle East—reveal comparable
conflict over ethnoracial group exclusion or marginalization in justice-
related occupations, drawing on the suppressed symbolic and substantive
benefits of equal representation in policing, courts, prisons, legislatures,
and other fields.[15] For example, faced with protests intensified by police
violence in Black communities, the British government has been forced to
confront its failure to develop a justice workforce representative of ethnoracial diversity in the population. In a series on "The Changing Face of
Justice" in Britain and Wales, the chief constable of South Wales Police
acknowledges that "for 150 years [the police] have been a white, male
organisation" and suggests confidence will be won by its diversification.
Reforms notwithstanding, critics still protest a "[British] criminal justice
process in which mainly white professionals arrest, prosecute, sentence
and hold in prison a disproportionate number of black defendants."[16]

In summary, ethnoracial group representation in justice administration
has been a subject of much interest and debate, not only across time and
sectors of the U.S. justice workforce but also in racialized societies worldwide. Related discourse reveals a debate between whether substantive distinctions or merely symbolic changes, if any, result from diversification.
There is no consensus on this question, but the retired Judge A. Leon Higginbotham best captures the nature of prevailing sentiment. Lamenting
that Presidents Ronald Reagan and George H. W. Bush appointed just two
African Americans to the U.S. Court of Appeals in their combined twelve
years in office, a rate surpassed even by the apartheid government of
South Africa, Higginbotham argued,

> It is difficult to have a court that in the long run has the respect of most seg-
> ments of the population if the court has no or minuscule pluralistic strands.
> Of course, pluralism does not absolutely and forever guarantee an effective
> and fair judiciary. Nothing really does. However, pluralism is a sine qua non

in building a court that is both substantively excellent and respected by the general population. In other words, judicial pluralism breeds judicial legitimacy. Judicial homogeneity, by contrast, is more often than not a deterrent to, rather than a promoter of, equal justice for all.[17]

Tendencies and Limitations of Prior Research

Embedded in claims that diversity bolsters the actual performance and perceived legitimacy of justice systems are at least two key assumptions. First, it is assumed that ethnoracial characteristics meaningfully distinguish the professional orientations and behaviors of justice professionals, or at least hold significance to observing publics. Second, it is assumed that these actual or perceived distinctions translate into significant differences in substantive or symbolic outcomes (i.e., in distributions of justice system services and sanctions, the perceived legitimacy of justice systems, etc.). In other words, a conflation of statistical, substantive, and symbolic representation is somewhat common to discussions of ethnoracial diversity in the justice workforce.

These two assumptions present empirical questions begging more systematic and *systemic* research. As noted earlier, scholarship on race, crime, and justice typically engages ethnoracial minorities as passive subjects of justice processes, operationalizing race as a characteristic of offenders, crime victims, and those subject to discrimination. The justice workforce is usually held constant in race-related research, despite the reality and debated significance of its racial variation. This limits insight into the racialization of social control in many ways, but especially by centering attention on the distribution of outcomes (i.e., arrest and sentencing decisions) and away from "the justice of institutional organization" itself, which is effectively assumed as given (i.e., a legal, rational process).[18]

Of course, numerous studies have considered the scope and significance of ethnoracial minority representation in justice administration, especially in the United States. Research on racial differences in professional orientation often finds that status characteristics (including race) of justice workers hold limited significance in comparison to occupational roles, political ideology, and professional goals.[19] Yet others suggest that ethnoracial minorities do bring distinct perspectives to bear on the idea and practice of justice, including particular sensitivity to fairness.[20]

Research is less extensive on the consequences of diversity for justice system outcomes, including justice system processes themselves and their perceived legitimacy by relevant publics. Several studies, focusing on police, judges, and corrections officers, find no substantial race-related differences in patterns of conduct.[21] Others report marginal or more substantial differences in relevant outcomes.[22] Studies of judicial decision making have found that minority judges do not treat minority defendants more leniently than White judges but do sentence defendants more consistently than White judges, who in contrast sentence minorities more severely.[23]

Nearly without exception, however, existing research focuses on specific occupational contexts.[24] The occupation drawing greatest attention is law enforcement, with several books and numerous articles addressing diversity and policing in various social and historical contexts. This literature offers the greatest theoretical depth, comparative perspective, and array of research questions and methodologies, due likely to more sustained research support and attention.[25] Closest to the policing literature in size and scope is a body of work addressing ethnoracial group representation in the legal professions, including lawyers, judges, and legislators, where again the focus is on isolated occupational contexts.[26] There have also been several studies of ethnoracial minorities in corrections, a subject of increasing interest in the wake of growing and racially disproportionate rates of incarceration.[27] Little research has addressed other relevant groups, such as probation and parole officers, legal scholars, criminologists, or law and criminal justice students.[28]

The atomized study of race and the justice workforce has generated rich insights on ethnoracial diversity within select occupations, and across social-historical contexts. But the study of isolated occupations is also a major limitation of prior justice workforce research, as it falls short of addressing how ethnoracial group representation operates across contexts of justice administration to affect the performance or perceived legitimacy of justice *systems*.

Decision makers operate within complex social and organizational contexts with processes significantly beyond their individual control. These sociological dynamics can override individual inclinations at the point of system outcomes, and are not entirely determined by occupational categories. Early cohorts of African American police officers, for example, were employed as managers of the racial status quo, assigned to police Black people and communities, and given severely limited authority, especially in policing Whites.[29] These dynamics—established (and contested) by legislators, lawyers, police supervisors, and others—conditioned, diminished, and otherwise distorted the significance of an increased Black police presence. Racial histories of policing in other societies similarly reveal the distorting effects of social and organizational circumstance. In colonial Australia and apartheid South Africa, for example, aboriginal and Black police under the direction of White government officials and supervisory officers were routinely enlisted in national campaigns of racial domination.[30]

Social organizational forces continue to condition the nature and relevance of ethnoracial group representation in justice administration. Research demonstrates, for example, that judges are typically recruited from the "establishment center of the legal profession," a process mitigating against a judiciary with diverse political orientations.[31] Selection does not work alone to regulate differences in orientation and outcome, as law and bureaucracy themselves tend to restrain alternative approaches. As the retired judge Bruce Wright observed, "[N]o matter how 'liberal' black judges may believe themselves to be, the law remains essentially a conservative doctrine, and those who practice it conform."[32] Law and policy, organizational norms, resources, and other factors condition the possibilities justice workers confront, and thus the significance of their diversity. Importantly, however, these conditions are the product of numerous decision makers acting simultaneously to define, maintain, challenge, and otherwise (re)organize the justice system from various points of influence. Recall in the example of the U.S. Department of Justice's effort to diversify lawyers that minority representation in the legislature has proven critical.

It may be impossible to isolate race effects on the orientations and behaviors of justice workers, and on outcomes of justice processes. However, similar to the progressive "waves" of race and sentencing research, workforce research will benefit from closer examination of the way race effects operate across multiple and interdependent contexts of justice administration.[33] Studies of isolated occupations provide fundamental and constructive insights, but fully appreciating the scope and significance of diversity in the justice workforce requires a systemic perspective.

Race and the Justice Workforce: Toward a System Perspective

Justice systems are networks of agencies and institutions collectively engaged in the definition and administration of justice. Sectors of a justice system are populated by workers whose input is ordered by various factors, including system responsibilities of particular fields and their professional, administrative, and service roles. Beyond a loosely integrated collection of various occupations, then, justice systems present hierarchical divisions of justice-related labor. But on what bases can we define this hierarchy, what occupations does it include, and what does the resulting framework reveal of ethnoracial group participation in justice administration?

The Division of Justice-Related Labor

The 2000 U.S. census lists over two million Americans employed in several justice-related occupations, though it does not specify the nature of the work these judges, lawyers, legal assistants, police, and corrections officers perform. We can, nevertheless, identify these and other occupations as particularly relevant in defining, interpreting, and enforcing the rule of law. We can further distinguish these occupations according to their hierarchical distribution.

I propose a hypothetical division of justice-related labor with three dimensions: power, prestige, and risk. *Power* refers to influence upon the formal organization of justice systems, with emphasis on system influence (i.e., through legislation, legal rulings, planning, budget decisions, etc.) rather than on influence over individual cases. Powerful occupations tend to involve "task definition," while less powerful occupations are more confined to "task execution."[34] *Prestige* refers to the social status, professional requirements, and compensation of the occupations. Finally, *risk* refers to occupational hazard, specifically the likelihood of exposure to violence.

Considering ten justice-related occupations included in the 1990 U.S. census, Figure 4.1 outlines a hypothetical division of justice-related labor. The pyramid shape in part symbolizes numerical distributions of workers in relevant sectors. In 1990 there were 796,742 individuals employed in what are defined as top-tier occupations (94 percent were lawyers), compared to 956,990 middle-tier workers (61 percent in policing), and 970,178 lower-tier workers (81 percent as private guards or police).[35]

The figure also illustrates the hierarchical ordering of the justice workforce by distinguishing occupations into top, middle and bottom tiers according to inferred levels of power, prestige, and risk. *Top-tier* occupations include positions with relatively high influence and prestige, all being held by elected officials and highly educated professionals. These

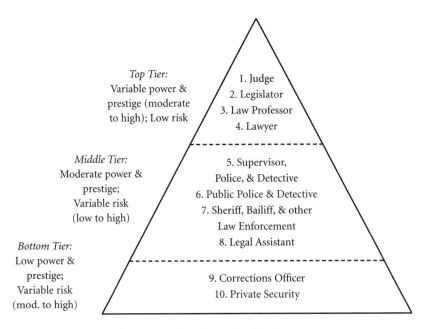

Fig. 4.1. A Hypothetical Division of Justice-Related Labor

positions involve relatively greater opportunity to define the tasks that they and others (i.e., middle- and bottom-tier workers) execute, and are further distinguished by a relative absence of occupational risk.[36] The *middle tier* consists of public law enforcement officers (administrators and officers) and court workers who provide primary services in justice administration (probation and parole would be included here). Middle-tier occupations enjoy moderate levels of power and prestige, and widely varying but in some cases extremely high exposure to risk. Finally, a *bottom tier* includes service personnel exclusively, such as corrections officers and private security guards. Bottom-tier occupations provide only case-level managerial and other limited custodial and security support, with generally no involvement in system administration. These positions are largely limited to the execution of tasks established by others, are less prestigious, and involve variable but generally moderate to high levels of risk, owing to their case-managerial, custodial, and security functions.

The division of justice-related labor considered here is exploratory and conceptual. It is expected that future research will empirically validate and refine this conceptual framework. Meanwhile, this tentative framework proves useful in gaining systemic perspective on the present scope and significance of ethnoracial diversity in the U.S. justice workforce.

Race and Representation in the U.S. Justice Workforce, 2000

The 2000 U.S. census provides some insight on the current statistical representation of (non-Hispanic) Whites, Blacks, Asians, American Indians, and Hispanics (any race) in the U.S. justice workforce.[37] This section considers ethnoracial group representation within and across six occupations from the proposed division of justice-related labor (Figure 4.1). To consider systemic distributions of group influence, occupations of two comparative types are considered: "professional and administrative" (judge, lawyer, and administrative police), and "service" occupations (public police and detective, legal assistant, and corrections officer). Although representing top, middle, and lower tiers, these occupations are distinguished conceptually according to their "task defining" versus "task executing" roles. Table 4.1 reports total numbers of workers by ethnoracial group and proportional rates of representation in each occupation per hundred thousand of each group in the overall U.S. population.

TABLE 4.1

Ethnoracial Group Representation in Occupational Sectors of the U.S. Justice Workforce, 2000

		Occupational Sector						
		Professional & Administrative			Service			
Race	Count	Judge	Lawyer	Supervisor, Police, & Detective	Police & Detective, Public	Legal Assistant	Corrections Officer	Totals
White	N*	49	777	86	455	226	251	1,842
(NH)	Rate**	24.94	399.18	43.98	233.67	115.98	128.84	946.59
Black	N	5	34	10	70	25	86	230
(NH)	Rate	15.19	99.76	29.12	205.76	72.42	253.86	676.10
Hispanic	N	3	29	6	52	23	32	144
(Any Race)	Rate	7.51	81.09	16.90	147.54	66.41	89.40	408.84
Asian & Pacific	N	1	20	.8	8	8	3	41
Islander (NH)	Rate	9.55	192.43	7.54	74.55	75.31	29.59	388.96
American	N	.5	2	.8	5	1	3	12
Indian, Eskimo,	Rate	22.48	83.62	39.15	229.11	66.22	160.47	601.05
Aleut (NH)								

* Ns in 1000s.
** Rates per 100,000.
SOURCES: U.S. Census 2000a, 2000c.

Although trend data are not provided, it should be noted that these figures reflect substantial twentieth-century changes in both the number of people employed in justice-related occupations overall, and ethnoracial group distributions. Lawyers are illustrative of this shift. In 1900, there were around 113,000 lawyers in the United States, 99 percent of whom were White men. In 1940, there were nearly 177,000 lawyers in the United States, and 97 percent were White men. By 1990, the total number of lawyers grew to 747,000, with the proportion White men decreasing to 71 percent. By 2000, there were approximately 870,000 lawyers in the United States, 65 percent of whom were White men (about 11 percent of lawyers in 2000 were non-White, and almost 30 percent were women).[38] Women account for much of the increase in the justice workforce generally, and its racial and ethnic diversity in particular. Non-White women approach statistical parity with or surpass male counterparts in sectors of the justice workforce, trends especially apparent in the case of African-American women in the judiciary and corrections.[39]

While the size and stratification of the justice workforce has changed dramatically over the past century, data presented here reveal the limited integration of ethnoracial minorities across sectors of the justice workforce. Non-Whites are heavily concentrated in service sectors of the justice workforce, and underrepresented in professional and administrative roles. Consider the distribution of African-American workers. Probably reflecting pressures to integrate police organizations, the greatest parity in Black and White representation is among police officers. Yet, there is a high concentration of African American workers in corrections, and substantial underrepresentation relative to non-Hispanic Whites among judges, lawyers, police administrators, and legal assistants. A similar but more extreme pattern of occupational concentration is apparent among Hispanics.[40]

Asians and American Indians present slightly different patterns of distribution in the justice workforce. Like Hispanics and to a lesser extent Blacks, Asian Americans are significantly underrepresented among judges and legal assistants, and even more so among police (administrators and officers) and corrections officers. However, Asian Americans have relatively high rates of representation among lawyers, thus reducing their service sector concentration compared to Black and Hispanic justice workers. American Indian justice workers approach statistical parity with Whites in the judiciary, policing, and corrections, a trend undoubtedly reflecting American Indian employment in tribal policing, courts, and correctional institutions. Owing to underrepresentation among lawyers, who play less significant roles in tribal courts, American Indians are concentrated in service sectors of the justice workforce at rates comparable to Blacks and Hispanics.[41]

Two main observations should be emphasized regarding patterns of ethnoracial stratification in the U.S. justice workforce. First, current distributions reflect substantial increases in the representation of racial and ethnic minorities and women in the U.S. justice workforce, particularly in professional and administrative roles. Second, and contrary to this apparent progress, non-White justice workers, with the partial exceptions of Asian Americans and American Indians, remain concentrated in service sectors of the justice workforce. Two-thirds of all Black, Hispanic, and American Indian justice workers are in service-oriented occupations considered here, compared to one-half of White and Asian American workers. While this stratification has been noted in prior research on individual occupations, its systemic dimensions are only visible when multiple occupations are considered.[42] Analyzing ethnoracial group representation across the division of justice-related labor yields a more comprehensive perspective on the scope and significance of diversity in the contemporary justice workforce.

Beyond Assumptions and Statistics: On the Impact of Diversity

Several assumptions were identified regarding the significance of diversity in justice-related occupations. On the whole, these assumptions suggest that increased "statistical representation" of a group in a given field relates to that group's "substantive and symbolic representation" in the given field, as well as its perception of justice system legitimacy.[43] Data presented here relate to statistical representation in the justice workforce, offering nothing directly about substantive or symbolic representation. In light of contemporaneous changes in U.S. criminal justice systems, however, these data offer some basis for reflection on the substantive significance of increased statistical representation to systemic outcomes.

The presence of ethnoracial minorities and women in the justice workforce increased substantially over the twentieth century, and particularly in the past several decades. Yet minority workers remain concentrated in service sectors of the justice workforce, relegated largely to execution of assigned tasks. Two contemporaneous developments have implications for our interpretation of this increased statistical representation, on the one hand, and pattern of occupational segregation, on the other: (1) increasing penal managerial objectives of criminal justice systems; and (2) the standardization of decision-making routines in criminal justice administration.

There is broad awareness of the increasingly punitive thrust of American criminal justice, and its disproportionate impact on ethnoracial minorities.[44] It is not necessary to elaborate on this development here, except to emphasize that systems once more inclined toward rehabilitative objectives, crime prevention, and alternatives to incarceration (in broad if not racially generalizable terms) have moved toward more retributive principles of criminal social control. Thus, probation and parole agencies have in recent decades "de-emphasized the social work ethos that used to dominate their work and instead present themselves as providers of inexpensive, community-based punishments, oriented toward the monitoring of offenders and the management of risk."[45] Juvenile systems long distinguished by rehabilitative philosophies and apparent emphasis on the offender's "best interest" have turned to more exclusionary penalties in the name of "accountability-based" sanctions. It remains unclear how the new rhetoric and related reforms have affected practices, but U.S. justice systems have been reoriented in past decades by "penal managerial" impulses.[46]

Coinciding with these shifts is a reorganization of decision making in justice administration. The public and politicians have become distrusting of certain "custodians of justice" over the past half-century, determining not to leave so much to their discretion. The result has been an increased involvement of the executive branch in criminal justice decision making, a shifting balance of discretion from the judicial to the prosecutorial role, and various efforts to routinize decision making, such as sentencing guidelines, prescribed enhancements, mandatory waivers of jurisdiction, and the introduction of various actuarial or less scientific classification instruments.[47] This reorganization redistributes if not diminishes discretion in justice processing, and thereby the relevance of decision-maker characteristics and orientations to decision-making outcomes.

The ethnoracial diversification of the U.S. justice workforce accelerated after 1960, coinciding with political and organizational shifts. Given this context, there is cause to question the impact of ethnoracial diversity in the contemporary justice workforce. Insofar as minority workers are uniquely inclined toward equitable and progressive crime control in minority communities, itself an unresolved question, they are "swimming upstream" against tides of criminal justice policy emphasizing punishment and incapacitation—in the midst of "wars" on crime and drugs. Whatever unique sensitivities these "new voices" might bring to justice administration are further muted and distorted by the routinization of decision making, especially considering their concentration in occupations charged with executing tasks defined elsewhere.

Taken together, the shifting goals of criminal social control, the reorganization of decision making, and patterns of occupational segregation suggest that an increased statistical representation of ethnoracial minorities in the justice workforce has not fundamentally altered prevailing ideas and practices of justice in the United States. While increased representation has probably contributed some to a more equitable distributions of justice services and sanctions, and to the democratization of decision making, systemic factors appear to limit and distort any ethnoracial minority group influence.

Conclusion: A New Agenda for Race and Justice Workforce Research

The equitable representation of racial and ethnic groups in justice-related occupations has been proposed as a means to bolster the actual performance and perceived legitimacy of justice systems. Yet a limited and disjointed body of research has been advanced to evaluate and guide this reform strategy. Existing research and anecdotal evidence tends to challenge assumptions about relationships among race and ethnicity, professional orientation, and eventual outcomes in justice processes, but findings on these questions are mixed, and the subject is worthy of far more systematic engagement. Research has neglected issues of agency in race, crime, and justice research generally, and nearly all we know about the scope and significance of diversity in the justice workforce comes from studies of isolated occupations.

This chapter argues for a more systemic analysis of race and the justice workforce, where patterns of racial and ethnic stratification are examined within and across the division of justice-related labor. This framework considers the hierarchical organization of the justice workforce itself, thus expanding our ability to assess the scope and significance of diversity to justice system processes and outcomes. Data presented here reveal the occupational segregation of minority justice workers in service-related fields characterized by limited power and prestige, greater exposure to risk, and a relegation to the execution of tasks established elsewhere. Considering this concentration in service occupations, as well as broader and contemporaneous developments concerning the politics and organization of criminal social control, it seems unlikely that marked statistical increases in the representation of ethnoracial minority justice workers have yielded major changes in the administration of U.S. justice systems. Though these "new voices" are probably an important presence, whatever unique sensitivities they bring to the idea and practice of justice appear to be muted and distorted by social organizational constraints on their influence. Future research should further examine expectations regarding the significance of diversity in the justice workforce and test the empirical questions they raise.

These are more than academic concerns. The United States and other racialized societies have witnessed incredible increases in the number of people in prisons, jails, and detention facilities, a vastly disproportionate segment of whom are ethnoracial minorities.[48] Various collateral damages have been associated with racialized mass imprisonment, including diminished employment opportunity, access to public housing and education, and political representation, as well as the breakdown of community social structure, all of which further marginalize racial and ethnic minority individuals, families, and communities.[49]

If increased diversity in the justice workforce offers to promote more equitable and legitimate justice system outcomes, it is urgent that conditions essential for these contributions be clarified and achieved. If we develop more systematic and systemic research on race and representation in the justice workforce, as well as address other dimensions of ethnoracial group agency in justice processes, the next wave of race, crime, and justice research may provide constructive insight into some of the most pressing social problems of our time. To this end, I close by specifying four key challenges awaiting future research on race and the justice workforce:

(1) Defining the Justice Workforce

Future research should refine the conceptualization and operationalization of the "justice workforce." What are the relevant occupations, how should we understand their hierarchical distribution, and what methods of analysis are appropriate for determining patterns of representation therein? This chapter offers an exploratory framework that requires empirical validation and invites further research at various levels of analysis (i.e., local, state, federal, and global entities). Improved data would not only expand and refine occupational distinctions in the proposed workforce but also facilitate analysis of stratification within occupations.

(2) Conceptualizing and Operationalizing Substantive Representation

Another major challenge is further conceptualizing and operationalizing "substantive representation." There are at least two dimensions to this challenge: (1) developing more robust measures of racial background, differentiating ascribed racial characteristics from racial identification (some research draws such distinctions, yet most measure race as a static, ascribed characteristic of decision makers, as here); and (2) relating measures of professional orientation and behavior to comparable data on constituent interests and expectations, and considering how race and other status or contextual characteristics relate to their convergence and/or dislocation over time.

(3) Measuring the Impact of Diversity on Outcomes

It is noteworthy that the overrepresentation of ethnoracial minorities among the criminally accused and punished has continued and in some ways intensified over the past half-century, as the justice workforce has grown more diverse. Future research should focus on the significance of diversity in the justice workforce to outcomes in justice administration, including this apparent paradox. Diversification may have had a net-widening effect, considering concentrations at intake (i.e., arrest) and custodial stages, and contemporaneous changes in criminal justice policy. Selective integration of minority justice workers—and particularly ethnoracial minority police deployed in previously underserved minority communities—may increase minority contact with criminal justice systems, intensifying their disproportionate arrest and incarceration.

(4) Developing Comparative-International Research

Finally, there is both need and unique opportunity for comparative and international research on race and the justice workforce. Issues of ethnoracial group representation in justice administration are salient in the vast majority of modern societies. Difficulties facing transnational research on race/ethnicity and crime may be less pronounced in justice workforce research, where need to reconcile incomparable laws and customs is diminished. The challenge facing comparative justice workforce research is reconciling the range of group representational interests with the realities of justice in action.

NOTES

1. Hughes 1932.

2. Walker 1980.

3. Ibid.:253.

4. Walker 1998:236–37.

5. In corporate work environments, Thomas and Ely (2001) find a similar array of perspectives (discrimination/fairness; integration/learning; and access/legitimacy) on the significance of diversity.

6. Marshall 1993:xi. Black justice workers of varied political persuasion have long reflected on the praxis of legal activism. See Alexander 1974; Cochran and Fisher 2002; Smith 1998; Styles 1934; Washington 1994; Wright 1973, 1984, 1987.

7. Smith 1993:3; also see Edwards 1982 [1959]:133; Washington 1972.

8. Harper 1991:3.

9. Napolitano 2001.

10. See Byers 2002; Holdaway 1996; Irwin 1980; Pope and Lovell 2000; Snyder-Joy 1995.

11. Jacobs and Cohen 1978:168. Also see Fridell et al. 2001. That riots were caused by White police is a gross simplification. As Blauner (1972) and others point out, White officers along with "Negro police and 'responsible' moderate leaders . . . were objects of the crowd's anger," being agents of an illegitimized social order (cited in Cashmore and McLaughlin 1991:90).

12. U.S. Department of Justice 2003.

13. Conyers and Nadler 2003; Office of the Inspector General 2004; Serrano 2003; U.S. Department of Justice 2002.

14. Herman 2002:1. Also see the typology of "corrections consumers" in Aguirre (2004). Wilkins (2004) notes a rise of "market-based diversity arguments" in the context of corporate law.

15. Fels 1988; Hansson and van Zyl Smit 1990; Holdaway 1996; Holdaway and Barron 1997; Kituai 1998; Weitzer 1995; World Policy Institute 2004.

16. Gould 2002:1–2.

17. Higginbotham 1992. He asks, "How is it that in President F. W. de Klerk's less than three years in office, one of his 31 appointments to South Africa's courts

is a black lawyer, while of the 115 Bush and Reagan appointments to the Courts of Appeals in 12 years, only two have been African-American?"

18. Young 1990:198. In this vein, it is important to look beyond distributions of racialized actors across occupations and examine the justice of this division of labor itself. This chapter does not attempt such an analysis but should inform its development.

19. Crouch and Alpert 1980; Jacobs and Kraft 1978; Raganella and White 2004.

20. Bennett and Johnson 2000; Cullen et al. 1993; Jurik 1985; Smith 1983.

21. Fisher-Giorlando and Jiang 2000; Mastrofski, Reisig, and McCluskey 2002; Spohn 1990a, 1990b; Uhlman 1978, 1979; Walker and Barrow 1985.

22. Dulaney 1996; Gottschall 1983; Luna-Firebaugh 2003; Weitzer 2000b.

23. Holmes et al. 1993; Welch, Combs, and Gruhl 1988.

24. Examples of studies engaging multiple categories of justice workers include Balbus 1973; Britton 2003; Dulaney 1996; Sachs 1973.

25. Alex 1969; Bolton and Feagin 2004; Chapman 1912; Fels 1988; Greene 2000; Holdaway and Barron 1997; Weitzer 1995, 2000b.

26. Hero and Tolbert 1995; Smith 1983; Welch 1990.

27. Irwin 1980; Jacobs and Kraft 1978; Philliber 1987.

28. But see Greene and Gabbidon 2000; Phillips and Bowling 2003; Russell 1992; Young and Greene 1995.

29. Dulaney 1996; Rudwick 1961a.

30. Brogdon and Shearing 1993; Day 2001; Hansson and van Zyl Smit 1990; Kituai 1998; Reynolds 1998.

31. Uhlman 1978:893; cited in Walker, Spohn and DeLone 2004:238.

32. Wright 1973:22–23; cited in Walker et al. 2004:238.

33. Zatz 1987.

34. See Young 1990:216–17.

35. U.S. Bureau of the Census 1990.

36. Law (and other) professors contribute to the interpretation of law and training of legal professionals, both of which may vary according to the diversity of the professoriate. See Crenshaw 1989b; Russell 1992.

37. The U.S. Census offers useful but limited data on the justice workforce. Occupations are not disaggregated by jurisdiction, area of legal practice, or other relevant distinctions (i.e., rank). Key occupations are not enumerated (probation and parole officers), or are inconsistently included.

38. Epstein 1993:4; Smith 1993:625–37; U.S. Bureau of the Census 1990, 2000c.

39. U.S. Bureau of the Census 1990, 2000c; But see Sokoloff 1992: ch. 7.

40. "Other" and mixed-race workers are excluded for simplification. These respondents are disproportionately Hispanic, but coding other and mixed-race respondents as Hispanic does not substantially alter distributions reported here; Hispanic concentration in service sectors decreases from 74 percent unadjusted to 72 percent as adjusted.

41. Deloria and Lytle 1983.

42. Biskup 1973; Dulaney 1996; Hansson and van Zyl Smit 1990; Holdaway and Barron 1997; Rudwick 1961a, 1961b; Sachs 1973; U.S. Department of Justice 2002.

43. For definitions of "representation," see Hero and Tolbert 1995; Swain 1995.

44. Fagan and Zimring 2000; Feld 1999; Garland 2001; Simon 1997.

45. Garland 2001:18.

46. Wacquant 2001.

47. Champion 1994; Silver and Miller 2002; Travis 2002; Zatz 1987.

48. Broadhurst 1997; Mauer 1999; Sudbury 2004.

49. Mauer and Chesney-Lind 2002; Roberts 2004.

Part II

Populations and Intersectionalities

Toward an Understanding of the Lower Rates of Homicide in Latino versus Black Neighborhoods

A Look at Chicago

María B. Vélez

Criminologists have paid considerable attention to explaining the high levels of crime in Black neighborhoods.[1] Unfortunately, very little work has extended this research to Latino communities. In fact, scholars have been slow to recognize and explain why levels of crime appear to be significantly lower in Latino than in Black neighborhoods.[2] One study found that homicide rates across El Paso, Miami, and San Diego were between .6 and two times lower in Latino than in Black neighborhoods.[3] The pattern of lower homicide rates in Latino neighborhoods also holds for Chicago. In this city, the average homicide rate was .43 per thousand persons across all Latino neighborhoods, or about one homicide for every two thousand people.[4] The rate in Black neighborhoods was nearly double that, averaging .84 homicides per thousand people. Such differences in homicide rates in Chicago exist regardless of the level of neighborhood poverty, an important correlate of crime.[5] Among extremely poor neighborhoods, for example, Latino areas averaged .61 fewer homicides per thousand people than African American neighborhoods.[6] Similar patterns are observed for low- and high-poverty areas.

The purpose of this chapter is to investigate in a preliminary manner why homicide rates are lower in Latino than in Black neighborhoods in Chicago. My central argument is that the lower rate of violence is due to the relatively advantageous structural position of Latino neighborhoods. Specifically, compared to Black neighborhoods, Latino communities in

Chicago have (1) lower levels of concentrated disadvantage (e.g., male joblessness, female-headed families), (2) a greater prevalence of immigrants who appear to provide protective mechanisms against crime, (3) better relationships with economic officials, the police department, and local politicians, and (4) greater spatial proximity to White, more advantaged neighborhoods. Thus, I propose that, even in the same city, Latino neighborhoods provide structurally distinct milieus that are not as vulnerable to crime-producing conditions as is the case for African American communities.

A focus on Latinos helps us better understand neighborhood criminological processes by commenting upon the generalizability of important structural concepts, such as concentrated disadvantage and racial residential segregation, to populations other than African Americans. As I argue in this chapter, these concepts do indeed seem generalizable to Latinos because the relatively low rates of killing in Latino neighborhoods correspond to relatively low levels of crime-producing structural conditions. Extending research in this manner is important for the general discipline of criminology given that Latinos are the largest minority population in the United States and their population share will only continue to increase. In 2000, Latinos made up 12.5 percent of the U.S. population and demographers estimate that this share will nearly double by 2050.[7] Given this dramatic growth, any understanding of the link between neighborhoods and crime will be grossly incomplete if Latino neighborhoods are not incorporated into the analysis.

This chapter will also hopefully broaden our understanding of the structural sources of crime. Past work has tended to overemphasize a limited repertoire of explanatory variables such as poverty and male joblessness. In contrast, this chapter takes a fresh look at the conceptualization of social structure in two regards. First, I examine how immigration—a concept largely neglected in the race-crime literature—creates neighborhood environments that reduce criminogenic conditions. Although particularly important for Latinos, immigration is theoretically relevant for Black neighborhoods that experience immigration from places like Haiti and Somalia. In fact, more than 6 percent of self-identified Blacks were foreign born in 2000.[8] Second, I incorporate structural factors like the responsiveness of city officials and racial residential segregation that have been underanalyzed in the race-crime literature. In doing so, I seek to provide a richer understanding of the structural correlates of crime.

Examining Black and Latino homicide rates in Chicago has both limitations and strengths. In terms of limitations, scholars need to assess whether the findings presented here apply to other cities in the "Rustbelt" such as New York and Philadelphia as well as settings in the South and the West where most Latinos reside. Yet, a focus on Chicago has two advantages. It is difficult to contrast Latinos and Blacks in locations where one group is very small because there are too few neighborhoods to compare. This is not the case in Chicago, where Blacks and Latinos comprise 36 and 26 percent of the city's residents, respectively.[9] Another strength is that Chicago has received arguably the most empirical and theoretical attention by criminologists. Focusing on Chicago allows work on Latino neighborhoods to be integrated more thoroughly into existing theoretical and empirical work.

The Racial Invariance Thesis: An Emphasis on Social Structure

This chapter is guided by the racial invariance thesis—the idea that criminological processes are the same for all neighborhoods regardless of racial composition.[10] In other words, factors that affect crime, such as employment opportunities, concentrated disadvantage, and informal social control, should apply equally regardless of whether the neighborhood is predominantly White, Latino, or Black. Therefore, for example, the relatively high levels of structural disadvantage in African American neighborhoods are responsible for their high levels of crime, especially in comparison to White neighborhoods.

The racial invariance thesis necessitates a focus on structural conditions. Factors that have received attention include concentrated disadvantage and the presence of public housing. Research has shown strong support for the role of these factors in explaining the Black-White gap in neighborhood crime. For example, a study of Columbus, Ohio, neighborhoods found that once neighborhood levels of disadvantage were taken into account, there were no significant differences in property-crime rates in Black versus White neighborhoods.[11] Concentrated disadvantage also accounted for a large portion of the higher levels of violent crime in Columbus's Black communities than in its White communities. Similarly, a study of Atlanta neighborhoods found that the percentage of African Americans in a neighborhood was related to homicide, assault, and public order crimes only within a mile of public housing.[12] Moreover, property crime rates were not significantly different between Atlanta's White and

Black neighborhoods once adjustments for disadvantage and proximity to public housing projects were made. Studies like these suggest the usefulness of examining structural characteristics of neighborhoods to explain crime disparities across racial/ethnic populations.

Structural Explanations of Black-Latino Crime Differences

This chapter highlights four promising structural features linked to neighborhood levels of crime that differentiate Latino and Black neighborhoods in Chicago. To be consistent with the racial invariance thesis, the lower rates of killing in Latino neighborhoods should correspond with lower levels of structural disadvantage. As I demonstrate below, this is indeed the case.

Concentrated Disadvantage

Concentrated disadvantage is a central explanation of the Black-White gap in crime.[13] Concentrated disadvantage refers to the simultaneous presence of heightened levels of poverty, male joblessness, female-headed families, and a dearth of professional/managerial role models. When disadvantage is concentrated across these dimensions, it leads to acute levels of social isolation, which refers to the lack of sustained contact with mainstream institutions and individuals.[14] In turn, socially isolated neighborhoods cannot organize effectively against crime (e.g., mobilize block watches), experience an increase in "ghetto related behavior" like drug dealing, and eventually experience heightened levels of violent and property crime. Research has consistently supported the role of disadvantage in producing crime.[15]

In accordance with the racial invariance thesis, Latino neighborhoods should have lower levels of concentrated disadvantage than Black neighborhoods.[16] At least in Chicago, this is clearly the case. Figure 5.1 shows that there are more than twice as many Black as Latino neighborhoods with extreme levels of poverty. This pattern of Latino advantage persists when one looks at levels of male joblessness and female-headed families. Only the presence of professionals and managers does not significantly differ across the two types of neighborhoods. The overall lower level of concentrated disadvantage in Latino neighborhoods is further evidenced when the four dimensions are combined to make an index. The average

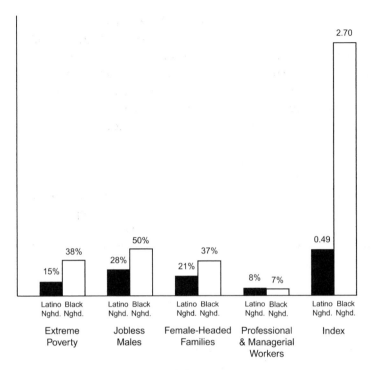

Fig. 5.1. Means for Dimensions of Concentrated Disadvantage and Index of Concentrated Disadvantage

score of Latino neighborhoods on the index of concentrated disadvantage —a measure that standardizes and sums the four dimensions—is less than one-fifth the average score for African American neighborhoods.

The Presence of an Immigrant Population

An emerging body of work suggests that a structural factor that provides protection against crime is the presence of immigrants.[17] Immigrants have lower rates of criminal involvement than nonimmigrants. One study, for instance, found that Haitian, Jamaican, and *Mariel* immigrants had lower homicide-suspect rates than the overall rate for Miami residents in 1990.[18] Similarly, a study of San Diego demonstrated that recent immigrants had significantly lower rates of homicide offending than their native-born counterparts.[19] These city-level findings seem to apply to the neighborhood as well. Communities with large shares of immigrants tend to have lower levels of violence than similarly situated neighborhoods with few immigrants.[20] A study of areas in El Paso with relatively high percentages of immigrants had lower homicide-victimization rates than neighborhoods with few immigrants.[21] This study also found that homicide levels in Miami's African American neighborhoods decreased as the percentage of new immigrants increased. This latter finding is of particular relevance to the racial invariance thesis because it demonstrates that immigrants provide a buffer against crime regardless of the race/ethnicity of the immigrant population in question.

One recent study refines our understanding of the immigration-crime link by distinguishing between communities with long-standing versus recently arrived immigrants. It found that Miami neighborhoods with large shares of 1960s immigrants, presumed to be more established, were less likely to be drug areas (having at least two drug homicides).[22] In contrast, neighborhoods with many recent arrivals in San Diego were more likely to be drug areas. Thus, this study indicates the need for further investigation of the conditions under which immigrants serve as a protective mechanism against crime.

While research has yet to fully uncover *why* the presence of immigrants in a neighborhood helps to control crime, two factors stand out. First, some immigrant communities that are well established have large numbers of immigrants who have been in the United States a long time and have created and sustained an ethnic enclave economy. An ethnic enclave is characterized by the presence of immigrants with sufficient capital to create new opportunities for economic growth and an extensive ethnic division of labor.[23] Typical businesses in enclaves are restaurants, street vendors, and open-air markets that arise in response to the needs of the growing immigrant population. Enclaves provide social capital for their residents by creating job opportunities and higher wages not available outside the enclave for immigrants and nonimmigrants.[24] While many residents may still be poor, the majority are working and should have greater attachment to the labor market. The presence of immigrants, in fact, may explain in part why male joblessness is so much lower in Latino than in Black neighborhoods (see Figure 5.1).

Second, an influx of immigrants may expand community institutions such as churches, schools, and immigrant-focused agencies like legal counseling and job placement.[25] Community institutions are integral in facilitating the control of crime because they organize activities that create networks among residents, provide programming for community youth, help connect communities to mainstream individuals and institutions, and facilitate the recruitment of external resources for the community.[26]

As is the case for the United States, a considerably higher proportion of Latinos than Blacks in Chicago are immigrants. Across Chicago neighborhoods in 1990, on average, 32 percent of residents in Latino neighborhoods were foreign born compared to just 2 percent for Black neighborhoods. The greater presence of immigrants across Chicago's Latino neighborhoods suggests another structural reason why they have lower levels of homicide than Black neighborhoods.

The Responsiveness of Economic Officials, the Police, and Local Politicians

Latino neighborhoods appear to have more favorable ties than Black areas to three key actors: economic officials, the police department, and local politicians. These ties, in turn, lead to an infusion of external resources that place Latino neighborhoods in a more favorable structural position than Black neighborhoods to have lower levels of violence.

Economic Officials. Neighborhoods with favorable relationships with banks are more likely to be allocated residential bank loans. This resource is crucial given that loans profoundly affect neighborhood viability.[27] Neighborhoods that receive few loans, for instance, are unable to build new housing, repair dilapidated housing, recruit new home buyers, sustain existing businesses, and attract new businesses. These events heighten criminogenic conditions because they lead to neighborhood depopulation, a decline in local economic opportunities, a weakening of local social ties, and the deterioration of community institutions like schools and churches. Given their importance to neighborhood viability, an infusion of these monies provides incentives for residents to stay in the neighborhood because they allow residents to renovate and/or refinance their homes. Encouraging residents to invest further in their neighborhood should make them more willing to participate in local activities such as block watches or community associations. These types of activities, in turn, stimulate the kinds of community control needed to reduce crime and victimization. Furthermore, strengthening organizations should allow such groups to more effectively lobby for additional external resources, which will reduce crime even more.[28]

Presumably because of better ties, banks clearly allocate more loan

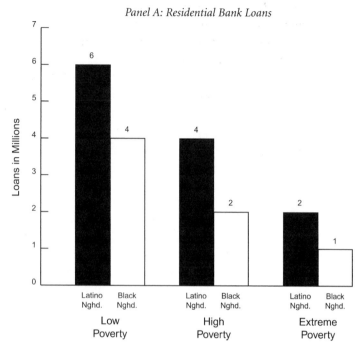

Panel A: Residential Bank Loans

Fig. 5.2. (*above and opposite*) The Responsiveness of Economic Officials, the Police, and Local Politicians in Latino and Black Neighborhoods

dollars to Latino than to Black neighborhoods. On average, in fact, banks allocated $2 million more to Latino neighborhoods than to Black neighborhoods in Chicago.[29] Panel A of Figure 5.2 shows the distribution of loans at varying levels of neighborhood poverty. Banks award significantly higher amounts of loans—between $1 and $2 million more—to Latino than to Black neighborhoods within all three poverty categories.

Police Department. A favorable relationship between a neighborhood and the police occurs when residents trust that the police are responsive to the needs of the community and treat residents in a fair, equitable, and just manner. People are likely to trust the police when officers are active players in helping the community control crime, such as by patrolling the neighborhood or by quickly responding to calls. Factors such as these minimize the opportunity for crime to take place without sanction. In addition, residents in neighborhoods with better ties to the police feel more comfortable and safe[30] and thus are more likely to engage in informal acts

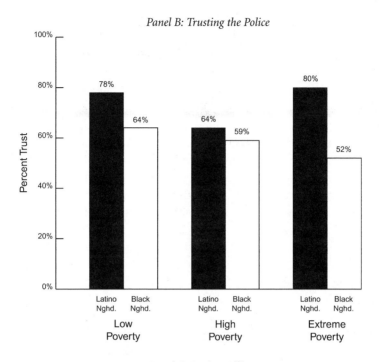

Panel B: Trusting the Police

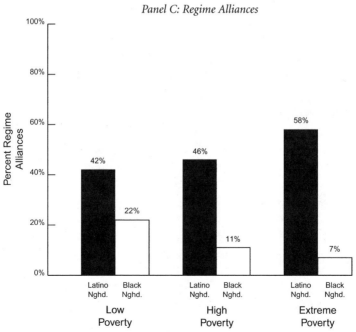

Panel C: Regime Alliances

of social control such as watching out for neighbors' property and questioning strangers in the neighborhood. The police can also help increase informal social control by attending community meetings and facilitating neighborhood watch groups.

One way to gauge the relationship between a neighborhood and the local police is to examine the percentage of area residents that report trusting the police. Overall, in 2000, nearly 70 percent of those living in Chicago's Latino neighborhoods reported trusting the police compared to only 58 percent in African American neighborhoods.[31] Panel B of Figure 5.2 shows that this pattern holds true at different levels of poverty. For instance, 80 percent of residents in extremely poor Latino neighborhoods trust the police compared to just 52 percent of residents in extremely poor Black neighborhoods.

Local Politicians. Neighborhoods that are represented by elected officials who are part of the formal and informal governing coalition of a city should receive a disproportionate share of city-allocated resources. While local Black or Latino officials both seek to secure resources for their respective constituencies, their ability to do so depends upon whether they are a part of the local governing regime.[32] Neighborhoods with powerful political connections should be able to secure greater city resources that equip them with tools to effectively control crime. For example, neighborhoods can utilize city-allocated funds to subsidize community organizations that provide programing like after-school recreation, facilitating the supervision of youth and thus curbing delinquency. Likewise, neighborhoods with regime alliances should be able to more effectively pressure city agencies to remove physical disorder such as graffiti than neighborhoods with no regime alliances.

To examine whether Latino neighborhoods are more strongly tied to the governing regime, I assess whether the neighborhood's alderperson serves as chair of one of the nineteen standing committees of the Chicago City Council in 1991.[33] In Chicago, Latino neighborhoods are more closely tied to the governing regime than Black neighborhoods. Specifically, nearly four times more Latino than Black neighborhoods had an alderperson that chaired one of the nineteen standing committees. Panel C of Figure 5.2 shows that the political advantage of Latino neighborhoods holds true at all poverty levels. For instance, Latino neighborhoods that are extremely poor are eight times more likely to have regime alliances than African American neighborhoods.

Racial Residential Segregation

The extent to which a minority population is residentially segregated from Whites can heighten neighborhood levels of crime.[34] Racial residential segregation concentrates disadvantage within minority communities, which, in turn, undermines a community's ability to organize effectively against crime. It also creates conditions that encourage individuals to act violently. In highly segregated minority communities, for instance, residents may adopt strategies like the "code of the street" that increase the likelihood of using violence to resolve interpersonal conflict.[35]

Latinos are clearly living under less segregated conditions than Blacks.[36] Data from the 2000 census and the Lewis Mumford Center for Comparative Urban and Regional Research show that African Americans in the United States live in communities that are hyper-segregated, with a dissimilarity index of 62.[37] In contrast, Latinos across the United States live in communities with modest levels of segregation, indicated by a dissimilarity index score of 48.[38] The pattern is somewhat different in Chicago for 2000 in that both Blacks and Latinos live in hyper-segregated communities; both have dissimilarity indices above 60. However, the index for Chicago's Latinos is 62, barely above 60, whereas for Chicago's African Americans it is substantially higher at 81.[39]

Latino neighborhoods are also less isolated from White neighborhoods than is the case for African American neighborhoods. This can be seen in two ways in Chicago. First, Latino neighborhoods serve as "buffer zones" between White communities and Black communities.[40] Predominantly Latino neighborhoods are located mostly in the north central and central areas of Chicago, situated between White and Black neighborhoods. African American neighborhoods, in contrast, are located in the central west and southern areas of the city—far removed from predominantly White neighborhoods, which largely encompass the outer ring of the city, and upper-income areas adjacent to Lake Michigan. Second, extremely poor Latino neighborhoods are less clustered together than their Black counterparts. In particular, extremely poor Latino neighborhoods are more widely distributed in the Chicago area while extremely poor Black neighborhoods are more closely clustered together.

Spatial advantage means that Latino neighborhoods are in a better position to protect themselves from crime because they benefit from the spillover of nearby more affluent and socially organized neighborhoods.

Socially organized neighborhoods are characterized by strong networks both among residents and with local political and economic officials that facilitate the control of crime.[41] This line of thinking is supported by a study of child-centered collective efficacy across Chicago neighborhoods.[42] In neighborhoods with child-centered collective efficacy, there are substantial connections between adults and children, exchanges between neighbors regarding child rearing, and a willingness to intervene on behalf of local children. This study found that Latino/mixed neighborhoods were more likely to be fully efficacious than African American areas.[43] They also found that, even if Latino/mixed neighborhoods had low levels of child-centered collective efficacy, they were 1.5 times more likely than Black neighborhoods to be surrounded by neighborhoods with high levels of collective efficacy. In fact, the authors found Black neighborhoods to be spatially *vulnerable*—even if an African American neighborhood had a high level of child-centered collective efficacy, it was three times more likely than a Latino area to be surrounded by neighborhoods with low levels of collective efficacy.

Discussion

Latino neighborhoods in Chicago, and in other cities as well, have lower homicide rates than African American neighborhoods. To account for this disparity, I have developed a line of theoretical reasoning that hinges on the different structural positions of Latino and Black neighborhoods. In particular, I argue that Latino neighborhoods are structurally advantaged vis-à-vis Black neighborhoods, situating them to have lower levels of homicide. To make this argument I point to how, compared to Black neighborhoods, Latino neighborhoods have less concentrated disadvantage, more immigrants, better ties to economic officials, the police department, and local politicians, and less segregation from White affluent neighborhoods. The structural approach adopted here is in line with criminological theory that emphasizes social structure to explain racial/ethnic crime disparities. It also pushes researchers to more fully capture the neighborhood dynamics of other minority populations and thus move beyond the traditional set of structural variables that are based on the African American experience.

The structural approach I use speaks directly to the racial invariance thesis. Some scholars have suggested a racially variant approach by arguing that key concepts that underlie explanations of Black-White crime differences are not applicable to Latinos.[44] The argument is that economic restructuring and the exodus of a middle class are not salient for the understanding of crime in Latino neighborhoods. Moreover, this perspective views immigration as a structural feature unique to Latinos. While these claims have some merit, searching for racially variant causal processes is misguided in two ways. First, it is important to separate a theoretical concept from its operationalization. I suggest that many traditional concepts used to understand criminological processes are indeed generalizable to Latino neighborhoods but may need to be operationalized differently to capture their unique historical experiences and contemporary circumstances. This argument can be illustrated with the theoretical concept of the availability of job opportunities that is central to explanations of crime. For African Americans in "Rustbelt" cities, job opportunities are hypothesized to be influenced by deindustrialization and thus can be measured by the resultant loss of manufacturing jobs. However, for Latinos living on the U.S.–Mexican border, job opportunities are tied closely to the health of the Mexican economy and thus may be measured by the number of retail jobs and businesses that serve Mexico's upper- and middle-class shoppers.[45] Such historically sensitive operationalizations do not mean that we have to abandon the racial invariance thesis because the underlying concept remains the same.

Similarly, even if a particular concept does not seem to characterize the typical historical experience of a specific racial or ethnic population, this does not mean that the concept does not *theoretically* apply. For instance, an exodus of the middle class because of an infusion of immigrants does not generally characterize Latino communities. However, where depopulation of the middle class has occurred, we would expect it to heighten local crime for Latino neighborhoods. Similarly, while immigration is not a particularly salient aspect of many Black neighborhoods, where it has occurred, it should reduce crime in Black neighborhoods. In fact, research shows that this is the case for Miami's Black neighborhoods.[46] In sum, I argue that we do not need to develop unique theories to explain crime in Latino versus Black neighborhoods any more than we need to develop unique theories to explain crime in Black versus White neighborhoods.

Drawing on these insights, I offer two general avenues for future work. First, more research is needed so that we can better understand the link between immigrant communities and crime. Quantitative studies should evaluate whether neighborhoods with large shares of immigrants do indeed have lower levels of crime ceteris paribus, across a variety of cities and immigrant populations. To date this observation has been made in only a handful of locations. This can be done by matching census tract data on the percentage of foreign-born residents and their recency of arrival with official crime data. Furthermore, future research should determine what specific characteristics of immigrant communities provide protective buffers against crime. Is it because predominantly immigrant communities have more job opportunities that connect residents to the formal labor market? Is it because they have strong community institutions like the Catholic Church and immigrant-serving agencies that promote formal social control? Is it because these communities have strong ties among neighbors that facilitate informal supervision of the neighborhood? One strategy for investigating the protective nature of immigration would be to conduct an ethnography, much like Pattillo-McCoy's *Black Picket Fences,* that compares Latino neighborhoods that differ in their levels of immigrants.

Second, the rich diversity among Latino subgroups affords a strategic opportunity to test the racial invariance thesis. The three largest populations—Mexicans, Puerto Ricans, and Cubans—differ on important structural dimensions. Compared to Cuban Americans, for instance, both Mexican Americans and Puerto Ricans have considerably lower family incomes and higher poverty rates.[47] Census data suggest other ways in which Latino subpopulations differ on theoretically relevant dimensions, such as foreign-born population share, educational attainment, occupation, and family structure.[48] A straightforward test of the racial invariance thesis could be conducted with regression decomposition. This technique assesses the extent to which crime rate differences among different racial ethnic populations are due to variation in the means (indicative of racial invariance) or their effects (indicative of racial variance) of structural disadvantage factors.[49] Taking Latinos and the structural characteristics of their neighborhoods seriously will undoubtedly broaden our understanding of the race-crime link, and help criminologists keep pace with the ever changing racial and ethnic composition of the United States.

NOTES

1. Krivo and Peterson 1996; McNulty 1999; McNulty and Holloway 2000; Pattillo-McCoy 1999; Sampson and Wilson 1995; Shaw and McKay 1942, 1949; Wilson 1987, 1996.

2. There is a larger body of research that compares offending rates between African Americans and Latinos (i.e., Bradshaw et al. 1998; Martinez 2002; Martinez and Lee 2000a). This work consistently shows that rates of criminal involvement by Latinos are lower than for African Americans.

3. Lee, Martinez, and Rosenfeld 2001.

4. Homicide data for 1993–1995 were downloaded from the Chicago Homicide Data Set at the Inter-University Consortium for Political and Social Research (ICPSR) data archive (http://www.icpsr.umich.edu). These data are from police counts that were geo-coded according to the address of the incident, collected originally by Block and Block (1998). African American and Latino neighborhoods have 50 percent or more Blacks or Latinos, respectively. The homicide differences noted in the text, and all other comparisons between Latino and African American neighborhoods in Chicago reported in this chapter, are significant at the $p < .05$ level.

5. Krivo and Peterson 1996.

6. I utilize the cut-off points provided by Wilson (1987, 1996) to characterize neighborhood poverty. Neighborhoods with *extreme* levels of poverty are those with 40 percent or more of their residents living below the poverty line. Nineteen (15.57 percent) Latino neighborhoods and 122 (38.01 percent) African American neighborhoods fit within this category. Neighborhoods with *high* levels of poverty are those with poverty rates between 20 and 39 percent. Seventy-two (59.07 percent) Latino neighborhoods and 116 (36.14 percent) Black neighborhoods fit within this category. Neighborhoods with low levels of poverty are those with less than 20 percent of their residents living below the poverty line. Thirty-six (29.51 percent) Latino neighborhoods and eighty-three (25.90 percent) African American neighborhoods fit within this category.

7. Ramirez and de la Cruz 2002.

8. U.S. Bureau of the Census 2002a.

9. Ibid.

10. Bursik and Grasmick 1993; Krivo and Peterson 1996; Sampson and Wilson 1995; Shaw and McKay 1942.

11. Krivo and Peterson 1996.

12. McNulty and Holloway 2000.

13. Krivo and Peterson 1996; McNulty and Holloway 2000; Sampson and Wilson 1995; Wilson 1987, 1996.

14. Wilson 1987:60.

15. See, for example, Krivo and Peterson 1996; Peeples and Loeber 1994; Peterson, Krivo, and Harris 2000.

16. Data for the variables that comprise the concentrated disadvantage index are from the 1990 census (U.S. Bureau of the Census 1991). The geographic identifier for neighborhood is the census tract. The variable, male joblessness, is based on the percentage of civilian noninstitutionalized males ages sixteen to sixty-four

with or without work disabilities who are either unemployed or not in the labor force in a census tract. The variable, female-headed families, is based on the percentage of households that are female-headed families in a census tract. The variable professionals/managers reflects the percentage of persons in a census tract age sixteen and older employed in professional and managerial occupations.

17. Lee et al. 2001; Martinez 2002; Martinez and Lee 2000a, 2000b; Martinez, Lee, and Nielsen 2004.

18. Martinez and Lee 2000a.

19. Martinez 2002.

20. Lee et al. 2001; Martinez et al. 2004.

21. Lee et al. 2001.

22. Martinez et al. 2004.

23. Portes and Bach 1985.

24. Portes and Jensen 1989.

25. For an illustration of this see Chinchilla, Hamilton, and Loucky 1993.

26. Bursik and Grasmick 1993; Vélez 2001.

27. Kim 2000; Massey and Denton 1993: Skogan 1990; Squires and O'Connor 2001.

28. For example, see Dawley 1992 and Rabrenovic 1996.

29. The variable, residential bank loans, is based on the total dollar amount of residential loans averaged over two years (1992–1993) allocated to each census tract. I utilized the total dollar amount rather than number of loans because it captures a bank's monetary investment in a neighborhood. These loans are for multifamily, home-improvement, and refinancing loans, conventional purchases, and loans made through the Veterans Administration and Federal Housing Administration. These data are compiled from the 1992–1993 issues of the *Community Lending Fact Book,* published by the Woodstock Institute.

30. Reisig and Parks 2004.

31. Data on police trust are from the 2000 wave of the Chicago Metro Survey, which involves interviews with a serial cross-section of adults ages eighteen and older residing in the six-county metropolitan Chicago area.

32. See Browning, Marshall, and Tabb 1984; Miranda and Tunyavong 1994.

33. Data for this measure come from City of Chicago 1991.

34. Logan and Messner 1987; Massey 2001; Massey and Denton 1993; Peterson and Krivo 1993, 1999; Sampson and Wilson 1995.

35. Anderson 1999; Peterson and Krivo 1993, 1999.

36. See also Charles 2003; Clark and Blue 2004; Massey and Denton 1993.

37. The dissimilarity index describes the degree to which a group is evenly distributed across neighborhoods, and indicates the percentage of either group that would have to move into another neighborhood to obtain within-neighborhood population distributions that correspond with the city. A score above 60 is considered to be hyper-segregated.

38. Charles 2003.

39. Ibid.

40. Squires et al. 1987:109–12.

41. Bursik and Grasmick 1993; Vélez 2001.

42. Sampson, Morenoff, and Earls 1999.

43. Although I disentangle the findings for minority neighborhoods, Sampson et al. (1999) focus their discussion on general differences between White and minority neighborhoods. They found that minority neighborhoods are more spatially vulnerable vis-à-vis their levels of child-centered collective efficacy. This means that even if a minority neighborhood has a higher than average level of collective efficacy, it is more likely than a comparable White neighborhood in Chicago to be surrounded by neighborhoods with low levels of collective efficacy.

44. Moore 1989; Moore and Pinderhughes 1993.

45. See Valdez (1993) for an illustration of this dynamic.

46. See Lee et al. 2001.

47. Ramirez 2004.

48. Ibid.

49. See Phillips (2002) for an example of the use of regression decomposition to test racial/ethnic differences in crime.

Chapter 6

Extending Ethnicity and Violence Research in a Multiethnic City

Haitian, African American, and Latino Nonlethal Violence

Ramiro Martinez, Jr., and Amie L. Nielsen

At the twilight of the last century and the dawn of the new one, researchers of the race and violent crime linkage broadened their focus beyond Black and White differences to include studies of other racial and ethnic groups. For example, research on Asian, Native American, and, in particular, Latino crime became progressively more frequent.[1] Still, at least one ethnic group was consistently underrepresented in studies of crime in general and violence in particular: Afro-Caribbeans.[2] This is especially true for Haitians, one of the largest groups in the United States with origins in the Caribbean[3] but a group that has been largely ignored. This oversight has not gone unnoticed in the criminological literature. In the introduction to his recent edited book, Darnell Hawkins[4] notes that prior race and crime research is challenged "by studies that show much variation in rates of interpersonal violence among persons of African ancestry in the United States and Africa in the past and within the black population of the United States today," a racial/ethnic/immigrant distinction that scholars can no longer ignore.

Although Afro-Caribbeans (and persons from sub-Saharan Africa) comprise a smaller proportion of the U.S. population than native-born Blacks, the growing Black diversity in urban America requires attention because it parallels the growth in the Latino and Asian populations that is in large part due to immigration.[5] The Afro-Caribbean population has increased by over 60 percent since 1990, and is concentrated on the East Coast in the New York City and greater Miami metropolitan regions, where immigrants now account for one-quarter to one-third of the total Black population.[6] In fact, in some Miami Black communities, Haitians outnumber native-born African Americans, rendering simple Black-White comparisons obsolete and requiring scholars to move beyond analyses of such racial dichotomies.[7] Failing to do so may result in false conclusions or generalizations based on inaccurate assessments of the racial/ethnic/immigrant makeup of U.S. society. In this chapter, we illustrate the necessity of moving beyond a continued reliance on a Black-White dichotomy by comparing diverse Black groups and Latinos in Miami, Florida. In particular, we examine how nonlethal victimization rates, and the varying contexts in which these occur, differ for Haitian, African American, and Latino communities in Miami.

Although we utilize the case of Haitians in Miami to demonstrate our point, the study of Haitians and Afro-Caribbean groups in general is warranted for reasons beyond just their substantial growth in population in the United States during the last two decades. Namely, most are probably subject to the same structural impediments or disadvantages as native-born Blacks (e.g., African Americans) and other ethnic minorities, including Latinos.[8] That is, they reside in economically disadvantaged communities and are vulnerable to legal and economic exploitation while settling in areas that disproportionately expose them to youth gangs, drugs, criminal activity, and intergroup violence.[9] Additionally, many Haitians encounter obstacles and difficulties that most ethnic minorities routinely avoid.[10] Not only are they foreign-born newcomers but they are also Black and speak French-Creole, a language rarely used by others. Further, federal agencies and the popular media have singled them out and stereotyped them as public health threats (e.g., AIDS-prone and drug abusers), resulting in severe discrimination and, relative to others, a negative reception from the government.[11] These barriers to accommodation and absorption suggest that Haitians have endured and continue to endure a great deal to enter and reside in the United States. Yet, even with these problems in mind little is known about how, or if, they respond to the same crime-generating conditions as other racial or ethnic groups in similar situations.

Moreover, the study of Afro-Caribbean (immigrant Black) crime is important not only because of the light it may shed on within-race variation in crime but also because of its potential for illuminating the role of variation in nativity for understanding crime. In this regard, the study of Haitians presents a race and crime paradox. Being Black, Haitians confront discrimination and prejudice much like African Americans. These social forces, combined with residence in highly segregated Black areas and severe isolation from Whites[12] suggest that Haitians should have high levels of involvement in violence. Yet, research has established that immigrant groups have lower crime than native minority populations.[13] Along with other immigrant groups, Haitians may be less crime involved than expected despite their isolation and disadvantage.

Below, we address two specific questions that contribute to the nascent immigrant Black crime literature: Are Black immigrants more or less crime prone or victimized than native-born Blacks? How do Haitians fare relative to another heavily immigrant group, namely, Latinos? In this chapter, we attempt to provide answers to these questions by exploring possible variations in violent crime for the city of Miami. We examine aggravated assault and robbery victimization among Haitians, African Americans, and Latinos for 1996–1997 in a place with multiple immigrant groups (e.g., Afro-Caribbean groups and Latinos) and immigrant and nonimmigrant Blacks (e.g., Haitians and African Americans). Hence, this chapter moves beyond the traditional and simple Black-White dichotomy that characterizes much criminological research, and represents one of the first attempts to compare violence among these distinct racial/ethnic/immigrant populations.

We draw on two prominent theoretical approaches within the violence and immigration literatures, respectively. Scholars of violent crime offer various explanations for higher levels of crime among ethnic minority groups. At the community level, criminologists direct attention to social disorganization theory. The original focus of this line of inquiry was to illustrate the role that poverty and other social conditions play in shaping crime-inducing contexts in immigrant European and southern Black migrant communities in urban Chicago.[14] Shaw and McKay's[15] work showed that areas with high levels of (European) immigrants had higher delinquency rates than other areas, a finding they attributed to the deleterious conditions of the disorganized areas into which the immigrant groups settled rather than to the groups themselves. In line with this literature, socially disorganized communities may be particularly important for explaining Haitian violent crime victimization.

While we draw from the social disorganization perspective, we also pay attention to the immigration literature. Specifically, the ideas put forth in segmented assimilation perspectives are especially important when immigrant groups are being considered within the study of race and crime.

According to this perspective, "social capital," or the ability to gain access to resources by virtue of membership in social networks and social structure, is a key element in explaining the achievements or difficulties faced by immigrant groups such as Cubans in Little Havana or Haitians in Little Haiti. Some immigrant communities are very poor, but they may be able to assist coethnics in adapting to the new area while buffering deleterious factors typically associated with crime (e.g., extreme disadvantage). Segmented assimilation also describes processes through which the second generation may become assimilated into different race, class, and immigrant groups (e.g., inner-city Black vs. immigrant ethnic enclave) rather than only into the American (mainstream) middle class, processes we describe in more detail below.[16] Before extending this discussion we provide a brief history of Miami's immigrant/racial/ethnic groups, followed by a discussion of their socioeconomic positions.

Origins and Theoretical Elaborations

The city of Miami, Florida, provides an appropriate context for this work, not only because Haitians are the second largest immigrant group in the area behind Cubans[17] but also because most city residents are foreign born (e.g., Cubans, Nicaraguans, Haitians). The city also contains older, more established African American communities. Admittedly, it is difficult to know precisely how many Haitians reside in Miami or the larger metropolitan area because of census undercounts. However, the population grew during the 1990s, and more than half of the Afro-Caribbean population in the Miami region is now Haitian. The largest Haitian concentration is in the Little Haiti neighborhood in the northeastern section of the city.[18]

Having arrived since at least 1977 fleeing political violence and economic turmoil, the vast majority of Haitians were treated as economic migrants and denied asylum hearings by the U.S. government.[19] Interdiction aside, other obstacles have undermined Miami Haitians' absorption and incorporation into the local economy and political arena. Most live in predominantly poor Black areas, most have less social capital (economic and educational opportunities) than others, which damages their economic advancement, and their group's socioeconomic condition overall has long been described as "dismal."[20]

Immigrant communities have long been portrayed as unpleasant places to live. For example, the founders of the Chicago School of Sociology described the immigrant European communities in the St. Stanislaus district, Pilsen, Halsted Street, and other places as undesirable due to their high population density, proximity to industrial areas, proliferation of tenement housing, and higher levels of crime.[21] However, recent illustrations of immigrant communities have changed. For example, while contemporary immigrant Cuban and Haitian communities are populated by newcomers with few economic resources or opportunities, the former group has more of the types of social capital and dense network ties that are helpful in accommodating newcomers.[22] Thus, while early social disorganization theorists described immigrant communities as highly disorganized and subject to processes that create crime, some poor contemporary immigrant areas with high levels of social capital are able to withstand these obstacles. Social capital allows for the relatively successful economic and social incorporation of newcomers. This is a positive aspect of segmented assimilation that many immigrants encounter and one that Latino immigrants in Miami have benefited from in adapting to everyday life.[23]

In contrast, several factors place many Haitians, especially the children of immigrants, at risk for downward mobility and segmented assimilation into poor African American culture.[24] These include the reception by the United States, lack of economic mobility, residential proximity to poor ghettos, and racial discrimination. Pushed to forge an identity, some second-generation youths living in such communities choose to "cover-up" and identify as Black Americans rather than face ostracism from peers because they are Haitian.[25] This leads to assimilation into norms and values of poor inner-city areas, including heightened awareness of racial discrimination, devaluing of education, and an oppositional culture.[26] As a result, chances for upward mobility, especially via education, are limited and downward mobility is likely.

Moreover, segmented assimilation may have implications for violence. Indeed, some research suggests that segmented assimilation, specifically assimilation of immigrants into poor community values and norms,[27] is associated with heightened community-level violence. In the present case, if similar patterns of criminal activity are evidenced for Haitians and African Americans, it would suggest that the consequences of race are stronger than those of immigration. It also suggests that the implications of having connections with and living in socially disorganized African American communities would impact Haitians. That is, if Haitians in Miami are, in fact, assimilating norms and values found in disadvantaged African

American communities, we should expect greater use of violence[28] and thus see similar levels of violent victimization for immigrant and non-immigrant Blacks. Conversely, to the extent that immigrants may enhance community organization and provide a buffer from assimilation into poor-community norms, despite impoverished conditions, immigrant concentration may lead to lower levels of violence.[29]

Community Portrait

While the city of Miami has many unique communities, at least three neighborhoods (Overtown, Liberty City, and Little Haiti)[30] are important for the study of immigrant and nonimmigrant Blacks.[31] Almost three-quarters (71.3 percent) of the city's Blacks live in these neighborhoods, which are inhabited almost exclusively by Blacks. Little Haiti was established in the late 1970s and early 1980s in an area known as "Lemon City" in the northeastern section of Miami. Based on support from various organizations and middle-class Haitians from other U.S. cities, Little Haiti developed some small businesses that employ one or two people and some service agencies. Yet, it is populated by poorer people, it has virtually no business infrastructure, and the community has been described as economically and politically "weak."[32] Similarly, the other two predominately Black neighborhoods (Overtown and Liberty City) also primarily consist of small shops that employ only one or a few people. Rather than large established businesses that offer essential services (e.g., grocery stores, banks, etc.), these areas have small stores, such as pawn shops and liquor stores. There are few restaurants; most places that sell food are small take-out businesses. Many buildings are vacant (boarded up, covered with graffiti and fire damage), while some of the existing businesses appear dilapidated (e.g., peeling paint). In contrast, Latino neighborhoods in Miami (Little Havana, Wynwood, and the Latin Quarter) offer more businesses and services, including more job opportunities. They also do not appear to be as run down as Black areas.[33]

Methods

To examine the ways in which contextual conditions affect violence among the three diverse groups (Haitians, African Americans, and Latinos), we use data for seventy communities (i.e., census tracts with at least five hundred residents) in the city of Miami. All victims of robberies and aggravated assaults reported to the Miami Police Department (MPD) in 1996 and 1997 classified as Haitian, African American, or Latino were examined (the relatively few victims of any other race or ethnicity are excluded). We determined the race/ethnic background of each individual based upon self-reported identities of victims and use of Spanish and French-Creole surname dictionaries.[34] Unfortunately, the surname method does not allow us to distinguish between Latino subgroups. Using addresses of the exact location of each robbery and aggravated assault, we computed the number of victims of each of these two crimes within each community for the three race/ethnic groups.

Several characteristics derived from 1990 census data were used to determine factors associated with community levels of Haitian, African American, and Latino aggravated assault and robbery victimization. Drawing on recent neighborhood research and theory, we examine the roles of economic disadvantage (percent of persons in poverty, percent of female-headed households, and percent of jobless males), residential instability,[35] the percent of the population that is recent immigrants (1980–1990), and the presence of young (18–24 years old) males.[36] We also examine whether tracts with greater victimization tend to be located near other communities with high victimization.[37] Finally, we assess whether ethnic neighborhoods in Miami (Little Haiti for Haitians, Overtown and Liberty City for African Americans, and Little Havana, the Latin Quarter, and Wynwood for Latinos) have different levels of violence than other areas after all of the above local socioeconomic conditions are taken into account.

Results

In Figure 6.1 we provide a descriptive portrait of two economic-disadvantage elements that compare the heavily (40 percent or greater) Haitian, African American, and Latino tracts to each other and to the entire city. Our comparisons reveal that immigrant and nonimmigrant Black communities alike have much higher percentages of residents living in poverty and in female-headed households than Latino areas and the city as a whole. Yet all heavily "Black" communities do not have the same extent of all types of economic disadvantage. While poverty rates are the same in the heavily Haitian and African American communities, notably higher

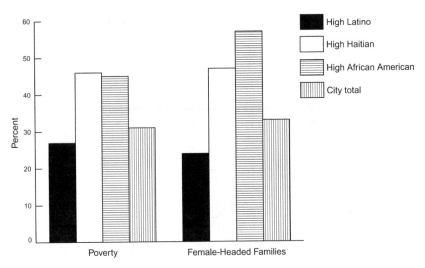

Fig. 6.1. Percent Poverty and Percent Female-Headed Families in Heavily (40 percent or more of the population) Ethnic Minority Communities and in Miami Overall

percentages of residents in African American than Haitian areas live in households headed by a female. These differences are consistent with our argument that the reality of crime and community context is best captured in comparisons within *and* between multiple racial/ethnic groups and even immigrant groups when possible, rather than just in comparisons of Blacks and Whites.

The overall (i.e., not group-specific) violent-crime rates also reflect important differences across racial/ethnic/immigrant groups. Figure 6.2 presents rates of aggravated assault and robbery across Miami's heavily (i.e., 40 percent or more) Latino, Haitian, and African American communities. We start by comparing overall violent-crime victimization rates (per thousand total residents) across the communities. The rates of nonlethal violence are lowest in Latino communities and highest in African American areas, while levels in Haitian areas fall in between. Specifically, the aggravated assault rate is highest in heavily African American tracts (44) and lowest in Latino areas (11), with reported aggravated assaults in Haitian tracts in the middle (31). Robbery rates (per thousand residents) follow the same order. Also noteworthy is that the robbery rate (17) in heavily Latino communities is relatively lower than in other communities but higher

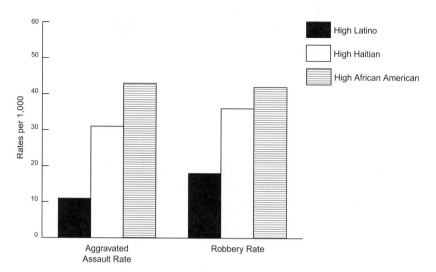

Fig. 6.2. Total Rates of Aggravated Assault and Robbery per 1,000 in Heavily (40 percent or more of the population) Ethnic Minority Communities

than the comparable rate of aggravated assault in Latino areas. Moreover, the Haitian community robbery rate (35) is twice that of Latino areas but is much closer to the African American tract rate (43) than is the case for aggravated assault. The rate for Black areas is very similar to the group's aggravated assault rate.

The *community* overall rates of assault and robbery do not take into account *group-specific* population sizes or group-specific victimization rates. To avoid highly skewed rates in tracts with few ethnic minorities we impose a minimum threshold of one hundred group-specific tract residents for inclusion in the calculations. In Figure 6.3 we show group-specific aggravated assaults and robberies based on group-specific populations. The rates for African Americans (52 African American assaults per thousand African Americans) are four times those of Latinos and Haitians, who have similar rates (13 per thousand Haitians and Latinos, respectively). This pattern suggests that the two heavily immigrant groups have much more in common, at least in terms of aggravated assault, than is evident in Figure 6.2. The results are similar in the case of robbery. Much like aggravated assault, the group-specific average Latino (23) and Haitian (19) robbery rates (per thousand) are very similar. In this case, Latinos have a slightly higher robbery rate than Haitians. The African Amer-

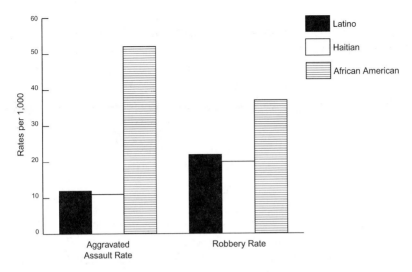

Fig. 6.3. Ethnic-Specific Rates of Aggravated Assault and Robbery per 1,000 Ethnic-Specific Residents. NOTE: 100 group-specific persons minimum per tract.

ican robbery rate (35) is higher than the rates of other groups but the disparities are not as great as for aggravated assaults.

To determine significant predictors that may be responsible for the differences noted above in aggravated assault and robbery rates for Haitians, Latinos, and African Americans, we conducted multivariate analyses.[38] The most important finding from these analyses is that economic disadvantage is a positive and significant predictor of ethnic-specific numbers of aggravated assault and robbery. That is, tracts with higher levels of disadvantage have more group-specific victims of violence for all cases except African American robberies. Not surprisingly, the number of (ethnic-specific) residents is positively related to all group-specific violence outcomes, such that there are more ethnic-specific assault and robbery victims in tracts with more group-specific residents. Additionally, the results indicate that victimizations tend to be clustered in space: tracts with greater numbers of aggravated assault and robbery victims, respectively, tend to be located near each other. There are also some findings unique to each group. Haitians are more likely to be assaulted, and there are more African American and Latino robbery victims in tracts with unstable residential populations. More African Americans are assaulted in tracts with a smaller proportion of young males, and communities with lower percentages of newcomers have higher African American robbery rates. This suggests that immigration buffers some types of violence. Consideration of the neighborhood measures indicates that there are more victims of Haitian assault but not robbery in Little Haiti. While the numbers of Latino victims do not differ in the three Latino neighborhoods, there are fewer African American robbery victims in Liberty City than elsewhere across the city. The latter may reflect the relatively disadvantaged status of the community, such that people there may not be viewed as viable targets.

Discussion/Conclusion

Our preliminary research affirms the significance of focusing on Haitian violence, not only because doing so moves us beyond the Black-White dichotomy but also because we explicitly differentiate a key Black immigrant group from similarly situated Latinos and native-born Blacks. Our analyses indicate that, on average, overall rates of two types of nonlethal violence are two to three times higher in heavily Haitian than in Latino communities, but they are lower than in heavily African American tracts. Yet, with regard to group-specific victimization, Haitians and Latinos report almost identical rates of aggravated assault and robbery. Given that immigrant and nonimmigrant Black communities in Miami have higher levels of disadvantage (e.g., percent poverty and female-headed households) than Latino areas and the "dismal" economic conditions of Haitians,[39] the lower Latino violence victimization rates in Latino communities are not surprising.

What is somewhat surprising is that despite discrimination and severe disadvantage, Haitian violence rates are not higher. The findings for Haitians are contrary to the conventional wisdom that immigration begets crime and to the expectations of negative assimilation. Instead, Haitian rates of nonlethal violence are in line with those of Latinos, most of whom are immigrant. In their chapter on growing up Haitian in Miami, Alex Stepick and colleagues[40] note, "The pain and shame of being a Haitian in Miami constantly assail second-generation Haitian youth in southern Florida." The youths describe how they routinely encounter prejudice and discrimination in everyday life. The long-term implications of this, along with exposure to disadvantaged community conditions, remain to be seen. The results here suggest that immigration status is more important than race and discrimination for Haitians with regard to nonlethal violence victimization. Yet, it is possible that in the future, as increasing numbers of Haitian youths confront racism and discrimination, or participate in the low-paying service sector economy, violence might increase among this group.[41] Indeed, as a result of downward mobility, segmented assimilation into poor African American norms, and adoption of an oppositional culture and "code of the street,"[42] an explicit anticipated consequence for Miami's Haitian population is that violence will become a key part of the search for respect in disorganized and severely disadvantaged communities.

Additionally, social disorganization proponents would argue that Little Haiti is an economically disorganized community (similar to Liberty City) that cannot exert social control over the behavior of the area's residents and visitors. This is supported by the greater number of Haitian aggravated assaults in this neighborhood. Little Haiti is also politically weak (unlike Little Havana). The combination of economic disorganization and political weakness means that increased levels of violence are probably unavoidable and should be expected in the future.

However, we must be careful to draw this conclusion from empirical evidence, and not from our speculative views. As both social disorganization theory and the segmented assimilation perspective argue, understanding outcomes for immigrants requires considering the settings and contexts they move into upon entry into the United States. This is no less true for Haitians than for other groups. More research is clearly needed to better understand the structural factors and processes that shape Haitian violence (and that of other immigrant Black groups), and this line of inquiry should borrow from immigration research. For example, segmented assimilation research and theory would suggest that the low level of Latino (and especially Cuban) violence reflects the positive aspects of assimilation given the advantages of economic, cultural, and political institutions in generating social networks that successfully enabled multiple waves of immigrant Cubans to merge relatively easily into the local community.

In sum, our chapter addresses and elaborates upon at least one crucial aspect of the race and crime literature: studies of crime can no longer ignore the increasing ethnic diversity across the United States. Black and White racial dichotomies do not reflect the reality of race and ethnicity in America, and scholars must acknowledge the impact of "new" immigrants and develop research agendas that direct attention to the relationships among race/ethnicity, assimilation/adaptation, and crime. This should include consideration of the history of immigrant movement into an area, the speed of acculturation/assimilation among families, and barriers to adaptation and access to resources to confront these obstacles.[43] Any of these effects can be exacerbated when, for example, some racial and ethnic groups are welcomed with (relatively) open arms while others are not. This also suggests that the adaptation of newcomers is shaped to a large extent by local context, the presence of a well-developed immigrant economy, and the existence of a vibrant immigrant community that can help buffer exposure to crime. The results of these analyses highlight race and ethnicity as well as the unique position of Black immigrants for crime in urban areas in the United States as an important topic for research. More generally, we must accurately incorporate distinct racial, ethnic, and immigrant groups such as Black Haitians, Dominicans, and Somalis into our research agendas.

NOTES

1. This is not to suggest that work on non-Black ethnic minorities has proliferated. However, some important work has emerged on Native Americans (Bachman 1992; Martinez 2002) and Asians (Yoshioka, DiNoia, and Ullah 2001).

2. The Afro-Caribbean population in the United States is almost exclusively Black (or Mulatto) and largely comprised of immigrants from English-speaking Jamaica and French-Creole-speaking Haiti.

3. See the important report by Logan and Deane 2003.

4. See Hawkins 2003:xxii.

5. Logan and Deane 2003.

6. Logan and Deane 2003:4.

7. Dunn 1997.

8. Martinez 2002.

9. Rumbaut and Portes 2001:6.

10. Stepick et al. 2001.

11. For more background see Stepick et al. 2001.

12. Logan and Deane 2003.

13. Lee and Martinez 2002; Martinez 2000.

14. Those who study immigrant violence also introduce concerns associated with acculturation, culture conflict, or severe alienation from society. Still others suggest that individual-level theories based on biopsychological factors, family socialization, and subcultures of violence or poverty play important roles in generating high levels of crime. Our emphasis is in a different area of focus and tradition.

15. See for example Shaw and McKay 1969 [1942].

16. Portes and Rumbaut 2001.

17. Stepick 1998.

18. Logan and Deane 2003; Stepick et al. 2001.

19. Stepick 1998.

20. Ibid.

21. Shaw and McKay (1969) described the body of work on this topic.

22. Portes and Stepick 1993.

23. Ibid.

24. Portes and Rumbaut 2001.

25. Stepick 1998; Stepick et al. 2003.

26. Portes and Rumbaut 2001.

27. Ibid.

28. Anderson 1999; Sampson and Wilson 1995.

29. Ibid.

30. Each is comprised of multiple census tracts. For the sake of presentation, our use of the term "neighborhood" refers to these areas while "community" refers to census tracts.

31. There are other Black neighborhoods in the larger Miami-Dade County. Dunn (1997) elaborates on many of these in an historical context, including the Black section of Coconut Grove in the city of Miami. See Portes and Stepick 1993 for more on the Latino/Cuban neighborhoods in Miami.

32. Portes and Stepick 1993; Stepick 1998.

33. Dunn 1997; Portes and Stepick 1993; Stepick 1998.

34. A Haitian student was also hired to recheck cases coded as racially "Black" by the MPD but not as French-Creole in the surname dictionary.

35. Economic disadvantage and residential instability are indexes created on the basis of standardized values. The items included in the economic disadvantage measure are noted in the text; the items comprising residential instability include percent of vacant housing and population in the neighborhood five or fewer years.

36. Data are from the 1990 census.

37. Negative binomial regression analyses with corrections for spatial autocorrelation (i.e., inclusion of a fitted spatial lag) are used.

38. Details of analyses are available from the author upon request.

39. Stepick 1998.

40. Stepick et al. 2001.

41. We are examining victims, rather than offenders, so we tentatively offer this possibility. Moreover, as we should expect, Little Haiti is a key area for Haitian assault victimization.

42. Anderson 1999.

43. Portes and Rumbaut 2001.

Chapter 7

Crime and Deviance in the "Black Belt"

African American Youth in Rural and Nonrural Developmental Contexts

Alexander T. Vazsonyi and Elizabeth Trejos-Castillo

The Black Belt

In the current study, we are interested in comparing rural African American youth who reside in the "Black Belt" to nonrural minority youth from the same geographic vicinity who reside in a small city outside the "Black Belt." The Black Belt is a crescent-shaped, particularly disadvantaged, rural-nonmetropolitan region that stretches from Virginia to Texas in the South. It includes forty-five million residents and comprises an area of 623 counties with high rates of poverty, unemployment, infant mortality, and poor health, and low rates of educational achievement. This region is known as the Black Belt, as the term originally was utilized to describe the rich, dark soil that was found in southern counties. Subsequently, the term has been associated with extreme rates of poverty and an extremely high proportion of African American residents. Census data indicate that of the approximately 3.8 million African Americans that reside in rural areas in the United States, 3.5 million live in the rural South, in the Black Belt region.[1]

Urban Bias

Little empirical work on crime and deviance exists that has focused on minority youth residing in rural areas of the United States, particularly on poor African American youth who reside in the Black Belt.[2] Thus, our understanding of what it means to be an African American adolescent from the Black Belt is severely limited. Most previous work that has tested the utility of applying the social disorganization framework to the problem of crime and deviance has been based on official data and lacks individual and other proximate explanatory mechanisms.[3] Alternatively, the remaining efforts have largely studied minority youth residing in inner-city contexts of the Midwest or the Northeast.

One of the principle rationales for studying rural/nonmetropolitan youth lies in the potential replication of correlates and risk factors associated with crime and deviance that have been identified on the basis of work in the urban developmental context. This is important because national school-based data that compare rates of crime reported to the police between urban and rural areas indicate few differences in levels of crime, especially in less serious violent crimes or nonviolent crimes (eleven per thousand in urban areas, nine per thousand in urban-fringe areas, ten per thousand in towns, and nine per thousand in rural areas).[4] Furthermore, because of the general paucity of work on rural youth, it is important to further investigate levels of, as well as the etiology of, crime and deviance in this population. This work clearly has theoretical implications, as much of the evidence that has shaped theories of crime is based on data from nonrural, metropolitan, or urban contexts. Additionally, and of equal importance, this work has profound policy implications. Though rather modest efforts exist at the state and federal levels to address the issue of destitute poverty and substandard living conditions in the Black Belt, little policy has been directed at targeting rural poor minority youth and their families. Thus, findings from the current study provide initial direction as to whether or not efforts directed at residents of the Black Belt need to differ from those utilized in nonrural areas of the United States.

Similarities or Differences in Developmental Process

In the current investigation, we compared African American adolescents who resided in a rural Black Belt county in Alabama to youth residing in a small city of a nonrural county in Alabama. Our goal was to further examine whether the developmental context differentiates levels of crime and deviance, and perhaps more importantly, whether it moderates the relationships between known predictors of crime and deviance, namely, measures of neighborhood effects (e.g., neighborhood cohesion) and family processes. In addition to a paucity of research conducted on rural African American youth, previous comparative efforts with similar goals as ours have compared African American to Caucasian youth; such comparisons inherently include multiple potential confounds, namely, race as well as neighborhood differences or differences in socioeconomic status. In the following sections, we briefly review studies that have relevance to the current effort.

Whether known risk factors replicate in the rural developmental context remains an empirical question. For example, even within inner-city developmental contexts, previous work has identified different relationships between family processes and violent inner-city versus urban poor youth.[5] Few community-based surveys of child mental health have been conducted in the African American population, and a number of small-scale studies of behavioral-emotional problems in African American children have been done in school settings.[6] Findings from a study of rural minority youth have implications for theory, policy making, and the potential effectiveness of prevention and intervention trials.[7] A number of complex challenges remain in assessing neighborhood effects, namely, differential selection of individuals into communities, indirect pathways of neighborhood effects, measurement error, and simultaneity bias.[8]

Neighborhood Effects, Parenting Behaviors, and Adjustment

Sampson, Morenoff, and Gannon-Rowley have synthesized the cumulative findings of neighborhood-effects on social processes, problem behaviors, and health-related outcomes.[9] One important finding from recent research is that community-based surveys can yield reliable and valid measures of neighborhood, social, and institutional processes. The authors found very little consistency across studies in the way neighborhood, social, and institutional processes are operationalized or theoretically situated. Many indicators of neighborhood mechanisms are intercorrelated. Sampson et al. identified four general classes of neighborhood mechanisms that, although related, appear to have independent validity: (1) social ties/interaction: social capital; (2) norms and collective efficacy: willingness of residents to intervene on behalf of children; (3) institutional resources: quality, quantity, and diversity of institutions in the community that address the needs of youth; and (4) routine activities: how land use patterns and the ecological distributions of daily routine activities bear on children's well-being.[10] In the current study, we used a measure of neighborhood social ties and interactions, namely, measures of neighborhood attraction and neighborhood cohesiveness.

The empirical literature provides both direct and indirect evidence concerning the effects of poverty and low socioeconomic status (SES) on the socio-emotional functioning of African American children and adolescents. Residing in a lower-SES neighborhood during early and middle childhood has been linked to lower adaptive functioning, diminished self-confidence and self-esteem, strained peer relationships, increased temper tantrums, and higher levels of symptomology, social maladaptation, and psychological distress. In addition, low SES and economic hardship during adolescence has been linked to diminished adaptive functioning with respect to relationships, school, work, delinquent behaviors, self-image, and depression.[11] The evidence also suggests that poverty and income status have effects on children's socio-emotional functioning (i.e., externalizing problems) independent of SES. McLloyd has identified three potential mediators in the link between socioeconomic disadvantage and children's socio-emotional functioning, namely, discrete and chronic stressors, experiences of inferiorization, and, of greatest relevance for the current study, nonsupportive and punitive parenting behaviors.[12]

A number of empirical studies have examined this issue. Even though variations in parenting styles have been documented in several studies associated with child adjustment to environments that vary in incidents of violence, for example, there is robust evidence supporting the connection of positive parent-child relationships with children's positive outcomes across investigations.[13] In addition, some work has also linked parents' educational level and the level of family income in addition to neighborhood effects to the development of child and adolescent measures of competence and adjustment, including behavior regulation.[14]

Parenting Effects across Contexts

Only a handful of studies have attempted to directly examine whether neighborhood context or urbanicity moderates the relationship between parenting behaviors and measures of deviance in African American youth. For example, Brody et al. examined how neighborhood disadvantage moderated the associations of parenting and older sibling problem attitudes and behavior with conduct disorders in African American children.[15] The authors found that the primary caregivers' parenting practices were significantly associated with the target children's conduct disorder symptoms. Harsher, more inconsistent, less nurturing, and less involved parenting practices were associated with higher symptom levels. Furthermore, parenting practices high in harshness and inconsistency and low in the nurturance and involvement dimensions were associated more strongly with children's conduct problems among families who lived in more disadvantaged neighborhoods.

Similarly, Forehand et al. examined the role of two parenting variables, namely, monitoring and communication, in adolescent deviant behavior in four samples: African Americans living in Montgomery (Alabama) and the Bronx and Hispanics living in the Bronx and San Juan (Puerto Rico).[16] Level differences in parenting variables and measures of adolescent deviance were found across all four groups. However, with the exception of the associations between communication and deviance for African Americans from New York, all correlations were significant. Lower levels of communication and monitoring were consistently associated with greater levels of deviance. Identical findings were made in four samples that differed by ethnicity, location, various demographic variables, levels of parenting variables, and levels of deviance.[17] In conclusion, positive parenting behaviors are predictive of positive development and positive developmental outcomes; a lack of closeness, monitoring, and discipline is predictive of problem behaviors, crime, and deviance. However, there exists inconclusive evidence about the role of neighborhood effects and the effects by the context (e.g., locality or urbanicity) across studies. This inconsistent finding is an important issue that requires further study. On the one hand, studies indicate that the effects of parenting may vary by context—that parenting is conditioned by the neighborhood or the developmental context. On the other hand, some studies find that parenting efforts and their effects on adolescent development are in a sense universal across settings. Positive parenting is associated with positive development, while ineffective parenting is associated with, among other indicators, crime and deviance.

Part of the reason why this is such an important issue is that according to the latter perspective, urban poor minority families and their children are "at risk" simply because of where they reside and simply because they lack resources; analogously, parenting is different, perhaps deficient, simply because the parents are poor and live in the urban developmental context. Of course, a similar argument can be made for rural youth, though almost no work exists on these families. Thus, this deficit thinking permeates the way these families and their children are viewed, studied, and treated; it also influences the way policy makers from the local to federal levels make decisions regarding how to assist such families. Yet, studies have also documented the level of resilience among youth who reside in poor neighborhoods, whether the inner city or the rural context. One way to further assess this issue is to examine two samples of African American youth who reside in very different developmental milieus, one in an extremely impoverished rural area and one in an average, small-city, nonrural area.

Thus, the current study examined (1) levels of crime and deviance in rural and nonrural African American samples; (2) levels of perceived community/neighborhood constructs and parenting in the rural and nonrural samples; (3) the importance of perceived community/neighborhood constructs in the variability of crime and deviance across rural/nonrural samples; and (4) the importance of maternal/caregiver family processes in explaining crime and deviance. These comparisons allowed inferences regarding the importance of the rural versus nonrural developmental contexts in both the relationships between perceived community/neighborhood constructs and crime and deviance as well as between family processes and crime and deviance.

Method

Samples

In the current study, data were collected from 398 African American adolescents (mean age 16.7 years) in a rural public school in grades nine through twelve.[18] The rural school, which included seventh through twelfth grades (N = 851), was located in a small town in a Black Belt county in Alabama. In 2000, the county in which the school is located was predominantly African American (73.1 percent) and had a high unemployment rate (8.1 percent), a median household income of $20,605, and an overall poverty rate of 33.5 percent.[19] The county also had a low population density, namely 18.7 persons per square mile. Historically, all African American children and youth attended the public school system, in this case the county school, while White youth attended a private academy.

The study school was over 99 percent African American.[20] In addition, about 90 percent of the student population was eligible for free and re-duced meals; because it is customary to underreport the actual percent-age of eligible students in cases where almost the entire student body qualifies, it seems reasonable to assume that almost all students were eligi-ble for free or reduced meals on the basis of their family's socioeconomic status.[21]

Data for the nonrural sample were collected from adolescents who attended a high school outside the Black Belt in Alabama in a small uni-versity town.[22] The county in which this school is found was predomi-nantly White (73.2 percent), had a median household income level of $30,952, and had an overall poverty rate of 21.8 percent.[23] It is worth not-ing, however, that families residing inside the city limits of the target school are known to be "better off" in comparison to families residing in the rural areas of the county, and thus, the census figures are somewhat misleading. The total student population at the high school was 1,134, of which 289 were African American.[24] All students in the school were invited to participate, and 877 students provided usable data (77 percent of the school population, 95 percent of the surveyed sample). Only African American youth were included in the current analyses, resulting in a final sample of 182 students (mean age of 16.5 years). In the year the data were collected, the school reported that about 12 percent of students were eligi-ble for free or reduced-price meals. Information on the race of students eligible for free or reduced-price meals was not available.[25]

Measures

All participants in both the rural and nonrural samples filled out the same questionnaire, which included questions about crime and deviance, family processes, and neighborhood cohesion; the survey also included items tapping demographic characteristics (age, sex, family structure, and socioeconomic indicators) and a question determining whether the stu-dent resided in a rural or nonrural area.

Deviance. Total deviance was measured by the 55-item Normative Deviance Scale (NDS).[26] The NDS assessed a broad spectrum of deviant activities and criminal behaviors. A total deviance score was computed by averaging the fifty-five items. The items also assessed seven separate sub-scales, each consisting of between six and eleven averaged items, namely, vandalism, alcohol use, drug use, school misconduct, general deviance, theft, and assault. Responses for all items in the NDS were given on a 5-point Likert-type scale and identified lifetime frequency of specific behaviors; responses included 1 (*never*), 2 (*one time*), 3 (*two to three times*), 4 (*four to six times*), and 5 (*more than six times*). Reliability estimates indicated good internal consistency across all subscales (all alphas above .83) and the total deviance measure (for rural sample, alpha of .98; for non-rural sample, alpha of .97).

Family Processes. The Adolescent Family Process Measure assessed adolescents' perceptions of their relationship with their mothers (mother, stepmother, or female caretaker).[27] Only maternal parenting was assessed because so few youth in the rural sample reported a traditional family structure. The measure included six subscales, namely closeness, support, communication, monitoring, conflict, and peer approval. Responses for closeness, support, and monitoring were given on a 5-point scale, ranging from 1 (*strongly disagree*) to 5 (*strongly disagree*).[28] Responses for communication, conflict, and peer approval were given on a separate 5-point scale ranging from 1 (*never*) to 5 (*very often*). Subscales were internally consistent in both samples (all above alpha of .75).

Neighborhood Measures. Neighborhood attraction and neighborhood connection are based on Buckner's Neighborhood Cohesion measure.[29] Our own analysis of the original seventeen items comprising this indicator of neighborhood cohesion showed that it reflects two separate constructs, neighborhood attraction and neighborhood connection. Respondents rated all items on a 5-point Likert-type response scale ranging from 1 (*strongly disagree*) to 5 (*strongly agree*). Neighborhood attraction is a 13-item scale that assesses how attracted the individual is to his or her neighborhood. Neighborhood connection is a 4-item scale that measures how close the individual feels to his or her neighborhood. Reliability estimates indicated that each scale was internally consistent in both samples (alphas range from .73 to .81 for both measures in the two samples).

Age (in years), sex (1 = male, 2 = female), family structure, and socioeconomic status are all included in our analysis. Family structure differentiates students whose home structure includes two biological parents, a biological mother only, a biological father only, a biological mother and stepfather, a biological father and stepmother, a biological parent and significant other, and any others. Socioeconomic status is a standardized scale combining the student's family income from 1 (*under $20,000*) to 5 (*$100,000+*) and the job type of the primary wage earner in the family—from 1 (*laborer*) to 6 (*executive*).[30]

Results

Each sample was approximately equally divided by sex though a slightly larger number of females participated in the rural sample. A large difference between the two samples was found in family structure; less than one-third of rural youth indicated that their parents were married in comparison to almost half of the nonrural sample. In addition, different indicators of SES also documented how the rural sample was significantly poorer in comparison to the nonrural sample. One substantial problem in both samples, especially in the rural sample, was that many youth did not reply to measures of family income or the primary wage earner. This was not surprising in a sense since many adolescents were poor and received free and reduced-price meals at school.[31]

To examine differences between the rural and nonrural African American students in parenting processes, neighborhood cohesion, and deviance, we conducted a series of one-way analyses of variance. In general, the results indicate that youth reported very similar levels of family processes in rural and nonrural areas. Two differences were found, namely, nonrural youth indicated affectively closer relationships with their caregivers than rural youth while rural youth reported higher levels of communication than their nonrural peers. Both neighborhood connection and neighborhood attraction were significantly higher among the rural than the nonrural African American youth. Finally, with the exception of school misconduct and general deviance, overall and all subtypes of deviance are significantly higher among the rural than the nonrural adolescents. However, these differences are modest in size.

In a second step of our analysis, we examined whether the developmental context, namely, residing in a rural area versus residing in a nonrural area, is associated with measures of family process, neighborhood cohesion, and deviance. After taking into account age, sex, SES, and family structure, results indicate that "context" is associated with one aspect of family process, both neighborhood measures, and all deviance measures. Consistent with what we found in mean level comparisons, residing in a rural developmental context is associated with higher levels of communication, higher levels of neighborhood attraction and neighborhood connection, and consistently higher levels of deviance. This finding provides some basis for further examining how and whether the rural versus nonrural developmental context moderates the associations of family process measures and neighborhood connection with crime and deviance. This is examined more extensively in hierarchical regression analyses. In these regressions, we analyze only two dependent variables for space considerations, total deviance and assault, which we selected because it is the most severe conduct included.

We use hierarchical analyses because they allow us to partial out potential effects by sex, age, family structure, and SES. Thus, the effects of these variables are examined first, followed by those for family processes, and finally, rural versus nonrural context. Initial analyses with all variables demonstrate that family structure, socioeconomic status, and neighborhood structure do not have effects on deviance. Thus, to be conservative, we explore a model that excludes these four variables. In this analysis, we do not find a statistically significant effect of rural-nonrural context on deviance.

Finally, we test whether family process measures have different effects on deviance in the rural and nonrural contexts. Findings from this third model indicate one significant interaction term for total deviance, conflict, and context, and one interaction term between context and monitoring. Hence, these relationships are conditioned, to some extent, by context; in both cases, the term is negative, indicating a smaller effect by the parenting variable on the deviance measure in the rural context in comparison to the nonrural one. Yet, adding these interactions results in a number of previously significant main effects losing their significance. Given the modest evidence of interaction effects and their effect on previously significant main effects, we focus on findings from the trimmed model without the interaction terms.

Table 7.1 includes the findings from these analyses for both the total deviance measure and assault as the dependent variable. We found that most family process measures are important, even when considered simultaneously with the others, in predicting total deviance as well as assault. Only communication and peer approval has no effect on deviance. In particular, greater closeness, support, and monitoring are associated with less deviance, while greater conflict is associated with more deviance. These findings are almost identical for both dependent variables. Importantly, after the effects by age, sex, and the family process measures are accounted for, "context" has no additional explanatory power for either total deviance or assault, although a trend is found in the regression that included assault as the dependent variable. In terms of explanatory power,

TABLE 7.1
Hierarchical Regression Analysis (Total Sample, Final Trimmed Model)

	Total Deviance			Assault		
	b	β	Change in R^2	b	β	Change in R^2
Age	.065*	.090	.017	.042	.054	.008
Sex	−.517*	−.273	.100	−.442*	−.216	.065
Closeness	−.134*	−.142	.142	−.125*	−.121	.116
Support	−.184*	−.216		−.180*	−.195	
Monitoring	−.138*	−.151		−.121*	−.123	
Communication	.071	.076		.061	.061	
Conflict	.102*	.106		.108*	.103	
Peer Approval	.057	.066		.027	.029	
Rural/Nonrural	−.127	−.063	.004	−.176ᵗ	−.080	.006
	Model R^2	.263		Model R^2	.195	

NOTE: * $p < 0.05$; ᵗ trend ($p < 0.1$).

the variables included explain about 26 percent and 20 percent of the total variance in total deviance and assault respectively, of which about 14 percent and 12 percent are accounted for by the family process variables.

To further examine the issue of how similarly the models worked for both total deviance and assault, we graphically plotted the standardized partial regression coefficients for the effect of each family process measures on total deviance versus its effect on assault in the total sample (Figure 7.1). This figure includes a best-fitting regression line as well as an estimate of the total amount of variance explained. The figure dramatically illustrates how family process measures predict the two measures (total deviance and assault) in an almost identical manner.

Discussion

In the current study, we examined the potential contextual effects on the levels of and the etiology of crime and deviance in samples of African American youth in a poor rural developmental context and in a more affluent, nonrural developmental milieu. Key findings included that (1) rural youth consistently reported higher levels of deviance, including total deviance, in comparison to their nonrural peers, (2) levels of neighborhood cohesion were perceived to be higher among rural youth, and (3) six distinct family process measures—closeness, support, monitoring, communication, conflict, and peer approval—were largely similar for the youth in the two contexts, though rural youth reported higher levels of communication and nonrural youth reported a greater amount of closeness. Though some evidence was found of an association between developmental context (rural versus nonrural) and measures of neighborhood cohesion and deviance in simple bivariate analyses, subsequent multivariate analyses indicated that neighborhood effects (as well as measures of SES) no longer accounted for unique variability in crime and deviance. In addition, consistent with some previous work,[32] we found that "context" did not explain variance above and beyond the effects of demographic variables and family process measures. In addition, family processes explained crime and deviance in a largely invariant fashion in these samples of rural and nonrural African American youth. Though a statistical trend was found for a context effect, we interpret this nonsignificant finding as a substantive one and not related to low statistical power, which was not an issue. Lastly, the study also provided evidence that key family processes, namely, closeness, support, monitoring, and measures of parent-adolescent conflict, were similarly predictive both of a general index of deviance as well as of assault.

The importance and implications of these findings can be best summarized by the following observations. First, the study documents that crime

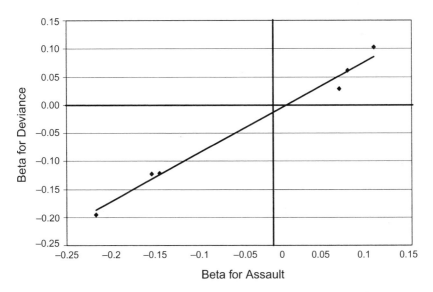

Fig. 7.1. Similarity in the Association between Six Family Processes and Measures of Deviance (Total Deviance and Assault). $R^2 = 0.987$, # points = 6

and deviance is also a serious problem in rural areas, one that appears comparatively more serious in the rural context than in the nonrural one. This is somewhat consistent with recent work completed by Osgood and Chambers on general samples of nonmetropolitan populations.[33] As they have pointed out, much work has called for more sophisticated empirical investigations outside metropolitan areas that include self-reports as well as a greater breadth of individual and community-level variables to establish whether ideas consistent with social disorganization theory find empirical support in rural areas.[34] In this sense, the current findings provide a very strong impetus to further study rural African American youth, a population that has been ignored too long in favor of an urban focus in both research efforts, and in ensuing policy decisions and social programs designed to address the unique risks and needs.

Secondly, though the current study did not comprehensively assess how social disorganization theory applies to rural and nonrural contexts, we believe that the current findings do have implications for theory. It is important to note that previous work in this area, including the work by Osgood and Chambers,[35] was based on official data.[36] In contrast, the current study was based on two separate original data sets collected in rural and nonrural contexts. The advantage of these data is the assessment of more comprehensive measures of known etiological factors that are a part of specific theories or simply known to be important in our understanding of crime and deviance. We found no evidence of effects of family structure on crime and deviance based in multivariate analyses. We also found no effects of socioeconomic status on crime and deviance. Finally, we found no effects of two measures of neighborhood cohesion. These findings were observed despite "level differences" in these measures across contexts; they do not provide much support for social disorganization theory. At the same time, this lack of support is not completely unexpected as it parallels previous work by Sampson and Laub that documented that when structural variables are considered together with more proximate measures in the explanation of crime and deviance, such as family processes, their effects are largely mediated through the proximate processes, and as a result, they largely disappear.[37]

Finally, and perhaps theoretically most interesting, parenting efforts in both contexts operate in a highly similar fashion across these very different developmental milieus. This suggests that socialization pressures and specific processes are highly salient when considered along with structural and community-level constructs in the explanation of crime and deviance. It also provides some evidence that applying the social disorganization framework to the problem of youth crime and deviance among African Americans, at least according to these rural and nonrural samples, may be of limited utility. Thus, explanatory models and theoretical work that includes more proximate mechanisms, such as individual-level constructs (e.g., low self-control) as well as family-level mechanisms, hold more promise in the understanding and explanation of crime and deviance in minority populations located in different developmental contexts.

At the same time, the findings from the current study also reinforce that the application of a "deficit perspective" to youth who grow up in minority families, to youth who grow up in severe poverty, and to youth who grow up in nontraditional families may not be useful—not useful for the social problems themselves, not useful for theoretical work, and not useful for potential prevention and intervention efforts. This also means that though African American youth from this extremely destitute Black Belt county in Alabama grow up in largely nontraditional, poor families, what may define their success as individuals—whether they engage in serious criminal and deviant behaviors—is to some extent determined by their affective ties with their caregivers and whether these take an interest in their lives and monitor their behaviors. Though some might label these findings as evidence of resilience to some extent, we believe that this concept itself implies a deficit perspective as a starting point, which we have argued is not useful.

From a policy perspective, the findings also indicate that prevention and intervention efforts should be directed at strengthening relationships with parents and other important adults who care for these youth, as well as strengthening other more proximate social control mechanisms, such as the school, to provide adolescents with the necessary tools to succeed in life. We realize that this study represents only a modest first step in work that attempts to study the importance of both socio-structural correlates and more proximate mechanisms in the etiology of crime and deviance of poor, rural, African American youth. Thus, we look forward to future studies that assess the potential impact of the community and the neighborhood together with proximate mechanisms on crime and deviance. We also look forward to simply more empirical and theoretical work that incorporates and considers populations of youth and young adults in the United States who have been ignored for too long.

NOTES

1. Wimberly and Morris 1997.
2. Osgood and Chambers 2000.
3. Shaw and McKay 1942.
4. U.S. Department of Health and Human Services 2001.
5. Gorman-Smith, Tolan, and Henry 1999.
6. McLloyd 1997.
7. Elliot, Williams, and Hamburg 1998; Flannery and Huff 1999; Thornton et al. 2000.
8. Sampson, Morenoff, and Gannon-Rowley 2002.
9. Ibid.
10. Ibid.
11. McLloyd 1997.
12. Ibid.
13. Armistead et al. 2002; Ceballo and McLloyd 2002; Pinderhughes et al. 2001; Pittman and Chase-Lansdale 2001.
14. Brody et al. 2002; Smetana, Crean, and Daddis 2002.
15. Brody et al. 2002.
16. Forehand et al. 1997.
17. For related work, see also Armistead et al. 2002; Forehand et al. 2000.
18. Vazsonyi and Crosswhite 2004.
19. U.S. Bureau of the Census 2003a, 2003b.
20. Alabama State Department of Education 2003; National Center for Education Statistics 2003.
21. National Center for Educational Statistics 2003.
22. Vazsonyi and Pickering 2003.
23. U.S. Bureau of the Census 2003b.
24. Alabama State Department of Education 2003.
25. Ibid.
26. Vazsonyi et al. 2001.
27. Vazsonyi et al. 2003.
28. Responses for the support subscale were reverse coded so that a high score indicated a large amount of support.
29. Buckner 1988.
30. For example, Capaldi et al. 2002.
31. The effects of SES were studied in subsequent analyses; however, because no consistent association was found between indicators of SES and measures of crime and deviance, final analyses did not include SES; therefore, the level of missing data for these two variables did not present a problem.
32. For example, Forehand et al. 1997.
33. Osgood and Chambers 2000.

34. For example, Smith and Huff 1982.

35. Osgood and Chambers 2000.

36. Specifically, research relies on crime data available through the FBI's Uniform Crime Reports, and sociodemographic data available through the U.S. Bureau of the Census.

37. Sampson and Laub 1993.

Chapter 8

Crime at the Intersections
Race, Class, Gender, and Violent Offending

Stacy De Coster and Karen Heimer

Race and gender differences in crime rates are well established. It is common knowledge that minorities and males are overrepresented in arrest statistics, and that this overrepresentation is most pronounced for violent crimes. However, we know surprisingly little about the nature and causes of gender differences in violence within race, or race differences in violence within gender. Empirical research on gender and violence often ignores race, or at best treats it as a nuisance variable to be controlled. And, most research on race and violence ignores gender, focusing mainly on the behavior and experiences of males. Yet, official statistics show that for serious violence, such as homicide and aggravated assault, the rates of offending by Black females are closer to the rates of White males than White females.[1]

Feminist criminologists have been calling attention to the importance of race-class-gender intersectionalities for well over a decade, pointing out that gendered experiences of crime—both offending and victimization—cannot be understood without consideration of race and class.[2] Indeed, studies of gender and crime that ignore race may describe mainly the experiences of Whites. Studies of race and crime that ignore gender risk missing the unique experiences of women of color. Yet, despite the calls for attention to intersectionalities, almost no research has examined the ways in which race, class, and gender simultaneously operate to shape experiences of crime and violence.

The purpose of the present chapter is to review research and offer some theoretical groundwork that may be useful for thinking about how to unpack the complexities of intersectionalities and violent offending. We begin with the basic tenets of feminist theorizing about race-class-gender and then cull important insights from research on masculinities and femininities. The scope of this chapter is limited to violent offending, in part because much of the relevant work on masculinities and femininities has focused on violence. We next sketch the outlines of a structural interactionist perspective, which focuses on how individuals make meaning of their social worlds within the context of cross-cutting social inequalities. We suggest that this framework may offer one direction for research on intersectionalities and violent crime.

Feminisms and Intersectionalities

Intersectionalities became a central topic in feminist social science in the 1990s, with the observation that race-class-gender inequalities "are not separate and additive, but interactive and multiplicative in their effects."[3] The impetus for this focus is often attributed to work on Black feminist theory and multiracial feminist theory. A central tenet of Black feminist theory, as developed in the early work of Collins, is that perceptions of the social world are constructed by individuals and thus, by necessity, are affected by the social positions of individuals.[4] In her recent work, Collins highlights the ways in which racism and sexism are inextricably intertwined.[5] She emphasizes that understanding racism requires understanding sexism, and vice versa, because race impacts African American men and women in different ways. For example, Black women are subordinated to White women, as well as Black men, who themselves experience restrictions of social power.

Similar points are made by multiracial feminism. For example, Baca Zinn and Dill propose that race, class, and gender are interweaving dimensions of inequality that shape individuals' experiences.[6] The experience of race, therefore, depends on class and gender, and the experience of gender depends on race and class. Black feminist approaches emphasize the social construction of race-class-gender experiences in everyday life. However, Black feminist theorists maintain that these experiences are profoundly shaped by structural constraints—they are embedded within structures of inequality. Understanding intersections thus requires consideration of the simultaneous contributions of macrolevel interlocking structural inequalities and microlevel interactions that define racialized, classed, and gendered positions.[7]

Criminology at the Intersections

Feminist criminologists have followed the lead of feminist scholars more generally and called for research that takes intersectionalities seriously. Some feminist criminologists have maintained that race, class, and gender should not be viewed as separable and additive; rather, their combined effects on crime necessitate an experience-based approach that examines the lives of people embedded within intersections.[8] Others have suggested the use of quantitative methods to parse the effects of race, class, and gender and to examine their combined effects.[9] But, what is common to both approaches is the idea that "everyone is located in a matrix of multiple social relations, i.e., that race and gender are as relevant to an analysis of [crime by] White men as they are to [crime by] black women."[10] Nevertheless, studies of criminal offending that explicitly take a race-class-gender approach are rare, to date.

The foundation for such work, however, has been laid by research on masculinities and violence and by feminist studies of women's and girls' offending. These studies quite often have focused on the experiences of a particular race-gender group, and thereby offer insights into the experiences of crime among disadvantaged people of color. What remains unclear is how these experiences might be similar and different for poor White women and poor women of color, as well as how they compare with those of men. Because of practical limitations, very little ethnographic and qualitative research has been able to include comparisons across race, class, and gender groups within a single study.[11] There have been a few attempts to use quantitative analyses of survey data to explore the ways in which race, class, and gender structure crime and violence.[12] These studies have not, however, been able to address many of the core issues raised in the qualitative research because they have relied on existing data that were not collected for the purpose of studying either race or gender in depth. Yet, understanding intersectionalities and crime more completely will require comparisons of processes across race, class, and gender groups.

We suggest that one route toward a better understanding of intersectionalities and crime (and thus, of crime more generally) may come through a focus on socially constructed identities and experiences that are embedded within structures of race, class, and gender inequality. Research on masculinities and femininities offers an important foundation for developing such an explanation.

Masculinities and Violence

The literature on masculinities and crime begins with the premise that males must demonstrate masculinity routinely in their daily interactions. They are expected to "do gender" and are held accountable to cultural standards of what this means.[13] Precisely what this means varies by race and class, a fact that leads to the construction of different types of masculinities.[14]

Connell proposes that masculinities are arranged in a power hierarchy, with hegemonic masculinities being the culturally idealized masculinity of the most powerful group in a given society.[15] Other masculinities are constructed in relation to this ideal. Of particular relevance for studies of race and class are the marginalized masculinities constructed through the actions of oppressed groups as they use the resources and strategies in their environments to resist and/or accommodate hegemonic masculinity.[16] Of course, oppressed groups have limited access to legitimate resources and strategies for achieving the idealized form of masculinity. In such situations, crime and violence may serve as resources for achieving or demonstrating masculinity.[17] Messerschmidt suggests that the use of violence to claim masculinity in these situations eventually may become part of what it means to be masculine within these settings or groups.[18] In short, oppressed groups may construct marginalized masculinities that are linked to violence. Males subsequently are held accountable to these masculinities.

Understanding marginalized masculinities requires consideration of hegemonic masculinities because the two forms are constructed in relation to one another.[19] The hegemonic masculine ideal in our contemporary society is constructed and enacted by White middle-class males, for the most part. This masculinity is characterized by professional/managerial labor, competition through expertise, whiteness, heterosexuality, violence, and dominance over others.[20] Violence is included in this definition because, while hegemonic masculinity may not actively encourage certain forms of violence, it does require that men *not* avoid or condemn violence and aggression. According to Franklin, the middle-class White male stance on violence is captured by the phrase, "Never start fights . . . but always finish them."[21]

In attempts to claim masculinity, White middle-class males typically have access to legitimate resources and strategies. Middle-class socialization and adult male role models provide the capital needed to compete in schools and in professional/managerial careers. As a consequence, many middle-class males can project hegemonic masculinity through academic and career success, and thus can avoid displaying masculinity through violence.[22] As Messerschmidt notes, Chambliss's classic study, "The Saints and the Roughnecks," illustrates this point. The White middle-class Saints were successful in school and engaged in only minor forms of delinquency, avoiding violence completely.[23]

Working-class White males do not have access to these same resources and strategies for accomplishing masculinity. Research by Willis and others finds that White working-class British boys who have difficulty claiming hegemonic masculinity react by forming an oppositional masculinity that defines mental labor and competition through expertise as "sissy stuff."[24] Instead, Willis's boys claim masculinity through violence, vandalism, and pranks. These same patterns are found among Chambliss's White working-class Roughnecks.[25] Several authors have further noted that racist and antigay hate crimes in Western industrialized societies are disproportionately committed by White working-class males as they publicly display masculinity through hostility toward groups who have less structural power.[26]

Notably, both working- and middle-class White males construct masculine identities rooted in paid labor. Many scholars suggest that paid labor and masculinities have not been as closely linked for disadvantaged Black males as they have been for these other groups. bell hooks argues that this is because Black underclass males perceive that economic opportunities will always be restricted by racism, no matter how hard they work.[27] This perception is clearly tied to the reality of life in segregated urban ghettos in which there are few role models who have succeeded occupationally.[28] The restricted resources and lack of successful role models in disadvantaged communities create a situation where an oppositional or marginalized masculinity emerges, which is characterized by competition through physical fights, heterosexuality, the use of violence, and dominance over others.[29] Anderson argues that claiming masculinity under such circumstances requires demonstrating "nerve" in various ways, including "throwing the first punch, getting in someone's face, or pulling the trigger."[30]

Consistent with this, Wilkinson's interviews with disadvantaged minority male offenders reveals that these men see public displays of violence as a way to construct street identities.[31] Similarly, Katz notes that street robberies are a form of masculinity accomplishment for disadvantaged Black males because robberies provide an opportunity to demonstrate dominance over intended victims.[32] Furthermore, Mullins and his colleagues find that extremely marginalized African American men living in a high-crime neighborhood rationalize their retaliatory violence against other men as necessary to preserve (or restore) honor and reputation.[33]

In short, the masculinities displayed by some disadvantaged Black males can be traced to a history of racial oppression and continued denial of access to education and occupations that would allow them to claim hegemonic masculinity. Studies suggest that men in these circumstances are held accountable to marginalized masculinity on the basis of both gender and race. For example, Anderson argues that some disadvantaged Black men begin to confuse their masculine street identity with racial identity; he found that boys who worked to succeed at school risked being accused of "acting white." This suggests that disadvantaged Black males have not simply constructed a marginalized masculinity, but rather have created *racialized masculinity* that is specific to their history and structural position.[34]

Overall, the concept of multiple masculinities, structured by interlocking race and class inequalities, seems to be consistent with empirical research. But, we note three points of caution. First, our emphasis, like that of others, has been primarily on masculinities and their relationship to definitions of violence, rather than other, more positive aspects of masculinity.[35] As seen through this lens, definitions of masculinity appear to encompass definitions of when violence is appropriate. The hegemonic masculinity of White middle-class males includes a definition of violence as appropriate for self-defense and "finishing fights"; the racialized masculinity of extremely disadvantaged Black males includes definitions of violence as appropriate for self-defense and finishing fights, as well as sometimes starting fights to display nerve or "juice," and so on. We will argue later that the two notions embedded in this conceptualization of masculinity—gender identities and norms or attitudes favoring violence—are analytically distinct from a symbolic interactionist perspective.

Second, research indicates that masculinities are not monolithic within race-class groups and, indeed, vary in their content *within* groups and *across* situations. For instance, Wilkinson's interviews with very disadvantaged men of color uncovered three major social identities, defined in terms of their use (or nonuse) of violence. These masculine identities were hierarchical, with identities promoting violence being associated with the most power.[36] This study is important because it demonstrates heterogeneity among disadvantaged African American men and reveals masculine identities that are not associated with violence. Messerschmidt also reports heterogeneity among White working-class boys who engaged in aberrant sexual and physical assaults (e.g., of younger children).[37] Because of abusive family and school experiences, these boys were unable to accomplish masculinity through mechanisms defined as normative within their race and class group.

Third, as Jody Miller notes, masculinities' research too often gives the impression that violence results simply from adherence to masculinity norms.[38] This is related to the point above, but goes further. Specifically, the argument here is that the masculinity approach to explaining violence runs the risk of depicting an oversocialized actor who responds as a member of a category rather than as an individual making choices within social and structural constraints.

We propose later in this chapter that recasting the masculinities approach from within a structural symbolic interactionist framework can offer a more elaborated view of definitions of situations, identities, and agency that can address the cautionary notes above. The framework can be used to explain, for instance, why the majority of disadvantaged African American men living in ghettos are *not* violent, why White middle-class men sometimes *are* violent despite access to other resources to claim hegemonic masculinity, and why *no* man is violent across all situations.

Femininities and Violence

Most research that speaks to femininities and violence focuses more on gender than race. Although there are theoretical statements about how race and class may shape femininities, most empirical studies focus on disadvantaged women and girls of color. We know little about femininity and violence among Whites or middle-class females. Yet, the findings of studies of disadvantaged women and girls of color offer crucial insights that must be accommodated by any attempt to explain race-class-gender and crime. We discuss some of the insights from this body of research here.

Explanations of gender differences in violence have proposed that violence transgresses normative conceptions of femininity.[39] Thus, traditional gender identities control female violence but promote male violence. This argument, however, is based on the assumption that femininity is synonymous with "emphasized femininity," the culturally idealized femininity of the White middle class.[40] This femininity complements hegemonic masculinity and is characterized by marriage, child care, sexual discretion, sociability (rather than competition), whiteness, heterosexuality, and submissiveness.[41]

Recent discussions suggest that, as in the case with masculinities, there are multiple femininities.[42] That is, females use the resources and strategies available to them to construct femininities in relation to emphasized femininity and in relation to masculinities. Although Connell posits that these femininities are not hierarchical, Simpson argues that White, middle-class females actively "join the oppressor" by constructing a femininity that complements hegemonic masculinity. They do so because it affords them power and status relative to subordinated (e.g., non-White and homosexual) women.[43] Thus, the submissive feminine ideal controls White middle-class females more than it does disadvantaged women and girls of color.

By contrast, research suggests that disadvantaged Black females construct a femininity that is rooted in self-sufficiency and independence. Some posit that the marginalized femininity of disadvantaged Black women is an accommodation to the racialized masculinity of disadvantaged Black males discussed earlier.[44] Independence and self-sufficiency are necessities for females when males have limited resources to construct masculinities rooted in work and family responsibilities. This marginalized femininity also may arise because White middle-class femininity offers little to racially and economically marginalized women—they have nothing to gain by submitting or giving up their voices.

Consistent with these themes, feminist criminologists propose that females engage in crime and violence to accommodate or resist masculinities and masculine environments. For instance, several studies of poor, minority girls reveal that abuse in their homes is a precursor to gang involvement.[45] Once in the gang, girls must portray toughness and crime to avoid further victimization on the streets.[46] Beth Richie's study of adult African American women offenders reveals a similar story about the connections between prior abuse and women's offending.[47] Under such circumstances, violence by women and girls emerges because it is impractical and dangerous to portray oneself as submissive and unwilling to use violence. But, these uses of violence are *not* a part of feminine identity, per se.

Miller's study of disadvantaged girl gang members supports the argument that being tough is a response to violent street environments.[48] For example, she points to the greater respect given to gang girls who were jumped in rather than sexed in; jumped-in girls have proven their tough-ness and can be trusted to help protect others in dangerous situations. Toughness and the willingness to fight among these girls confers status. Harris also reports that among the minority gang girls she studied, "bad girl" femininity conferred status whereas the "dud" femininity of girls who did not fight reduced respect.[49] Thus, marginalized girls of color, like their male counterparts, gain status through demonstrating the ability and will-ingness to fight.

There may be, however, some important gender differences in the way status and respect are conferred. For example, Mullins et al. report that women must simply show that they can and will use violence when neces-sary, whereas marginalized men can gain status from "throwing the first punch."[50] In other words, extremely disadvantaged females are more likely to try to settle disputes through nonviolent means, but use violence when necessary, whereas males use violence more readily. This difference may arise because violence by females is not viewed as normatively laudable, but rather is viewed as a legitimate protective response in a violent street environment. By contrast, violence is linked to masculine identities for males in the street environment.

A second gender difference centers on the importance of using violence and fearlessness for gaining respect, status, or "juice" in extremely disad-vantaged, socially isolated communities. Although demonstrating juice is key for masculine status and respect, these displays are only a small part of what respect means for females. Studies of marginalized women of color suggest that respect also accrues through being "respectable"—being dis-crete and monogamous in sexual relations.[51] Both women and girls in street environments police the sexual behaviors of other females, and aggress against those who threaten their own or friends' reputations as respectable or "decent."[52] Interestingly, the females in these studies use violence as a tool to protect feminine identities, even though violence is not considered by them to be normative feminine behavior. For males, however, violence is used to simultaneously protect and display masculine identities because it *is* considered normative masculine behavior. In sum, violence appears to be distinct from definitions of femininity, even mar-ginalized femininities. Females are more apt to use violence as self-protec-tion than to claim gender.

Miller proposes that some gang girls actually may be crossing gender boundaries and constructing masculine identities—becoming "one of the guys" rather than simply using violence as a protective mechanism while still maintaining a feminine identity.[53] She argues that if such a possibility is disregarded, the femininities-masculinities framework becomes open to criticisms of gender dualism and tautology. There is limited empirical research, however, on the situational dynamics that might lead females to construct masculine identities versus "bad girl" (or dud) femininities. Miller posits that one factor for girls in gangs may be gang structure; girls in mixed gangs and female gangs may be more likely to do masculinity than girls in gangs that are auxiliaries to male gangs, who may be more likely to construct "bad girl" femininities. Interestingly, gang structures appear, in turn, to be associated with race, with Black girls more likely to report being in all-girl or mixed gangs and Latina girls more likely to report being in auxiliary gangs.[54]

In the following section, we suggest that it may be fruitful to separate motives and justifications for violence from gendered identities. We suggest that feminine and masculine identities may well vary across and within race-gender groups, but that justifications for violence are analytically distinguishable from gendered identities. This framework may help explain links between femininities, as well as masculinities, and violence.

Inequalities, Situations, Identities, and Violence

The primary focus of research on masculinities and femininities is not on explaining intersectionalities per se but rather on articulating differences in identity and behavior *within* gender. Yet it is clear that studies of masculinities and femininities can contribute importantly to our understanding of race-class-gender and violent crime. In the remainder of this chapter, we suggest that insights from these studies can be reframed and extended from a structural symbolic interactionist perspective.

The starting point of our analysis is the Black feminist observation that human experience emerges at junctures of intersecting inequalities. Dimensions of inequality are not simply additive; the experience of being an African American female is not understandable if race and gender are considered separately. Rather, intersecting inequalities shape human interactions in ways that we are only beginning to understand. We present here a framework that maintains that intersecting inequalities affect the situations encountered by people, and thus their negotiated meanings of selves and the social world.

The interactionist perspective focuses attention on the definition of the situation, which is produced collaboratively through communication and coordinated interaction between people. As proposed in the work of Mead, Stryker, McCall, and Simmons, and others, interactionist analyses center on the role-taking process, through which actors consider how others view situations.[55] Specifically, actors engage in a cognitive process in which they cast themselves in the role of others and determine how these others are likely to view events, people, and possible lines of action in the situation. Through this process, actors define or give meaning to themselves and situations. Definitions of self and identities are built up over time through ongoing role taking of the perspectives of others, or seeing oneself through the eyes of others.

This general approach has been applied to develop an interactionist theory of crime and delinquency.[56] Drawing on interactionist research and theory more generally, Heimer and Matsueda specify a set of cognitive outcomes of role taking that may be particularly relevant in situations that lead to crime and violence.[57] Specifically, they propose that when people encounter situations that offer opportunities to solve problems through crime or violence, they consider how others would view the situation, and through this process negotiate the following: definitions (e.g. rationalizations, attitudes) of law violation as appropriate or inappropriate in the situation; perceptions of how others are likely to respond to different behaviors, including law violation; and the implications for identities if they were to engage in crime or violence. In short, like research on masculinities and femininities, our interactionist perspective views violence as a strategy to resolve problematic situations that can have consequences for definitions of self and relationships to others.

Social structures play a critical part in the process because they determine communication networks and, thus, the outcomes of role taking.[58] In other words, race, gender, and class shape opportunities for interaction and determine the others with whom we come into contact, thus affecting definitions of violence, perceptions about others' reactions to violence, and implications of using violence for identities and definitions of self. This interactionist perspective on crime has been used to address some aspects of gender and race differences in self-reported delinquency, although these have been preliminary attempts and have not realized the potential of the perspective for understanding the race-class-gender nexus with regard to offending.[59] Here we discuss how the general perspective may help us to understand intersectionalities and violence, particularly some of the intriguing findings from the research on masculinities and femininities.

We focus first on definitions of the self, which we view as encompassing gender identities (feminine or masculine), as well as other identities. Consistent with the work on masculinities and femininities discussed above, gender identities can vary across race and class due to inequalities in opportunities and resources. In other words, there are probably differences in "average" gender identities across race-class groups because of social constraints that accompany structural inequalities.

As discussed above, studies of marginalized masculinities suggest that, on average, there is heightened emphasis on using violence or threats of violence to claim gender in disadvantaged communities. Violence becomes a prime way to negotiate masculinity because extreme structural inequalities create severe restrictions on resources available for doing gender in alternative ways (e.g., respected jobs). Resources for negotiating femininity also are restricted in these communities. Specifically, it often is impractical for females in these communities to be submissive and dependent on others, as required by idealized (stereotypical White, middle-class) femininity. Thus, some girls negotiate "bad girl" femininities through asserting themselves and showing that they are capable of using violence to defend themselves when necessary.

An interactionist analysis reveals the dynamics of these situations in ways that are consistent with, yet unarticulated by, most research on masculinities, femininities, and violence. Specifically, the intersecting constraints of economic and racial inequality produce situational constraints on claiming gender. Definitions favoring violence and aggression become more *salient* across a range of social interactions as an alternative way to negotiate gender identity. For example, threats to reputation from others are more likely to trigger definitions favoring violence to deal with the threats, as has been reported by research on both masculinities and femininities.

However, most interactions in extremely disadvantaged communities do *not* eventuate in violence—even interactions involving threats to reputation or honor. If they did, we would see rates of violence higher than those observed in these communities. Indeed, violence is often avoided in many situations by the same individuals who use aggression in other situations to restore threatened honor and reputation. And, some individuals avoid using violence altogether. These points become somewhat blurred in an analysis that equates forms of masculinities with violence. Nevertheless, some empirical research supports our arguments here. For example, Wilkinson's study uncovers two major social identities among extremely disadvantaged, young, minority males that are defined in terms of their calculated, infrequent use and nonuse of violence.[60] "Holding your own" is an identity in which the man gives the impression that he *can* use violence, but chooses to do so only when necessary for protection. These men are respected on the streets because of the many challenges they must overcome to attain this status. Wilkinson also identifies a "punk" or "herb" masculine identity, which is associated with avoiding violence and toughness; these males are stigmatized and are often targets of victimization.

Importantly, the "holding your own" identity is the most common identity in Wilkinson's study and clearly is a respected way of claiming masculinity. This reveals a potentially important parallel between definitions of violence by many extremely disadvantaged minority males and White, middle-class males doing hegemonic masculinity. Specifically, in both circumstances, claiming masculinity is associated with defining violence as appropriate to *end* fights, *not* to start them. Moreover, the definitions of violence negotiated by "herbs" or "punks" promote violence less often than is the case among many White men. In sum, while men experiencing poverty, isolation, and racial exclusion may use violence more often to resolve problematic situations, it is not required. The view of marginalized masculinities as subsuming violence obscures the important point that in most interactions, even the most disadvantaged men refrain from violence, and some marginalized men refrain from violence altogether.

An interactionist analysis distinguishes between gender identities (masculinity and femininity) and definitions that favor using violence to resolve problems. In other words, gender definitions are analytically distinct from definitions of when and why it is appropriate to use violence to solve problems.[61] Thus, individuals can claim masculinity through other practices—such as through wit, humor, or athletics—in situations where they define violence as inappropriate. And, disadvantaged men may define violence as inappropriate when the threat to honor comes from women on the streets, as in the case of the research on retaliatory violence by Mullins and colleagues. Yet they may simultaneously define domestic violence against women as acceptable. Or, as in Wilkinson's study, some men may claim masculinity by threatening violence at times, yet defining it as unnecessary in most situations.

The decoupling of gender identities and violent definitions allows for variation across individuals in response to multiple dimensions of inequality. It also allows for variation in the use of violence across situations, even by individuals who resort to violence fairly regularly. The power to negotiate different solutions to problems of claiming gender is key for allowing individuals agency in their interactions and avoiding oversocialized conceptions of behavior.

Analytically distinguishing between identities and definitions may be especially helpful for making sense of femininities and violence. Here, individuals can claim femininity in situations where they also define violence as appropriate, even though it may be counter to most constructions of femininity. For instance, research on extremely disadvantaged minority females suggests that they define violence as appropriate when they are faced with femininity challenges, or situations wherein others question their reputations as "decent women." They also may define violence as appropriate when necessary to protect the neighborhood or as a form of protection for themselves and their friends in the streets.[62] The behaviors of these girls may be counter to culturally normative definitions of gender, but they are justified or rationalized on grounds sometimes unrelated to gender or as means by which to protect feminine identities.

The interactionist approach that we employ proposes that another important outcome of role taking is the perception of how others are likely to respond to various lines of behavior. If actors perceive that others are likely to reward violence—that it would enhance their prestige or repair damaged honor—then definitions favoring violence to solve problems may become more salient. If, however, they perceive that others would disapprove of their use of violence in the given situation, definitions against using violence may be called up. Or, actors may refrain from violence even if they themselves consider it to be appropriate in the situation. By contrast, the perception that others would approve of and perhaps even expect violence in response to a status threat can lead to violence even when the individual does not favor violence as a way to solve the problem. Mullins et al.'s analysis of retaliatory violence among disadvantaged African American men and women offers several examples of these various outcomes of role taking.[63]

Clearly, the outcomes of role taking identified here—gender identities, definitions of violence, and expected reactions of others to violence—will merge and appear fluid in reality. Conceptually disentangling them, however, has the advantage of recognizing that multiple inequalities can structure attempts to claim gender in ways that lead to a variety of outcomes, of which violence is but one.

According to both the interactionist and masculinities/femininities perspectives, behavior is at least in part determined by resources for claiming gender, which are in turn a product of intersecting structural inequalities. However, the question of whether race *itself* affects the negotiation of violence, above and beyond the effects of extreme economic disadvantage and social isolation, remains unanswered. The examples offered in this chapter often confound race and class, and thus their separate contributions to understanding the crime of females and males are largely unknown. For example, in the masculinities literature, we learn of the use of violence among working-class White males, and greater use of violence among extremely disadvantaged African American men and boys. We do not know, however, whether the use of violence by Whites would be similar to that of Blacks if they experienced similar levels of poverty. Is it race and class, or just class that matters for violence? The notion of intersecting inequalities conceptually allows for racial discrimination to limit resources for negotiating gender, above and beyond the limitations imposed by economic disadvantage. But because race and class inequality so often overlap in American society and thus in our research, it is difficult to know whether gender differences in crime and violence are racialized, in addition to being classed.

The perspective proposed here is rooted in the long-standing symbolic interactionist tradition. We suggest that this perspective might offer a broad platform from which we can build a more complete explanation of race-class-gender than exists to date. Yet, we intend this chapter to raise the possibility, not to develop a complete theory. We simply suggest that structural symbolic interactionism offers an overarching framework that can subsume masculinity and femininity perspectives, and at the same time offers the basis for identifying specific elements of situations that may help to understand race-class-gender differences in interactions leading to violence. While structural inequalities create average differences across race-class-gender groups, a detailed analysis of gender identities, definitions favoring violence, anticipated reactions to violence, and other dimensions of situations can offer a framework for pushing forward our understanding of heterogeneity in violence within and across race-class-gender groups.

Directions for Research

Understanding race-class-gender intersections is critical to understanding violence. Although feminist criminologists have called for such research for more than a decade now, we have seen little empirical research that takes intersectionalities seriously. There is a growing body of research that examines the experiences of men and/or women of color with crime and violence, but because the focus is typically on one race-class-gender group, we know little about how groups compare with one another. We also know little about how the experiences of disadvantaged women of color, for example, cannot be understood as the simple summing of the experiences associated with race, gender, and class inequality.

Clearly, it is difficult to conduct research that allows for study of a variety of race-class-gender groups simultaneously. Ethnographic and qualitative studies face practical barriers to including as many neighborhoods and respondents as would be necessary to examine such diverse groups. And, while we could compare findings from ethnographies and qualitative studies focused on all possible race-class-gender intersections, existing studies have tended to focus on disadvantaged African Americans and, to a lesser extent, Latinos; studies of violence among White middle-class males and females are hard to come by, but are essential comparisons, if we are to understand intersectionalities completely. Indeed, the weekend sprees of destruction and violence by White male students on college campuses clearly show that aggression is alive and well even in the White middle class.

Until recently, quantitative analyses of survey data were hamstrung by sampling strategies that produced too few respondents of color to generate meaningful comparisons across race-class-gender groups. More recently, surveys with larger and more diverse samples have been conducted, but these studies have not targeted the issues most relevant for understanding intersectionalities and crime. It is difficult, therefore, to move beyond an examination of patterns of offending to ask questions about causal mechanisms.

Yet, it can be argued that we cannot understand violence generally until we understand the reasons for race-class-gender patterns. Embarking on such a mission, in our view, requires the guidance of a theoretical perspective, as well as a careful review of relevant research. In this chapter, we have focused on the literatures on masculinities and femininities because most research taking both gender and race seriously is found here. We propose an interactionist analysis of situations within structural constraints, this type of approach may serve as a springboard for future theory development and research. We choose this perspective because it is an established tradition in sociology and criminology, and is quite consistent with feminist views on race, class, and gender as well as work on masculinities and femininities.

Of course, other perspectives may work equally well or better. The important point is that moving forward will require theory-guided, empirical research. In our view, the best route to follow empirically would be to combine qualitative and quantitative studies of race-class-gender and violence. Each research style brings important insights, and the synthesis of their findings allows us to learn more than we could with each methodological approach alone.

NOTES

1. Bureau of Justice Statistics 2004.
2. Daly 1997; Simpson 1991.
3. Saltzman Chafetz 1997:115.
4. Collins 1989.
5. Collins 2004.
6. Baca Zinn and Dill 1994.
7. For example, Collins 2004; Glenn 1999.
8. Daly 1993, 1997.
9. Simpson and Gibbs 2005.
10. Daly 1997:35.
11. One notable exception is Maher's (1997) ethnography of a neighborhood drug market that included poor White, African-American, and Latina women.
12. Heimer 1995; Simpson and Elis 1995; Simpson and Gibbs 2005.
13. Messerschmidt 1993, 1997.
14. Connell 1987, 2000; Kimmel 1996.
15. Connell 1987, 2000.
16. Connell 1987.
17. Collison 1996; Copes and Hochstetler 2003; Messerschmidt 1993; Mullins, Wright, and Jacobs 2004.
18. Messerschmidt 1993, 1995.
19. See Demetriou 2001.
20. Connell 1990; Franklin 1984; Messerschmidt 1993.
21. Franklin 1984:50.

22. Willis 1977.
23. Chambliss 1973; Messerschmidt 1993.
24. Willis 1977; see also Mac an Ghaill 1994.
25. Chambliss 1973; Messerschmidt 1993.
26. McRobbie 1980; Messerschmidt 1993; Willis 1977.
27. hooks 1981; see also Franklin 1984.
28. Anderson 1999; Wilson 1996.
29. Anderson 1999; Goodey 1997; Majors and Bilson 1992; Mullins et al. 2004; Oliver 1994.
30. Anderson 1999:92; see also Goodey 1997; hooks 1981; Majors and Bilson 1992.
31. Wilkinson 2001.
32. Katz 1988.
33. Mullins et al. 2004.
34. Mirande 1997.
35. Hall 2002.
36. Wilkinson 2001.
37. Messerschmidt 2000.
38. Miller 2002.
39. Heimer and De Coster 1999; Simpson and Elis 1995.
40. See critiques by Miller 2002 and Simpson and Elis 1995.
41. Connell 1987.
42. Ibid.
43. Simpson 1991:127.
44. Collins 2004; Simpson 1991.
45. For example, Joe and Chesney-Lind 1995; Miller 2001; Portillos 1999.
46. Fishman 1988; Laidler and Hunt 1997; Lauderback, Hansen, and Waldorf 1992.
47. Richie 1996.
48. Miller 2001.
49. Harris 1988.
50. Mullins et al. 2004.
51. Campbell 1984; Laidler and Hunt 1997; Miller 2001; Miller and Mullins 2005; Mullins et al. 2004.
52. See Miller 2001; Miller and Mullins 2005; Mullins et al. 2004.
53. Miller 2001, 2002.
54. Compare with Campbell 1984; Laidler and Hunt 1997; Lauderback et al. 1992; Miller 2001; Venkatesh 1998.
55. See, for example, McCall and Simmons 1978; Mead 1934; Stryker 1980.
56. Heimer and Matsueda 1994; Matsueda 1992.
57. Heimer and Matsueda 1994.
58. Stryker 1980.

59. For example, Heimer 1995, 1996.
60. Wilkinson 2001.
61. Heimer and De Coster 1999.
62. Miller 2001; Mullins et al. 2004.
63. Mullins et al. 2004.

Chapter 9

Race, Inequality, and Gender Violence
A Contextual Examination

Toya Z. Like and Jody Miller

Much contemporary criminological research continues to treat race and gender uncritically. Most often, race and gender function as control variables, rather than as important sources of structural and situational inequality that must be understood and accounted for in their own right.[1] Yet, the last decade has witnessed the development of increasingly sophisticated research on these issues. With regard to race, this is evidenced by the contributions of scholars such as those included in this volume. Likewise, feminist scholarship has grown tremendously. However, these works have been slow to incorporate advances from sociological research and theory, as seen in the paucity of criminological work that attends to the intersections of race, gender, and class.[2]

As demonstrated by Sojourner Truth's nineteenth-century speech "Ain't I a Woman?"[3] the insistence that feminism (and, by proxy, feminist scholarship) address race has been a visible critique from its inception. This position—that it is misguided to assume uniformity in the experiences of and inequalities faced by women, and that doing so often results in an exclusive focus on White middle-class women—took root in academia with the publications of such scholars as bell hooks, Patricia Hill Collins, and Elizabeth Spelman.[4] The primary goal of these works was to interrogate the limitations of feminist scholarship, and the primary audience was feminist scholars. As a result, attention to race and class is often a requirement for scholars who publish in leading feminist outlets. Among feminist criminologists, there is now widespread agreement that women's experiences of gender inequality can best be understood when simultaneously situated in the contexts of intersecting inequalities.

The same cannot be said for research on race and racism. Despite innovations in the study of race, crime, and criminal justice, this area of study often remains gender blind. The goal of this volume is to promote a paradigmatic shift in the way criminologists study and address race and racism; our goal in this chapter is to demonstrate the importance of incorporating gender into this agenda. Specifically, we argue that researchers cannot fully examine and explain the impact of race and racism without serious consideration of its gendered dimensions. To demonstrate this position, we draw from a qualitative study of violence against African American girls in a distressed urban community. Situating our analysis in the context of criminological research on race, neighborhoods, and violence, we examine the nature, circumstances, and meanings of violence against young women, asking the following question: How do race and class inequalities *differentially* affect young women by structuring risks for violence that are gendered?

Social Ecology and Violence against Urban African American Girls

Lauritsen's analyses of the National Crime Victimization Survey (NCVS) reveal a stark reality for African American girls. Their risk for nonfatal violent victimization is dramatically higher than for other adolescent females, and is nearly equal that for African American boys. In fact, their risk for nonstranger violence—including in their neighborhoods—is *higher* than that of any other group, including their African American male counterparts.[5] This finding counters conventional wisdom in criminology assuming that while women's fear of crime is greater than males', their risks for victimization are consistently lower. While White and Latina girls' victimization risks appear considerably lower than their male counterparts' in the NCVS, the same is not true for African American girls. Moreover, Lauritsen's area-level analyses reveal that this relationship between race and victimization risk is accounted for, in large part, by factors associated with highly distressed urban communities. She concludes, "Communities will have the most difficulty protecting youth from victimization if they are highly disadvantaged, and more specifically, if they have high proportions of young people and single-parent families."[6]

The impact of community context is an important, though not surprising, finding. Scholars have shown that disadvantage in urban Black neighborhoods is unmatched. Robert Sampson and Wilson, for example, failed to find a single city in which African Americans and Whites lived in ecological equality. They conclude, "The *worst* urban contexts in which whites reside are considerably better than the *average* context of black communities."[7] Thus, African American girls living in inner-city communities face unique circumstances associated with racial and class inequalities. Wilson's work suggests that there are unique pressures in inner-city communities, driven by structural inequalities such as unemployment and unbalanced gender ratios, that increase cultural support for the victimization of women and encourage young Black males to sexually exploit young women.[8] These arguments are evident in research on the urban street world, where researchers have provided consistent and extensive evidence of the salience and institutionalization of gender inequality, including violence against women.[9]

Unfortunately, little research examines how disadvantaged community contexts shape girls' exposure to gender-based violence.[10] Work on violence against women has only recently explained women's differential experiences across race and community contexts.[11] Moreover, scholars who seem well situated to examine violence against young women in disadvantaged communities, as seen in theoretical sensitivity and sophistication in examining male-on-male violence, are rarely attentive to young women and gender inequalities. For example, Anderson's *Code of the Street* discusses young women primarily as girlfriends, sexual partners, and teen mothers. This partly results from the peripheral space allotted to females on the streets, which remain a male-dominated terrain. But it also reflects a broader tendency in criminological research, including that on race and racism, to pay insufficient attention to gender and gender inequality.

Here we bring a gendered lens to bear in our analysis of violence against African American girls. While research on urban violence typically focuses on serious physical violence, particularly homicide, with an emphasis on men, our focus is specifically on the widespread nature of sexual violence in distressed urban neighborhoods. While young women face other forms of violence, we look at sexual violence to vividly illustrate our key argument: To understand the impact of race and class inequalities on crime, research must consider their intersections with gender inequality. We examine the nature, circumstances, and meanings of sexual violence, including coercion, sexual assault, and gang rape. Our goal is to draw attention to the ways in which disadvantaged social contexts translate, all too often, into a continuum of sexual violence that many young women witness and experience in their daily lives.

Methodology and Study Setting

Data for this chapter come from surveys and in-depth interviews with thirty-five young women in north St. Louis, Missouri,[12] ranging in age from twelve to eighteen with a mean age of approximately sixteen. Young women were recruited to participate in the project with the cooperation of several organizations working with at-risk and delinquent youths, including a local community agency and two alternative public high schools. The community agency was a neighborhood-based drop-in center, where youths from the neighborhood were free to congregate and socialize. The two alternative schools drew youths from the St. Louis public school catchment area, and were designated to serve youths expelled from St. Louis public schools for chronic in-school disruptive behavior or violence.

We study urban African American youths because our knowledge is particularly limited with regard to violence against adolescent girls in highly distressed urban African American neighborhoods. St. Louis typifies highly distressed urban areas, having large concentrations of extreme disadvantage that result in social isolation, limited resources, and high rates of violent crime. Table 9.1 provides census data comparing girls' neighborhoods, St. Louis City, and St. Louis County.[13] As illustrated, young women were drawn from neighborhoods characterized by intense racial segregation, as well as disproportionate rates of poverty, unemployment, and female-headed families. These are precisely the contexts associated with high rates of violent victimization risk for women noted above.

Sampling was purposive in nature. We sought to interview youths at risk to be involved or already involved in delinquent activities, as previous research suggests these youths have a higher risk for victimization.[14] Data collection began with a survey, and young women were then asked to participate in an audiotaped in-depth interview, typically on the same day. During the survey, young women were asked whether they had experienced verbal or physical sexual harassment, and about their experiences with sexual coercion and sexual assault (see Tables 9.2 and 9.3 below). The survey responses helped guide the conversation in the in-depth interviews. These were semistructured, with open-ended questions that allowed for

TABLE 9.1
Select Neighborhood Characteristics

	Respondents' Neighborhoods	St. Louis City	St. Louis County
Percent African American	82.6%	51.2%	18.9%
Percent Poverty	33.8%	24.6%	6.9%
Percent Unemployment	18.0%	11.3%	4.6%
Percent Female-Headed Families with Children	43.1%	28.8%	10.7%

considerable probing. In-depth interviewing provided a method for understanding the social world from the participants' points of view.[15] Reliability was strengthened through triangulated data collection, with youths being asked about their reports at multiple points across two interviews, and being asked for detailed accounts during the in-depth interviews.

In the in-depth interviews, young women were first asked to describe the nature of conflicts between girls and boys at school. Those who reported experiencing sexual harassment were asked to provide detailed descriptions of the events and their consequences. The same sequence was followed regarding interactions with men in their neighborhoods. With regard to sexual assault and coercion, girls were reminded of their survey responses and asked whether they would be comfortable talking about the event(s) in more detail. They were then asked to describe what happened, how the experience affected them, and whether they told anyone or sought assistance.[16] Though not generalizable, the study raises significant issues that may guide further inquiries into the contexts and nature of sexual violence experienced by African-American adolescent girls, and highlights the importance of studying the way gender shapes the experience of urban disadvantage and crime victimization.

Findings

Here, we describe the extent of sexual victimization among the young women we spoke with, and highlight the social contexts in which such violence emerges. As illustrated in Table 9.2, both sexual and gender harassment were common experiences for the young women. More than two-thirds reported experiencing verbal sexual harassment, and nearly half reported being touched inappropriately. In addition, half of the girls had been subject to nonsexual derogatory comments, and nine out of ten

TABLE 9.2
Prevalence of Sexual and Gender Harassment Experiences

Sexual and Gender Harassment	N (Percent)
Have boys ever made sexual comments that made you feel uncomfortable?	25 (71%)
Have boys grabbed or touched you in ways that made you feel uncomfortable?	17 (49%)
Have boys ever called you names or said things to make you feel bad about yourself?	18 (51%)
Respondents who answered yes to one or more of the above	31 (89%)

had experienced some form of harassing behavior.[17] Verbally harassing behaviors included routine and sometimes graphic sexual "come-ons," derogatory comments that were often sexual in nature, threats of sexual violence, and sexual rumors spread to other youths. Physically harassing behaviors consisted of touching or hitting girls in their buttocks, breasts, and genitalia, and sometimes escalated to physical violence when the girls challenged boys' actions.

Girls experienced sexual harassment both in their schools and in their neighborhoods. Just over half of the girls (54 percent) described experiencing such incidents in the community, and more than three-quarters (77 percent) reported such incidents at school. While sexual harassment is not the focus of this chapter, it is important to note at the outset, because it sets the stage for more serious forms of sexual abuses through the routine sexualization of young women. Girls' discussions demonstrated that harassing incidents were not rare events, but were an everyday part of the cultural milieu in their neighborhoods and at school. For instance, Yvonne said there were a lot of conflicts between girls and boys that stemmed from the young men "like touching and stuff, trying to touch on your booty or your breasts or whatever." She said this occurred "like every day. Every day." Likewise, Vanessa said, "I see it every day," and Tami concurred that it happened "all the time."

One notable feature of the harassment of young women is that such events are highly public in nature, and typically occur in the presence of other youths and even adults. However, girls rarely reported that young men face negative repercussions for their actions. Rather, they noted that other youths often incite the offender toward further action. Moreover, gender and sexual harassment are commonly intertwined. Incidents that are highly sexual at the onset often shift to derogatory name calling when a young woman responds negatively to a young man's sexual advances. These dynamics, likewise, were described as escalating in the presence of others, as young men seek to put girls "in their place" when their rebuffs are read as disrespect. Furthermore, young women who fail to adequately challenge young men's comments develop reputations as individuals who seek out or enjoy sexual attention; with this comes the attribution that they are sexually available, "rats," or "ho's." As discussed below, similar dynamics that put the onus of responsibility on young women's behaviors are found in girls' accounts of more serious forms of sexual mistreatment.

Likewise with sexual rumors: These center around accounts of girls' sexual activities and are troubling for girls because they damage their reputations. Sexually based rumors, regardless of their validity, facilitate the continuation of sexual harassment of the particular girl about whom the rumors are spread, and often escalate the harassment to include more young men than the original source of the rumor. In fact, as we will discuss below, the spreading of sexual stories about particular girls often leads to more exploitative sexual behaviors by boys, with quite detrimental effects. These "milder" but widespread forms of sexual mistreatment, coupled with an absence of mechanisms for holding young men accountable, lay a contextual foundation for more serious forms of sexual abuses. Thus, we conceptualize the sexual victimization of young women along a continuum that begins with sexual harassment but also includes sexual exploitation, coercion, sexual assault, and gang rape. These more serious incidents are the basis of the remainder of the chapter.

Sexual Exploitation and Coercion

Young women experience and witness serious forms of sexual exploitation that often are coercive in nature. In these cases, young men purposely take advantage of girls known or believed to be particularly sexually vulnerable and easily manipulated. For example, though Kiki noted that, in general, "most of the boys is disrespectful" towards girls, and "basically always want to mess with the girls, touch on 'em and all that stuff," she later clarified that "it's just the girls that's disrespectful to theyself. So they just, the boys they disrespect them and stuff." Her description of one such incident highlights how harassment escalates into sexual exploitation for such young women.

> *Kiki:* Just like this one girl that use to go here, she dropped out or whatever. She was going here, doing fine and stuff. She a real pretty girl, she had a

whole lot of talent, rap and everything, I mean, wasn't nothin' wrong with her. It's just the simple fact—and she did it—I mean, and they use to say they took pictures, they brought it to school. . . . She'll like 'em and then they'll make her think that they like her but they got a girlfriend and stuff like that. . . . They'll do it to her [have sex with her] then she'll just suck they stuff. . . . I mean, it's so many people that she just dropped out 'cause it just like, 'cause everybody be like, "You a dick suckin' girl," callin' her all stuff. . . . She gone [left school].

Interviewer: And when you said they had pictures, you mean they had—

Kiki: Yeah, they took pictures of her doing it in a van. Pictures of her doin' it in a van. They was like, "I'll bring it and show you." And I'll be like, "Why y'all gone do that." . . . It's nothin' wrong with her . . . why would you do it because y'all—she know her self-esteem is so low. She just doin' it so people could like her.

Sexually exploitative behaviors are most commonly reported as occurring at social functions such as parties and get-togethers. These social functions typically include youths' friends but also peers that they are acquainted with but have less intimate ties to. Most often, adults are not present, and youths consume alcohol and marijuana. It is under these circumstances that some girls are sexually fondled or mistreated by male peers. For example, Dawanna said that she and her friends typically get together to party every weekend. Asked whether her friends ever try to take advantage of girls in situations "where everybody's drinking and smoking," she explained,

Yeah there's been a time that some females drink and then smoke and [they are] mixed up and sometimes they don't know what they doin' and somebody take 'em home or walk 'em down the street to their home or whatever. . . . Some of the males will you know, some of the males would try to you know, take advantage of 'em 'cause they drunk.

Recounting one such incident, Dawanna noted that after a party, she rode home with friends that she described as a "little couple." Dawanna explained that the girl

was so intoxicated that, you know, she didn't care what she was doin'. She just yellin' out his name and then all of a sudden she had just took off her clothes and junk and he just, they was just at it [having sex in the car while

Dawanna was present]. And then he had . . . threw her clothes outside [the car] . . . and drove her home and laid her down in the front [of the house naked]. But I mean, I was like "you trippin'," so I had to take off the extra shirt that I had on and gave it to her.

Dawanna said the next day she "had told [the girl] everything and she don't know what happened. But she ended up getting on [confronting and fighting] the boy." Similarly, Destiny discussed a get-together with friends where "the girl drunk too much and stuff and was lettin' [two boys] feel all over her and stuff." Lisa recalled a get-together in which her boyfriend's friend urinated on a young woman:

> *Lisa:* They got drunk, they got real drunk. He peed on this girl, made her go to his house, take a shower, then he had sex with her. That's how they do girls. . . . All of 'em were drunk. But see that's just how they do girls. That's just how his friends are with girls.
> *Interviewer:* So she, she was his girlfriend?
> *Lisa:* Naw, she wasn't his girlfriend. She wasn't nothin' like that. She was just one of the girls out there. And all them girls . . . down there where they stay, that's the way they like to be treated. 'Cause that's where they head at.

Lisa continued, "everybody laughed, and it wasn't nothin' [the girl] could do. . . . Then, [the young man who peed on her was] like, 'come on baby, you want me to take you, you can go take a shower in my house, come on, come on baby.' She was like, 'huh uh,' but she went anyway." Lisa's assumption was that when the young man got the girl to his house, "he had sex with her."

Such incidents are clearly exploitative and degrading to the young women involved. However, they are not viewed by participants or witnesses as sexual assaults. At worst, the girls feel taken advantage of or mistreated, and the victims are held accountable as much as or more than the perpetrators. Such incidents occur in the presence of others who do little, if anything, to intervene. Like Kiki, some young women disapprove of such behavior and feel sorry for girls they see as having "low self-esteem"; however, blame is placed on these girls for "disrespecting" themselves and allowing such mistreatment to occur. Young men rarely face sanction for such actions—instead they are perceived as engaging in activities that many young men do when the opportunity arises.

TABLE 9.3
Prevalence of Sexual Assault and Coercion (N = 35)

Sexual Assault and Coercion	N (Percent)
Have you ever been sexually assaulted or raped?	9 (26%)
Has anyone ever tried to sexually assault or rape you?	6 (17%)
Has anyone pressured you to have sex when you didn't want to?	13 (37%)
Has anyone had sex with you when you didn't want to, but you were unable to stop them because you were high or drunk?	3 (9%)
Has a group of men or boys made you have sex with them when you didn't want to but felt like you didn't have a choice or couldn't say no?	2 (6%)
Have you been pressured or forced to have sex with a boyfriend when you didn't want to?*	9 (27%)
Respondents who answered yes to one or more of the above	19 (54%)
Respondents who answered yes to more than one of the above	11 (31%)

* N = 33; Two girls reported never having had a boyfriend.

Sexual Assault

As Table 9.3 demonstrates, many young women reported serious forms of sexual coercion and assault. One-quarter of the girls reported having been the victims of a sexual assault. In addition, fully half of the young women stated that they have been forced or pressured into unwanted sex in at least one situation, and nearly a third reported multiple assaults. The predominant forms of sexual assault reported by young women are acquaintance rapes, sexual coercion or assault in dating relationships,[18] and rapes involving the use of drugs and alcohol. In addition, two young women reported having been the victim of a gang rape. Notably, 40 percent of the young men we interviewed reported that they had "run trains" on young women. Although none of the young men defined these as sexual assaults, as we describe below, both young women who were victims of such assaults defined them as rape.

Acquaintance Rape

The majority of girls who disclosed a sexual assault had been victimized by an acquaintance. This included friends, friends' relatives or friends, or friends of the victim's family. These assaults typically take place at someone's residence, and the victim is often alone with the attacker. Janelle's experience is typical:

> I was over at a friend's house, this girl, and he [the girl's friend] came over there and, you know, he was sitting down and he was talking to me and

conversating with me at first, you know, and then he got to trying to touch on me and stuff and I was like "no, go away," pushing him and trying to avoid the whole situation, but me being a female, males have more strength, so he holds me down and there's not too much I can do about it because you know, I'm not as strong as him.

At the time of the assault, Janelle's friend "had went to the store." Afraid of reprisals, Janelle did not call the police, and told her family only a couple of years later. She explained, "I thought if he found out that I told somebody he would somehow try to do something else to me."

Cherise described a similar assault in which, when she was fourteen, she was raped by an adult acquaintance in her neighborhood. She said her friends would routinely go to the man's house to "play Nintendo games, come over and watch TV. . . . I was over at his house watching *Xena*, I remember exactly what was on, *Xena*, and this guy forced himself on me." Cherise said that she "felt scared so I just let him do it." She described resisting at first, but "when he made like a facial expression I was too scared. I mean, I felt like if I was to tell him 'no, stop' maybe he would've hit me or beat me up or did something to me . . . so I just went along with him. And that was when I lost my virginity." Like Janelle, Cherise did not report the assault to the authorities. However, unlike Janelle, she did not keep the assault to herself. Instead, she told family members what had happened, and "my big brother beat him down."

Rapes Involving Drugs and Alcohol

Given our description of the types of sexual exploitation that occurred in the context of parties or get-togethers involving alcohol and drugs, it is not surprising that some young women described sexual assaults in these settings as well. Young women are more likely to report being present when such assaults take place, but several have been victims as well. Kristy recalled, "we were at a party, there was a lot of drinking and we were using some drugs. I had passed out. So like I'm coming to, I seen myself somewhere I know I shouldn't be." Specifically, she found herself underneath a young man she "hardly even know," who had had sex with her while she was passed out. She continued, "so I began fighting my way up, you know, put up a little fight, then I was like, you know, leave the party, go to a relative's house, sober [up] a little." Once she was sober, Kristy said she "told a true friend and we went and retaliated . . . [and] jumped him." To her surprise, though, "jumping that dude got us into a little bit more trouble than we imagined. 'Cause he called the police and well, two of my friends got assault charges." As a consequence of the assault, Kristy said, "I don't trust people and I don't drink."

Other young women witnessed sexual assaults taking place while they were at parties. Twelve-year-old Shauntell witnessed her cousin rape a girl during a party they attended. She explained that the girl "got high and drunk," but that her cousin was not. She recalled,

> She was just sittin' there on the couch, just chillin', listening to music, and my cousin told her to "come here." She got up and went to him. He was like, "come sit here with me for a minute." She was like, "for what?" He said, "come here." [Then] he said, "well come here Shauntell." So I went with him, and we went down . . . [to] the basement.

The young women appeared "scared" when Shauntell's cousin tried to send Shauntell back upstairs, asking " 'why she can't come in here with me?' And my cousin said 'she can sit right there.' " Shauntell sat down, and her cousin started kissing the girl. She explained,

> At first she started likin' it. But when he started takin' off his clothes and taking off her clothes, she started tellin' him to stop. And I [was] like, "man, don't do that man." He was like, "Shauntell go upstairs." She was like, "naw, Shauntell don't leave me." So I just sat there, closed my eyes and covered my ears.

Shauntell said that she "kept hearing her say stop," and that it was "scary. 'Cause I was just imaginin', I was just thinking what if that was me in that position."

When Shauntell talked to her cousin about the incident later, "he said that she wanted it and she deserved it. . . . He was like, 'because she was comin' on to me before we got to the party, and she tried to front me out in front of my boys, and that's what she get.' " Shauntell's cousin described the young woman's behavior before the party and in front of his friends as justifying the rape to teach her a lesson. What is perhaps most disturbing about such incidents is that they occur in fairly public settings, where others are nearby and aware of what is taking place. Shauntell felt unable to intervene when her older cousin raped the young woman in her presence, but others simply choose not to because such acts are not unexpected and often deemed "deserved."

Gang Rape

As noted in Table 9.3, two young women reported having been the victims of a gang rape, though the phenomenon appears to be widespread.[19] Sheron was at home when her sister's boyfriend, Sheron's ex-boyfriend, and several other of their friends came over. Of her ex-boyfriend and the rape, she explained,

> We went together but we had broke up. He came in the room [that night] and we did whatever. And then it was dark in there so somebody else, I saw the door and somebody else came in there and they was just like, "if you gonna do it to him then you have to have sex with me too." And I was like, "Why?" And he was like, "Well if you don't have sex with me then you gonna have to give me oral sex." So I knew that I wasn't gonna do that, and [her ex-boyfriend] said, "We not gonna leave until you have sex with him." So I feel that, you know, I ain't have no other choice.

Cherise described being gang raped by a group of her male friends after going out with them, though she explained, "I don't remember nothing about it." She recalled,

> [I] got drunk. They raped me. Came home, don't know how I got home. I know I was in a car though. And woke up, [and my] privacy was swolled. I knew they had did something. They put something in my drink, maybe to make me forget and the only how that I did know was because my privacy was swolled. [I] told my cousins about it, [and the young men] came over there. I believe the reason they came over there was because they know they put something in my drink and they thought I didn't remember about it. Maybe they was planning on doing it again. So we called them over there and they got beat down. Beat down!

As with other sexual assaults that took place at parties, a number of young women also reported witnessing or being aware that such incidents were taking place when they were at get-togethers. Once at a hotel party,

Felicia reported that a young woman was forced to perform oral sex on all the young men in the room. An acquaintance of Felicia's

> picked her up and held her off the balcony from her feet and told her that if she didn't give all the dudes in the room a blow job, he was gonna drop her. So she got down, she gave all the dudes in the room blow jobs, and one of the boys stuck his finger up in her and was like, "well, she's a virgin, who wants to sleep with her?" She was like, she wasn't no virgin, and he was like, he don't care, she was tight and [he] want to sleep with her. She said no and he smacked her and tossed her up [raped her].

Felicia said that there "were about fifty of us" in the room, but no one intervened to stop the gang assault. She explained, "most of the girls was like 'you didn't have to do her like that.' It wasn't necessary. I mean, that's how we was and a lot of boys said the same thing. I mean it was like three boys out of the whole crew that said she deserved it." Nonetheless, the strongest reaction anyone had to the incident was "to have no part of it" rather than putting a stop to it. In fact, Felicia herself reflected on the incident and surmised, "that's on her. 'Cause I feel she put herself in that position. I mean, you put yourself in a position for this. She put herself in that position."

Discussion

The sexual violence experienced by African American girls living in concentrated disadvantage is extensive, encompassing acts that range from sexual harassment to gang rape. Three-quarters of the young women we spoke with reported having been sexually harassed; one-quarter, raped; and half, some form of sexual assault or coercion. Moreover, one in three girls reported multiple incidents of sexual assault or coercion. These figures indicate a disproportionate amount of sexual violence—particularly given that the mean age of our sample was only sixteen. By comparison, Koss and her colleagues found that 12 percent of the college students they surveyed self-reported having been raped; our sample of African American adolescents in high-risk urban settings report a rate more than double their findings.[20]

Additionally, our research suggests that violence in one setting or of one type often served to reinforce and justify additional violence.[21] Though not discussed in detail, sexual harassment was pervasive among the girls and highly public, routinely taking place in the presence of other youths, and often in front of community adults or school officials. The public nature of these events facilitated feelings of embarrassment and humiliation among some young women. Moreover, girls' responses to this harassment, if assertive or aggressive, often resulted in more vicious mistreatment, especially in the form of gender harassment: incidents quickly escalated into hostile confrontations when girls rejected boys' sexual overtures. Girls who did not resist such treatment were often targeted for further abuse by both male and female students. A lack of negative response by the victim could easily lead to further sexual harassment. Moreover, girls who did not reject sexual harassment were often seen as deserving of the treatment or blamed for it by other youths. These incidents often spilled over into other social contexts that were even more violent in nature.

In community social settings, the mistreatment girls faced sometimes intensified to include sexually coercive and degrading acts. At parties and get-togethers—which were not supervised by adults and typically included the consumption of drugs and alcohol—some young men seized the opportunity to sexually exploit vulnerable girls. As with sexual harassment, these incidents occurred in the presence of others, and seemed to be aimed specifically at expressing blatant devaluation for the girl. Such maltreatment of girls appeared to act as a status enhancement for boys. Perhaps most troubling is the extent of gang rape documented in our investigation. Nearly half of the young men we spoke with reported having "run trains" on girls, though none defined it as a sexual assault. Most of the girls had either witnessed or heard about such events, and several had been the victims of such assaults. Drugs and alcohol, as well as the lack of adult supervision, were important factors that made parties conducive to such incidents. A striking feature of the events described by young women was their public character. In fact, the most common theme in the entire range of sexual violence reported was that much of girls' victimization occurred either in the presence of or with the knowledge of their peers. Yet, few witnesses did anything to prevent the victimization or intervene on the victim's behalf.

These findings fit well with our broader understanding of how distressed neighborhood contexts heighten levels of violence and hinder the development of sustained mechanisms for intervention. Research on social capital and collective efficacy, for example, compares neighborhoods' abilities to generate social ties and protective mechanisms among their residents. Neighborhoods must have conditions present—such as institutional, political, and economic resources—to facilitate the development of "mutual trust and shared expectations among residents," in order for neighborhood processes, like the willingness to intervene on behalf of others and monitor the behavior of young people, to thrive.[22] Distressed urban communities, where African Americans are disproportionately located—including the young women in our study—often lack these requisite resources. This helps explain why so many social opportunities for sexual violence were present, while necessary protections and interventions were often absent.

In a recent study of domestic violence and community context, Benson and colleagues suggest that violence against women is linked both to the social isolation present and the difficulties disadvantaged neighborhoods have in developing collective efficacy:

> Even if most residents of disadvantaged neighborhoods personally disapprove of spouse abuse, they may not openly express their disapproval to the offender, because in these neighborhoods people are expected to mind their own business and to stay out of the personal affairs of others. In neighborhoods low on collective efficacy it is not customary for residents to take action for the common good. Hence, no one feels responsible to intervene on behalf of victimized women. Additionally, residents may hesitate to intervene in these situations because they fear that they will become targets of violence themselves.[23]

However, our research suggests that it is also necessary to understand the overlay of gender inequality with community context. This includes powerful ideologies about women and gender that place young women at risk. Youths' lack of intervention into incidents of sexual violence appeared tied to their gendered perceptions of the event and the parties involved, including their belief that the victim's behavior—at that moment or in general—was conducive to violence. The ability to stand up for oneself is a key avenue for respect in disadvantaged communities, and for young women, this includes standing up to protect one's sexual integrity. Young women who "failed" to do so—particularly when their actions rendered them culpable in some way in the eyes of others—faced sanction, at the very least in the form of lack of empathy and lack of intervention.

Ironically, young women espoused strong victim-blaming attitudes, including those who had been victims of sexual assault. Analyzing their own victimization, girls focused primarily on aspects of their behavior that they have since modified to prevent future assaults (e.g., "I don't drink no more"). In general, young women did not approve of boys' exploitive actions. However, they did report that "boys will be boys"—believing that many young men would disrespect and take advantage of girls whenever the opportunity existed. Thus, they held other girls accountable for failing to avoid such opportunities. The expectation that men and boys will mistreat young women had a strong impact on girls' perceptions of victims. Comments such as "girls should have more respect for theyselves," "if you dress like a 'ho' you get treated like a 'ho,'" and "stupid girls deserve what they get" illustrate both the nature and severity of girls' beliefs. Such tactics may act as mechanisms by which girls achieve a greater sense of personal security in situations where sexual victimization is likely: rather than focusing on males (whom they have little or no control over), they attempt to shape their own behaviors to prevent or reduce their risks for victimization. Girls who fail to do so are thus seen as deserving what they get.

Research consistently shows that rape myth acceptance and victim blaming remain problematic throughout U.S. society.[23] Nonetheless, the degree of fatalism about young men's behaviors, and its relation to girls' victim-blaming belief systems, is probably exacerbated by the urban street milieu they must negotiate. Gender stratification is widespread, as is the visible devaluation of women, and the strong element of status hierarchy among young men. The degradation of women and girls appears to be an avenue for both status enhancement and male bonding among young men in impoverished urban communities. The public nature of the sexual violence we documented illustrates that young men obtain rewards for committing these acts in front of their peers.[24] Because these communities provide few opportunities for legitimate sources of success and prestige, alternative means become normative. This particular avenue for male peer recognition and respect is of great detriment to the young women in these communities.

What has been missing from much previous research on race, inequality, and crime is specific attention to the way gender inequality overlays with neighborhood dynamics to heighten victimization risks for young women. While often conceptualized in gender-neutral terms or assumed to be male-on-male, our research demonstrates that urban violence is a gendered phenomenon, and that the social and institutional dynamics in disadvantaged communities shape violence against the women and girls who reside there. This study provides a needed foundation on the issue; future research on the linkages between urban inequality and violence against women is clearly warranted.

If a paradigmatic shift in the study of race and crime is to occur, it is essential that research be grounded in an understanding of the way gender and racial inequalities intersect to shape the meanings and opportunities for violence. For this research agenda to move forward, *comparative* qualitative studies—across race, class, and community contexts—are necessary. While our study allows us to offer preliminary suggestions about the role of racial inequalities in shaping gender-based violence, our specific focus on urban African American youth precludes us from making decisive claims about the role of race/ethnicity and class in gender violence. Moreover, new avenues for examining these issues from a quantitative perspective are needed. The strength of qualitative research lies in the insights it provides on the situational contexts and meaning systems surrounding violence; however, broader patterns can only be identified and tested through quantitative analysis. This research will be strengthened when gender and gender inequality are integrated into the study of race, inequality, and violence.

NOTES

1. Daly 1998; Holdaway 1997.

2. Collins 1990. For notable exceptions in criminology, see Maher 1997 and Steffensmeier, Ulmer, and Kramer 1998.

3. "Sojourner Truth's Speech to the Akron Convention, 1851."

4. Collins 1990; hooks 1981; Spelman 1989.

5. Lauritsen 2003. This pattern holds for adult African American women as well. See also Lauritsen and White 2001.

6. Lauritsen 2003:10. See also Lauritsen and Shaum 2004.

7. Sampson and Wilson 1995:42 (our emphases).

8. Wilson 1996. See also Anderson 1999.

9. Maher 1997; Miller 2001.

10. Burt et al. 1997.

11. For a promising recent example, see Dugan and Apel 2003. Their research suggests that American Indian women face levels of violence strikingly higher than rates experienced by African American women.

12. We were unable to complete in-depth interviews with two study partici-

pants, although their survey responses are included. The broader study also investigates peer and neighborhood violence, dating violence, and police conflicts, and includes interviews with forty young men.

13. To ensure anonymity, we did not obtain girls' addresses; instead, we asked them to provide the names of two cross streets near to where they lived. Data presented in Table 9.1 come from census block data for these cross-street locations. Thus, it is not a precise measure of girls' neighborhoods but provides a rough match. We were unable to obtain this information for five girls, because the street names they gave were parallel. However, in four of the five cases we were able to narrow down to their zip codes. These data were not included in the calculations in Table 9.1, though it is notable that these four girls lived in zip codes with comparable neighborhood conditions to those for whom we gathered block-level data. The figures for St. Louis County do not include those of the city, as the city is its own county.

14. Lauritsen, Sampson, and Laub 1991. Our initial goal was to compare troubled youths to those integrated in their communities in more prosocial ways. Despite nearly two years of effort, we were unable to obtain necessary permissions to gain access to a comparative group of "resilient" African American youths in north St. Louis.

15. Miller and Glassner 2004.

16. Young women were provided with a contact sheet of victims' service agencies that provide services to adolescent girls, the agency functions were outlined, and they were offered assistance in contacting them.

17. Excluding gender harassment, three-quarters of the girls reported having experienced verbal and/or physical sexual harassment.

18. Due to space constraints and our focus here on broader peer dynamics, sexual violence in dating relationships is not discussed in this chapter.

19. As noted earlier, forty young men were also interviewed, and close to half reported having "run trains" on girls. It may be that girls underreported such events, because only two young women said they were victims of such an assault. This would not be surprising. This type of sexual victimization is especially stigmatizing for young women, and underreporting has been found in previous research for such events as sex-for-crack exchanges and sexual initiation for girls in gangs. However, these numbers are probably close to accurate: by definition, gang rapes involve multiple perpetrators and a single victim. So, for example, if five young men, on average, participated in a train on a single girl, the ratio of perpetrators to victims is 5 to 1. In all, sixteen boys reported having engaged in such events, leading us to expect to find two or three girls in our sample of thirty-five who had been victimized in this way.

20. Koss, Gidycz, and Wisniewski 1987.

21. See also Miller and White 2003.

22. Sampson, Morenoff, and Gannon-Rowley 2002:457. See also McNulty and Bellair 2003b.

23. Benson et al. 2003:210.

24. Scully 1990.

Part III

Contexts and Settings

Chapter 10

Is the Gap between Black and White Arrest Rates Narrowing?

National Trends for Personal Contact Crimes, 1960 to 2002

Gary LaFree, Robert M. O'Brien, and Eric Baumer

In response to the massive civil disorders in much of the United States in 1967, President Lyndon Johnson established the National Advisory Commission on Civil Disorders (the Kerner Commission) and charged it with determining what happened, why it happened, and how to prevent it from happening again.[1] Perhaps the most memorable phrase from the commission's voluminous 1968 report is the conclusion that "our nation is moving toward two societies, one Black, one White—separate and unequal."[2] The image of two separate societies was especially striking with regard to crime. For example, in a study of Chicago neighborhoods included in the report, researchers found that a low-income, predominantly Black neighborhood had thirty-five times as many serious crimes as an upper-income, predominantly White neighborhood.[3] More generally, Blacks were arrested on average four times more frequently than Whites in 1966 for the seven street crimes routinely tracked by the Uniform Crime Reports (UCR).[4]

It has been four decades since the civil disturbances of the mid-1960s rocked the United States. Has the gap between Black and White arrest rates significantly narrowed during this time period? No published study has provided a definite answer to this question, which is especially surprising given the tremendous amount of theoretical attention devoted to Black-White differences in crime commission and criminal justice processing. Here, we rely on econometric time-series methods to test two competing perspectives that make contrasting predictions about changes in

Black and White arrest rates for four major personal crimes (homicide, robbery, rape, and aggravated assault) from 1960 to 2002. Our results show significant convergence between Blacks and Whites for rape and aggravated assault arrests reported in the Uniform Crime Reports (UCR), and for rapes reported in the National Crime Victim Survey (NCVS). We also find that the gaps between Black and White homicide and robbery UCR arrests and Black and White NCVS robbery offenses generally declined during this period, although these convergences are not statistically significant. The main contrary finding is that Black-White aggravated assaults (NCVS) significantly diverged from 1973 to 2002. Our explanation for these findings emphasizes differences between offending rates and police discretion over time.

Assimilation and Conflict Perspectives on Black-White Crime Trends

Assimilation Perspective

The classic work of Shibutani and Kwan[5] defines assimilation as a change of mental perspective in which an immigrant group eventually perceives the world from the point of view of a host group. They argue that assimilation between ethnic groups eventually results in all cases where one group does not simply exterminate the other. Wilson[6] provides what is perhaps the best known argument for racial assimilation. He notes that during the 1960s and 1970s, the United States entered a new period in which class increasingly supplanted race as the major determining characteristics in the lives of African Americans. Whereas previous barriers to African Americans had been designed by the dominant culture to control and restrict the entire Black population, Wilson claims[7] that economic barriers after the 1960s mostly affected the Black "underclass." In short, Wilson argues that race relations in America have undergone a progressive transition from racial inequalities to class inequalities. This transition may be seen especially in the growing strength of the African American middle class and in the unprecedented progress Blacks have made in securing positions of power in government and business.

Other supporters of an assimilation view have pointed to evidence of a narrowing gap between Blacks and Whites in educational attainment and earnings. Thus, Wattenberg and Scammon[8] argue that a fundamental change in American society took place after 1960 as Blacks increased their educational attainment, moved into skilled blue-collar or white-collar jobs, and began earning salaries ever closer to those of Whites. Similarly, Moynihan[9] showed that young, Black, husband-wife families living outside the South have incomes that are about the same as comparable White families.

In one of the most comprehensive comparisons of Blacks and Whites regarding education, employment, and earnings, Farley[10] concludes that Blacks have narrowed the gap with Whites in educational attainment, placement in high-prestige jobs, and earnings. The Black-White gap in educational attainment was cut in half from the end of World War II until the early 1980s. During the same period, the proportion of Blacks in managerial and professional jobs doubled. By the early 1980s, the racial gap in earnings for Black and White women had all but disappeared and the gap in earnings for Black and White men, while still large, had clearly lessened. Farley, his general conclusion notwithstanding, points out that other indicators show little evidence of Black-White convergence over time (especially unemployment rates).[11]

Conflict Perspective

Conflict theorists[12] have long claimed that political power, in close association with social class position, is the basic determinant of organizational rewards and constraints. Access to scarce resources is determined, in part, by membership in subgroups, defined especially by class and race. Following Sellin's[13] influential argument that racial discrimination is a critical ingredient in the application of U.S. law, conflict theorists have traditionally linked race directly to criminal justice processing by arguing that criminal law is a tool created and enforced by powerful subgroups to maintain their own favorable access to organizational rewards and to limit the access of less powerful subgroups to these rewards. Thus, Chambliss[14] and Chambliss and Seidman[15] argue that the "administration of the criminal law is a highly selective process that involves the use of a wide range of discretion" that results in "systematic bias in law enforcement."

The conflict perspective is supported by recent studies showing either continuing inequality or a widening rift between Blacks and Whites in access to housing and education and in overall income levels. For example,

Massey and Denton argue that racial segregation in the United States has been so pervasive in perpetuating racial inequality that it can fairly be compared to the South African system of apartheid:

> [Residential segregation] forces blacks to live under extraordinarily harsh conditions and to endure a social world where poverty is endemic, infrastructure is inadequate, education is lacking, families are fragmented, and crime and violence are rampant.[16]

Massey and Denton claim that high levels of Black-White segregation had become universal in American cities by 1970. Despite passage of the Fair Housing Act in 1968, this situation had changed relatively little in the nation's largest Black communities through the early 1990s. Moreover, levels of Black-White segregation do not vary significantly by social class. Massey and Denton suggest that the "hypersegregation" of Blacks in American society creates the structural conditions for the emergence of an oppositional culture that devalues work, schooling, and marriage, and that stresses attitudes and behaviors that are antithetical and often hostile to success in the larger economy.

Many such predictions can also be found in Wilson's[17] work. He argues that the structural transformation of the urban economy away from manufacturing to services, and the flight of jobs from central cities to suburbs, had an especially negative effect on predominantly African American communities, concentrating disadvantages and setting Black neighborhoods apart from other areas. Moreover, the migration of middle-class Blacks out of the central city further weakened the stability of Black inner-city neighborhoods. The intense social isolation of such neighborhoods cuts their residents off from a wide range of social benefits, including access to marriageable partners, involvement in quality education, and exposure to conventional role models.

According to Farley,[18] Blacks made much progress in family income in the 1960s, but the economic status of Black families deteriorated substantially after the 1970s, mostly because of changes in living arrangements. After the 1970s, the proportion of Black families headed by women increased dramatically, as did the proportion of separated and divorced Black women with children outside of marriage. These changes have widened the income gap between Black and White families because female-headed families typically have much lower incomes than husband-wife families.

Empirical Implications for the Black-White Arrest Gap

The body of research on inequality between Blacks and Whites in major social institutions during the second half of the twentieth century is a study in contrasts. Those who support an assimilation perspective point to obvious Black gains in earnings, middle-class employment, and educational attainment. Those who support a conflict perspective point to growing residential segregation, continuing gaps in Black-White unemployment, continuing and perhaps increasing segregation in schools, and a growing gap in family income linked, in turn, to rapid changes in the Black family. More specifically, each of the social forces emphasized in the assimilation and conflict perspectives has been linked in various ways to violent offending and the use of formal social control. Consequently, if the Black-White gap in these social conditions has changed over time, we would expect to see corresponding changes in the Black-White gap in arrest and crime rates. But the two perspectives outlined above point to divergent predictions. Those supporting an assimilation perspective would predict growing *convergence* in Black-White arrest and crime rates for personal contact crimes, while those supporting a conflict perspective would predict *divergence or little change* in the long-standing Black-White arrest and crime gaps. Our analysis is directed at evaluating these competing empirical predictions.

Prior Research and the Current Study

While there is a voluminous literature on Black-White differences in criminal offending and criminal justice processing,[19] virtually all of this research has been cross-sectional. Such cross-sectional studies of crime rates can be divided into two broad categories: those that include race in models predicting overall rates,[20] and those that disaggregate rates by offender's race and estimate separate models for Blacks and Whites.[21] Blau and Blau[22] found that, while the proportion of Blacks accounts for much of the variation in violent crime rates in large metropolitan areas, the effect of race is greatly reduced when other variables, especially racial socioeconomic inequality, are controlled. Thus, they argue that racial inequality leads to strong pressures to commit acts of criminal violence and to weak social controls against doing so.

In an analysis of city, metropolitan, and state homicide rates for 1960,

1970, and 1980, Land, McCall, and Cohen[23] found that among their measures of resource deprivation, percent Black population is the most consistently associated with high homicide rates. They also found that connections between resource deprivation measures (including percentage Black) and homicide rates were larger in 1980 than in 1970. They interpret this as supporting Wilson's[24] arguments about the growing importance of concentration effects for African Americans in the 1970s. Thus, their analysis provides indirect evidence for a widening gap between Black and White arrest and crime rates during this period.

Starting in the late 1980s, much of the cross-sectional research on the racial gap in crime has addressed the issue of whether Black and White arrest and crime rates are affected by the same factors.[25] Sampson[26] used UCR arrest data to develop models of race-specific rates of robbery and homicide by juveniles and adults in 150 U.S. cities for 1980. He found that the scarcity of employed Black men increases the prevalence of families headed by females in Black communities. Moreover, Black family disruption substantially increases rates of Black murder and robbery, especially by juveniles. These effects are independent of a wide range of demographic and economic controls, and are similar to the effects of White family disruption on White violence.

As more researchers have disaggregated models of crime by race, they have generated research on the "racial invariance" question: whether Whites would exhibit the same crime rates as Blacks if Whites faced the same structural disadvantages as Blacks. Some recent city-level analyses support the assumption of race invariance,[27] while others do not.[28] Still others report some support depending on the specific measures of disadvantage and crime examined.[29] While racially disaggregated cross-sectional research has increased our understanding of the dynamics of racial differences in crime, and provided important insights into Black-White outcomes at particular points in time, it has not been very useful for formally analyzing the relationship between Black and White crime trends over time.

Several recent descriptive studies of Black and White arrest rates over time provide some evidence for convergence. LaFree[30] presents the annual ratio of Black to White total arrests for seven crimes from 1946 to 1990, and concludes that the gap between Black and White arrest rates has been narrowing for most crimes since the 1960s. Similarly, Cook and Laub[31] compare Black and White juvenile (ages 13–17) arrest trends for four violent crimes (murder, rape, robbery, and aggravated assault) from 1965 to

1999 and find evidence that the Black-White gap has considerably narrowed. Compared to White juveniles, Black juveniles were arrested for violent crimes more than ten times as often in the mid-1960s and early 1970s. This ratio dropped to less than four times as often by 1999. However, Cook and Laub found much different patterns for homicide. Here the gap between White and Black juveniles widened during the late 1980s and early 1990s and began to move back to its former levels after the mid-1990s. Importantly, neither LaFree nor Cook and Laub offer statistical tests for convergence or divergence between Black and White arrest rates over time. In the current study, we respond to the limitations of prior research by examining annual Black and White arrest rates for a 43-year period; adopting specific statistical tests for convergence and divergence between Black and White arrest and crime trends; and focusing on the relationship of individual Black and White rates to each other over time.

Data and Methods

Race-Specific Violent Crime Measures

In the United States, the two major longitudinal data sources for crime by offender's race are UCR arrest statistics and NCVS reported victimizations.[32] Unfortunately, NCVS data are only available since 1973 and hence miss the steep increases in crime that began in the early 1960s. We focus here on the four serious personal contact crimes included in the UCR (homicide, robbery, rape, and aggravated assault), which, with the exception of homicide, are also included in the NCVS. We assembled an annual time-series data set of UCR personal contact crimes for the United States from 1960 to 2002 and for the NCVS from 1973 to 2002.

Researchers have long argued that UCR arrest data by race probably reflect a mixture of actual criminal behavior and the processing decisions made by police.[33] Thus, Hindelang[34] distinguishes between "behavioral" and "labeling" interpretations of UCR arrest data and O'Brien[35] differentiates between "offender-generated" and "recorded" crimes. We note that using UCR arrest data to explore whether the long-term arrest gap between Blacks and Whites is changing has important implications for both theory and policy regardless of the combination of actual behavior and police bias represented by arrest rates. However, prior studies have concluded that the four personal contact crimes emphasized here exhibit meaningful differences in the extent to which they reflect actual criminal behavior by race as opposed to the recording decisions of police.

Compared to the other personal contact crimes, researchers agree that homicides are more likely to be reported to police, are recorded by police as bona fide crimes, and receive the most time and resources from criminal justice agencies.[36] Accordingly, we assume that homicides come closest to measuring actual criminal behavior while also recognizing that the classification, reporting, and recording of homicides also involves some discretion and error.[37] By contrast, rape and aggravated assault rates are greatly affected by changes in citizen reporting to police and police recording decisions over time.[38] Finally, when compared to homicide, robbery is more susceptible to changes in reporting and recording over time. Nevertheless, compared to rape and aggravated assault, robbery is more likely to be reported to the police and recorded as criminal by police.[39] Consistent with prior research, in the analyses that follow we assume that arrest trends for homicide and robbery are more likely to reflect changes in actual criminal behavior; and that arrest trends for rape and aggravated assault are more likely to reflect changes in victim reporting and police recording practices.

We also perform parallel analyses using the NCVS data. Because the NCVS obtains data on offender's race directly from victims, it excludes police discretion in its race-specific estimates of offending. The NCVS data, however, also have important limitations: they exclude homicides; they are susceptible to the usual limitations typical of survey research;[40] and they are based on a relatively small sample of rape cases.

Testing for Convergence and Divergence

To test for convergence between Black and White arrest and crime rates, we use methods recently adopted by O'Brien[41] and LaFree and colleagues.[42] Briefly, we first compute the yearly logged difference between Black and White arrest or crime rates. We then classify the resulting "convergence scores" as stationary, trend stationary, or difference stationary.[43] A stationary time series has a mean, variance, and autocovariance that are constant over time;[44] scores vary by year, but never move far away from their mean. If a series of convergence scores is stationary, the relative difference between the two component arrest rates does not change significantly over time. A stationary series therefore represents neither convergence nor divergence between Black and White arrest rates. A trend stationary process resembles a stationary process except that it also includes a significant deterministic trend (either positive or negative). Fluctuations are short term and always return to a linear trend line. By contrast, a difference stationary (or unit root) series does not vary around a constant mean (stationary) or a constant trend (trend stationary), but instead "wanders" from a mean level with no tendency to return to that level once it has moved.

We use the augmented Dickey-Fuller procedure to test for the presence of a unit root.[45] For stationary and trend-stationary series, we report coefficients and significance tests for the slopes of the linear trend terms. A significant negative slope indicates that the component arrest rates are converging while a significant positive slope indicates that the component arrest rates are diverging.

If a series is difference stationary, we apply a procedure explicated by O'Brien[46] that tests for convergence/divergence on the basis of the regression of first differences of the convergence scores on an intercept and sufficient lags to remove autocorrelation among the residuals. If the intercept is significant and negative, we conclude that the relative difference between the two component arrest rates has been declining on average (i.e., converging) during the time period. If it is significant and positive, we conclude that the relative difference between the two rates has been increasing on average (i.e., diverging). Thus, for difference-stationary series, we report coefficients and significance tests for the intercepts of the regressions using first differences. This process amounts to determining whether the mean yearly increase or decrease in a series is statistically significant over a period of years.

African American and White Arrest Trends, 1960 to 2002

In Figure 10.1, we compare African American and White UCR arrest *ratios* for homicide, robbery, rape, and aggravated assault from 1960 to 2002. A declining slope represents convergence between Black and White arrest rates, a rising slope represents divergence, and a flat slope indicates no change. Evidence for convergence is clearest for rape (c) and aggravated assault (d). At its highest point (1965), the ratio of Black to White rape arrests was more than eight to one. By contrast, at its lowest point (2002) this ratio had dropped to just over three to one. Similarly, the ratio of Black to White aggravated assault arrests stood at twelve to one in 1960,

(a) Ratio of Black Homicide Rates to White Homicide Rates: 1960 to 2002

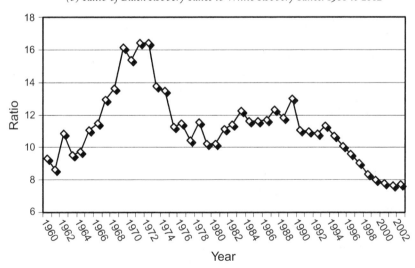

(b) Ratio of Black Robbery Rates to White Robbery Rates: 1960 to 2002

Fig. 10.1. (*above and opposite*) Ratio of Black to White UCR Arrest Rates for Four Personal Contact Crimes, 1960 to 2002

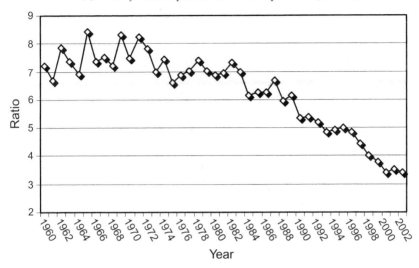

(c) Ratio of Black Rape Rates to White Rape Rates: 1960 to 2002

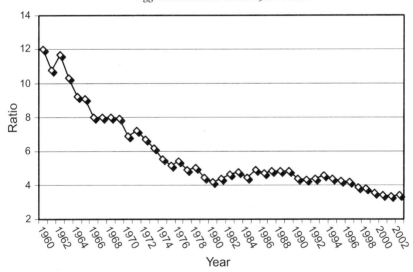

(d) Ratio of Black Aggravated Assault Rates to White Aggravated Assault Rates: 1960 to 2002

but had fallen to three to one by 2002. However, note that the large drop from the 1960s through 1980 was not as pronounced for rape arrests.

The Black-White arrest ratio is more variable in the case of homicide and robbery. While both still have a declining (i.e., converging) slope, the general downward trends in the ratios include two major countertrends. In the case of homicide, the Black-White arrest ratio increases gradually after 1960, reaching a series high of more than 13.72 in 1971. It then falls considerably to a low of 5.91 in 1984 before again increasing to a high of 9.43 in 1993. Following these shifts, it has a generally downward slope again until the end of the series. If we divide the homicide series in half— 1974 and before and 1975 and after—we find that the ratio of Black to White arrests in the first part of the series *always* exceeds the ratio in the second part.

We see a similar pattern for robbery. The robbery ratio increases from 1960 until the early 1970s, peaking in 1972; declines from the early 1970s until the early 1980s (although reaching a low point in 1979 rather than 1984); increases again from the early 1980s to the late 1980s (reaching a peak in 1989 rather than 1993); and then generally declines for the remainder of the series. In short, both the homicide and robbery series can be characterized as a generally declining ratio that experiences two major interruptions: a large increase in the arrest gap from the start of the series until the early 1970s and a more minor (at least in the case of robbery) increase in the arrest gap from the mid-1980s to the early 1990s.

Figure 10.2 shows the ratio of Black to White offending rates using NCVS data from interviews with robbery, rape, and aggravated assault victims. The most striking difference between the NCVS and the UCR trends is that the NCVS data show less consistent evidence of Black-White convergence. In fact, the slope for the robbery (a) and aggravated assault (c) series are essentially flat. By contrast, the slope for Black to White rape (b) is more strongly negative (i.e., converging); it declined by nearly 300 percent from its peak in 1973 (6.36) to its low point in 1993 (1.94). However, increases in the Black-White rape ratio in 2001 and 2002 have left it much closer to its original 1973 peak.

While the NCVS and UCR Black-White ratios for these three personal contact crimes are clearly different, the differences are not nearly as great when we consider the fact that the NCVS data begin in 1973. If we reexamine the UCR arrest ratios for robbery, rape, and aggravated assault (Figure 10.1), it is clear that much of the decline from their peak levels happens before 1973. This is especially true for robbery and aggravated assault.

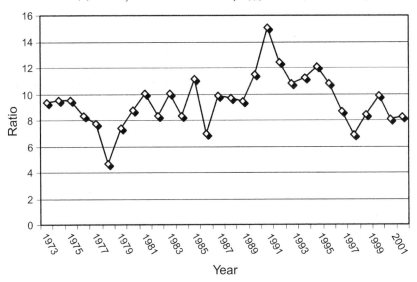

(a) Ratio of Black to White Robbery: 1973 to 2002 (NCVS DATA)

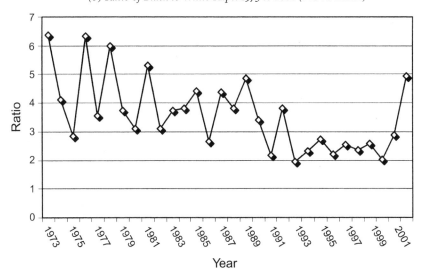

(b) Ratio of Black to White Rape: 1973 to 2002 (NCVS DATA)

Fig. 10.2. (*above and overleaf*) Ratio of Black to White Offenders from NCVS, 1973 to 2002

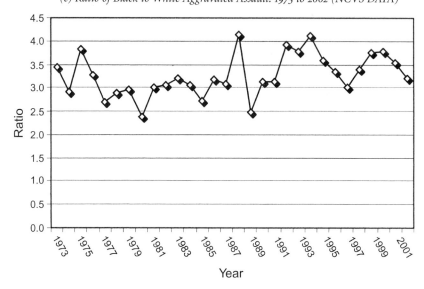

(c) Ratio of Black to White Aggravated Assault: 1973 to 2002 (NCVS DATA)

Fig. 10.2. (*continued*)

Interestingly, the most consistent declines in the UCR ratio of Black to White arrests from 1973 to 2002 is for rape, the NCVS crime that most clearly has a negative trend.

Taken together, a review of the UCR and NCVS series permits three main conclusions about the Black-White crime gap. First, UCR arrest data show substantial evidence of convergence for all four personal crimes, especially during the 1970s and the 1990s. Second, this convergence is much greater before 1973 than after. And finally, the UCR data show that the Black-White arrest gap actually increased substantially during the 1960s and after the mid-1980s for homicide and robbery, the two contact crimes that are most likely to measure actual criminal behavior. Definitive conclusions about convergence and divergence, however, require more formal statistical tests, to which we now turn.

Formal Tests for Convergence and Divergence

Recall that our tests for convergence or divergence between Black and White arrest and crime rates require two steps. First, we determine whether the logged ratio of Black to White arrests (or reported victimizations) over time is stationary, trend stationary, or difference stationary (i.e., has a unit root). Second, we test each series using the convergence test that is appropriate for the type of distribution found. We tested for stationary, trend stationary, and difference stationary series for (1) the Black-White ratio from UCR arrest rates from 1960 to 2002 and 1973–2002 (to facilitate direct comparison with the NCVS) and (2) the ratio of Black to White offenders identified from crime victims responding to NCVS from 1973 to 2002. A full explanation of these tests is provided in the technical appendix. However, our main substantive conclusions are that all of the UCR arrest series may be appropriately treated as difference stationary (i.e., unit root) while all of the NCVS series are appropriately treated as stationary. This determination allowed us to apply the appropriate test for convergence to the UCR and NCVS trends.

We next tested the three series for convergence or divergence, using the procedures described above. For the analyses of the long (1960–2002) and short (1973–2002) UCR series, we first differenced each series and then tested whether there is a significant decrease or increase in the series over time (i.e., is the drift intercept significantly negative or positive). For the analysis of the NCVS series, we test whether each series contains a statistically significant trend.

Table 10.1 presents the estimated coefficients for both the UCR and the NCVS comparisons. Note that the coefficients are negative for both the short and long UCR series tests and for all of the NCVS tests except the aggravated assault series. Hence, all of the series except for NCVS aggravated assault are generally converging.

For the full UCR series (1960 to 2002), convergence for aggravated assault is significant (p < .01) and the series for rape is marginally significant (p < .10).[47] The results for the NCVS series (1973 to 2002) indicate that convergence for rape is significant (p < .01), but there is divergence in the rates for aggravated assault (p < .05). For the UCR short series (1973 to 2002), convergence for both rape and aggravated assault reach significance (p < .05), and convergence for robbery is marginally significant (p < .10).

Descriptively, these results suggest that over the period 1960 to 2002 there has generally been convergence in the rates of violent crime for Blacks and Whites as recorded in UCR arrest rate data. This convergence appears for both 1960–2002 and 1973–2002 (although the trend for homicide is not significant in either the long or short UCR series or the robbery long series). The NCVS data (1973 to 2002) indicate convergence for

TABLE 10.1

Intercepts (α) from First Differenced Logged Ratios of Black to White Rates for the
Difference Stationary Series (superscripted d) and Trends (δ) for the
Nondifference Stationary Series (superscripted t)

	Estimated Value of α or δ	Number of Terms Used to Correct for Autocorrelation
UCR Data (1960–2002)		
Homicide[d]	−.0131	0
Robbery[d]	−.0045	0
Rape[d]	−.0239[a]	1
Aggravated Assault[d]	−.0300[c]	0
NCVS Data (1973–2002)		
Robbery[t]	−.0057	1
Rape[t]	−.0225[c]	0
Aggravated Assault[t]	.0064[b]	0
UCR Data (1973–2002)		
Homicide[d]	−.0213	0
Robbery[d]	−.0249[a]	0
Rape[d]	−.0279[b]	0
Aggravated Assault[d]	−.0224[b]	0

For the difference stationary series, based on the test results reported in Table 10.1, we used a specification in which the first differenced series was the dependent variable and it was regressed on the intercept and zero, one, two, or more lagged difference terms, depending upon the number of lagged terms needed to correct for autocorrelation.

For the series that were not difference stationary series, we used an equation in which the dependent variable (logged ratio of Black to White rates) was regressed on a constant, a linear trend, and no autoregressive term, a first-order autoregressive term, or a first- and second-order autoregressive term, depending upon the number of terms needed to correct for autocorrelation.

[a] Reject the null hypothesis at the .10 level.
[b] Reject the null hypothesis at the .05 level.
[c] Reject the null hypothesis at the .01 level.

robbery and rape (although the trend for robbery is not significant). The trend for aggravated assault is toward divergence and is significant. Taken together, ten of the eleven comparisons in Table 10.1 are in the direction of convergence.

Discussion and Conclusions

We began by contrasting assimilation and conflict perspectives of long-term changes in the post–World War II arrest gap between Blacks and Whites in the United States. An assimilation perspective predicts that as Blacks and Whites gradually become more similar in terms of economic, political, and social conditions, their arrest rates will also converge. By contrast, a conflict perspective predicts that, compared to Whites, the disadvantages faced by African Americans have generally not lessened during the past half-century and may in some cases have worsened. To the extent that these disadvantages are linked to arrest rates, a conflict perspective predicts either further divergence or little change between Black and White crime rates. In general, our results strongly support the assimilation perspective. Of eleven convergence tests estimated (eight for the UCR and three for the NCVS), ten were negative (i.e., converging) and six were significant. Only one test was significant for divergence (aggravated assault for the NCVS).

As noted earlier, there is long-standing disagreement in criminology about the extent to which UCR arrest rates by race measure actual behavior or police discretion. One of the practical effects of this disagreement is to discourage the use of arrest statistics in studies of race differences in criminal justice processing. However, the differing predictions of assimilation and conflict perspectives regarding the ratio of Black to White arrests are the same whether rates reflect actual behavior, police discretion, or some combination of the two. That is, regardless of their source, the assimilation perspective predicts converging Black-White rates while a conflict perspective predicts divergence or little change. Moreover, there is widespread agreement in criminology that of the four personal contact crimes examined here, homicide most likely reflects actual behavior, and rape and aggravated assault most likely reflect police discretion, with robbery intermediate between these two.

To obtain some sense of the potential effects of police discretion in reducing the ratio of Black to White offenses, we first examine the long UCR series and then compare the short UCR series with the NCVS series for the same years. We would expect police discretion to be a potent factor only in the UCR series. In the long UCR series, only two of the offenses that are converging show statistically significant convergence: rape and aggravated assault. As noted, these offenses are more likely to be subject to police discretion than homicide or robbery. When the short UCR series is compared with the NCVS series, there is a statistically significant (albeit at the .10 level) convergence for the UCR but not the NCVS series for robbery. For rape, both series show convergence, with the coefficient being just slightly greater for the UCR series. For aggravated assault, the UCR data show convergence while the NCVS data show divergence.

In short, it appears that during the period spanned by our data, there is more evidence for Black-White arrest/crime convergence for offenses that have been more directly linked to *police discretion* than for offenses more directly linked to *actual criminal behavior*. The evidence for convergence was strongest for the types of data most likely to reflect police discretion (i.e., UCR) and for the UCR crimes most likely to reflect police discretion (i.e., rape and aggravated assault). The main reason why Black-White arrest convergence is less for homicide and robbery is the rapid increase in Black rates of these offenses during the 1960s, and to a lesser extent, the rise in Black rates during the mid-1980s. While both Black and White arrest rates for homicide and robbery grew rapidly during the 1960s, the Black rate grew faster than the White rate. Similarly, homicide arrest rates for both groups grew rapidly after the mid-1980s, but the Black rate increased faster than the White rate. These findings underscore the importance of research that can explain both why the gap in arrest inequality for rape and aggravated assault has substantially narrowed, and why the inequality gap in homicide and robbery has been much more resistant to change during the past four decades.

The results also suggest that the strongest support for a conflict view of the arrest gap is found for Black and White homicide and robbery arrest rates in the 1960s and early 1970s—the only major examples of a growing divergence between Black and White arrest rates observed in these data. This was a period of great social change and unrest regarding race relations in the United States. Interestingly, it is also the period when conflict perspectives were especially influential in criminology.

In general, we see much support for growing assimilation both from the two crimes that are more likely to reflect actual criminal behavior and the two crimes that are more likely to reflect police discretion. This conclusion is strengthened by the considerable agreement between the two major longitudinal sources of crime data in the United States. Moreover, the UCR and NCVS changes also appear to be substantively important in absolute levels. Thus, from their high points until 2002, the Black-White UCR arrest ratio fell by 52 percent for homicide, 53 percent for robbery, 60 percent for rape, and 72 percent for aggravated assault. The declines in Black-White robbery and rape ratios from the NCVS are smaller but still substantial; from their high points until 2002, the Black-White NCVS robbery rate fell by 45 percent, and the rape rate fell by 22 percent.

On the other hand, even with these changes the current trends do not suggest that parity in arrest and offending rates for African Americans and Whites will come anytime soon. In fact, the Black-White homicide arrest ratio was actually greater in 2002 than in 1984; the Black-White robbery arrest ratio was only slightly lower in 2002 (7.77) than in 1961 (8.62); and much of the decrease in the Black-White ratio for aggravated assault arrests happened before 1975. Similarly, NCVS data show that the Black-White ratio for robbery was actually lower for several earlier years (1977–1979, 1986, 1998, and 2001) than in 2002; the Black-White ratio for rape increased dramatically after 2000; and the Black-White ratio for aggravated assault has actually increased somewhat since the series began in 1973. Given these long-term trends, it may be many years before the concerns about two separate societies enunciated in 1968 by the Kerner Commission are finally put to rest.

NOTES

1. National Advisory Commission on Civil Disorders 1968.
2. Ibid.:1.
3. Ibid.:267.
4. Ibid.:269.
5. Shibutani and Kwan 1965.
6. Wilson 1978.
7. Ibid.:2.
8. Wattenberg and Scammon 1973.
9. Moynihan 1972.
10. Farley 1984.
11. Ibid.:202.
12. For examples, see Chambliss and Seidman 1971; Quinney 1970; and Turk 1969.
13. Sellin 1928.
14. Chambliss 1969.
15. Chambliss and Seidman 1971.
16. Massey and Denton 1993:15.
17. Wilson 1987, 1996.
18. Farley 1984:199.
19. For reviews, see Hawkins 1995; Kleck 1981; and Zatz 2000.
20. Land, McCall, and Cohen 1990.
21. Parker and McCall 1999; Sampson 1987.
22. Blau and Blau 1982.
23. Land et al. 1990.
24. Wilson 1987.
25. Krivo and Peterson 2000; Sampson 1987.
26. Ibid.
27. Krivo and Peterson 2000.
28. Harer and Steffensmeier 1992; Ousey 1999; Shihadeh and Flynn 1996.

29. LaFree and Drass 1996; LaFree, Drass, and O'Day 1992; Messner and Sampson 1991; Phillips 2002.

30. LaFree 1995.

31. Cook and Laub 2002.

32. Rand, Lynch, and Cantor 1997.

33. For example, O'Brien 1985; President's Commission on Law Enforcement and Administration of Justice 1967.

34. Hindelang 1981.

35. O'Brien 1996, 2003.

36. O'Brien 1996; Riedel 1999; Sellin and Wolfgang 1964.

37. For example, see Maltz 1999.

38. LaFree 1989; O'Brien 1996, 2003.

39. Blumstein, Cohen, and Rosenfeld 1991; Gove, Hughes, and Geerken 1985; O'Brien 1985.

40. Cantor and Lynch 2000; O'Brien 1985; Sparks 1981.

41. O'Brien 1999.

42. LaFree 2005; LaFree and Drass 2002; LaFree and Hunnicutt 2005. A full technical description of these methods is available from the author upon request.

43. Hamilton 1994; Nelson and Plosser 1982.

44. Enders 1995.

45. Ibid.; O'Brien 1999.

46. O'Brien 1999.

47. Based on the results in Table 10.1, we can interpret the annual rate of decrease as 2.36 percent $[= (e^{-.0239} - 1) \times 100]$ for the long UCR series for rape, while the annual rate of decrease for aggravated assault is 2.96 percent $[= (e^{-.0300} - 1) \times 100]$.

Chapter 11

Race, Labor Markets, and Neighborhood Violence

Robert D. Crutchfield, Ross L. Matsueda,
and Kevin Drakulich

Theories of the spatial distribution of rates of violent crime typically include race and ethnicity as well as labor market participation as key explanatory concepts. For example, in his underclass thesis, William Julius Wilson argues that a history of migration of southern Blacks to capitalize on manufacturing jobs in northern cities, a subsequent loss of jobs in the transition to a service economy, and a movement of upwardly mobile middle-class Blacks out of the inner city resulted in high concentrations of poverty, joblessness, disrupted families, and violence.[1] More generally, social disorganization theory suggests that neighborhoods with high concentrations of racial and ethnic minorities may have high rates of violence in part because of low socioeconomic status, resulting from joblessness and low-quality jobs, which contribute to community disorganization, loss of control over youth, and high rates of crime and violence.[2]

While this literature has focused on the social and economic marginalization of African Americans and subsequent violence, similar processes probably affect both the economic circumstances and the levels of violence of other racial and ethnic minority groups. This is particularly likely for Latino populations. In recent decades, the size of the Spanish-speaking population in the United States has swelled dramatically, largely because of immigration from Mexico. Latinos, especially recent immigrants, frequently find work at the margins of the labor market[3] and have levels of violence that some find to be higher,[4] and others find to be lower,[5] than for the general population. Unfortunately, estimates of labor market participation and other social characteristics fail to distinguish recent immigrants from native Latinos or immigrants of longer residence. Nor do they differentiate among Hispanic national groups. We know that the immigrant experiences of Puerto Ricans, Dominicans, Cubans, Mexicans, and Central and South Americans are very different, as are their labor market experiences, residential patterns, and violence rates.

Another important change in the American population results from the post–Vietnam War stream of immigrants from Southeast Asia. Historically, American criminology has paid little attention to Asian communities, accepting the image of low crime communities that Takagi and Platt characterized as "gilded ghettos."[6] In reality, there has always been substantial heterogeneity among Asian populations in the United States, today even more so than in the past. Yet, we know little of the nature and levels of violence within these communities.

If we consider simultaneously changes in the ethnic composition of the U.S. population and the way the economy affects neighborhoods and violence, the following question arises: What are the key labor market characteristics associated with high rates of violence that help to explain high crime rates in minority neighborhoods? Crutchfield posed one answer: High concentrations of secondary sector jobs, as defined by dual-labor market theory, along with high unemployment, produce high rates of community violence.[7] His empirical research supports the proposition that high concentrations of job instability characteristic of secondary-sector jobs produce high rates of violence. Subsequent articles on labor market participation and violence also provide general support for this relationship.[8] Crutchfield argued that the association between rates of job instability and violence across neighborhoods is mainly due to a "situation of company" in which high concentrations of young men experiencing unstable employment are conducive to violence. Although his arguments were forceful, he was unable to marshal evidence supporting this mechanism over competing ones.[9]

This chapter builds on the literature on race, labor markets, and violent crime in three ways. First, it reexamines the empirical relationships among neighborhood racial/ethnic composition, labor market indicators, and violent crime using more recent data on census tracts within Seattle, a city whose population dynamics reflect changing U.S. demographics. Second, it capitalizes on data from a new survey on over four thousand households nested within census tracts to test the "situation of company" hypothesis. Third, it tests the extent to which the "labor-market concentration" mechanism accounts for racial differences in neighborhood violence rates.

Dual Labor Markets, Race, and Crime

Dual Labor Market Theory and Race

Dual labor market theory was developed by economists such as Bluestone and Piore[10] to address problems of underemployment and urban poverty not captured in models of neoclassical economics.[11] Essentially, it is argued that the economy can be divided into two sectors—primary and secondary—on the basis of job characteristics. The primary sector contains good jobs with high wages, good work conditions, and job stability.[12] Chances for advancement exist and are governed by administrative and due process rules through internal labor markets within organizational units, rather than solely by free market forces through external markets. The stability of primary sector jobs fosters strong social relationships with others in the workforce.

In contrast, the secondary sector contains less desirable jobs with low wages, poor work conditions, and, most importantly, job instability.[13] Chances for advancement are poor, discipline is based on personal relationships and can be harsh and capricious, and job turnover rates are high.[14] As a result of job instability, workers fail to develop strong ties to their coworkers and the workplace. For dual labor market theory, job stability is the crucial difference between primary and secondary sector jobs. Because primary sector jobs tend to be stable, enduring, and often part of an occupational career, primary sector workers are required to show up for work regularly and on time. Such is not always the case with secondary sector jobs, which tend to be intermittent, erratic, and short in duration.

Dual labor market theorists maintain that Blacks disproportionately begin their careers in the secondary labor market. This occurs in part through statistical and systemic discrimination. For example, employers making hiring decisions tend to use information that is readily and inexpensively available to them, such as race or demeanor, which may be correlated with job performance in the aggregate, but in individual cases results in discrimination. Piore points out that such discrimination increases the pool of secondary laborers, exerting a downward force on wages, and reduces the pool of primary sector workers, exerting an upward force on wages.[15] Thus, secondary employers and primary workers have incentives to favor such discrimination. Quasi-experimental audit studies have found strong effects of racial discrimination for entry-level jobs.[16] Indeed, Pager found stronger effects of employment discrimination against Blacks than against felons.[17] Once a worker is relegated to a secondary sector market, it is very difficult to move out. Erratic and unstable work conditions reinforce absenteeism and tardiness, making workers ill prepared for the regularity of primary jobs. Poor relationships with co-workers and supervisors make workers ill equipped to manage relationships and institutional regulations of primary jobs. Such patterns also set the stage for difficulties outside of the workplace.

Neighborhoods, Race, and Labor Markets

Labor market sectors help structure patterns of income, career trajectories, and social networks. In most cities, patterns of residential mobility have created spatial distributions of primary and secondary workers. Generally, secondary sector workers lack the income and other resources to live in affluent neighborhoods, and end up relegated to low-income housing located near commercial sectors in the central city. On this point, Kasarda found that welfare recipients are less likely to move from inner-city impoverished areas to suburban areas, where entry-level job opportunities are greater.[18] Primary sector workers, in contrast, have historically used their higher incomes to settle in more affluent neighborhoods, typically located away from the central city in peripheral or suburban areas.[19]

Such patterns help to explain residential segregation patterns. Indeed, racial assimilation theories argue that assimilation along the lines of increasing human capital, better jobs, and better English-language skills help explain residential mobility of minorities. Competing explanations, such as place stratification models, argue that racial discrimination in the housing market plays an important role in residential segregation.[20] Research has found support for this argument. Blacks seeking to move to better neighborhoods face barriers such as discrimination by mortgage lenders and real estate agents,[21] which, in part, reflect preferences of residents. The preferences of White residents—generally against integrating their neighborhoods—in turn, derive from their negative stereotypes of ethnic and racial minorities.[22]

These processes have led to enduring residential segregation in major cities, in which high concentrations of Black impoverished neighborhoods persist. Quillian has described recent trends in such residential patterns.[23] He finds that upwardly mobile Blacks are moving into nonpoor White neighborhoods at a higher rate than Blacks moving out of such neighborhoods. But as Blacks move into these neighborhoods, the White population declines at an even higher rate, which prevents the proportion of Blacks in White neighborhoods from increasing. These net flows produce new impoverished neighborhoods, contribute to increasing populations in Black impoverished neighborhoods, and produce greater concentration effects. The recession of the early 1980s, in which a drop in labor demand disproportionately affected secondary sector laborers in moderately impoverished neighborhoods, also increased concentration effects.

Neighborhood Race, Labor Markets, and Violent Crime

Our argument to this point is that racial discrimination in the labor market along with residential segregation have produced neighborhoods with high concentrations of African Americans, secondary sector workers, and unemployed workers. These neighborhoods are at risk of high rates of violence.[24] But what is the theoretical link between labor market characteristics and violence? We build on arguments of Crutchfield[25] and Crutchfield and Pitchford[26] to identify two mechanisms by which unemployment and secondary sector employment are associated with high rates of violence.

The first mechanism occurs at the individual level among workers. Secondary sector jobs have low wages, low skill levels, and bleak promotion prospects, and as such are unlikely to engender the kinds of job commitments and interpersonal ties to coworkers enjoyed by primary sector occupations. Secondary sector workers have time on their hands, and are unconcerned with losing their jobs or losing the respect of their coworkers. In contrast, primary sector workers receive higher wages, have more complex jobs, or have promotion and career prospects; therefore, they are likely to develop strong job commitments and ties to coworkers, and are less likely to do anything to jeopardize their jobs or their employment relations. On this point, Sampson and Laub found that job stability, rather than employment, is associated with desistance from crime,[27] and Crutchfield and Pitchford found that primary sector workers are less likely to engage in crime.[28]

The second criminogenic mechanism described by Crutchfield occurs when relatively large portions of marginally employed people live in proximity to one another.[29] Residential segregation produces neighborhoods with high concentrations of jobless and secondary sector male workers, who move in and out of the labor force, work less than full time when employed, and develop few commitments to jobs. Freed from commitments to work, they have time on their hands with little to do. Such "workers" frequently pass the time by hanging out on street corners, in pool halls, and in local taverns, bars, and nightclubs—places that are often staging grounds for violent encounters. According to Cohen and Felson's routine activities theory, their location in the social structure makes them "suitable targets"—that is, potential victims of violent "motivated offenders" —in the absence of "capable guardianship."[30] The absence of constraints from labor market and educational institutions may free such individuals to become "motivated offenders," as well. Difficulties arise, in particular, when conventional institutions are unable or unwilling to resolve the disputes of such uncommitted men. In neighborhoods, concentrations of marginally employed secondary sector workers result in a situation of company where suitable targets, motivated offenders, and a lack of capable guardianship come together, making crime more likely.

The above mechanisms imply a specific model of how neighborhood racial composition is related to rates of violence, which unfolds in four steps. First, macro processes of dual labor markets and residential segregation give rise to neighborhoods with concentrations of marginally unemployed Black adults and youth. Second, high rates of job instability and the accompanying low levels of economic resources in such neighborhoods give rise to a "situation of company," in which high concentrations of jobless and marginally employed Black males have time on their hands and weak institutional commitments. Third, labor instability and low levels of economic resources result in increased violent crime through the presence of these "situations of company." Finally, collectively these processes produce the association of neighborhood racial composition with violent crime. Research on these topics has focused on African American and White communities. Here we move beyond that racial dichotomy by including Latino and Asian populations in our analyses.

A link between the aggregate distribution of labor market participation and violent crime rates has been established in the literature,[31] as has a connection between individual labor market participation and criminal involvement.[32] Research has not, however, examined the extent to which the racial composition effect on violent crime can be explained by labor market participation. Indeed, in most major industrial cities, extreme residential segregation makes it impossible to disentangle racial composition from structural disadvantage. Also, research has not established empirically whether the mechanism relating labor market processes to rates of violence involves large concentrations of marginally employed young men freed from institutional controls and forming a "situation of company" conducive to violence.

This Study

Hypotheses

To determine if higher levels of violence in minority communities can be explained by higher unemployment and the allocation of workers who live in minority neighborhoods into secondary sector jobs, we analyze a set of models that are illustrated by Figure 11.1, which displays the interrelationships among factors described above. Social disorder, which includes young men conspicuously socializing in public places that are unregulated by legitimate institutions, refers to neighborhood conditions that capture the presence of "situations of company." The hyphenated line between racial composition and violent crime depicts the often observed higher levels of violence in minority neighborhoods when compared to predominantly White communities. Here the line is hyphenated because we hypothesize that when labor instability and social disorder are "taken into account" the "often observed" connection between neighborhood racial composition and violence will be shown to be illusionary.

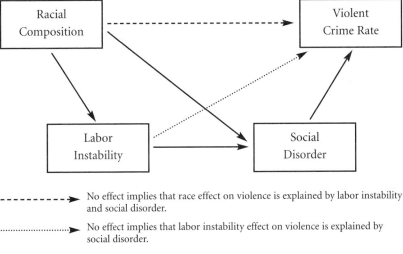

No effect implies that race effect on violence is explained by labor instability and social disorder.

No effect implies that labor instability effect on violence is explained by social disorder.

Fig. 11.1. Neighborhood Model of Race, Labor Markets, Social Disorder, and Violence Rates

What do we mean by "taken into account?" We take other factors "into account" when we analyze their influence simultaneously with racial composition and violent crime. The solid arrow between "racial composition" and "labor instability" represents the higher unemployment rates and disproportionate secondary sector employment of people of color, resulting in higher labor instability in neighborhoods with more minority residents. The dotted line connecting "labor instability" and the "violent crime rate" represents the results of past research, showing that neighborhoods that are high on the former are also high on the latter. Here, the line is dotted because we expect an important mechanism through which labor instability causes violent crime to be present. This is because the places where disadvantaged workers live have more social disorder, and will thus have more of the "situations of company" conducive to crime. Social disorder then is here represented as the mechanism through which labor instability affects crime. The higher levels of social disorder, resulting from labor instability, are depicted by the solid arrow. Racial composition also leads to neighborhood social disorder because of disadvantages experienced by residents, so a solid line connects these two variables in the model. Finally, our prediction that neighborhood social disorder leads to high levels of violence is illustrated with a solid line.

In summary, we hypothesize that (1) labor instability leads to neighborhood social disorder, which in turn leads to higher rates of violent crime; (2) the connection between racial composition and social disorder can, in part, be explained by higher levels of labor instability in minority neighborhoods; and (3) the connection between racial composition and violent crime rates can be explained by higher levels of labor instability and social disorder in minority neighborhoods.

Measures

Our measures of local workforce composition, as well as the other measures of local structural disadvantage and race and ethnic composition, come from the 2000 U.S. census. We created a measure of neighborhood labor instability by combining the proportion unemployed and the proportion of workers employed in secondary sector jobs.[33] Though the association between secondary sector employment and unemployment has dropped in Seattle since Crutchfield's original paper,[34] it is still high enough to warrant the creation of a combined measure. We use census tract median income as a measure of neighborhood economic well-being.

We also use a set of census characteristics as control variables, including the proportion of the population who are young males (age fifteen to twenty-four) and the proportion of the population age five and above who lived in the same house five years ago (residential stability). Finally, we include measures of the respective proportions of the neighborhood that are African American, Asian, and Hispanic. Seattle has a large Asian-immigrant population, and the tract-level correlation between proportion Asian and proportion immigrant is .944. For comparability with the other racial groups only proportion Asian is used, but empirically, the effect of the proportion Asian cannot be disentangled from the effect of the proportion immigrant.

The Seattle Neighborhoods and Crime Survey (SNCS) is a survey of 4,904 residents of 123 Seattle census tracts conducted in 2002 and early 2003. This survey provides the measures of neighborhood disruption. We rely on reports of survey respondents, who are neighborhood residents, to signal the presence of "situations of company" within their neighborhoods. Residents were asked about local problems in the neighborhood, including groups of teenagers hanging around on the street and neighbors who cause trouble and make noise. The resulting measure of social disorder is the sum of valid responses to the two 3-category items.

Finally, the crime measure is the yearly average for 2002 and 2003 of the sum of robberies, aggravated assaults, rapes, and murders adjusted by the census tract population. The violent crime rate measure is highly skewed so a logged variable is used in the analyses. The measure is based on Seattle Police Department data.

Results

Race and Ethnicity and Seattle Neighborhoods

It is useful to begin by describing the ethnic composition, topography, and community organization of the city of Seattle. All are relevant for our consideration of the effects that labor market participation has on neighborhoods and violent crime. The most striking characteristic of Seattle's ethnic composition is the large percentage of White residents. At the time of the 2000 census, Asian Americans were the largest minority group at 13.1 percent. African Americans were 8.3 percent of the city's population; Latinos were about 5.3 percent; and, 16.9 percent of city residents were foreign born. Less than 1 percent of those reported in the census were Native

Americans. The largest groups of immigrants were of Asian descent, and many lived in neighborhoods that included Asian Americans. This residential pattern prevents us from separating the effects of Asian Americans from immigrant populations. The Latino population, while small compared to some other western cities, is largely a result of people who moved to Seattle between 1990 and 2000. This new group of residents is concentrated in a small area in the southwest section of the city. While the total percentage of the non-White population is small when compared to other large cities, the racial/ethnic diversity of the non-White population makes Seattle a good location for studying race, neighborhoods, and crime while going beyond the Black/White dichotomy or the White/non-White comparisons that have historically characterized criminological research.

Seattle's topography is important for understanding residential patterns. The city (note Figure 11.2) sits between Puget Sound, a saltwater inlet off the Pacific Ocean, and Lake Washington, a 20-mile-long freshwater lake to the east. Lake Union and canals connecting the sound and Lake Washington divide the city's northern and southern sections. Originally Seattle was built on seven hills; early on, high-pressure hoses were used to sluice some of the hills into the Sound. The surviving hilly terrain affects residential patterns as much as or more than the bodies of water. The hillsides, which are proximate to the water, are today the location of high-priced "view" property. In the south end of the city, two of the larger concentrations of minority residents, the Central District and the Rainier Valley, are separated by ridges from high-end lake-view neighborhoods, some of which have considerable racial integration. To the east, facing the lake, are very expensive houses; to the west (in addition to some increasingly expensive houses as a result of gentrification) are inexpensive houses and neighborhoods with the poorest citizens of the city. There are similar patterns elsewhere in the city, in which middle- and upper-middle-class people live in houses facing the water, while middle-class and even working-class people live on the nonview side of the hill. Rarely are these neighborhoods separated by anything more than a few transitional residential or minor commercial blocks.

Seattle can also be described as a "city of neighborhoods." While elsewhere realtors use this phrase as a code for "segregated," this is less the case in Seattle. There are discernible neighborhoods with unique character that are well known to residents. For example, Ballard was once a Scandinavian logging village before annexation into the city; Beacon Hill, until the 1990s, was characterized by nearly equal populations of Asians, African

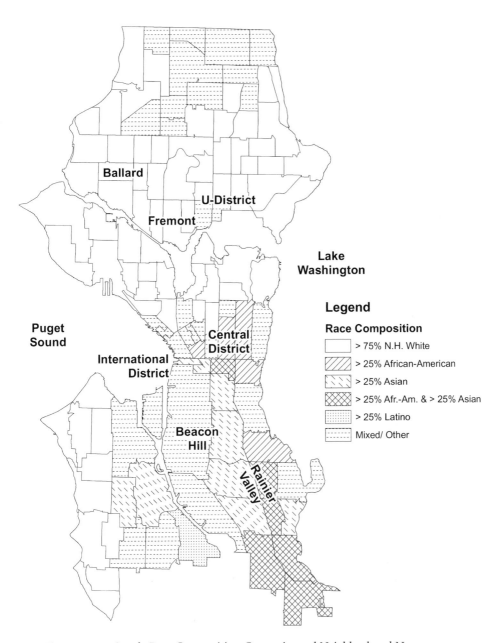

Fig. 11.2. 2000 Seattle Race Composition Categories and Neighborhood Names

Americans, and Whites but is now nearly 50 percent Asian as a result of immigration; and, Fremont is an artsy, formerly "hippie" neighborhood that advertises itself as the "center of the universe." These and other neighborhoods are meaningful because of the racial and ethnic composition of residents, but they also have social meaning. Ballard, where people of Scandinavian descent are but a small minority today, is more socially conservative than Fremont just to the east, which annually holds a solstice parade that includes nude bike riders. The Central District, the historic center of the city's African American community, has never been more than 50 percent Black, and the Rainier Valley is home not only to Seattle's poorest residents but also to stable, racially integrated neighborhoods, large communities of recent immigrants, and a revitalized trendy restaurant and club district. Figure 11.2 displays the distribution of minority populations in Seattle census tracts. Clearly, most people of color live in the south end, but all regions of the city have minority residents, and all tracts have White residents.

Figure 11.3 presents the distribution of violent crimes in Seattle as well as the distribution of labor instability, a measure of the secondary labor market that will be described below. Neighborhoods with high levels of violent crime and high labor instability are clustered in the central and southern parts of the city, as is much of the non-White population. The important question for this research is to what extent are high levels of violence in minority communities explained by high levels of labor instability in these neighborhoods?

Labor Instability Disorder and Crime

Can social disorder help us understand the effect of labor instability on crime, and can labor instability and social disorder help us understand the association of neighborhood racial composition and crime? To answer these questions, we construct two sets of models. The first predicts neighborhood levels of social disorder with the race and ethnic composition of the neighborhoods as well as controls for the proportion of young males and the residential stability of the neighborhood. Then labor instability and median income—which represent, in part, the economic resource consequences of labor instability—are introduced. A second set of models predicts neighborhood violent crime rates. An initial model again uses race and ethnic composition, young males, and residential stability. Then labor instability, median income, and finally social disorder

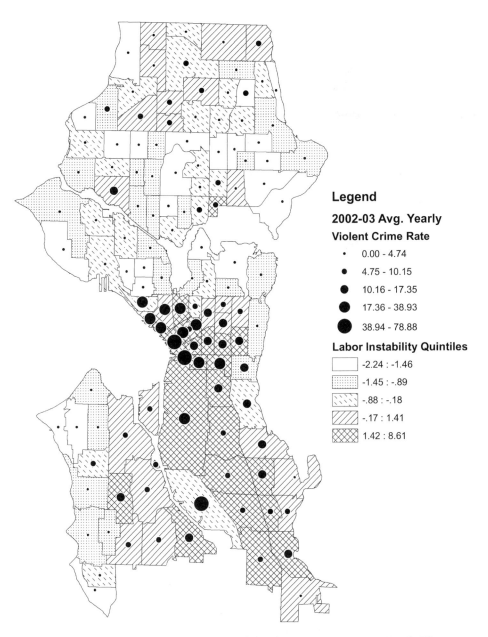

Legend

2002-03 Avg. Yearly
Violent Crime Rate

·   0.00 - 4.74

●   4.75 - 10.15

●   10.16 - 17.35

●   17.36 - 38.93

●   38.94 - 78.88

Labor Instability Quintiles

-2.24 : -1.46

-1.45 : -.89

-.88 : -.18

-.17 : 1.41

1.42 : 8.61

Fig. 11.3. 2000 Seattle Labor Market Instability by 2002–2003 Average Yearly Violent Crime Rate

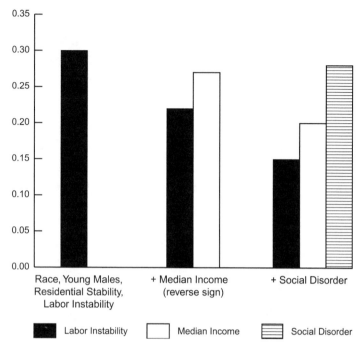

Fig. 11.4. Selected Standardized Coefficients from Regressions of Logged Average Yearly Violent Crime Rate on Race, Young Males, Labor Instability, Median Income, and Social Disorder

are added to the model. Key findings from each of these models are highlighted below.

The first question is whether the effect of labor instability on crime, previously established by Crutchfield,[35] can be explained by the intervening mechanism of social disorder. The results indicate that both labor instability and lower median income are important in determining neighborhood levels of social disorder. In turn, it appears that social disorder does mediate some of the effect of labor instability and median income on violent crime. Figure 11.4 presents selected standardized effect sizes from the models predicting crime. In the first model, when race and ethnic composition, young males, and residential stability are controlled, labor instability has a moderate positive association with violent crime. Adding lower median income to the model, hypothesized to capture the economic resource effects of labor instability, decreases somewhat the association of labor instability and violent crime. Finally, adding social disorder reduces further the effects of both labor instability and median income on violent crime. This appears to support the notion that the association of labor instability and violent crime can be understood, in part, through local social disorder.

Explaining the Association of Race and Violent Crime

The second question of this research is whether we can understand the association of race and violent crime through this process of labor instability, resource deprivation, and social disorder. We begin this analysis by considering whether, in fact, neighborhoods with larger minority populations have high levels of social disorder and whether they also have more people working at the margins of the local labor market. Our thesis is that observed correlations between violent crime rates and the percentage of the population that is African American, Latino, or Asian/immigrant will be explained, at least in part, by higher levels of social disorder brought on by relatively high levels of economic marginalization.

The Effects of Racial Composition on Social Disorder

In Figure 11.5, we present the results from an analysis designed to explain variation in neighborhood social disorder. The unstandardized effect sizes for the percents African American, Hispanic, and Asian from this model are presented. Here (the left-hand set of three histograms), the ability to predict social disorder from the size of minority populations is displayed, first with percent young males and residential stability held constant, then with labor instability taken into account (the middle set of histograms), and finally with the median income of tracts taken into account (the right-hand set). We should note that the average levels of social disorder for neighborhoods with relatively large Asian and immigrant, African American, and Latino populations are higher than in non-minority neighborhoods. This pattern holds even after residential mobility and the age composition of neighborhoods are taken into account. We note also that, with rare exception, these neighborhoods, even those typically thought of as minority communities, still have substantial White populations.

Next, we introduce a measure of the degree of labor instability present in neighborhoods, and then the median income of tracts. The explanatory

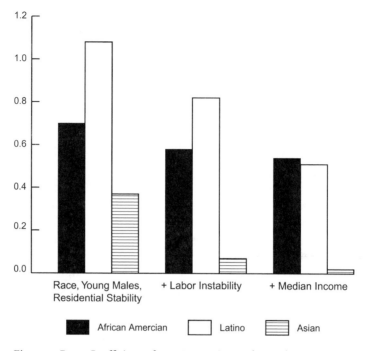

Fig. 11.5. Race Coefficients from Regressions of Social Disorder on Race, Young Males, Labor Instability, and Median Income

power of each measure of racial composition of neighborhoods declines when economy, jobs, and income are considered, but the changes in effect sizes are not the same for each group. The effect of the percent Asian and immigrant on social disorder is explained by labor instability, suggesting that these communities have higher levels of disorder because residents are more likely to be unemployed or working in secondary sector jobs. Greater labor instability also helps to account for higher social disorder where African American and Latino residents live, but the presence of these race/ethnic populations is still significantly related to disorder even after employment is considered.

The amount of social disorder declines as the income of census tracts increases. And, taking income into account further reduces the effect of racial and ethnic composition on neighborhood social disorder. Of course, we know that economic marginalization is a direct result of labor market marginalization (labor instability). The predictive ability of percent African American, while still significant, is reduced slightly. The effect of percent Latino is also reduced substantially when median income is taken into account. So, these results indicate that the economic marginalization of people of color in Seattle helps to explain why minority group members are more likely to live in neighborhoods with more social disorder. But, even after labor instability and income are taken into account, African Americans and Latinos are still more likely to live where there is more social disorder. Our next question concerns how much of observed higher levels of violence in minority neighborhoods is due to economic factors and social disorder.

Does Labor Instability Explain the Race-Violence Connection?

As in most cities across the United States, violent crime rates are higher in Seattle neighborhoods where more people of color live. We expect that these higher levels of violence are explained, at least in part, by neighborhood labor instability and low income because these factors create greater disorder, which in turn leads to crime. Figure 11.6 displays what happens to the association between the sizes of racial/ethnic minority populations, first when we consider the percentage of the population that is young, male, and residentially stable, and then when we additionally consider labor instability, median income, and social order in turn. The figure presents the unstandardized effect sizes from the respective regressions of logged violent crime.

Just as we saw when we examined social disorder, the effects of race and ethnicity can, to some extent, be explained by considering other factors. Neighborhoods with more African Americans, Latinos, and Asians/immigrants have higher violent crime rates. However, the pattern differs for the minority groups when we introduce additional factors. Higher levels of labor instability help to explain why minority communities have higher crime rates. Once we take employment into account, communities with more Asians and immigrants have no more violent crime than other neighborhoods. It appears that the employment disadvantage of neighborhood residence completely accounts for higher violent crime rates where more Asians and immigrants live. The relationships between the percentage of neighborhood residents who are African American or Latino and violent crime rates remain when we take into account the labor instability of those living in the community, but the effects of both are substantially reduced.

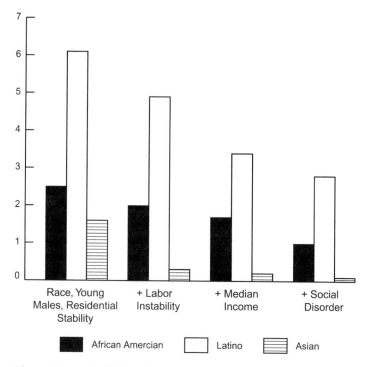

Fig. 11.6. Race Coefficients from Regressions of Logged Average Yearly Violent Crime Rate on Race, Young Males, Labor Instability, Median Income, and Social Disorder

The same is true when income and neighborhood disorder are considered. When median income is introduced into our consideration of neighborhood violent crime the effects of racial composition are again reduced. The reduction is larger where Latinos live than where African Americans live. In other words, taking both labor instability and income into account helps to explain the higher crime rates in these neighborhoods, with percent Latino being impacted more strongly. What of social disorder? Above we showed that these same economic factors explained some of the higher levels of disorder in minority communities. Here (Figure 11.6) we see that when social disorder, which results from labor instability, is taken into account the association between violent crime and percent African American or Latino is reduced further.

These analyses help to tell an important story that links the economic circumstance of residents to levels of social disorder in neighborhoods, which together explain, in part, why the communities in which more minorities live have higher violent crime rates. Their neighborhoods have more labor instability and that causes more violence because it lowers income and increases social disorder. But this does not complete the story.

Summary and Conclusions

Our analyses yield five key findings, which help to explain the relationship between macrolevel labor market processes operating at the neighborhood level and rates of violence. First, we find that labor market participation affects the level of social disorder in neighborhoods. Second, minority communities have higher levels of social disorder. Third, higher levels of disorder in minority communities are explained, in part, by higher levels of instability and lower median incomes. Fourth, higher violent crime rates in minority neighborhoods can, in part, be accounted for by the higher levels of social disorder there. And fifth, these patterns are different for racial and ethnic groups.

In Figure 11.1 we presented a diagram depicting the interrelationships of the variables in these analyses. That figure can be used to summarize important differences in patterns for the ethnic groups. We predicted that racial composition's effect on neighborhood violent crime rates would operate through labor instability and social disorder. Neighborhoods with higher percentages of racial and ethnic minorities would have more labor instability, which in turn would lead to social disorder, which would then directly increase violent crime rates. We found that taking these factors into account completely explains why violent crime rates are higher in Asian American and immigrant communities relative to other communities. Neighborhoods with large percentages of Asian Americans and immigrants have higher rates of violence because they have higher levels of labor instability and social disorder. In contrast, social disorder and labor instability explains part, but not all, of the effects of the percentage of African Americans and Latinos on neighborhood violence. Even after taking into account labor instability and social disorder, African American and Latino neighborhoods still have higher rates of violence than other neighborhoods.

Our conceptual model, following from research on the underclass and "American apartheid" theses, emphasizes the spatial distribution of secondary sector and underemployed residents throughout the city of Seattle.

We argue that overlapping concentrations of labor instability in neighborhoods with concentrations of racial and ethnic minorities are produced by residential patterns, some of which entail discrimination. These residential patterns produce concentrations of social incivilities, disorder, and "situations of company" that are conducive to high rates of violence. Thus, the causal mechanisms in our models operate at the neighborhood or community level, and we find support for those mechanisms. Researchers can extend this model by integrating an individual-level mechanism that explains individual violent acts. Here, one might posit that individuals at the margins of the paid economy, and their offspring, might themselves be at risk of greater violence, regardless of their community of residence. One could test this hypothesis using individual-level measures of labor market participation and violence as well as contextual measures of labor instability and social disorder.

Our major findings point to additional directions that we believe criminologists should pursue. First, because labor instability and social disorder do not completely explain why violence rates are higher in African American and Latino communities than elsewhere, criminologists should explore alternative mechanisms. One such possibility might entail cultural processes such as Anderson's code of the street.[36] Here, ethnographic research could prove crucial for unearthing new causal mechanisms involving cultural processes, structural mechanisms, and the interaction between the two.[37]

Second, our analyses highlight the importance of moving beyond the Black-White dichotomy in consideration of race and crime. The labor market and residential histories of African American, Asian, and Latino people are very different, so our results should come as no surprise. To gain a real appreciation of how labor market participation affects crime indirectly through income, social disorder, and alternative mechanisms, we must study the members of unique racial and ethnic communities. For example, we should disaggregate Asian, Latino, and Black groups, making distinctions among Japanese, Chinese, Filipinos, Southeast Asians, Puerto Ricans, Dominicans, Cubans, Mexicans, Central and South Americans, African Americans, Jamaicans, Somalis, and Ethiopians.

Third, the changing nature of the economy, immigration, and residential patterns of cities across the United States provides opportunities to build on our research on ethnicity, labor markets, and violence. To illustrate, earlier we described Seattle's neighborhoods. The industrial transition that has affected America's blue-collar workers has not had as devastating effects in Seattle as in many other places, presumably because of the presence of good aerospace and shipping industry jobs. Nevertheless, there are blue-collar neighborhoods where residents have lost economic ground. How might blue-collar neighborhoods, like predominantly White Ballard and predominantly minority Beacon Hill, be differentially affected by labor market changes? How are Seattle's extremely heterogeneous south end neighborhoods affected by these changes? These neighborhoods include middle-class Whites and minorities living in close proximity to the poor and working class—people most affected by labor market transitions. Perhaps most interesting of all, there is a group of neighborhoods in the southwest of the city that ten years ago was heavily populated by immigrants from southeast Asia. Now, the writing on the facades of formerly Vietnamese storefronts is giving way to Spanish, a reflection of Seattle's new Latino population moving into the area. A very rapid racial transition is being accompanied by an economic transition. These changes in Seattle, and similar changes elsewhere, provide rich opportunities for developing better understandings of how race, ethnicity, employment, and economic circumstance affect violent crime.

NOTES

1. Sampson and Wilson 1995; Wilson 1987.
2. Sampson and Groves 1989; Sampson and Raudenbush 1999.
3. Wright and Dwyer 2003.
4. Jasinski, Asdigian, and Kantor 1997.
5. Martinez 2002.
6. Takagi and Platt 1978.
7. Crutchfield 1989.
8. Bellair, Roscigno, and McNulty 2003; Crutchfield, Glusker, and Bridges 1999; Crutchfield and Pitchford 1997.
9. Crutchfield 1989.
10. Bluestone 1970; Piore 1970, 1975.
11. Kalleberg and Sørenson 1979.
12. Bluestone 1970; Piore 1975.
13. Bluestone 1970; Piore 1970.
14. Andrisani 1973; Bosanquet and Doeringer 1973.
15. Piore 1970.
16. Bendick, Jackson, and Reinoso 1997; Cross et al. 1990; Turner, Fix, and Struyk 1991.

17. Pager 2003.
18. Kasarda 1989.
19. For example, Fuguitt and Brown 1990.
20. Alba and Logan 1993.
21. Shlay 1988; Yinger 1995.
22. Bobo and Zubrinsky 1996; Farley et al. 1994.
23. Quillian 1999.
24. Crutchfield 1989; Sampson and Wilson 1995.
25. Crutchfield 1989.
26. Crutchfield and Pitchford 1997.
27. Sampson and Laub 1990.
28. Crutchfield and Pitchford 1997.
29. Crutchfield 1989.
30. Cohen and Felson 1979.
31. Crutchfield 1989; Crutchfield et al. 1999.
32. Bellair et al. 2003; Crutchfield and Pitchford 1997; Uggen 2000.
33. See Crutchfield 1989.
34. Ibid.
35. Ibid.
36. Anderson 1999.
37. Bourgois 1995; Sullivan 1989.

Chapter 12

Drug Markets in Minority Communities
Consequences for Mexican American Youth Gangs

Avelardo Valdez

The dynamics and consequences of illicit drug markets on urban minority communities in the United States are best understood within the context of inequality and race. Participation in drug-related criminal behavior among today's ethnic and racial minorities parallels that of the Irish, Italians, and Jews during the first half of the twentieth century who were involved in "organized crime," especially during Prohibition.[1] Criminal involvement by these earlier immigrants as well as contemporary poor Blacks and Hispanics is associated with the community's exposure to criminogenic structural conditions often imposed by majority society. Commenting on contemporary drug markets, Kornblum states, "Drug markets became hypertrophied in minority ghettos for a series of highly interrelated reasons, all having to do with race and class discrimination and with the history of deviance in America."[2] In this chapter, I explore how the macrosocial patterns of inequality, ecological containment of the truly disadvantaged, and changing drug markets in a Mexican American barrio exacerbate drug use, crime, and other deviant behaviors.

The increasing presence of minorities in the drug market during the last thirty years (1970–2000) has coincided with the economic restructuring that moved jobs from central cities to suburbs and reduced pools of low-wage labor. These economic changes exacerbated inequality and, as byproducts, poverty, joblessness, and welfare dependency in urban minority neighborhoods. As an adaptation to these structural realities, certain segments of low-income minority communities have chosen to participate in sectors of the illegal economy.[3] Concomitantly, the supply and demand for illicit drugs has increased despite harsh prohibitionist policies in the

United States and many other countries.[4] These policies are predicated on a drug prohibition ideology that distorts the immutable laws of supply and demand. Many argue that these policies are deliberately aimed at minorities, who suffer the most negative consequences, including a disproportionate percentage of drug arrests, imprisonment, and health problems such as HIV and Hepatitis C.[5]

Mexican American Youth Gangs and the Drug Market

Multiple studies offer insights into the participation of minorities in the illegal drug market, especially during the cocaine and crack epidemic in New York during the 1980s and 1990s.[6] Other studies have focused on gangs and then on members' participation in street-level heroin and other drug distribution markets.[7] Research on minority street gangs involved in drug selling and dealing have situated these groups in urban ghettos or barrios. For purposes of the chapter, the term "youth gang" is used to refer to groups of adolescents who engage in collective acts of delinquency and violence, and are perceived by others and themselves as a distinct group. Moreover, the group has a structured hierarchy with rituals, symbols (colors, signs, etc.), and a specific territory.[8]

The proximity of Mexico, a major source of heroin in the United States, has made illegal drugs more accessible to users in south Texas than in other regions. In 1988, the Office of National Drug Control Policy (ONDCP), pursuant to the Anti–Drug Abuse Act, designated the southwest border as a High Intensity Drug Trafficking Area (HIDTA). Such areas are identified as having the most critical drug trafficking problems that adversely impact the United States.[9] South Texas shares a border with Mexico, a primary staging area for large-scale binational narcotic trafficking operations. As a result, Mexican Americans living near the U.S.–Mexico border have more access to drug sources than those living away from the border. This produces highly decentralized drug markets in the Southwest characterized by numerous small-time drug entrepreneurs with ties to Mexican distributors along with larger international cartels. Although these drugs are primarily shipped throughout the United States, a substantial amount is targeted for consumers in the Southwest.

There have been few studies on Mexican American drug use and selling/dealing, especially among youth gang members.[10] The sparse existing literature suggests that most Mexican American street gangs are involved in drug markets as low-level sellers, with only a minority being engaged in profitable, midlevel drug enterprises.[11] Moore discusses the participation of adult gangs within the drug market of east Los Angeles.[12] As she states, "drug dealers did employ members . . . in a hierarchy that included non-addicted dealers, addicted dealers (who in turn would supply addict-push-ers who sold heroin for use rather than profit) and finally the consumer addict."[13] Her findings suggested that it was usually individual older gang members who used other members to market drugs to street consumers.

However, there is scarce information on the relationship of youth gangs to the larger drug markets in these communities, especially during the unsettled decades of the 1980s and 1990s. Some dynamics include the ebb and flow of the Mexican cartels as they respond to U.S. drug prohibition policies and enforcement activities. For instance, rigorous interdiction efforts along the U.S.–Mexico border have made it more difficult to smug-gle marijuana than cocaine or heroin.

This chapter describes heroin use and dealing among Mexican Ameri-can street gang members in a highly segregated and poor urban commu-nity. It is argued that participation in drug markets by youth gangs is part of a constellation of economic activities that flourishes in the context of concentrated poverty, social isolation, and vice market segregation. In the manner advanced by Sampson and Wilson,[14] I view the race and drug use (crime) linkage through contextual lenses that highlight the different ecological settings that Hispanics and Whites reside in regardless of indi-vidual characteristics. My focus is on the interaction between the larger community's drug markets (including adult criminals) and youth gangs, and the process that leads to specific debilitating consequences both for the gangs as organizations and for members. Presented is how this Mexi-can American urban community's characteristics lead to structural barri-ers and cultural adaptations that engender social disorganization and undermine social control. I discuss how the heroin market was restruc-tured by external and internal market changes and prohibitionary drug policy decisions.

Methods

This research evolved from a study of violence among Mexican American gangs in south Texas.[15] The study focuses on identifying and distinguish-ing the relationship between gang violence and drug use among male youth gangs. Data were collected from active members of twenty-six youth gangs in San Antonio, Texas, over a five-year period. Community researchers, trained indigenous paraprofessionals, went out daily to establish contact, observe gang activities, and develop gang rosters. Based on this fieldwork, the study developed a targeted quota sampling strategy to obtain a representative sample of this hidden population of gang members.[16] Personal data were obtained through a comprehensive life history questionnaire administered to a sample of 160 subjects recruited from twenty-six gangs. These data were combined with field notes and transcripts from twenty-four focus groups. The focus groups consisted of gang members, adult criminals, nongang delinquents, social service providers, public housing residents, and other neighborhood residents.[17] These multiple sources formed the base for our observations on patterns of individual drug use, drug dealing and selling operations, organizational rules, maintenance and transformation of the gang, and the gang's relationship to other criminal elements in the community. Additional qualitative data were collected from several other studies conducted in the community by this research team.

Drug Market Segregation and Heroin Use

The West Side community in San Antonio is comprised predominantly of Mexican-origin persons living in one of the poorest urban areas in the United States. According to the 2000 census, per capita income is $5,098, and the median household income is $14,352 for twenty-two census tracts that comprise this community. Fifty-five percent of West Side families have children living in poverty, and only 23 percent of the families receive public assistance.[18] The area that is the focus of this study is the smaller segment of the larger West Side consisting of eight census tracts with a population of around fifty thousand persons.[19] Neighborhoods in this area have the highest concentration of low-income Mexican-origin persons in the city.

This was the traditional settlement area for Mexican immigrants beginning in the 1920s when they arrived in large numbers escaping the political turmoil and poverty of Mexico. This migration steadily increased through the 1940s as San Antonio experienced urbanization. However, unlike other newcomers to the city, Mexicans were segregated into limited geographic areas primarily on the near West Side adjacent to the central business district. These neighborhoods suffered from inadequate housing, inferior infrastructure (water, sewers, electricity, etc.), and limited public services (schools, police, clinics, hospitals). In the 1930s, San Antonio's barrios had some of the highest rates of tuberculosis, venereal diseases, and infant mortality in the United States.[20]

The Mexican barrios of San Antonio were also where the city's vice was concentrated, especially in the Mexican businesses immediately adjacent to downtown. San Antonio is similar to other cities such as New York and Chicago, where vice districts were typically segregated in minority ghettos or barrios. According to one historian,[21] in the first half of the twentieth century, this area of San Antonio had over ninety bordellos, saloons, gambling dens, and small shacks where prostitutes plied their trade. These establishments were sustained by Anglo clients from throughout the city. The area simultaneously was the entertainment center for the Mexican population where Spanish-language theaters (vaudeville and film), cantinas, restaurants, outdoor markets, and dance halls were situated. It was the primary source of liquor during Prohibition and marijuana beginning in the late thirties. This red light district operated under the approval of the city until the early 1940s.[22]

For Mexicans in this city, opportunities to engage in illicit activities were facilitated by the proximity of the vice area and their group's limited access to other conventional opportunities imposed by a de facto Jim Crow social structure.[23] One criminal activity in which Mexican Americans were well positioned to flourish was drug trafficking. Within this market, Mexican Americans had an advantage over others in that they shared a common language and ethnic background with drug wholesalers in Mexico's border regions and interior. Beginning in the 1940s, Mexicans began to establish connections with drug market enterprises that extended throughout the United States.[24]

Accessibility to Mexico's drug wholesale distributors created highly decentralized drug markets in San Antonio and other parts of the Southwest characterized by multiple small-time drug entrepreneurs. These drug distribution activities were embedded in the highly isolated barrios of San Antonio and other smaller and medium-sized Texas cities and towns. An adverse consequence of these drug markets was that they made illicit drugs, especially marijuana, heroin, and cocaine, highly accessible to Mexican Americans in these barrios. During this period, heroin and opiate users were primarily older southern Whites and urban younger subcultural groups.[25] But it is highly likely that this period corresponds to the point in time when Mexican Americans began the practice of injecting heroin. Maddux and Desmond state that it was within "this initial center (vice district) that heroin trafficking and heroin use spread throughout much of the West Side."[26]

Over the last four decades, a drug market has evolved in San Antonio's Mexican American community that involves a highly diversified market-place with various actors operating at different levels. Exclusive networks of multigenerational family and friends carry out these drug activities. Some of these networks are small with operations limited to San Antonio. Others are larger organized drug networks with connections in Mexico and other cities throughout the United States where Mexican Americans migrated such as Chicago, Detroit, and Milwaukee. Although a hierarchical structure exists in this drug market, there has always been space for individual entrepreneurs to operate. Mexican American drug users in San Antonio looking to buy the more popular drugs (e.g., marijuana, cocaine, and heroin) do not have difficulty locating a seller or dealer in the immediate community.

During this period, the Mexican American drug-using population has developed a clear preference for heroin and other opiates and nearly universal use of intravenous injection as the route of administration.[27] As a result, a distinct heroin subculture developed in southwestern cities and towns among Mexican American users, or *tecatos*. The term "*tecato*" denotes a chronic or career heroin user with a criminal orientation and repeated involvement with the criminal justice system.[28] Therefore, *tecatos* have developed a distinct street identity revolving around a "*pachuco*" lifestyle characterized by heroin use, criminality, incarceration, unique style of dress, tattoos, and social networks. They have traditionally been stigmatized and socially isolated from the larger Mexican American and Anglo community.

The Social Isolation of Family-Based Heroin Users

This *pachuco/tecato* subculture is reinforced by the social isolation of this population in class- and ethnic-segregated barrios. This is the case for the specific area of the West Side previously described. Within these neighborhoods, networks of extended family members living in close proximity to each other are found. These networks are often multigenerational, including older members such as grandparents, step-parents, cousins, uncles, and aunts. Most of the families in these poor barrios are conventional and adhere to more traditional family characteristics associated with Mexican American families. Those families associated with street life, such as addicts, criminals, and gang members, are more unconventional or "*cholo*" families and are characterized by drug use, criminality, incarceration, and strong street connections. Many of the Mexican American heroin users among our respondents are associated with this type of family network.

Given the marginal economic status, social isolation, and close proximity of these families, most members are highly dependent upon each other for various forms of mutual assistance. Family members rely on each other for financial help and assistance when in need. For instance, when a gang member's girlfriend has a child, they commonly move in with family members, usually one of their mothers. Frequent visiting by family members is normative and expected. In this sense, there is a high degree of mutual expectations among members of these family-based networks. These social relations reinforce a common set of values and norms. Families with an antisocial value orientation provide a basis of tolerance for deviant behaviors such as drug use, crime, and high-risk sex. As suggested by others,[29] in these environments, the wider cultural values are simply not relevant—they become "unviable."[30]

Among those families where heroin is used, the use is usually a multi-generational phenomenon. Many of the gang members grew up in households where heroin was used by adults and older siblings. This may be why street gang members in this study voice ambivalent attitudes towards *tecatos*. Although Chicano adult heroin users are an integral part of the criminal scene in the barrios, they are marginally accepted by other participants such as gang members, juvenile delinquents, car thieves, drug sellers and dealers, "coke heads," and alcoholics. *Tecatos* have a reputation even among these networks as being untrustworthy and unreliable since most of their time is spent in criminal or quasi-criminal activities to generate resources to purchase drugs. This includes shoplifting, committing burglaries, fencing stolen merchandise, and scamming friends, neighbors, and relatives for money.

However, youth gang members are reluctant to completely reject *tecatos* because many are immediate and extended family members, neighbors, and friends. Therefore, many gang members know first-hand how an addict's behavior negatively impacts the lives of family and friends; they have personally experienced the way their heroin-dependent fathers, older brothers, or, in some cases, mothers discard their family obligations.[31]

As a result of such experiences, most gangs actively discourage the use of heroin through a no heroin rule that prohibits heroin use among its members. Nearly 70 percent of respondents reported that their gang has such a rule as part of the informal bylaws. Sanctions for violating the rule vary from a verbal warning to a severe beating. One gang member explains the no heroin rule in his gang:

> The rules were just something everybody knew. It was just understood that heroin was not allowed. If a person was known to have done heroin and the gang leadership found out about it, then a violation would be given to the gang member who was accused of doing heroin. The punishment depended on how bad the violation was.

However, not all the gangs had a no heroin rule nor was the rule always enforced among those that had one. For instance, the Nine-Ball Crew did not enforce such a rule because many of its members, including the leader, were selling heroin for adult family members. Thus, it was not in the gang's interest to have this kind of restriction. This inconsistency in enforcement encouraged other gang members to use heroin as they realized they might not be sanctioned.

Prison Gangs and the Drug Market Transitions

San Antonio's West Side heroin market radically changed when a Mexican American prison gang, Pura Vida, entered into this marketplace in the early 1980s. Pura Vida was one of three prison gangs with a presence in San Antonio's criminal scene. The entrance of Pura Vida in San Antonio corresponded with a dramatic increase in incarceration rates in Texas and the United States, largely as a result of federal and state drug laws passed during the last three decades.[32] Thus, the American prison population increased to approximately two million persons during the 1990s. Young Hispanics and Blacks disproportionately comprise this incarcerated population.[33] Eventually, this incarcerated population returned to communities that offered little opportunity, particularly for ex-felons.

According to interviews with ex-felons, when members of Pura Vida began to be released (paroled) from penal institutions, they organized themselves into a criminal network outside the prison. Under the leadership of members still inside the system, Pura Vida began to engage in drug dealing, extortion, fencing stolen property, and other illegal activities in San Antonio. Pura Vida's presence was most visible in the West Side core of San Antonio, home for many of the parolees. It was within this community, particularly in the city housing projects, that they established their presence in the drug marketplace.

During the course of this research (1995–1999), Pura Vida gradually gained control of a large portion of the heroin and cocaine market in these neighborhoods. The control of the heroin market was accomplished through a highly regimented vertical organization using ex-felons recruited in the prisons and connections in Mexico. The organizational structure is along paramilitary lines with a president, vice-president, general, captains, lieutenants, sergeants, and soldiers.

Independent drug dealers are allowed to sell in these geographic areas, but are assessed a 10 percent surcharge, known as *el diez por ciento,* on all drug sales by the gang. Pura Vida members enforce the surcharge through intimidation, physical threats, violence, and murder. In one highly publicized incident, Pura Vida soldiers killed an independent heroin dealer who refused to pay his *diez por ciento.* What made this incident so shocking was that the dealer's teenage daughter, boyfriend, and friends, who were not involved in the drug market, were also murdered. Weeks later the perpetrators of these killings were found, mysteriously murdered, their bodies dumped on the outskirts of the city.[34]

The Increased Use of Heroin among Youth Gangs Members

Part of Pura Vida's success in this market resulted from its well-established heroin connections in Mexico, organizational structure, and members' loyalty and commitment. Once they acquired these characteristics, Pura Vida began to market the drug, just like any retailer or wholesaler of legal commodities. Pura Vida consciously targeted heroin sales in two vulnerable populations: delinquent nongang youth and gang members. They did this by making the drug more accessible, putting more retail sellers into the community, lowering prices, offering higher purity levels, and using gang members and peers as sellers. One young heroin user, commenting on the accessibility of heroin, said, "You can get it anywhere in the neighborhood, from all kinds of people. Even young kids can get it for you." One gang member reported how easy it was to score a ten-dollar paper to snort a few lines of heroin to party or when they were just "kicking back." Increased purity allows users to ingest the drug in ways other than through injecting, a practice that is still frowned upon by most gang leaders and members. As a result, snorting heroin (or "sniffing") slowly became an acceptable alternative among many gang members, particularly as its availability increased.

While heroin use increased, many gang members remained ambivalent toward the drug. In contrast, the use of marijuana was highly normalized among gang members. Many smoke "weed" (marijuana) continuously throughout the day. Marijuana use is highly prevalent among gangs and other delinquent juveniles in many low-income minority neighborhoods. One field worker noted, "These guys smoke marijuana while walking to school, cruising, and even during pick-up basketball games at neighborhood playgrounds. Its just common behavior." Intranasal use of powdered cocaine is also an acceptable part of the gang member's lifestyle.

About a quarter of the gang members interviewed reported having used heroin in the preceding thirty days. Approximately 70 percent of these were injectors and the rest reported intranasal use (sniffing or snorting). A marked increase in noninjecting heroin use over the course of the study was observed. As mentioned previously, heroin is a highly stigmatized drug associated with being a *tecato*. In a focus group, one participant described *tecatos* as "dirty, sick, and always scratching themselves." Heroin addicts were chastised by gang members even though *tecatos* were part of the street scene in these neighborhoods. In fact, many gang members had older adult relatives who were heroin addicts. These attitudes about heroin users changed as gang members began to increase their use of heroin. This was done either by snorting it or by "shabanging," a method in which a solution of heroin and water is prepared and sprayed into the nasal passages with either a syringe or an eyedropper.

Sixty percent of noninjectors eventually transitioned to injecting heroin.[35] This is an exceptionally high rate compared to other noninjecting samples that have been studied.[36] Many of those who began injecting became addicted, a status that led to personal problems and impaired functioning with respect to obligations as gang members.

Gang members who are addicted begin to engage in compulsive drug-seeking behavior that is irresponsible, and become indifferent to their responsibility as gang members. Moreover, they become unable to sustain non-heroin-related personal relationships. They begin to engage in crimes that are geared towards getting resources to buy drugs, such as burglary, shoplifting, low-level drug selling (for one's own profit), and other, less "gang-related" crimes. This behavior invariably leads to conflicts with the gang's leadership, who often continue to enforce the *no heroin* rule. This rule becomes increasingly more difficult to enforce because ever larger numbers of members are using heroin.

Some gangs experience such high numbers of members drifting into the heroin *tecato* subculture that the gang's viability is threatened. The gang that best illustrates this transformation is the Chicano Dudes. Approximately thirty of its members became addicted to heroin during the study. This gang initially had a very strict no heroin rule; however, as the leadership and older gangsters (OGs) began using and selling large quantities of heroin, the rule was no longer enforced. Heroin use became so prevalent that the Chicano Dudes acquired a reputation among other gangs as a "bunch of *tecatos*" and has nearly disintegrated.

Another major consequence of heroin use among members is the disproportionate incarceration rate compared to nonusers. Many heroin users are arrested and incarcerated for two primary reasons. One is directly associated with the selling and dealing of heroin. A gang member who sells heroin eventually will get "snitched on" by a disgruntled customer, a neighbor, or even a fellow heroin dealer trying to rid himself of competition. One of these persons will turn his name over to law enforcement, an action that often ends in arrest. The other reason for arrest and incarceration is the high volume of burglaries, robberies, and car thefts committed by users. While incarceration negatively affects the individual, it is even more detrimental for the organization of the gang as many of its members and leaders are removed from the community.

Several gangs experienced a complete dissemination as a result of heroin addiction. A critical number of the leaders and members became either heavy users or addicts. Many of these then became unable to fulfill their obligations to the gang. Unable to provide protection to their members or defend their territories from encroachment by other gangs, they become easy prey for rival gangs.

Cooptation and Recruitment of Gang Members by Adult Prison Gangs

Another consequence of the dominance of the heroin market by Pura Vida in San Antonio is the practice of recruitment and cooptation of members of the youth gangs. Pura Vida has recruited gang members either as independent sellers or as more formal associates of the gang. The association may range from a "probationary" or "apprentice" status to the status of a full-fledged member. Many delinquent barrio youth have been eager to join the Pura Vida, given the prison veteran's warriorlike status within the street culture of the West Side of San Antonio. The *pinto* (prison veteran) is seen by many as having a highly disciplined code of conduct and a philosophy of life attuned to the values of many street-oriented young men. In addition, many of these delinquent youth assume that by joining Pura Vida they have access to more lucrative illegal enterprises and increased levels of protection from street rivals.

Most young gang members were initially recruited into Pura Vida when they were sent to Texas state correctional facilities. In the prison, they develop a close solidarity with the organization and participate in the group's illegal activities. They are also tutored on Pura Vida philosophy, codes of conduct, and principles of the organization. Upon release from prison, they become the *soldados* (foot soldiers) of Pura Vida and usually do not return to their street gang.

Another common mechanism of recruitment is kinship. Gang members who are recruited into Pura Vida often have a close relative—a brother, father, uncle, or cousin—already in the gang. The case of Jaime, the leader of the Nine-Ball Crew, illustrates the influence of family on the recruitment of gang members. Jaime's stepfather, a high-level member of Pura Vida, controlled the drug trafficking for the prison gang in the neighborhood in which the gang was located. Jaime mentioned in interviews the respect he had for his stepfather and the position he had in Pura Vida and his ambition of eventually becoming a member. By the end of the research project, Jaime, as well as many other gang members, had been recruited by Pura Vida mostly through familial ties, such as cousins, uncles, and brothers.

Pura Vida also recruits associates into its organization by "fronting" drugs to potential earners. Fronting is a technique that is commonly used by drug dealers. It is somewhat similar to giving credit to someone. Pura Vida will "front" some drugs to a gang member and then the gang member is obligated to pay his debt after the drugs are sold. If the gang member does not pay his full debt in the agreed manner, he may be forced to continue to sell for Pura Vida even after his debt is paid. Many times just the intimidation Pura Vida yields in the neighborhood obligates the gang member to sell for them. The positive side of fronting for the gang member is that he now has the protection of the prison gang in the neighbor-hood from rival youth gangs and other adult criminals in the same area.

Discussion and Conclusion

The major thesis of this analysis is that the ecological context is important for understanding the link between race and crime, regardless of individual characteristics. In this regard, context must be understood from both an historical and a contemporary framework. In this chapter, an argument is made that decades of deviance containment as illustrated by the location of vice districts in minority communities—a specific form of institutional racism—shape perceptions, cultural patterns of learning, and opportunities. Moreover, the social isolation and structural inequality experienced during the most recent two decades by poor urban minorities has engendered adaptive behaviors that often include crime and deviance.[37] The result is what is controversially referred to as social disorganization—defined as a decrease in conventional social rules of behavior.[38]

What this chapter suggests is the spread and persistence of intravenous heroin use by Mexican Americans in San Antonio was facilitated by the proximity of the vice district to the West Side. One can only speculate that heroin's initial diffusion into the fabric of the Mexican American community in the 1940s was a product of direct contact between them and White heroin addicts looking to sell and buy the drug, since this is where the city historically chose to concentrate its other illicit activities (i.e., prostitution, gambling, etc.). There is evidence documenting that heroin was predominantly used by Whites prior to the 1940s and was rare for minority groups, with the exception of Blacks from New York.[39] During the decades that followed, however, heroin use decreased for Whites, but increased for Mexican Americans and Blacks.[40] This increase corresponded to the association of heroin with markedly deviant and minority subcultures located in highly segregated ghettos and barrios such as those discussed here.

The behaviors discussed in this chapter are exacerbated by deliberate public policy decisions that target minorities, such as U.S. drug laws.[41] Specifically, the negative consequences of drug policies have disproportionately affected poor minority areas such as the Mexican American neighborhoods examined in our work. During the last two decades, south Texas has become a major staging area for large-scale binational narcotics operations. In response, there has been an escalation of interdiction efforts by law enforcement agencies in this region. The effects of these prohibitionary policies on the drug market in San Antonio, and possibly other southwestern cities, are reduced prices and higher quality of heroin and cocaine. This has created increased opportunities for poor minorities living in these communities to engage in drug selling and dealing (and related crimes), and drug abuse and addiction.[42]

Another significant factor that influenced the heroin market in San Antonio is the large number of Mexican American men incarcerated during the last two decades. Most of these men have been convicted and incarcerated for nonviolent drug offenses related to punitive drug laws passed by state and federal lawmakers.[43] Many Mexican American men, upon being released as convicted felons, return to communities such as the West Side of San Antonio that offer few opportunities for them. This problem has occurred throughout the United States.[44] As a result, many have begun to take advantage of opportunities offered by drug markets centered in low-income barrios, often under the umbrella of the prison gangs. It was in this context that Mexican American adult prison gangs were able to dominate the heroin market and other street-based drug sellers and dealers such as Mexican American youth gangs. The larger implications of these punitive criminal justice policies for Mexican Americans and other minorities merits further study of issues such as the impact drug policies are having on political disenfranchisement, increased welfare dependency, persistent poverty, and the growth of an increasing Mexican American underclass. These issues have been addressed somewhat in regards to African Americans, but less so for U.S. Hispanics.[45]

The illegal-drug industry consists of competing profit-making enterprises in a capitalist-based world economy. Each is in constant search for new markets, often targeting consumers in minority communities and other vulnerable populations. The existence of these drug markets in U.S. low-income neighborhoods creates substantial economic opportunities for many residents. Urban minorities are vulnerable to these market opportunities given the economic losses experienced by deindustrialization during the last three decades, the transfer of thousands of jobs to other countries, and the growth of the informal economy.[46]

Drug markets seem to have their most pernicious impact when they are organized and dominated by corporate-style drug dealing organizations rather than more street-level sellers and dealers such as youth gang members. The existence of corporate-style dealers in economically marginalized communities is more likely to contribute to the breakdown of community-based institutions including the economy, family, and peer-based friendship groups such as gangs. As demonstrated by this study, corporate-style dealers in these types of drug markets may also lead to greater levels of serious drug use and addiction by young gang members. The extent to which this happens in similar communities in different regions of the United States and other places in the world needs further study.

Lastly, this chapter illustrates the important contribution that research incorporating race, inequality, culture, ecology, and public policy makes in advancing our knowledge of crime. Understanding this complex intersection can be best achieved by implementing research designs that integrate both quantitative and qualitative data collection and innovative analytical strategies. Approaching this issue in this manner will highlight those urban structures and institutions that are linked to contextual and cultural patterns that better explain the association of race and crime.

NOTES

1. Bell 1960.
2. Kornblum 1993:117–18.
3. Kasarda 1985; Wilson 1996.
4. Gray 1998.
5. Brownsberger 2000; Zule and Desmond 1999.
6. Curtis 2003; Hagedorn 1998; Hamid 1990; Williams 1989.
7. Bullington 1977; Moore 1978; Sanders 1994.
8. There are varying definitions of what constitutes an adolescent gang (Klein 1971; Miller 1975; Moore 1978; Yablonsky 1962), often based on the researcher's relationship to the gang and source of information. The definition used in this study is based on our experiences in working with gangs in San Antonio.
9. *Drug Trafficking* 2001; Office of National Drug Control Policy 2003.
10. Bullington 1977; Sanders 1994.
11. Valdez and Sifaneck 2004.
12. Moore 1978.
13. Ibid.
14. Sampson and Wilson 1995.
15. This study was sponsored by the National Institutes of Health, National Institute on Drug Abuse.
16. Yin et al. 1996.
17. Valdez and Kaplan 1999.
18. U.S. Bureau of the Census 2000b, 2001, 2002b.

19. Brischetto 2000.
20. Garcia 1989.
21. Bowser 2003.
22. Ibid.
23. Montejano 1987.
24. Redlinger and Michel 1970.
25. Ball 1965.
26. Maddux and Desmond 1981:36.
27. Bullington 1977; Casavantes 1976; Desmond and Maddux 1984; Moore 1978; National Institute of Justice 1996.
28. Quintero and Estrada 1998, 2000; Ramos 1995; Valdez, Kaplan, and Cepeda 2000.
29. Anderson 1978; Horowitz 1987.
30. Sampson and Wilson 1995:50.
31. Valdez et al. 2000.
32. Gray 1998.
33. Harrison and Beck 2003.
34. This information was gathered initially from field work and later confirmed by police reports and articles in the *San Antonio Express-News*.
35. Valdez et al. 2001.
36. Neaigus 1998; Valdez, Kaplan, and Codina 2000.
37. Wilson 1996.
38. Sampson and Wilson 1995.
39. Kornblum 1993; O'Donnell and Jones 1968.
40. There was an increase in heroin use by Whites in the late 1960s and 1970s that was associated with returning Vietnam veterans and emerging youth drug subcultures. But, this trend was short lived compared to the continual use of heroin by Mexican Americans.
41. Gray 1998.
42. Another example of this is the New York Police Department's decision to avoid street-level drug dealers because contact with them was thought to encourage corruption among police officers. Paradoxically, this policy has actually increased the supply of heroin as new distributors entered the market as a result of less policing (Wendel and Curtis 2000).
43. Beckett and Sasson 2000.
44. Clear, Rose, and Ryder 2001.
45. Uggen and Manza 2002.
46. Wilson 1996.

Chapter 13

Perceptions of Crime and Safety in Racially and Economically Distinct Neighborhoods

Lauren J. Krivo, Ruth D. Peterson, and Diana L. Karafin

Growing recognition that the character of neighborhoods affects the lives of individual residents has come to the forefront of research on crime. Indeed, a focus on neighborhood effects appears to be "all the rage" in scholarship on crime and other social dislocations.[1] This is true of studies examining the role of race/ethnicity in these outcomes and of general analyses of criminal involvement, violence, and other social concerns.[2] Thus, it is puzzling that neighborhood characteristics are not given much attention in explorations of the importance of race and ethnicity in residents' perceptions of the degree to which their communities are safe or crime-free. Here, scholars have focused mainly on the influences of individual attributes and experiences in isolation from the local context of daily life. Consequently, we know much more about what personal factors relate to views on crime and safety than about the ways that settings give rise to such perceptions. The exceptions are studies that focus on the relationship between neighborhood racial composition and social disorder and social disorganization within communities. These analyses demonstrate important contextual effects.[3] Yet, these works are limited in helping us to understand racial and ethnic variation in perceptions of crime and safety because they fail to conceptualize the entrenched interconnections of race, ethnicity, and economic status in differentiating neighborhood contexts. In this chapter, we argue that conceptualizing these broad interrelationships will shed light on the significant ways in which internal conditions and external structures and social dynamics of communities are inequitable by race and class in ways that affect residents' perceptions and actions.

The combination of dramatic levels of racial residential segregation coupled with racial inequality in other social and economic domains defines the urban landscape in the United States. As a result, many neighborhoods are racially *and* economically distinct; this fact has important implications for community structures that impact residents' views. Several scholars conclude that differences across racial and ethnic communities in social status and organization are the most important sources of group disparities in violence.[4] Yet, Pattillo-McCoy demonstrates poignantly that what happens in one particular race-class neighborhood, the Black middle-class community of Groveland, is dramatically affected by both its own racial and economic composition and the social and economic vulnerabilities of surrounding poor Black areas.[5] That is, the geographic, social, and political positioning of a community within the overall urban space probably influences individual and community dynamics. Findings for Groveland further suggest that the combination of Black racial composition and middle-class character has unique implications for the way community (internal and external) dynamics play out. Unfortunately, most empirical research has not been structured to investigate the complex role of different aspects of neighborhood context, or the combined impact of race and class composition, for understanding how the realities and perceptions of crime and safety are racially/ethnically differentiated.

Here, we ask, How do we better understand whether and how race- and class-varying contexts are connected with subjective safety of neighborhoods? Do residents of middle-class Black neighborhoods differ significantly in their perceptions of crime and safety from those living in middle-class White neighborhoods, or do the residents of these two types of areas feel equally safe and free from crime? Similarly, do the residents of poor, predominantly White communities fear for their own safety as much as those in poor Black neighborhoods, or does the racial context differentiate these two types of poor areas? In structuring our analyses to answer these questions, we begin with the premise that race and class are organizing principles in the United States that together affect the situations of communities of varying colors. Drawing on this notion, we compare four specific neighborhoods that are differentiated by their racial and class composition to assess what implications race, class, and their intersection have for the way internal characteristics and social relations affect local areas and their residents. Because the four communities also vary in their external positions and connections in ways that reflect the combinations of race and class, we can then point to the way outside forces are likely to impact residents' perceptions. Heretofore, studies of community perceptions and fear of crime have generally relied on samples of neighborhoods in which these explicit comparisons are not made. The comparative analyses we present should, therefore, provide new insights and set the stage for more comprehensive investigations that build on our conclusions by measuring external conditions and examining residents in a larger sample of strategically chosen communities.

Residents' Perceptions in Context

As noted, a small body of literature considers fear and perceptions of crime as dependent on internal aspects of the neighborhood context. One of the most commonly explored factors is the racial composition of neighborhoods. In particular, a number of studies examine the social-threat hypothesis that the size of minority populations, particularly Blacks, increases fear and lessens feelings of safety.[6] Findings generally support this view. Individuals are more fearful and believe that there is more crime in their neighborhoods when African Americans (or non-Whites and sometimes Latinos) comprise (or are perceived to make up) a larger share of the population. However, results are not conclusive as to whether these relationships hold only for Whites, thereby reflecting White stereotyping and racial threat, or also apply to Blacks and Hispanics, implying more broadly held stereotypes regarding criminality and race.

Studies also focus on the extent to which disorder and social disorganization (e.g., weak social integration, lack of neighborhood attachment) explain fear and perceptions of crime and safety. Here, the argument is that more socially disorganized areas and places with greater disorder induce fear and increase perceptions that crime abounds. Results show that residents feel less safe and think there is more crime when there is more real or perceived disorder.[7] In contrast, aspects of neighborhood integration have been found to affect fear of crime in some studies but not in others.[8]

Findings regarding internal neighborhood conditions are informative but do not take into account the fully systemic nature of racial and ethnic inequality. For example, studies of crime and fear perceptions look at neighborhoods as if they are independent entities in which their separate and internal characteristics, including racial composition, are the full set of conditions that affect how residents feel. However, this is unlikely to be the case in contemporary U.S. cities. Rather, the social conditions that arise in neighborhoods and reactions of residents to crime and urban life may stem differentially from the following factors: where neighborhoods are located relative to other neighborhoods; the social and economic characteristics of residents of nearby communities; connections with politicians and government agencies who serve areas; how businesses and merchants perceive the areas as opportunities for investment and withdrawal; and other ways in which neighborhoods are situated relative to external actors. These factors may be particularly important when one is considering racial and ethnic differentiation in community responses because of the extent of residential segregation by race, ethnicity, and class found in the United States.[9] Blacks and Whites are very highly segregated and hence tend to live apart from one another. Other ethnic groups are more modestly segregated although there is also some ethnic clustering. Economic segregation, which has been growing in recent decades, adds to the residential divisions found in urban areas.[10]

Separately and in combination, racial/ethnic and economic segregation have important consequences. Most notably, residents of White and Black (or other minority) neighborhoods reside in areas that are highly differentiated with regard to a variety of external characteristics. Minority, and often especially African American, communities have fewer and weaker connections with powerful political and economic actors, suffer from racial exclusion, neglect, and discrimination by authorities, and are more likely to be spatially situated near other less powerful and otherwise disadvantaged localities than areas that are populated primarily by Whites. The positioning of areas with respect to these factors can have important effects on the internal social dynamics emphasized in some studies of residents' views of community safety. As well, their direct influences may be equally or more pronounced.

Studies have also failed to address the broader systemic impact of racial/ethnic inequality by assessing how the interplay of racial composition and economic status influences perceptions of crime and safety, and alters the ways that internal and external neighborhood factors affect these perceptions. A wide range of research shows that poorer communities often lack the capacity to organize to diminish crime and create an environment that is perceived as a safe place to live. Conversely, middle-class areas are characterized by a greater availability of resources to keep crime at bay and reinforce the perception that residents are safe. However, the racial hierarchy in which Whites hold the most privilege and African Americans and other people of color suffer the greatest burden that runs throughout the social, economic, political, and spatial landscape may affect these class dynamics. Thus, compared to their White counterparts, African American middle-class communities bear the brunt of racism and accompanying diminished resources relative to their class status, with the result being higher levels of crime and greater perceived threats to safety and order. Similarly, Black poor areas suffer worse outcomes than White poor communities due to the added burden of race.

Often, analysts are unable to see how the complex interplay between racial and class composition affects neighborhood safety and perceptions. This blindness stems from both theoretical and empirical realities. Theoretically, the most prominent contemporary explanation of racial and ethnic differences in crime emphasizes that these group inequalities result from dissimilarities in class circumstances.[11] Remaining excesses for minority populations are then conceptualized as cultural adaptations to disadvantaged environments. By extension, views of crime and safety stem also from class and cultural differences across groups. However, this view fails to take seriously the role of racial structures that remain in play in a hierarchical society even when economic circumstances are equated. Of particular relevance is that individual residents and leaders, inside and outside of communities, respond in varying ways to combinations of race and class, not simply to either alone. If we do not theorize this point, we can overemphasize the role of culture and may fail to see the complex structural relationships that exist.

Empirically, racial/ethnic economic inequality combines with racial residential segregation to produce few predominantly non-White middle-class neighborhoods and few highly disadvantaged White areas. As a result, researchers are not often in a position to examine various racial/ethnic groups that are similarly disadvantaged or advantaged, or areas of similar economic status across the spectrum of race and ethnicity. This reality has tended to reinforce perceived stereotypes in which race and class are completely confounded as explanations for group differences in crime and safety because we are left comparing two extremes. That is, the contrast has been between the combined privileges of White race and middle- or upper-class status present in some areas versus the combined burdens of Black race and poor-class status that pervade in other localities.

The analysis that follows is designed to address these theoretical and empirical problems in extant work on perceptions of crime and safety. Thus, we conduct a study of four neighborhoods in Columbus, Ohio, specifically chosen to allow for comparisons between areas that are economically similar but racially distinct, and racially similar but economically distinct. In doing so, we illustrate the value of explicitly chosen comparisons for drawing sound conclusions about the relative role of race and class in community safety research.

Comparing Four Neighborhoods: Methods and Description

In 2001, we conducted a survey of residents in four neighborhoods in the city of Columbus, Ohio, to assess individuals' views of their communities, including what problems they perceived with crime and safety. We attempted to identify local communities as distinct areas with meaningful social boundaries. Our method entailed first utilizing census data (for 1990) to select potential neighborhoods that were homogenous by race and class.[12] Next, we physically observed areas, noting obvious distinct boundaries such as parks, intersections, rivers, and highways. Together, the census and observational information was used to finalize our selections and neighborhood boundaries. This process of choosing "real" neighborhoods allows for meaningful comparisons. In particular, the areas match two predominantly White neighborhoods that vary in economic status (poor and middle-class) with two economically similar, predominantly African American communities.

The middle-class African American neighborhood, Cosby Park, is on the southeast side of Columbus and has about nineteen hundred residents.[13] This "backyard living community" resembles a suburban subdivision; it is almost completely residential and has winding streets, ranch-style housing, and few sidewalks. Driving through the neighborhood, one is struck by the quietness and the fact that very few residents are seen on the streets or in the front yards. The community is currently 76 percent Black and has a median household income of just over $46,000 (up just $1,000 from 1990). The city's mayor and a number of prominent African American members of city government live in the neighborhood. The White middle-class area, Taft Heights, is on the north side of Columbus and has about five thousand residents. In contrast to Cosby Park, Taft Heights is a "front porch neighborhood" with a more historic feel. The majority of the housing was built in the early 1900s in a variety of styles.

Passing through the neighborhood, one sees an active street life with many residents walking, running, gardening, and playing with children. This community is 97 percent White with a median household income of approximately $78,000. The economic status of Taft Heights and Cosby Park were more similar in 1990 when the median household income in the former was $46,000. One of the city's major north-south arteries runs through the middle of the neighborhood, with businesses and other service organizations lining this thoroughfare.

These middle-class neighborhoods contrast sharply with the White (Joad Village) and Black (King Town) poor areas, which have median household incomes of about $29,000 and $25,000, respectively. King Town is just southeast of downtown Columbus. This area has slightly over forty-two hundred residents, with 89 percent being African American. What stands out when one visits the area is the degree of on-street activity involving children. Young children are observed walking around and playing ball or chase with few adults visibly present. Teens and young adults are seen congregating and moving through the area in small groups. Houses are smaller and of more variable quality than in either of the middle-class areas. In addition, there is a mixture of single-family homes and 2–3-unit structures. These vary from well kept to more run down, and some are even boarded up. Older and small businesses run along the main street that borders the area, but this strip also includes boarded up storefronts, a closed down theater, and vacant lots.

Joad Village is just south of downtown and not far from King Town. It has over twenty-six hundred residents, and approximately 79 percent of these are White. Similar to King Town, the residential dwellings in this neighborhood are a mixture of single-family homes and small, multi-unit houses and apartments that range from very well maintained to run down and/or boarded up. However, Joad Village has a much quieter feel than its African American counterpart, with fewer children and adults observed in the streets and yards. Numerous small local businesses are found along two main streets that bound the neighborhood on the east and west, but in this community, boarded up storefronts are not evident.

Within each of the four chosen communities, we interviewed approximately 150 adults (response rate of 63 percent). Three specific questions regarding subjective safety are examined: (1) How safe do you feel being alone outside in your neighborhood at night?; (2) How safe do you feel children are when they are outside in your neighborhood?; and (3) Overall, how much crime do you think there is in your neighborhood? Possible responses to the first two questions are "very safe," "safe," "unsafe," or "very unsafe"; answers to the crime perceptions question are "a lot," "some," "a little," or "none." Consistent with prior work on the importance of internal neighborhood social dynamics (e.g., disorder, collective efficacy), we include measures of neighborhood attachment, social disorder, physical disorder, social cohesion/control, and social ties/reciprocity.[14] Our analyses also control for several demographic and socioeconomic characteristics of respondents: sex, age, home ownership, and education.[15] Because our analysis is limited to four neighborhoods, we are not able to directly incorporate external community characteristics into our models. However, differences in levels of perceived crime and safety and in the effects of internal community characteristics on residents' views across neighborhoods that are racially similar but economically distinct, or economically similar but racially distinct, signal the potential importance of differential external contexts on perceptions of neighborhood safety and crime.

Views of Crime and Safety across Neighborhoods

Views of crime and safety by neighborhood type are presented in Figure 13.1 for the three subjective safety outcomes. These results highlight the importance of neighborhood class composition for all three indicators.[16] Compared to their middle-class counterparts, residents of Joad Village and King Town perceive that their communities are less safe and more crime ridden. Over half (52 percent) of those in Taft Heights and more than a third (37 percent) in Cosby Park report that they feel very safe when alone outside at night in their neighborhoods. These figures contrast sharply with the 17 percent and 23 percent of persons in Joad Village and King Town, respectively, who report feeling very safe outside at night. Similarly, a much larger percentage of residents of the middle-class than the poor communities believe that children are very safe outside in their neighborhoods (Panel B). Finally, almost no residents of the middle-class areas, irrespective of race, perceive a lot of crime where they live, while 18 to 30 percent of those in the poor communities think that crime is widely present (Panel C).

Though the dominant patterns in Figure 13.1 reflect class differences, important racial effects are also evident. Within the middle-class neighborhoods, notably fewer residents of Cosby Park than Taft Heights feel very safe regarding themselves.[17] Also, more residents of Taft Heights than

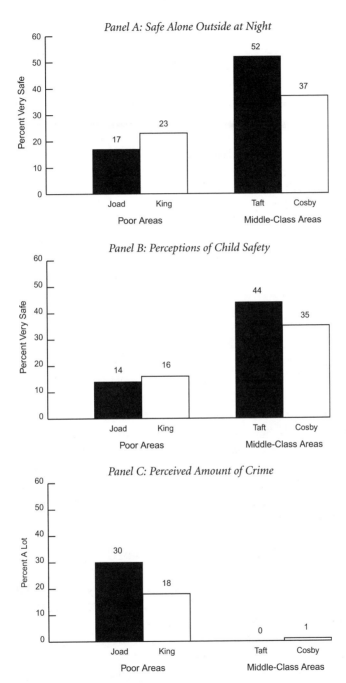

Fig. 13.1. Perceptions of Crime and Safety by Neighborhood Type

Cosby Park view children as very safe, but this difference is not statistically significant. Race does not play an important role in either of these outcomes for the poor communities. Similar proportions of those living in Joad Village and King Town view their areas as very safe for themselves and children. Regarding perceptions of levels of crime, racial composition takes on importance in the poor rather than the middle-class areas, with those in the White community perceiving more crime. Specifically, 30 percent of residents of Joad Village perceive a lot of crime while only 18 percent of those in King Town claim this to be the case.[18]

These descriptive results provide one indication of the importance of examining the interaction of race and class composition of areas when considering residents' perceptions. To provide a more nuanced understanding of such intersectionality, we explore whether the same conditions influence perceptions across the four distinct neighborhoods. The guiding question is whether variation in patterns across race-class composition of areas is observed, thereby suggesting that unmeasured external forces that differentiate the four neighborhoods might help to explain these differences. As noted, we examine the influence of several internal community characteristics: neighborhood attachment, social and physical disorder, cohesion/social control, and social ties/reciprocity. In Table 13.1, we present the results of these analyses, which also control for respondents' individual characteristics, for each of the four areas. The findings indicate which internal neighborhood factors affect each of the safety outcomes, with + representing a positive significant effect, – representing a negative significant influence, and NS indicating that the factor does not affect the outcome.

The multivariate findings demonstrate several distinct patterns by race and by class. They also underscore the importance of the race-class intersection. To begin with the unique race effects, social ties/reciprocity have effects in both Cosby Park and King Town. People living in African American areas, regardless of class, who describe their neighborhoods as having more social ties and a greater degree of reciprocity among residents, tend to feel that they and their children are safer outside. On the other hand, such ties do not appear to be relevant in White areas, whether middle-class or poor. Thus, strong local connections are uniquely important in views of safety for residents of Black communities.

Regarding the distinct influence of class, social disorder, as evidenced in conditions such as loud neighbors, public drinking, and the sale/use of drugs, stands out as having a relationship with views of safety for poor but not middle-class areas. In Joad Village *and* King Town, those who perceive

TABLE 13.1

Effects of Community Characteristics on Perceptions of Safety and Crime:
Poor and Middle-Class Neighborhoods[a]

	Panel A: Middle-Class Neighborhoods[b]					
	Taft Heights			Cosby Park		
	Safe Alone	Child Safe	Crime View	Safe Alone	Child Safe	Crime View
Neighborhood Attachment	NS	NS	NS	+	NS	NS
Social Disorder	NS	NS	NS	NS	NS	NS
Physical Disorder	−	−	+	NS	NS	NS
Cohesion/Control	+	+	−	NS	NS	NS
Social Ties/Reciprocity	NS	NS	NS	+	+	NS

	Panel B: Poor Neighborhoods[b]					
	Joad Village			King Town		
	Safe Alone	Child Safe	Crime View	Safe Alone	Child Safe	Crime View
Neighborhood Attachment	+	+	−	NS	+	NS
Social Disorder	−	−	NS	−	−	+
Physical Disorder	NS	NS	+	NS	NS	+
Cohesion/Control	+	NS	NS	NS	NS	−
Social Ties/Reciprocity	NS	NS	NS	+	+	NS

[a] All effects also control for sex (female), age, home ownership, and education.
[b] A + indicates a positive significant effect ($p < .05$), − indicates a negative significant effect ($p < .05$), and NS indicates no significant influence.

more social disorder feel less safe. For residents of King Town, observed social disorder also heightens perceptions of the amount of crime in their local area. Yet, when such disorder is present in middle-class communities, no effects on perceptions are evident.

Several patterns also reflect race-class intersectionality. First, some unique results are evidenced for the White middle-class community—Taft Heights. Here, two factors (physical disorder and cohesion/control) significantly influence views of safety and crime. Taft Heights's residents feel safer and perceive less crime when they observe less physical disorder, and see the area as characterized by greater cohesion and social control. Neither of these factors affect any of the three outcomes in Cosby Park. Further, physical disorder and cohesion/control only sporadically influence the outcomes in King Town and Joad Village (four of twelve nonsystematic effects).

The second pattern that reflects a unique combined effect of race and class composition is for neighborhood attachment. Within Joad Village alone, this predictor has a significant effect on all three perceptions. Residents who claim that they would *not* move from the neighborhood, even if they could afford to, tend to feel safer and perceive less crime in the area. No such effects emerge in the middle-class community of Taft Heights and only sporadic influences of attachment are found in the two Black areas. The final expression of a race-class intersection is reflected in the fact that almost none of the neighborhood factors has a significant influence on outcomes in the Black middle-class neighborhood. Only three of the fifteen potential effects are significant for Cosby Park. This contrasts with between six and eight for the other three areas. Consequently, it appears that conditions beyond those we have incorporated must be important in this particular type of race and class context. We discuss below how this might include specific external conditions.

Discussion and Conclusions

Neighborhoods in the United States are situated relative to one another on the basis of their racial/ethnic and class composition. This structural positioning influences a host of local conditions that, in turn, have implications for levels and perceptions of crime and safety. In line with this viewpoint, we posited that the structure of perceptions varies across racial/ethnic- and class-distinct neighborhoods. The above analyses provided evidence consistent with this theme. The findings confirm that differences in perceptions exist across neighborhoods due to the social structural position represented by racial composition, class composition, and the combination thereof. Those in middle-class neighborhoods feel safer and perceive less crime than those in poor areas. However, there are also subtle race differences in such perceptions, with residents of Taft Heights, the White middle-class community, feeling the most safe and crime free. Further, the central factors that lead to variations in perceptions are not uniform across the neighborhoods, and partly depend on race *and* class composition. In particular, physical disorder and social cohesion are important for the middle-class White area alone, and neighborhood attachment is central only for Joad Village, the poor White community. In addition, we are generally unable to explain perceptions in the middle-class African American neighborhood of Cosby Park with the internal social dynamics included here.

The results raise two significant questions. What other conditions may differentiate the communities and explain why commonly explored internal characteristics are of differential import across the neighborhoods?

What specific factors distinguish the middle-class Black area of Cosby Park from all of the others such that our current model seems so inadequate for explaining perceptions in this neighborhood? One might speculate that the root source of differences in perceptions of crime and safety across the four areas is actual crime rates, which we have not taken into account. However, reported crime rates for these neighborhoods do not align perfectly with the variations in perceptions of crime and safety reported by residents. For example, though residents in Taft Heights perceive the least crime in their neighborhood and have the highest proportion of residents who feel very safe, this community does not have the lowest crime rate of the four areas. Rather, the total and property crime rates for Taft Heights are higher than those for Cosby Park.[19] Thus, it is incorrect to assume that one may deduce how residents perceive crime and safety in their neighborhood simply by examining actual crime rates.

The fact that crime rates, and other internal conditions, do not fully explain differential patterns of perceptions across communities suggests a clear need for fresh frameworks to guide the analysis and interpretation of data. Our argument is that the most important undertheorized and empirically evaluated factors reflect external community conditions and the way these independently affect local safety and interconnect with internal neighborhood processes. Above we pointed to several types of external conditions that may be important in differentiating communities where residents feel safer from other areas: the social and economic character of surrounding neighborhoods; the extent to which businesses invest in and/or withdraw from the community; and the existence and nature of residents' connections with powerful politicians and government agencies. Scholars must articulate the relevant aspects of each of these, conceptualizing how the various dimensions interrelate with one another and with internal conditions in affecting communities, while also identifying any additional important external conditions.

With four cases, we were unable to integrate directly an external perspective into the above analysis. However, as noted, scholars have laid some foundation for anticipating a role for the characteristics we note. Further, descriptive data on some available indicators suggest important ways in which our four communities are indeed distinguished by external conditions. Regarding the socioeconomic character of surrounding areas, Pattillo-McCoy's study of "Groveland" (recall that this is a predominantly Black middle-class area) highlights the way this community faces unique risks (relative to most middle-class White neighborhoods) because of its close proximity to areas with higher levels of deprivation.[20] Neighborhoods clearly have permeable boundaries, and so Groveland is, to some degree, subject to the spillover of violence and other problems that result from greater disadvantage in nearby communities. Social relations also cross boundaries, particularly through links between young people attending the same high school. In Groveland, these foster a greater likelihood of risky behaviors including violence and, as such, may also make residents feel less safe. White middle-class communities are rarely in danger of these proximity effects. And, indeed, most have the advantage of relative distance from areas of urban disadvantage. The literature on concentrated disadvantage also indicates that African American poor neighborhoods are highly geographically concentrated, suggesting the possibility that they are more likely to be surrounded by extensive areas of poverty than is the case for poor White communities.[21]

Descriptive data for the four communities investigated here confirm the presence of such differential patterns of spatial proximity. Of the four neighborhoods, Taft Heights (the middle-class White area) has the lowest poverty rate (2.6 percent) *and* is surrounded by the lowest poverty areas.[22] The census tracts that border this community have an average poverty rate of 5.9 percent. This compares with a poverty population of 4.8 percent in Cosby Park, the middle-class Black community, and an average rate in the areas surrounding it of 11.8 percent—twice that of the tracts near Taft Heights. Moreover, all four of the areas that border Taft Heights have poverty rates below that in four of the five neighborhoods adjacent to Cosby Park.

The poor Black (King Town) and poor White (Joad Village) neighborhoods are obviously socioeconomically distinct from the two middle-class areas. However, they are more comparable to each other in both their own rates of poverty (29 percent and 24 percent, respectively) and those of the surrounding areas (on average, about 28 percent for each). Still, there is an important though subtle difference between these two localities. Notably, King Town is surrounded by a large number of disadvantaged, predominantly Black communities, and as such is part of Columbus's Black Belt. Only one of six bordering neighborhoods has low (9.7 percent) poverty (and it is an isolated low-poverty tract in this part of the city). By contrast, Joad Village is directly adjacent to just three census tracts, one of which has a notably lower poverty rate (13.8 percent) and itself flows into other, more advantaged tracts. Taken as a whole, these patterns of differential spatial proximity of advantage and disadvantage by race and class composition may be fruitful for explaining the differential role of the internal characteristics noted above. Future research will need to explore this possibility with a more comprehensive database.

It has been argued that the extent to which significant economic actors invest in (or withdraw from) communities helps to maintain the actual and perceived viability of areas. Vélez (in this volume) notes that variation in neighborhood viability has implications for social control in areas, which, in turn, affects how safe residents feel and how much crime they perceive. Thus, economic investments are a type of external condition that should be incorporated into community analyses of race, class, crime, and safety. Indicators of such investments that are available for neighborhoods throughout the country are the extent of residential loans and rates of denials of such loan applications.[23] The most striking observation regarding residential loans in 2000, across our four neighborhoods, is the dramatic influence of racial composition. Both of the African American neighborhoods have very high loan-denial rates; nearly half (47.1 percent) of loan applications in King Town are denied, as are over one-third (34.4 percent) of those in Cosby Park. Notably, this latter denial rate is higher than that for Joad Village, the *poor* White neighborhood, which has a rate of 28.0 percent. In contrast, one race-class type area is uniquely privileged in the loan market; the White and middle-class neighborhood of Taft Heights has a residential application denial rate of just 10.5 percent. Also of note, similar loan denial patterns prevail for the areas that border the different types of race-class neighborhoods; higher denial rates are evident in communities bordering Cosby Park (despite its middle-class status) and King Town, and particularly low denial rates are found near Taft Heights. These findings are consistent with the large literature on mortgage discrimination by race, although this literature does not address the race/class intersection.[24]

A third external factor that we suggest is important for understanding the effects of race and class composition, and their intersection, on communities is the extent and nature of connections with political and government agencies outside the neighborhoods. Here we are unable to provide specific indicators of such connections for the four communities examined in this chapter because data are hard to obtain. But the representation of residents as elected officials in city government, the strength of neighborhood associations and their connections with city agencies, and the numbers and extent of residents' ties with officials should all be considered as potential links that provide some communities with more favorable environments than others. These types of connections may also supply some areas with better knowledge and resources to combat local problems that make the area feel less safe and more crime ridden. Historically, White and middle-class neighborhoods have had the greatest power and connections to political and governmental officials. But increasing numbers of African American mayors, city council members, and the like (including in Columbus, where the mayor is Black and three of the seven city council members are African American) challenge us to explore more systematically and carefully how these factors are arrayed and differentially affect communities in contemporary U.S. society.

Evaluating the conceptual ideas set forth above will require investments in significant data collection that incorporates and expands upon the sample design used here. Our analyses uncovered important distinctions because we carefully chose Black and White neighborhoods that are as comparable as possible in their class composition. Significant findings in which the roles of internal neighborhood predictors are highly conditional by race and class structure may well have been missed in a general random sample of communities in which racial and class composition are simply statistically controlled.

Yet, it is important to move beyond studying only a few neighborhoods in a single city, however carefully chosen. Findings from such a small sample are only suggestive. Thus, we advocate expanding data collection to include larger samples of neighborhoods that are similarly situated along racial/ethnic and class lines, and that are embedded in a wider range of settings (e.g., areas outside of the Midwest, larger places, and smaller cities). The challenge, of course, is to identify appropriate samples in light of the rarity of predominantly White neighborhoods with large poor populations and minority communities with large middle-class populations. Successfully meeting this challenge will allow researchers to explore the generalizability of our patterns across varying urban contexts, and to assess how relationships compare for neighborhoods of multiple additional racial/ethnic makeups (e.g., Latinos and Asians). Broadening the samples in these ways will also help analysts avoid the pitfalls identified by Martinez and Nielsen and Vélez (in this volume) that are inherent in exploring Black and White neighborhoods alone.

An additional challenge will be to make sure that the variety of racially and economically distinct neighborhoods chosen have meaningful social boundaries. Utilizing census tracts to represent neighborhoods is convenient, but doing so compromises the meaningfulness of findings. One simple strategy for identifying "real" neighborhoods is to focus on geographic areas where the work of determining boundaries has already been done. For example, several researchers have worked extensively to identify neighborhoods in New York City and Chicago through an arduous process of interviewing local residents and observing physical boundaries.[25] For areas where this work has not been done, we recommend a two-fold process. Researchers should first identify potential racially and economically distinct neighborhoods in the areas of interest through an examination of census data. Next, they would decide upon neighborhood boundaries by carefully using Geographic Information Systems technology to take into account physical dividers such as parks, rivers, highways, major thoroughfares, and railroad tracks. Doing so should produce more meaningful definitions of local areas than the simple use of census tracts.

Here, we have attempted to set the stage for a new direction in research on perceptions of crime and safety among communities by demonstrating some ways that areas differentiated by race-class composition diverge in their views; highlighting some of the factors that influence these perceptions; and delineating critical steps that must be taken to advance research on this topic. These steps include purposive sampling, broader data collection across places and populations, and improved theorizing. Such goals will not be easy to achieve. Collecting data for a representative sample of individuals within a range of explicitly chosen types of race/ethnic-class communities across a variety of cities or metropolitan areas will require commitment of substantial resources. Developing appropriate conceptual tools (including identifying central explanatory factors and articulating their interrelationships) may require integrating multiple perspectives and collaborative efforts of individuals with diverse approaches.

Our own conceptual orientation has emphasized the potential importance of incorporating the role of external factors to help explain patterns like those we observe. Undoubtedly, colleagues drawing on different theoretical traditions can point to other potentially central, but unexplored, mechanisms to account for such patterning. We encourage them to do so (and to suggest strategies for addressing the difficult data problems). However, we argue that they must approach this endeavor with the conscious recognition that U.S. society is simultaneously structured by race/ethnicity *and* class, with perceptions (and levels) of crime and safety reflecting their interconnectedness. If we fail to take this into account, we risk that the resulting knowledge will make more obscure the meaning of race and class differences in perceptions, as well as the apparent safety-related actions taken by residents of different communities. To avoid this pitfall, we offer our work as a starting place for providing a nuanced understanding of how and why perceptions of crime and safety stem from the intersectionality of race/ethnicity and class in space.

NOTES

1. Sampson, Morenoff, and Gannon-Rowley 2002.

2. For example, see Lauritsen and White 2001; McNulty and Bellair 2003a, 2003b; and Sampson, Morenoff, and Raudenbush 2005 on race, ethnicity, and violence. For examples of general studies of neighborhood effects on crime, see Browning, Feinberg, and Dietz 2004; Lauritsen 2001; and Morenoff, Sampson, and Raudenbush 2001.

3. For example, Chiricos, Hogan, and Gertz 1997; Chiricos, McEntire, and Gertz 2001; Covington and Taylor 1991; Kanan and Pruitt 2002; Quillian and Pager 2001; Skogan 1990, 1995.

4. Krivo and Peterson 1996; McNulty and Holloway 2000; Sampson et al. 2005; Shihadeh and Shrum 2004.

5. Pattillo-McCoy 1999; see also Browning et al. 2004; Morenoff 2003; Morenoff et al. 2001.

6. For example, Chiricos et al. 1997, 2001; Covington and Taylor 1991; Liska, Lawrence, and Sanchirico 1982; Moeller 1989; Quillian and Pager 2001; Skogan 1990, 1995.

7. Covington and Taylor 1991; Kanan and Pruitt 2002; Perkins and Taylor 1996; Quillian and Pager 2001; Rountree and Land 1996; Skogan 1990.

8. For example, Kanan and Pruitt (2002) found no effects of various measures of social integration on multiple dimensions of fear of crime. In contrast, Rountree and Land (1996) demonstrated that greater social integration decreases perceived general risk of crime but increases fear of specific crimes.

9. Fischer et. al. 2004; Logan, Stults, and Farley 2004; St. John 2002; Wilkes and Iceland 2004.

10. Fischer 2003; Jargowsky 1996.

11. See Peterson and Krivo 2005 for a review of this literature.

12. When the communities were chosen, 2000 census data were not yet available. However, the descriptions below reflect their status in 2000 (U.S. Bureau of the Census 2002a) with comparisons to 1990 where noted (U.S. Bureau of the Census 1991).

13. Neighborhood names are pseudonyms.

14. To determine *neighborhood attachment,* respondents were asked, "If you could afford to spend twice as much money on housing, would you move to another neighborhood, move to another home in your neighborhood, or stay

in your current home?" Responses are grouped as a dummy variable in which 0 = resident would move to another neighborhood if s/he could afford to, and 1 = resident would *not* move out of the area even if s/he could afford to. *Social disorder* is an index comprised of measures of perceived problems with loud neighbors or noise, drinking in public, people selling or using drugs, and loitering teens. The *physical disorder* measure combines responses regarding the perceived extent of local problems with litter, graffiti, vacant houses or storefronts, broken windows, unkempt yards, and landlords who let property run down. *Social cohesion/control* is an index incorporating measures asking residents how close-knit the neighborhood is, whether or not people help their neighbors, how much neighbors can be trusted, and whether neighbors would stop children who were skipping school or doing graffiti. The *social ties/reciprocity* measure includes responses to questions about how often people visit in each other's homes or on the street, how often people watch over property when others are away, and how often people do favors for each other.

15. Sex is coded as 1 = female, 0 = male. Age is measured in years. Home ownership is a dummy variable coded as 1 = homeowner, 0 = nonhomeowner. Education is coded as the highest grade or year of school completed.

16. T-tests reveal that the differences in proportions between the middle-class and poor areas are significant for all three safety measures.

17. T-tests reveal that these proportions are significantly different.

18. T-tests reveal that these proportions are significantly different.

19. The 2000 total, violent, and property crime rates for Taft Heights were 49.31, 1.47, and 47.84, respectively. For Cosby Park these rates were 39.99, 3.59, and 36.4.

20. Pattillo-McCoy 1999.

21. Wilson 1987; Massey 1996; and Massey and Denton 1993.

22. All census tract poverty rates reported here are from U.S. Bureau of the Census 2002a.

23. Federal Financial Institutions Examination Council 2001.

24. For example, Ross and Yinger 2002; Yinger 1995;.

25. See Jackson and Manbeck 1998; Sampson, Raudenbush, and Earls 1997; and www.infoshare.org.

Chapter 14

Neighborhood, Race, and the Economic Consequences of Incarceration in New York City, 1985–1996

Alex R. Piquero, Valerie West, Jeffrey Fagan, and Jan Holland

Since the early 1990s, the United States has had an incarceration boom in terms of the number of inmates entering correctional facilities and the creation of new jails and prisons. Between 1995 and 2002, overall incarceration in the United States rose 3.6 percent to 2,033,331 inmates in jails and prisons.[1] The number of inmates in state prisons increased 2.9 percent to 1,209,640 during this time, and jail populations rose 4.0 percent to 665,475. As a result, the total incarceration rate per hundred thousand citizens went from 601 in 1995 to 701 in 2002. These increases took place during a time when serious violent and property crime rates both decreased significantly from the high levels of the mid-1980s.

This unprecedented increase in the use of incarceration has raised questions about its impact on reducing crime,[2] its intergenerational impacts on children and families,[3] and associated concerns about the prospects of newly released inmates avoiding crime and successfully returning to community life.[4] Several studies have shown that incarceration is concentrated among African Americans and Latinos;[5] suppresses earnings, especially for young African American males;[6] and, often, is a turning point that diminishes life prospects for stable marriage and employment.[7] Researchers now are examining the effects of the spatial concentration of incarceration, one of the byproducts of the imprisonment boom.[8] There has been both theoretical and empirical work on the unintended consequences of incarceration for individuals, families, and neighborhoods that experience the highest rates of incarceration.[9] This research suggests that there are unique effects of concentration beyond those from the aggregation of particular individuals within neighborhoods.

We are slowly learning that high rates of incarceration have negative consequences that offset their correctional benefits. However, research has not examined how these adverse effects are distributed across different racial and ethnic groups, or across neighborhoods whose racial composition varies. Much has been written about the mass incarceration of minorities *writ large*,[10] but prior work has not focused on the consequences of incarceration on aspects of neighborhood well-being, or on potential differences in impacts by race or ethnicity. Given the fact of racial residential segregation in most American cities and suburbs,[11] the intersection of the racial and spatial concentration of incarceration on minority citizens probably compounds the effects of incarceration on crime and other dimensions of social and economic well-being. In part, the concentration of incarceration is due to law enforcement policy choices, the concentrated drug enforcement in poor neighborhoods, and aggressive stop and frisk procedures.[12] Because of the way police allocate resources to neighborhoods, there are more Blacks and Hispanics in correctional institutions. This seems to hold true independent of differences in crime rates across racially distinct neighborhoods.

Recognizing that the community consequences of incarceration are racialized, research on the collateral outcomes of the interconnections among race, crime, and criminal justice should be keenly attuned to these race/ethnic differences in order to move the field forward. For the most part, conceptual and policy/descriptive analyses have been conscious of these differences, but empirical work has been severely limited. Indeed, no solid research has focused on the economic consequences of incarceration that affect not only individual residents but also the viability of neighborhoods themselves. This is one of the many "black holes" of criminological research, and this chapter takes a step to address this research gap.

Here, we examine the race-specific effects of incarceration on two specific dimensions of neighborhood well-being: median income and human capital. The research setting is New York City from 1985 to 1996, a period with a "perfect storm" of gun homicides, a drug epidemic, and very unstable employment patterns, all of which disproportionately affected minority citizens.[13] This chapter offers three specific contributions to our understanding of the effects of high rates of incarceration on neighborhoods. First, we examine whether incarceration exhibits negative effects on community well-being differentially among White, African American, and Hispanic areas. Second, we assess two dimensions of neighborhood economic well-being, median income and human capital, that are robust predictors of elevated crime. Third, we use a panel design to examine a period in New York City (1985–1996) that saw crime rates rise and then fall, while incarceration rates rose steadily in concentrated areas throughout the city. The chapter asks whether persistently high incarceration rates erode human capital and depress income, intensifying incarceration risks and threatening to create conditions where imprisonment and economic disadvantage become inherent features of certain neighborhoods. Importantly, we investigate this issue in a race/ethnic-specific manner. As our results reveal, the community consequences of incarceration, at least with respect to two economic outcomes, appear to be racialized.

Prior Research

Social scientists are only now beginning to investigate the effects of incarceration on communities for outcomes other than crime.[14] This first wave of studies suggests that incarceration affects individuals, families, and communities by increasing crime and decreasing economic stability, achievement, and family well-being. Several studies have examined one or more of these outcomes, but, importantly, none has disaggregated the effects of incarceration either by the race of the individual or by the racial composition of the neighborhood.

Incarceration and Crime

One of the first studies to show that incarceration is spatially concentrated and implicated in crime rates in communities was conducted for Tallahassee neighborhoods.[15] In this city, higher rates of *prison release* in one year were associated with higher community crime rates the following year. Also, low rates of prison admission had an uncertain impact on crime rates; moderate rates reduced crime, and higher rates increased crime. However, it is difficult to establish the causal order in this relationship because the high crime rates may have caused the high incarceration rates, particularly because the researchers failed to assess the impact of incarceration on community organization.

Another study examined the effects of neighborhood incarceration

rates on social organization in thirty Baltimore communities, and ultimately on crime.[16] First, they hypothesized that incarceration lessens the
capacity of communities to engage in social control. They found that
changes in neighborhood incarceration rates over time were not significantly associated with higher levels of collective efficacy. However, higher
incarceration was connected with less community solidarity.

Next, when researchers accounted for joint, but unmeasured causes of
prison admissions and crime, three specific findings emerged. First, they
demonstrated that more incarceration was associated with less neighborhood crime. Without this method, incarceration was positively associated
with crime. Second, reductions in neighborhood crime did not enhance
community organization and informal social control. Third, increases in
incarceration were associated with declines in some of the community
processes on which informal social control depends. Lynch and Sabol also
found that the positive effects of incarceration on informal social control/
collective efficacy continued to be significant, and the negative effects of
incarceration on community solidarity also held.[17]

Both the Tallahassee and Baltimore studies implicate incarceration as a
negative influence on community organization and informal social control. Rose and Clear hypothesized that concentrations of incarceration
may disrupt social networks and damage familial, economic, and political
sources of informal social control, mortgaging the community's social
capital and the social ties of persons living there (regardless of whether
they had been to prison). The perverse consequence of this damage may
be more, not less, crime.

The mechanism for the erosion of social capital is the dynamic of "coercive mobility," mobility induced by removal to and return from prison.[18]
Such mobility has long been implicated in higher crime in communities.[19] But Rose and Clear's recent contribution to this notion pinpoints
the mechanisms by which coercive mobility raises the risk of crime by
undermining the less coercive and more influential institutions of social
control, such as families, community associations, and a community's capacity to enforce norms to defend against crime.[20] These dynamics are
compounded systemically by the mobility of victims of crime who might
otherwise be participants in social regulation.[21] Thus, the churning effects of prisoners coming and going with limited job prospects may contribute to mobility in ways that increase the risks of crime. Finally, high
rates of incarceration may reduce incentives for citizens to participate in

informal social control by reducing the communicative value of sanctions, and delegitimizing law and legal actors, which invites further crime and intensifies the crime-enforcement-incarceration-crime cycle.[22]

Incarceration and Economic Well-Being

The prospects for stable employment and earnings of former inmates are dim.[23] As time spent in prison increases, the likelihood of disengagement from the legal economy increases.[24] One study found that, although growing levels of incarceration initially produced lower rates of conventional measures of unemployment, the recycling of ex-offenders back into the job market with reduced job prospects increased unemployment in the long run.[25] Further, serving time in prison is estimated to decrease levels of earnings by 10 to 30 percent, and to substantially diminish earnings growth.[26]

Incarceration not only lowers the work prospects of former inmates, but it has a corrosive aggregate impact on their neighborhoods.[27] In areas where former inmates are concentrated, individual barriers to meaningful employment for released prisoners and their peers may be compounded, further aggravating existing social and economic disadvantages.[28] This could become a collective problem if neighborhoods become stigmatized by high incarceration. Such stigmatization can complicate the ability of residents to access job networks to enter and compete in labor markets,[29] and deter businesses from locating in the areas.[30] Disruption of local networks of social control and economic activity can mean that, in the long run, incarceration will increase crime.[31] Finally, incarceration can affect the economic strength of a community by reducing the population that brings money to families and the neighborhood. As Lynch and Sabol argue, "[Incarceration] can also reduce the earning power of family left behind because they must tend to tasks formerly performed by the incarcerated family member."[32]

Incarceration and Family Integrity

Several writers have claimed that imprisonment damages human and social capital of the incarcerated, their families, and their communities.[33] For the most part, this line of theorizing and research has concentrated on individuals and families, but less on communities. However, community effects are evident in several studies. One ethnography of the social networks of Latino families and neighbors showed that incarceration weakens families by removing men from them, reducing the supply of marriageable men in the neighborhood, and, in turn, attenuating or skewing family formation toward unstable couplings.[34] The end result is that families may be less effective as socializing agents and less able to supervise teenagers.

Recent work with incarcerated males and the "fragile families" they leave behind suggests that imprisonment can disrupt family ties and social networks, aggravating vulnerabilities to crime through compromises to social control and, in turn, creating churning effects on social networks.[35] High rates of incarceration can destabilize crime networks and potentially introduce systemic violence associated with competition among crime groups for territory and market share.[36]

Some argue that incarceration contributes to the prevalence of Black families headed by single women.[37] Increases in incarceration of Black men were associated with about 20 percent of the increase in the number of Black families headed by single women during the 1980s.[38] Incarceration also tends to lessen the supply of marriageable men in inner-city ghettos and foster attitudes that are conducive to feeling little pressure to be married. As Wilson explains,

> Both inner-city black males and females believe that since most marriages will eventually break up and since marriages no longer represent meaningful relationships, it is better to avoid the entanglements of wedlock altogether.[39]

Current Focus

We are slowly learning that high rates of incarceration have negative consequences that may offset their correctional benefit. Incarceration is not simply a consequence of neighborhood crime, but instead may transform into an intrinsic part of the ecological dynamics of neighborhoods that actually elevate crime. Moreover, the spatial concentration of incarceration is believed to attenuate a neighborhood's economic fortune via at least four mechanisms:[40] (1) socially mediated processes that ensue from concentration effects such that ex-offenders find it difficult to forge links to legal work;[41] (2) compromises to social control that increase the number of single-parent households,[42] reducing the number of older males and straining citizens' relationships to law and social control; (3) depleting an area's social capital and further stigmatizing the community such that the economic life course of both ex-offenders and other residents is affected;[43] and (4) increasing voter disenfranchisement in poor, predominantly minority communities, which may adversely affect the political economy of neighborhoods.[44]

However, no work shows how these effects are distributed across different racial and ethnic groups, or across neighborhoods whose racial composition varies. Prior work has not focused on the consequences of incarceration on different dimensions of neighborhood well-being, or on how those impacts vary by race/ethnicity. Thus, much more work needs to be done on the effects of incarceration for smaller, community-level units like census tracts with particular attention to economic outcomes.[45]

We take steps in this direction by examining the effects of incarceration on income and human capital for census tracts in New York City over a 12-year period. We suspect that higher incarceration is associated with lower income and less human capital in tracts. Importantly, we also examine whether the hypothesized patterns operate differently across race. We suspect that incarceration has more and more rapidly occurring deleterious effects on income and human capital among minorities—especially Blacks—as compared to Whites. This acceleration effect probably emerges because of race-based preferences in the way some laws are enforced and the way police patrols are allocated to neighborhoods. Understanding how incarceration differentially influences groups is particularly important for assessing whether some groups are especially affected and hence need targeted policy responses.[46] Because evidence suggests that the growing social concentration of incarceration is tied to its spatial concentration in typically minority, poor, urban neighborhoods,[47] understanding the impact on local communities is central to understanding contemporary patterns of race and class inequality and the social problems of inner cities.[48]

Earlier work demonstrated that the spatial concentration of incarceration in New York City neighborhoods, its changes over time, and its sensitivity to drug enforcement, arrests, and incarcerations both for drug and nondrug crimes have long been spatially concentrated in the poorest neighborhoods.[49] During the mid-1980s in the heart of the city's incarceration run-up, just seven of fifty-five community board districts accounted for over 72 percent of all of the state's prisoners.[50] New York City's patterns of racial residential segregation all but ensure that the effects of racially skewed street-level police enforcement translate into racially and spatially concentrated incarceration in the poorest minority neighborhoods.

Herein, we present a race-specific analysis of the effects of incarceration on noncrime outcomes. First, we present baseline trends in race-specific incarceration and crime for New York City census tracts, 1985–1996. Then, our analyses examine the factors predicting median income and human capital, including race-specific prison and jail admissions, homicide victimization rates,[51] and variables that allow the influence of predictors to vary over time. Although our effort is a modest one, it provides the first empirical evidence of race-specific effects. We hope that this work spurs future studies to expand on our preliminary investigation.

Data

We used a longitudinal panel of incarceration and crime for New York City census tracts for 1985–1996 collected by Fagan and colleagues. These data include a 25 percent sample of all individuals sentenced to prison and a 5 percent sample of all jail sentences for cases with dispositions in New York City for the years 1985, 1987, 1990, 1993, and 1996. This yielded an annual sample of prison sentences of two to four thousand individuals, and an annual sample of jail sentences of three to four thousand persons. We obtained counts and locations of persons incarcerated in each year of the panel from the New York State Division of Criminal Justice Services, TRENDS file. Vital Statistics records on homicide victimizations for 1985–1996 were obtained from the New York City Department of Health, Vital Statistics. Drug arrest and other criminal history data were obtained from the New York State Division of Criminal Justice Services (DCJS). All other data are from the U.S. Bureau of the Census for 1980, 1990, and 2000. Census-tract equivalencies were developed to adjust for changes in census tract boundaries over time. Data for between-census years were linearly interpolated.

Variables

Two key outcomes are examined: median household income and human capital. Median income is race-specific, with household race reflecting that of the householder.[52] The human capital measure reflects both work experience and skills that tend to increase earnings among neighbor-hood residents.[53] Specifically, we combine measures of educational attainment (percent high school graduates), labor force participation (weeks worked by persons sixteen and over in the past year), and job skills (percent 16 and over with skilled occupations).[54] This conceptualization of human capital is similar to that found in other research.[55] We expect that higher incarceration is associated with lower median income and lower human capital over time.[56]

Race/ethnic-specific jail and prison incarceration rates represent our principal independent variables. The prison and jail admission records included the residential addresses of individuals along with their demographic (e.g., race, ethnicity) and case characteristics. The residential addresses for each prison or jail admission were geocoded and race/ethnic-specific counts were computed for all census tracts. These counts were converted to rates per hundred thousand race-specific tract population.

We also include factors that capture the level of neighborhood criminal/law enforcement activity. Unfortunately, spatially disaggregated data on felony crimes and arrests are not publicly available from New York's police department.[57] As one alternate measure of crime, we include homicide victimization.[58] On the basis of Vital Statistics records, victims' residential addresses were geocoded into spatial coordinates, assigned to census tracts, and aggregated to the tract level. Homicide rates per hundred thousand tract population for each year in the series were then constructed.

To address the theoretically significant contribution of drug enforcement to incarceration,[59] we constructed a time series on drug arrests as a measure of the intensity of drug enforcement.[60] Several studies provide evidence that drug arrests are reasonable proxies for overall drug enforcement and drug market activity.[61] The time series is based on drug arrest data for a 10 percent sample of drug arrestees charged with sale or possession of controlled substances, sale or possession of marijuana, or possession of drug paraphernalia from 1985 to 1996.[62] Each arrest record was geocoded to the residential address of the arrestee and then assigned to each census tract. Drug arrest rates per ten thousand tract population were calculated.

On the basis of data from the 1980, 1990, and 2000 censuses, we included a measure of social control/supervision that incorporates both the structural deficits of social areas and their dynamic processes of social control. This variable captures the density of supervision of young people within tracts, including (1) the concentration of the youthful population; (2) the percent of female-headed households with young children; and (3) the ratio of youth to adults. Finally, several control variables reflecting characteristics of the composition of the neighborhood are included: total tract population, percentage of the specific race/ethnic population, and the specific race-ethnic tract population greater than fifteen years of age.

Analytic Procedure

The data for all tracts within all years are combined into a single data set. Thus, the number of cases included equals the number of tracts times the number of years. To analyze these data, we use a model to account for the fact that observations for the same tract at different time points are not independent of one another. Specifically, we consider that the errors for observations that are closer in time are more highly correlated than those distant in time (i.e., an autoregressive process). In our multivariate analyses, we also specify a time trend in median income and human capital that is the same for all tracts. Further, we allow the effects of the other predictors to vary over the time period studied.[63]

Results

Descriptive Data

Table 14.1 shows trends in race-specific incarceration and crime in New York City census tracts between 1985 and 1996. For all three race/ethnic groups, prison admission rates peak in 1990 while jail admission rates peak in 1987. Importantly, African Americans and Hispanics have much higher rates of both jail and prison admissions than Whites/Others throughout the 12-year period. Of note, the Hispanic prison admission rate is always higher than the Black rate, while the inverse is true for jail admission rates. In short, the data in Table 14.1 show that prison and jail admission rates for the total population hide the large variation across race/ethnicity.

Regarding crime, misdemeanor arrest rates increase from 1985 to 1987, drop, and then rise to a high of 2,349 per ten thousand persons in 1996. The drug arrest rate, homicide victimization rate, and overall crime rate all increase up to 1990, at which point the homicide victimization and

TABLE 14.1
Trends in Race-Specific Incarceration and Crime, New York City Census Tracts, 1985–96

	1985	1987	1990	1993	1996
Prison Admission Rates*	134.4	186.0	262.5	245.2	194.5
Black	261.1	336.3	493.5	446.9	338.0
Hispanic	263.6	391.3	518.6	488.6	391.0
White and Other	22.7	24.9	25.9	23.1	19.9
Jail Admission Rates*	741.7	818.8	704.7	507.4	574.4
Black	1,486.0	1,578.5	1,351.5	946.1	1,160.4
Hispanic	1,329.4	1,575.9	1,263.6	907.2	914.6
White and Other	115.2	126.2	115.9	88.2	102.1
Misdemeanor Arrest Rate†	1767.7	1978.6	1620.1	1718.9	2349.9
Drug Arrest Rates†	77.7	109.2	110.5	88.8	128.6
Homicide Victimization Rate*	19.2	23.1	30.7	25.9	12.7
Crime Rate†	8,392.9	9,033.5	9,717.3	8,171.8	5,226.5

SOURCE: Criminal Justice Indicators, available at http://www.criminaljustice.state.ny.us. Prison and jail admissions are based on a 20 percent sample of prison admissions and a 5 percent sample of jail admissions.
  * Rate per 100,000 persons
  † Rate per 10,000 persons

overall crime rates drop sharply, while the drug arrest rate drops but picks up again in 1996.

Other descriptive data (see online technical appendix) indicate that there is a relationship between family poverty and prison sentences for African Americans and Hispanics in New York City for 1996. For both groups, areas with high percentages of families below poverty tend to have overrepresentations of prison sentences. The concentrations of African American and Hispanic incarceration in high-poverty neighborhoods also correspond with known patterns of racial residential segregation in New York City; the clusters of African American incarceration are in parts of New York City that are very heavily Black and the Hispanic incarceration clusters are found in areas that are predominantly Latino.[64]

Predictive Analyses

Next, we explore how race-specific incarceration rates in one year might predict tract-level median income and human capital in the following and later years within race/ethnicity, after accounting for the other important predictors (Table 14.2).

AFRICAN AMERICAN ANALYSES

As Table 14.2 shows, African American prison and jail admissions have deleterious consequences for neighborhood well-being. Higher African

American prison admissions are associated with lower median income among members of this group. Jail admissions among African Americans do not significantly predict median income. In contrast, higher jail *and* prison admissions are associated with lower levels of human capital. Regarding other factors, although a higher drug arrest rate is related to a higher median income, both the homicide victimization and drug arrest rates are associated with lower human capital. As expected, greater human capital means higher median income. Higher social control/supervision is associated with less median income but more human capital.

HISPANIC ANALYSES

Turning to the Hispanic-specific incarceration results, neither jail nor prison admissions significantly affect median income. Also, higher jail admissions among Hispanics are associated with lower human capital, a finding that was also true for African Americans. Both higher homicide-victimization and higher drug-arrest rates correspond to lower median income and human capital. As expected, greater human capital is associated with greater median income, while more social control/supervision is associated with greater median income and human capital.

TABLE 14.2

Race-Specific Effects of African Americans, Hispanics, and Whites/Other Incarceration on Median Income (MI) and Human Capital (HC): New York City Census Tracts, 1985–1996 (N = 9,855 tract-year combinations)

	African Amer.		Hispanics		Whites/Other	
	MI	HC	MI	HC	MI	HC
Intercept	−6.034*	−3.252*	11.035*	−2.399*	8.294*	−2.962*
Time	1.082*	0.076*	−0.026*	0.062*	0.233*	0.077*
Time^2	−0.013	0.000	−0.001*	0.000*	−0.001*	0.000*
Residual (Baseline Effects)	1.063*	1.030*	1.098*	1.036*	1.089*	1.030*
Tract Population (logged)	1.586*	0.398*	−0.125*	0.328*	0.167*	0.368*
Percent Race/Ethnic Specific Population	5.727*	0.324*	−0.643*	−1.452*	0.771*	0.059*
Race/Ethnic Specific Tract Population (> 15)	−0.001*	0.000	0.000*	0.000*	0.000*	0.000*
Race/Ethnic Specific Prison Admissions (lag)	−0.021*	−0.002*	0.001	0.000	0.001	0.001
Race/Ethnic Specific Jail Admissions (lag)	0.001	−0.001*	0.000	−0.000*	−0.001*	0.000
Homicide Victimization Count (lagged)	0.018	0.010*	−0.006*	−0.010*	−0.010*	−0.010*
Drug Arrest Rate (logged, lagged)	0.159*	−0.012*	1.098*	−0.009*	−0.013*	−0.013*
Human Capital	0.421*	NA	0.231*	NA	0.361*	NA
Social Control-Supervision	−0.404*	0.701*	0.072*	0.540*	−0.503*	0.635*
2 Log Likelihood	30066.0	−7699.5	−8909.5	−9046.0	−5042.2	−8438.5

* p < .05

NOTE: Models included interactions of all variables listed above with time. For Whites/Other, there are very few non-zero data points by tract and year for either jail (7.2%) or prison (8.2%).

WHITE/OTHER ANALYSES

Perhaps of greatest importance for Whites is that there are very few tracts within any year that have any Whites/Others admitted to jails (7.2 percent) or prison (8.2 percent). In other words, incarceration has not been applied extensively to Whites/Others in New York City. Nonetheless, one of the four incarceration effects is significant showing, that White/Other jail admissions are associated with reduced median income. Also, higher homicide-victimization and higher drug-arrest rates correspond to lower median income and human capital. As expected, greater human capital is associated with higher median income. More social control/supervision is associated with lower median income but higher human capital.

Discussion

This study builds on prior research examining the negative consequences of incarceration. However, unlike prior research, ours examined the *race-specific* effects of both jail and prison on *two measures of neighborhood well-being,* median income and human capital, over a 12-year period for New York City census tracts. Four key findings emerged.

First, for both jail and prison admissions, African Americans and Hispanics had exceedingly high rates of admissions compared to Whites/Others. Also, African Americans had higher jail admissions than Hispanics, but Hispanics had higher prison admissions than African Americans. Still, the key finding to emerge was the exceedingly low prison and jail admissions among Whites/Others. Second, we showed that nonetheless areas with higher White/Other jail admissions have lower median incomes. Neither jail nor prison admissions among Whites/Others influence levels of White human capital. Incarceration, then, does not appear to exert deleterious consequences among Whites/Others, at least with regard to the two measures of neighborhood well-being assessed herein. This may be due to the fact that so few areas have even one White/Other prison or jail admission in a year.

Third, African American prison admissions lead to lower median income, and both African American prison and jail admissions lead to lower human capital. Thus, the negative consequences of incarceration among African Americans appear quite pronounced in New York City between

1985 and 1996. Fourth, Hispanic jail admissions lead to lower human capital, but Hispanic prison admissions appear to do little to alter median income or human capital. This is true even though prison admissions for Hispanics are higher than for African Americans.

Though preliminary, our results are important because we took a new approach to studying the deleterious consequences of incarceration by conducting race/ethnic-specific analyses. Prior to this study, no research had examined how incarceration relates to neighborhood well-being across race/ethnicity. Further, we improved upon previous studies by exploring a local context *longitudinally*. The findings suggest some overall differences in the role of incarceration for neighborhood well-being, with its impact being especially important for African Americans. In short, our data suggest that the community consequences of incarceration, at least with respect to two economic outcomes, are racialized. At the same time, the questions posed and analyses presented open up several new avenues of research, theorizing, and data collection that should be undertaken to move this research agenda forward.

First, theory is needed to suggest how incarceration differentially influences local life chances of racial/ethnic groups through informal social control and/or opportunity structures. Second, data on incarceration, a broader array of indicators of neighborhood well-being, and individual perceptions are needed at the census tract (and block) levels to provide a foundation for better understanding the deleterious consequences of incarceration for overall communities, not just for the individuals that are incarcerated.[65] Third, studies are needed for other cities and types of places. To elaborate, one strength of our data is that they cover changes in one jurisdiction (New York City) for a 12-year period. This strength is also a weakness because New York City may be a particular and peculiar context. The 12-year period examined also suffers from some historical effects, namely, the rise and fall of the drug/crack trade. Additional studies should replicate our analyses using different cities and time periods.

Fourth, as with any analysis of this type, it is difficult to sort out causality. We attempted to minimize this problem as much as possible by selecting variables that may relate to either our key predictors or our outcomes. Still, further research using alternative statistical approaches (e.g., instrumental variables) must be undertaken. Fifth, our analysis did not examine how processes in one census tract may affect processes in neighboring areas. The importance of events in adjacent areas should be explored in future analyses of the localized spatial dynamics of incarceration (and crime). Finally, we only examined two measures of neighborhood well-being (income and human capital); clearly there are other outcomes such as neighborhood social interactions and collective efficacy that should be studied.

To conclude, our modest effort linking incarceration to neighborhood well-being in a race-specific fashion suggests that the effects of incarceration are not the same across race/ethnicity. Much as segregation leads to concentration effects for minorities that do not exist for Whites, mass incarceration produces negative economic consequences for communities, and these are especially potent for African Americans. Unless policy makers take action rather than simply watch things transpire, opportunities for entrance into the licit economy and meaningful work among Blacks in particular will continue to deteriorate, and the resulting negative consequences are likely to stack up for generations to come.

NOTES

1. Harrison and Beck 2003.
2. Spelman 2000.
3. Hagan and Dinovitzer 1999; LeBlanc 2003.
4. Visher and Travis 2003.
5. Mauer 1999.
6. Freeman 1996.
7. Sampson and Laub 1993.
8. Clear et al. 2003.
9. Lynch and Sabol 2004.
10. Mauer 1999; Tonry 1995.
11. Massey and Denton 1993; Logan, Stults, and Farley 2004.
12. Tonry 1995.
13. Karmen 2000.
14. Hagan and Dinovitzer 1999; Lynch and Sabol 2004.
15. Clear et al. 2003; Rose and Clear 1998.
16. Lynch and Sabol 2004.
17. Lynch and Sabol suggest that increases in incarceration encourage informal social control through mechanisms such as fear reduction. Because they failed to find that incarceration promotes interactions with residents, they suggest that the incarceration/informal social control linkage operates through individuals: "Residents may see or know of persons being incarcerated for crime, and this may increase their confidence in engaging in informal social control. They may feel

that the 'bad guys' are gone and that the criminal justice system is working with them to increase safety" (Lynch and Sabol 2004:24).

18. Lynch and Sabol 2004.
19. Shaw and McKay 1942.
20. Bursik and Grasmick 1993.
21. Dugan 1999.
22. Fagan and Meares 2000; Jackson 2001; Uggen and Manza 2002.
23. Fagan and Freeman 1999; Freeman 1996.
24. Freeman 1996; Grogger 1995; Hagan 1993.
25. Western and Beckett 1999.
26. Western 2002.
27. Western, Kling, and Weiman. 2001.
28. Ibid.:414.
29. Granovetter 1973, 1974.
30. Granovetter 1974.
31. Lynch and Sabol 2004.
32. Ibid.:273.
33. For example, Hagan and Dinovitzer 1999:122.
34. LeBlanc 2003; see also Wilson 1996.
35. McLanahan and Bumpass 1998; McLanahan and Sandefur 1994.
36. Curtis 1998.
37. Myers 2000.
38. Sabol and Lynch 2003.
39. Wilson 1996:104.
40. Fagan, West, and Holland 2003.
41. Hagan and Palloni 1990.
42. Hagan and Dinovitzer 1999.
43. Hagan 1993.
44. Thompson 2002.
45. Fagan et al. 2003; Lynch and Sabol 2004.
46. Western et al. 2001:416.
47. Sampson and Wilson 1995.
48. Western et al. 2001:425.
49. Fagan et al. 2003.
50. New York City Department of Planning 2003.
51. See Maltz 1998.
52. A uniform measure of median income by race is not available across all census years: 2000 census median income is measured as median household income by race of householder reporting one race alone; 1990 median income by race is measured as the midpoint of the census income category that at least half the households fall in by race of householder summing across income categories;

1980 median income by race is measured as the midpoint of the census income category that at least half the families fall in by race of householder summing across income categories.

53. Becker 1991.

54. The index was derived from principal components factor analysis.

55. Sanders and Nee 1996.

56. Because crime and incarceration are highly correlated over time, we used a measure of the tracts' joint propensities for both crime and incarceration at the outset of the time series. We estimated a regression equation to account for these differences in intercepts (starting points) for each tract at the baseline year in the time series, and used the unstandardized residuals from this model as a proxy for differences in tract risk. Census tracts varied at the outset of the study period in rates of incarceration and crime, and the trajectories of tracts were obviously influenced by their starting points. Failing to account for these propensities would bias estimates of the effects of incarceration over time. An initial analytic step was to develop parameters that would account for these differences and to control for such differences in explaining trajectories of incarceration over time. We used Ordinary Least Squares (OLS) regression models on the baseline (1985) panel to estimate the incarceration propensities of tracts based on their crime and social structural indicators, and included these propensities in later models of the effects of incarceration over time. We used the standardized residuals from these models as the measure of incarceration propensity, and included these residuals in the subsequent analyses.

57. Beginning in 1994, the New York City Police Department launched a computerized crime mapping system, COMPSTAT. Crime data before that date cannot be located to specific addresses other than through manual geocoding of complaint and arrest records, or manual coding of the records of arrestees. Even after the launch of COMPSTAT, these data were unavailable for research purposes, but were used internally for strategic analysis of enforcement practices.

58. Maltz 1998, 1999.

59. Tonry 1995.

60. Baumer et al. 1998.

61. Baumer et al. 1998; Ousey 1999; Rosenfeld and Decker 1999.

62. See Fagan and Davies 2002.

63. We included interactions of time with all the predictors as a way to examine changes in the effects of each variable over time. However, any interpretation of these interactions should be approached with caution. There were dynamic changes in New York City during the study period that were not included in these analyses, including changes in the demography and housing markets of the city. These unobserved variables are potential influences over time on the economic conditions of the city's neighborhoods that would compete with incarceration or law enforcement to change their economic fates. Therefore, we are concerned

about the possibility of biases from omitted variables in the meaning of time as the effects of increasing property values steadily increased. Their effects over time on the observed variables would complicate any interpretation of the time interactions with the observed variables.

64. Logan and Mollenkopf 2004. The online technical appendix with maps illustrating these relationships can be viewed at http://cjrc.osu.edu/race/bookappendix2006. These maps are also available from the authors upon request.

65. Lynch and Sabol 2004.

Part IV

Mechanisms and Processes

Chapter 15

Creating Racial Disadvantage
The Case of Crack Cocaine

Doris Marie Provine

Scholars concerned with the persistence of racial disadvantage have focused much attention on street-level bureaucrats in the criminal-justice
system. Police, prosecutors, and criminal-court judges deserve critical attention because they make policy at a day-to-day level. But it is important
to avoid the trap of assuming that these are the only relevant actors. Those
who initiate and frame the legislative process may also create racial disadvantage by their actions. Racism should be a focus for scholarly attention not just at the retail end of the policy process but also at its point of
origin.

This chapter focuses on policy formation by elites in the context of the
federal initiative against crack cocaine. In 1986, Congress set a five-year
minimum prison term for first-offense trafficking of five grams of a mixture containing cocaine base (that is, crack); the legislation set a ten-year
minimum for those caught selling fifty grams. In 1988 Congress criminalized possession of crack, creating a five-year mandatory prison term for
first offenders with five grams of a mixture containing cocaine base. Both
penalties are vastly disproportionate to what offenders receive for other
drug violations. Possession of any amount of any other drug can result in
no more than a year in prison. Trafficking the pharmacological equivalent
to crack, powder cocaine, requires a hundred times as much of the drug.
Congress intended, and law-enforcement agencies received, a powerful
message: focus as many resources as possible on crack cocaine arrests,
including arrest and prosecution of small-time users and sellers.[1]

The disastrous consequences of this policy for poor, urban minorities, particularly young African American males, are well known and have

received much critical comment. African Americans, who constitute only about 12 percent of the U.S. population, now comprise over 50 percent of new prison admissions, a rate of incarceration 8.2 times that of Whites. Drug arrests are a major contributor to this racial skew. African Americans constitute 63 percent of those sent to state prisons for drug offenses; in two states, they make up over 90 percent of new admissions. At the federal level, over 90 percent of those convicted for using or selling crack are African American. There are more African Americans in prison, for longer terms, than at any time in our nation's history.

Some observers see this build-up as evidence of a new American stance toward the underclass—a lock-away policy for minorities that helps to sustain a huge and growing White-dominated prison-industrial complex.[2] At the very least, this build-up is evidence of widespread tolerance for racial disadvantage and neglect. Prison has become a way station to adulthood in some poor urban communities. Despite the widespread perception that the war on drugs has failed, extraordinarily harsh penalties for possession and sale of crack appear to be a permanent part of the political landscape, particularly at the federal level, where the costs of incarceration are of little concern compared to the symbolism of being "tough" on crime.

What responsibility, if any, do policymakers have to avoid racial disadvantage when they design criminal-justice initiatives like this one? Do they acquire a responsibility to act when the racial implications of their policies become obvious? Definitive answers to such questions reach beyond the competence of the social sciences, but they suggest an appropriate ambit for scholarly concern. How, for example, do well-placed advocates shape public attitudes toward social problems? Why are public resources committed so heavily to punitive approaches that particularly affect Blacks and other already disadvantaged populations?

Appropriate analytical tools include legislative history and institutional analysis. It is crucial to examine the way issues get framed by policy-making elites and their supporters in the media. Focusing on the rhetorical presentation of issues helps to show what political interests are served by particular approaches and how options become limited. Scholars must take account of the important role that unconscious racism plays in motivating policy choices. It is safe to assume that participants will never openly express racial bias, nor experience it as a conscious state of mind. We live in a post–civil rights era in which it is no longer permissible to seek racial disadvantage through law. Indeed, the United States has gone further and expressed its commitment to racial diversity. Many people, including many policymakers, embrace that ideal. It would be naïve, however, to assume that racial stereotypes and biases have suddenly disappeared from the American scene after centuries of oppression. Criminologists have not made this assumption when they study policy implementation. Until there is reliable evidence to the contrary, we should assume that policy-making elites labor under the same racial misunderstandings and biases as street-level bureaucrats.

The goal of the analysis that follows is to encourage critical, race-sensitive thinking about the policy-making process. The crack cocaine saga is an appropriate illustrative case because the racial impact of the policy is clear. But this case should by no means be considered unique. In a nation divided by race, policy initiatives inevitably instantiate racial disadvantage unless they address the issue straightforwardly (which seldom happens). Here, I hope to provoke other studies that focus on the way negative racial stereotypes animate policy thinking and influence policy choices to the disadvantage of subordinate populations in our society.

My strategy divides the problem into two parts. The first section deals with the media and political interests who found common cause in portraying crack as a drug demanding harsh criminal controls. This alliance worked many times in the past to encourage punitive sanctions for illicit drug use by demonizing drug users. Crack proved an especially potent symbol because of its association with dangerous people, namely, young, unemployed, urban Black males. The second major section of the chapter focuses on congressional responses to this "new" drug. The crucial question is, What must Congress have been thinking when it enacted uniquely harsh penalties for crack offenses?

Racial Symbolism and the Rise of Crack

Drug use poses particular challenges to those seeking repressive controls. Illicit drug use is typically consensual, and tends to be a rather private activity. Moral entrepreneurs must work hard to create the sense of public unease and fear required to enact strong criminal controls. They must construct a frightening "other"—sullen, defiant, dangerous, and cut off from legitimate society—who responds only to the threat of a long prison term. The solution for over a century has been to link drug use to particular subordinated and distrusted populations in our society. Prohibition of alcohol, for example, became a matter for criminal legislation, rather than exhortation, only after it became linked to non-native-born Whites in the North and Blacks in the South.[3] Stereotypes about Chinese opium eaters, Mexican marijuana smokers, and Negro cocaine fiends have been crucial to the success of campaigns to criminalize these drugs. The media have played a facilitative role in this process, spreading a racialized picture of drug dangers without carefully looking into the matter.

The rise of concern about crack cocaine in the 1980s has strong elements connecting it to prior campaigns to criminalize the use of mind-altering drugs. This time, however, the negative racial images were covert. The demographics of crack made it easy to portray crack as a "Black" drug without sounding racist because the most visible sales occurred in Black urban ghettos, and the most visible sellers were Black. Timing also helped the case for strong criminal controls. Public opinion about drugs and crime was hardening in the 1970s, and by the 1980s the tenor of public debate had moved from deterrence to retribution. Between 1975 and 1989, the average prison term for violent crimes tripled. To be tough on crime became a political necessity.[4]

The Political Foundation for a War on Crack Cocaine

When the Reagan administration took office in 1980, it was not clear what drug would carry the most weight in the public mind. The administration, at the urging of parent groups, first focused on the problem of youthful marijuana smoking.[5] But patterns of drug use were changing. Marijuana use had been on the decline since the late 1970s, while cocaine was once again becoming fashionable, largely because prices were falling precipitously. By 1984, cocaine was cheap enough to be affordable to even the poor and homeless, and its purity had increased enough to make it smokeable. It was at about this time that crack, a solidified version of powder cocaine, was invented. Mixing powder cocaine with baking soda and water and heating the mixture in a microwave oven created a solid mass that could be smoked. "Rocks" of cocaine were easy to transport and sell in small quantities for a short, but intense, high. This new concoction was instantly popular among inner-city drug users.

President Reagan was determined to put drug dealing on the public agenda, not because it was popularly perceived as a serious threat at the time but because of the political message it communicated. A punitive drug war would play well among middle-class suburban voters concerned that their children might be attracted to drugs. The human costs of enforcement would be borne by people with whom they did not identify or sympathize. Religious conservatives found recreational drug use sinful. Newly powerful in Republican politics, they were anxious to strike a blow for moral responsibility and against the loosened moral standards of the 1960s. A new war on drugs would support and expand the Republican Party's post-Watergate base, which included both fiscal and moral conservatives.

Reagan appealed to his base by stressing individual responsibility for moral choices and downplaying structural factors at play in unemployment, urban decay, and other human troubles. It was easy to blame urban ills on crack and to demonize crack dealers as a scourge to civilization, threatening productive elements of society—a pattern familiar from previous drug wars. The strategy involved attacking policies targeted toward Blacks and minorities, without reference to race, but in a way that would polarize the electorate along racial lines. In retrospect, it is clear that crack was, in Reinerman and Levine's words, "a godsend to the Right," serving as "an ideological fig leaf to place over the unsightly urban ills that had increased markedly under Reagan administration social and economic policies."[6]

President Reagan invested heavily in the antidrug strategy. On October 28, 1986, he signed the $1.7 billion "Drug-Free America Act." The president's new drug czar, William Bennett, announced that prison capacities would be doubled and users, as well as dealers, would be incarcerated. A second, even more expensive spending bill was adopted just before the 1988 election. Democrats, on the defensive, competed with Republicans to be tough on drug crime.

The Federal Role in Fomenting the War on Crack

Federal officials actively encouraged the media to focus attention on crack as a drug arising from the Black urban ghetto that threatened the entire population. Government also benefited from the media's fascination with this new threat. The National Institute for Drug Abuse carried out an active campaign in 1986 to "increase public awareness" of the drug problem, offering public service announcements, news releases, and "ride alongs" on federal drug busts. The Drug Enforcement Administration's

New York representative, Robert Stutman, gave hundreds of interviews to encourage media interest: "I began a lobbying effort and I used the media. The media were only too willing to cooperate, because as far as the New York media was concerned, crack was the hottest combat reporting story to come along since the end of the Vietnam war." All of the major networks followed the reports of these agencies closely in their news programs.[7]

Katherine Beckett demonstrated the extent of government influence on media coverage of drug issues in the Reagan period by analyzing "interpretative packages" in television stories between 1982 and 1991. She found that most stories had their basis in government information, such as footage provided for the media by law-enforcement organizations. These stories tended to be more favorable to escalating the effort than those produced through private sources:

> The ascendance of the discourse of law and order in the news . . . was largely a consequence of officials' capacity to call attention to and frame discussions of the crime and drug issues. Conservative politicians and law enforcement personnel were particularly successful in defining themselves as the relevant "authorities" on the crime and drug issues.[8]

The tone of this coverage became increasingly moralistic and dramatic over time. It included many misleading and inaccurate claims about an "epidemic" of drug use, about crack as a violence-inducing drug, and about pathetic "crack babies" destined to struggle with addiction. The cocaine-related deaths of two Black celebrity athletes, Len Bias and Don Rogers, in the spring of 1986, precipitated more media attention. Crack was initially (incorrectly) blamed for both fatalities.

The extent to which government officials would go to promote the idea that itinerant crack dealers posed an imminent threat to the nation was illustrated in 1989 when newly elected President Bush, in a television address, dramatically held up a bag of crack he claimed had been bought in Lafayette Park, directly across from the White House. The clear implication was that it was for sale everywhere. President Bush stated, "It's turning our cities into battle zones, and it's murdering our children." The truth was that federal agents could not find anyone in the park selling crack. They had been forced to ask a local Black drug dealer to come there to make the sale; they gave him directions to Lafayette Park, paid him $2,400, and let him go.[9] The strategy was nevertheless successful. By September 1989, shortly after President Bush's speech, 64 percent of respondents to a New York Times/CBS News poll labeled drugs the nation's most important problem. In January 1985, only 1 percent had that opinion.[10]

Reading the Legislative Mind

Congress immediately embraced the sensationalized approach the media had taken toward crack. The metaphors of cancer, wildfire, and epidemic that had been effective in arousing public concern were also useful in justifying strong legislative action. The pumped-up, fear-inducing rhetoric, however, did not square well with the facts. Crack smoking never held much appeal beyond the ghetto. Sellers lacked the social capital to move into suburban areas. And even in ghettoized areas, crack had limited, and declining, appeal. Regular use rates were less than 1 percent throughout this period, and monthly use rates were less than 2 percent and declining through the late 1980s. The people who did use crack regularly tended to be those who were also attracted to heroin and other harmful drugs.[11]

In establishing special mandatory minimums for offenses involving crack cocaine, Congress was competing with the White House to put its own stamp on the problem of drug abuse. The two branches did not disagree, however, on the basic evil: drug dealers from the urban ghetto spreading the "cancer" of crack to the larger society. They also had consensus on the appropriate means for attacking the problem: tough criminal penalties for these recalcitrant members of the underclass. The idea that drug dealers might themselves be victims of the drug they were selling did not receive any attention.

Were members of Congress aware that they were attacking a racially specific target in setting particularly harsh criminal penalties for crack-cocaine offenses? The 1986 and 1988 Anti–Drug Abuse Acts are famous for their draconian mandatory minimum sentences for sale and possession of small amounts of crack. Virtually everyone has heard that sale of crack cocaine is punished one hundred times as severely as sale of powder cocaine. But the etiology of this legislation is not well understood. Members of Congress vehemently deny any racist leanings in voting for these penalties. The public record reveals no crude racial stereotypes or slurs. The effort was bipartisan and the legislation passed by wide margins.

Some members of the Black Congressional Caucus voted for the mandatory minimums.

Any inquiry into the emotional state of a legislative body is bound to be risky and filled with imprecision. Congress is a complex institutional actor, leaving behind only indeterminate signs of its motivation and decision-making processes. Members of Congress passed the 1986 legislation less than five weeks after initiating its effort, leaving few traces of their thinking. Congress held no committee hearings, hosted no major debates, and produced no reports justifying its action. News articles, rather than debate, fill most of the relevant pages of the *Congressional Record.* The speeches that were published are full of self-congratulation about the bipartisan spirit of the effort. The record is hardly more robust for the adoption of the 1988 law that penalized simple possession of five grams or more of crack.

There are, nevertheless, many clues about congressional intent in this record. The fact that this large body was in virtual unanimity in setting especially harsh penalties for crack is significant, revealing a common mindset. Another indication of what Congress was thinking comes from the published material members inserted into the record. A third indication of Congressional beliefs about crack lies in the remarks of members themselves. Those who expressed most alarm about crack received support from other members; the few with critical observations were ignored.

This section presents evidence that Congress knew it was going after a poor and largely Black population in criminalizing small-scale sales and possession of crack cocaine. Congress was also aware that many of those slated for punishment were addicted to the drugs they were selling. Congress knew that crack cocaine was part of a thriving drug business in poor non-White areas of big cities, made possible by the buying power of rich White areas. It was aware that drug sellers who were arrested would probably be replaced by other unemployed, undereducated youth without prospects for decent employment. It knew that few White middle-class purchasers would be affected by its new mandatory minimums.

The 1986 Anti–Drug Abuse Act

On September 8, 1986, Representative James Claude Wright of Texas introduced HR 5484 to the House of Representatives. Members of Congress were enthusiastic in their endorsement, hailing it as a significant bipartisan effort to deal realistically with the perceived crisis in illicit drug use through interdiction, education, rehabilitation, and increased spending on law enforcement. New criminal penalties for trafficking crack cocaine were a very small part of this bill. They were noncontroversial. The little debate that occurred focused on a proposed death-penalty provision for drug dealers and creation of an overarching "drug czar" to manage the federal government's efforts in this area. Less than two months after it was introduced, President Reagan signed into law the 1986 Anti–Drug Abuse Act.[12]

Most of the short lifetime of this bill was spent within House Committees, though there were some brief exchanges in both chambers. Many of the remarks were self-congratulatory, thanking members for their bipartisan leadership. There were a few criticisms. And reports were entered into the record indicating how politicians like Senator Moynihan debunked the argument that crack causes crime, calling it a scapegoat:

> If we blame crime on crack, our politicians are off the hook. Forgotten are the failed schools, the malign welfare programs, the desolate neighborhoods, the wasted years. Only crack is to blame. One is tempted to think that if crack did not exist, someone somewhere would have received a Federal grant to develop it.[13]

This observation was ignored in subsequent discussion, though Senator Evans criticized the rush to legislate and suggested that the crisis had been overdrawn. Representative Barney Frank of Massachusetts was the most critical: "I am afraid that this bill is becoming the legislative equivalent to crack. It is going to give people a short-term high, but it is going to be dangerous in the long run to the system and expensive to boot."[14] These concerns were brushed aside in an atmosphere of overwhelming accolades. New York Representative James Scheuer, for example, described it as "a great bill" and praised the "great consensus" on which it was built.[15]

The new law created a five-year minimum prison term for first-offense trafficking of five grams of a mixture containing cocaine base (crack) and a ten-year minimum for fifty grams. As Table 15.1 indicates, these thresholds were much more stringent than for most of the other drugs listed in the penalty section of the new legislation. The difference among penalties was alluded to only once, by one of the prime movers in the enactment process, Florida Senator Lawton Chiles. In a September 26 speech,

TABLE 15.1
Five- and Ten-Year Federal Prison Terms for Varying Amounts of Illegal Drugs[a]

Substance	At least 5 years of imprisonment	At least 10 years of imprisonment
Marijuana	100,000	1,000,000
Cocaine or derivatives	500	5000
Heroin	100	1000
PCP	10	100
N-phenyl-N	40	400
Cocaine base	5	50
Methamphetamine	5	50
LSD	1	10

[a] Mixture amounts in grams.

he expressed his appreciation for the Senate's recognition of crack's dangerousness:

> Those who possess 5 or more grams of cocaine freebase will be treated as serious offenders. Those apprehended with 50 or more grams of cocaine freebase will be treated as major offenders. Such treatment is absolutely essential because of the especially lethal characteristics of this form of cocaine. Five grams can produce 100 hits of crack. Those who possess such an amount should have the book thrown at them.[16]

No one took issue with this sentiment or with Chiles's pharmacological assertions. The small African American representation in the House was mixed in its assessment, with eleven of the House's twenty-one African American members voting in favor of HR 5484. No one addressed the sentencing issue directly for the *Congressional Record*. New York Representative Charles Rangel was an active supporter of the legislation as a whole; others were silent.

Congress had clearly made up its mind about crack before the bill came up for discussion in September, but it did so with little indication of serious discussion. The words "crack" or "cocaine" did not appear at all in the *Congressional Record* until March 21, 1986. The crack issue then enters the *Record* mostly through news articles and brief speeches by a few members of Congress in connection with bills they were sponsoring. The news sources posted to the *Record* vary from nationally focused media, including *Newsweek* and the *New York Times,* to more locally oriented outlets like the *Palm Beach Post and Evening Times.* The first clear indication of concern was a hearing on "The Crack Cocaine Crisis" in July. This hearing included a lengthy testimonial from a young woman recovering from addiction to a combination of crack and Valium, but did not range very far into the extent and seriousness of the crack cocaine problem.

The news articles members of Congress submitted for the *Record*, however, tell a much more compelling tale. They are uniform in describing crack cocaine in alarming terms, e.g., "Men have given up their paychecks. Women have prostituted themselves. Children have stolen from their parents. . . . Cocaine rocks have turned thousands of Floridians into addicts whose cravings are so strong, that, for some, crime becomes the only way to support their habit."[17] Crack was treated as cheap, instantly addictive, and devastatingly destructive.

There is a racial subtext to many of these stories. While Congress apparently believed that all classes and racial groups were vulnerable to crack abuse, it knew that the Black urban underclass sold the drug, and it apparently did not care why. Even the fact that many dealers were themselves addicted to crack failed to move advocates of harsher penalties.

Looking at the material that members of Congress inserted in the *Congressional Record* to inform themselves about the extent of the drug problem reveals three racially inflected themes. These three issues were reiterated in various news publications submitted to the *Record* in the months preceding passage of the 1986 law:

1. Crack is moving out of the ghetto and into the suburbs:
   - "Even though sellers usually set up shop in predominantly Black neighborhoods, their customers tend to be white. The ability to sell cocaine in rock form has lowered the price to where it is affordable to the middle class."
   - "Street sales of cocaine rocks have occurred in the same neighborhoods where other drugs were sold in the past: run-down Black neighborhoods . . . but the drug market is also creeping into other neighborhoods. . . . Less than a block from where unsuspecting white retirees play tennis, bands of young Black men push their rocks on passing motorists, interested or not. 'Rock houses' where the drug is sold but not smoked also are appearing in all kinds of neighborhoods."
   - "Crack has captured the ghetto and is inching its way into the suburbs. . . . The police are losing the war against crack, and the war is turning the ghettos of major cities into something like a domestic Vietnam."

2. While users are (now) of all races, crack dealers are generally Black:
   - "Most of the dealers, as with past drug trends, are Black or Hispanic, police said. Haitians also comprise a large number of those selling cocaine rocks, authorities said. . . . Whites rarely sell the cocaine rocks."
   - " 'I got some ear ring. You know, make yo' ears ring. It so good. . . . We goin' to smoke 'em good. Get you high. . . . Hey, you want girls, I'll get you girls, Black girls . . . I swear. I ain't jivin' you.' For the growing numbers of the white middle class who have become hooked on cocaine rock, buying the drug can be like stepping into a foreign culture."
   - "Although police said most dealers are Black, cocaine rocks are sold in all types of neighborhoods by all types of people."
   - "Dealers—'ounce men' as they are known in LA—organize small cells of pushers, couriers and lookouts from the ghetto's legion of unemployed teenagers."
   - "West 107th Street in Manhattan is a fringe neighborhood populated by low-income Blacks and Hispanics—and one of New York's open-air drug markets. . . . West 107th Street sees a steady stream of limos, taxis, and out-of-state cars. 'Sometimes you get the impression we're in New Jersey,' says Deputy Inspector Frank Bihler. . . . He jokes about blowing up the bridges and tunnels to keep the suburbanites out."

3. Crack is beginning to ruin the lives of the productive (mostly White) classes, including promising, college-bound youth:
   - "So the pretty young girl with dirty-blonde hair, deep blue eyes and a model's figure says she started stealing. She needed money to buy the rock."
   - "Art F was a 40ish San Francisco lawyer when cocaine took over his life. . . . He smoked $1000 worth of rock a day. Somewhere along the way he lost his wife, his two children and his Marin County home."

Noteworthy in these articles and in the remarks of members of Congress is the prevalence of testimonial evidence and the absence of any grounding of drug concerns in history or in the nation's experience with control of illicit drugs. Statistics are occasionally noted for shock purposes, but with no effort to appreciate the limitations of the data or its long-term significance. Medical evidence is virtually absent; the claim that crack is instantly addictive is taken for granted.

This disdain for evidence and critical reflection before the imposition of serious criminal penalties represents a failure in the democratic process. Most troubling is the framing of willful (generally Black) sellers and help-less (potentially White) users. The sellers—typically poor, without job skills, and often addicted—are presumed to be free to desist from the ugly business of drug dealing at any time. Their failure to do so is a legitimate cause for harsh criminal penalties. The drug buyer who drives to the ghetto from New Jersey in a limo or taxi, on the other hand, is morally blameless. The law set aside significant funds for their treatment.

More of the Same: The 1988 Anti–Drug Abuse Act Criminalizes Possession

Congress revisited drug policy in 1988, a period of urban violence, much of it associated with gang conflicts over drug profits. The 1988 legislation was, again, an omnibus affair. It contained more mandatory minimum penalties for drug offenses. The penalty most relevant for this discussion is for simple possession of cocaine base, with no evidence of intent to sell. A first-time offender, under the new law, receives at least five years in federal prison. This severe penalty is out of keeping with others in the federal system. Possession of any amount of any other drug can yield a maximum of one year in prison.

The new mandatory minimums came out of floor negotiations; the original bill did not contain them. Proponents cited the growing supply of crack, its harmfulness, and its links to violent crime, particularly gang-related crime. Creating penalties for possession, it was hoped, would help police officers catch traffickers. Anyone who possessed five grams, the legislators reasoned, might well be a trafficker.

The issue of mandatory minimums was somewhat more controversial in 1988. In both the House and Senate, some members questioned the wisdom of this approach, particularly in light of the guidelines approach to sentencing that Congress had embraced in establishing the Federal Sentencing Commission. Mandatory minimums were a blunt tool entirely out of keeping with this approach. Nevertheless, both the House and Senate passed the new legislation by large margins. The Black Congressional Caucus, once again, played a low-key role. It did not oppose this legislation.

Crack and Moral Panic

The "crack attack" that stirred Congress to enact harsh mandatory minimum sentences for possession and sale of small amounts of crack cocaine
was a moral panic. Moral panics create "folk devils," elements in society
who are stripped of all favorable characteristics and blamed for the condition. These harm-causing characters are selfish and evil; they must be
stopped.[18] In the epidemic of concern over crack, the folk devil was the
drug dealer, and to some extent, the drug itself. The media and political
leaders helped to create this panic and to focus it on ghetto drug dealers.
The press, as Reinerman and Duskin observe, developed "a cultivated in-
capacity for understanding drug problems" that fostered false stereotypes
about drug dealing and tended to support endless drug wars.[19] Officials
made the war metaphor work by locating the enemy in the disreputable
elements of society, and by promising victory. They generated comforting
feelings of solidarity by appealing to collective concerns with "our children," "our cities" and "our values."[20]

Drug scares pay handsome political benefits by focusing public attention on drugs and justifying government action. The passions surrounding alcohol prohibition helped elect presidents and assisted the White
South in disenfranchising its African American citizens. In the 1930s,
Harry Anslinger rose to political power, and stayed there for over thirty
years, by saying frightening things about drugs. Modern presidents, beginning with Richard Nixon, have also discovered the benefits of drug
scares because they allow conservative officials to blame the poverty and
despair of some segments of society on personal failure, rather than lack
of opportunity. That illicit drugs tend to be most visible in the poorest
neighborhoods of our nation only reinforces the point. Every president,
Franklin Zimring and Gordon Hawkins note, acts confident that the problem can be eradicated with enough law-enforcement effort; they describe
this unreasonable (but self-serving) optimism as "an amnesia that seems
to affect political leaders in regard to drug control."[21]

Race has framed every moral panic over drug use in the United States,
including concerns the American colonists expressed about the use of alcohol by their Indian neighbors. Race has always helped White Americans
determine which drugs will be considered dangerous and which will be
accepted as a normal part of society, regardless of their cost in death and
disability.[22] Race is an essential ingredient in the rhetoric of danger and
disrespect for middle-class norms that stirs up passion and ignites fears of

loss of control and dangerous characters. The irony is that middle-class White Americans have always been major consumers of illicit drugs, supplying crucial capital to this illicit industry.

Drug selling, like gambling and prostitution, is a traditional means of upward mobility for disadvantaged groups. Our failure to deal with the reality of a severe lack of opportunity in poor minority areas, criminologist John Hagan suggests, ensures that this business will continue to attract sellers as long as demand holds out:

> Until we confront the social and economic roles played by deviance service centers and vice industries in America's racial and ethnic ghettos, we will not be able to reduce the scale of their associated activities and stubborn persistence in these distressed minority settings. This is especially true in the context of the economic slowdown and transition that has characterized the last quarter of this century.[23]

What is distinctive about the anticrack campaign is not its focus on African Americans in impoverished urban areas but its harshness. The build-up of African Americans imprisoned for drug offenses represents an unprecedented assault on a ghetto vice industry, a high-water mark in the nation's episodic wars on drugs. Between 1987 and 1998, the federal budget for fighting drug abuse rose from $6 billion to $20 billion.[24] Two-thirds of this money went to law enforcement and prisons; only one-third, to prevention and treatment. Judges lost discretion to reduce sentences in light of extenuating circumstances. Congress gave law-enforcement agencies powerful inducements to seek forfeiture of drug-related assets. Those convicted of drug offenses were stripped, for life, of important rights, including the right to live in publicly assisted housing units and eligibility to receive education benefits. Families have been ripped apart by long prison sentences. The collateral damage to African American communities has been enormous.

Conclusion: Race and Public Policy

Congress might have been more successful in combating crack if it had focused more explicitly on the business of drug dealing and the psychology of drug use, including its racial dimensions. Illicit drug use is a lifestyle issue, and drug selling is an economic issue. Legislation designed to change these behaviors will always have strong class, regional, and racial dimensions. Drug abuse is a crisis in poor African American and some other minority communities.[25] Congress was well aware of some of these facts, as member submissions to the *Congressional Record* indicate. Congress should also have been aware of the racial implications of a criminalization approach to illicit drug use. This nation has had ample experience with the failures of making drug use a serious crime. And we have a well-known history of racially discriminatory law enforcement. Taking these facts about race in America into account should have counseled Congress to adopt another approach.

Our national experience creates a special responsibility for legislatures to avoid further disadvantaging groups that have already suffered discrimination. The constitutional guarantee of equal protection of the laws, enacted in the aftermath of slavery, also suggests a legislative responsibility to avoid discrimination on the basis of race. The starting place for such a discussion must be, not an assumption that race is irrelevant, but recognition that race is inevitably relevant. The nation cannot honor its commitment to racial equality unless it recognizes race.[26]

Yet in what little open discussion did occur in the effort to combat crack abuse, race was never broached. Those who support this kind of color-blind standard in public debate sometimes argue that highlighting racial advantage and disadvantage exposes political minorities to stigmatization. But in a race-conscious, racially organized society, color blindness simultaneously denies the importance of race, while allowing for its manipulation.[27] The failure of progressive voices to address the way social policy issues are raced allows conservatives to frame the issues. In this case, race, though banished from open consideration, instead entered into congressional thinking sub rosa, permitting legislators to embrace penalties they would never have considered had they been envisioning a respected, White target population.

The United States needs to start a new conversation about race. Along with frank talk about race, we need more empirical scholarship on how public policies come to be formed. Such analysis will reveal, as this chapter has, that societal racism is still available to those who want to drum up support for repressive policies. Racism helps convince policymakers and the voting public that nothing short of punishment will work. One can expect that racial images may be deployed whenever public support is lacking, as it often is in morals legislation.

This chapter also suggests that scholars should search for links between policy formation and policy impact. Racial disadvantage may begin with the way policy is formulated. It is not necessarily a problem of too much discretion at lower levels in the administrative hierarchy. And, at any level, racial disadvantage is not necessarily conscious. The implications of this approach reach beyond the criminal-justice arena. Policies that adversely affect minority populations, whether they concern health, the environment, or economic well-being, should undergo critical scholarly scrutiny that focuses on the assumptions made when the issues were debated, the framing that occurred, and the racial history of concern that the framing process reveals.

NOTES

1. U.S. Sentencing Commission 1995.

2. Garland 2001; Simon 1997.

3. Gusfield 1986; Provine 2003.

4. Steven Belenko (1993) offers a useful analysis of this development. See also Beckett 1997 and Mauer 1999.

5. Musto 1999.

6. Reinarman and Levine 1988. See also Edsall and Edsall 1991.

7. Quoted in Beckett 1997:56. See also Reeves and Campbell 1994, especially p. 165.

8. Beckett 1997:77.

9. Elwood 1994:23.

10. Ibid.:41; Jensen and Gerber 1998; Reinarman and Levine 1997, especially pp. 23 and 156.

11. Bourgois 1995; Goode 1990.

12. Public Law 570, 99th Congress, 2nd Session (October 27, 1986), *Anti-Drug Abuse Act of 1986.*

13. *Congressional Record.* 1986 (September 26). 99th Congress, 2nd Session, 132 (129) S 13741.

14. *Congressional Record.* 1986 (September 11). 99th Congress, 2nd Session, 132 (118) H 6679.

15. *Congressional Record.* 1986 (October 17). 99th Congress, 2nd Session, 132 (144) H 10777.

16. *Congressional Record.* 1986 (September 26). 99th Congress, 2nd Session, 132 (129) S 13741.

17. *Congressional Record.* 1986 (April 22). 99th Congress, 2nd Session, 132 (51) S 4668.

18. Cohen 2002; Goode 1990.

19. Reinarman and Duskin 2002:41.

20. Media scholar James Hawdon (2001) found this kind of rhetoric and its impact in 167 drug-related speeches and public statements by Presidents Reagan and Bush between 1981 and 1992. He concluded that "President Reagan masterfully incited the public and helped create a moral panic." President Bush was less gifted in stirring these passions, and by 1992, the panic was winding down. See also Goode 1990 and Tonry 2004.

21. Zimring and Hawkins 1992.

22. Lauderdale and Inverarity 1984.

23. Hagan 1995:39.

24. Gest 2001.

25. For example, Lusane 1991; Miller 1996.

26. To maintain an ideologically rigid color blindness in the face of sociological realities, legal scholars Lani Guinier and Gerald Torres (2002:37) argue, "inhibits the kind of democratic engagement necessary for confronting some of the most deeply entrenched problems facing our society." See also Omi and Winant 1994.

27. Omi and Winant 1994.

Chapter 16

Transforming Communities
Formal and Informal Mechanisms of Social Control

Wenona Rymond-Richmond

Well they're safe down there, where I come from, 5010. The houses that they building give them that. The ones across the street, make them stay back over there. That's how it was. It was just fine. They stay on their side, we stay on our side. You mix 'em up together it like putting oil and water [together]. Somethin' you not suppose to do. That's just like puttin' water and milk, it don't mix! It not a mixture, 'cause you, cause it gonna thin out, you feel me? You can't do that! A-1 sauce and barbeque. That's nasty. You can't do that. That's wrong. They [Chicago Housing Authority] know what they was doin' was wrong. What do they care? They want the land, they want the area. They don't really actually care. They— they . . . it's all about money. Money and politics.

—Resident of the Henry Horner Homes

Perceptions of high crime and chaos in "ghetto" neighborhoods often result in the assumption that poor, minority communities lack social organization and social control. This belief is a central tenet of some federal policies, including the "Plan for Transformation," a policy to demolish and redevelop public housing developments. Yet, as I argue in this chapter, policies that are enacted upon poor minority communities often fail to take into account the organizational structure and tools of the community itself. As a result, the implementation of structural changes may clash with and undermine community members' strategies of controlling and reducing crime. Hence, even well intentioned policies may contribute to unsafe and violent environments. This is the view expressed by LaKeisha[1] in the quote above, in which she explains that the Chicago Housing Authority ignored the fact that residents of her housing development possessed an internal system of social control centered on spatial boundaries as a means to reduce violence. As long as people "stay on their side," things will be "just fine." In fact, the Plan for Transformation has remapped established social spaces by dividing LaKeisha's neighborhood into two distinct and antagonistic communities, thereby increasing violence in the area, though the intention was to provide a better quality of life for residents.

The research reported herein is based on a case study of the Plan for Transformation of one public housing project in Chicago. The purpose is threefold. First, I seek to illustrate how social organization may be manifest in a context that to outsiders appears to be extremely disorganized. Studying the forced redevelopment of a community renders social order and the dominant mechanisms of social control more observable. In extremely disadvantaged minority contexts, less apparent forms of organization consisting of cognitive maps that proscribe and prescribe behavior may be set in motion by poor relations with authorities (police, the housing authority, etc.), yet serve as an effective mechanism for social control, thereby reducing violence and ensuring the safety of residents. Thus, a second goal of this research is to illustrate the nature of the cognitive maps prevalent in a dangerous public housing community. Third, this case study will also illustrate how violence itself (including gang violence) may be the consequence, unintended or otherwise, of ignoring the internal organizational structure of disadvantaged communities.

Developing a deeper understanding of the meaning of the link between race and crime involves not only assessing different patterns and contexts but also explicating the mechanisms by which the link occurs. While it is "difficult to study the intervening mechanisms of social disorganization directly,"[2] this chapter aims to identify mechanisms that residents in a dangerous public housing development devise in order to maintain social control and attempt to reduce violent crime. In this chapter, I posit that studying the forced redevelopment of a community provides a unique opportunity in which social order is rendered more observable, and dominant mechanisms of social control become apparent.

It is well documented that poor, minority communities have a strained relationship to law enforcement and the legal system, and thus have developed informal mechanisms of social control.[3] Informal social control has long been recognized as an important theoretical construct for explaining levels of crime in communities.[4] However, few empirical studies have been conducted to illuminate how social control operates on the ground level in actual communities. This chapter seeks to address this shortcoming by demonstrating the nature and role of cognitive maps in protecting individuals and families from victimization in a particular setting. Cognitive maps are a response to abandonment and discrimination by police and other formal mechanisms of social control, and they inform and restrict residents' daily travels by warning them of safe and dangerous physical and symbolic spaces. As such, these maps are "strategies that the urban poor devise to escape or circumvent the structures of segregation and marginalization that entrap them, including those strategies that result in self-inflicted suffering."[5] For example, gangs form in part as a device for circumventing marginalization; yet, they create invisible borders that individuals fear to cross, resulting in a form of self-inflicted suffering.

Only a handful of sociologists have considered cognitive maps as mechanisms of social control.[6] Suttles claims that residents devise cognitive maps both as a way to describe their neighborhood and as a mechanism for social control.[7]

> these cognitive maps are part of the social control apparatus of urban areas and are of special importance in regulating spatial movement to avoid conflict between antagonistic groups. In this respect, such cognitive maps provide a set of social categories for differentiating between those people with whom one can or cannot safely associate and for defining the concrete groupings within which certain levels of social contact and social cohesion obtain.[8]

Understanding cognitive mapping is important because it is connected to spatial behavior. Individuals use cognitive maps as a spatial navigation tool, for visiting, walking, or living.

As reported below, public housing residents living in one of the most dangerous, segregated, and deteriorating high-rise housing developments in Chicago have refused to be relocated from their high-rise apartments into single-family town homes. How can this be? To outsiders, public housing symbolizes America's social ills and failed policy decisions directed towards the urban poor. Many believe that any alternative to high-rise public housing would be better than the way we currently house the urban poor. Both journalistic and academic reports on the redevelopment process in Chicago follow a similar line: the lives of residents of Chicago Housing Authority (CHA) will be greatly improved by demolishing the old-style public assisted living and replacing them with single-family town homes. Words like "hulking," "dilapidated," and "eyesore" are frequently used to describe the high-rises,[9] while phrases like "architecture of normalcy"[10] are used to describe the new low-rise developments.

From these descriptions, one might assume that all public high-rise residents would be overjoyed by the opportunity to move. Yet, ethnographic research and interviews with residents from one public housing project in Chicago, the Henry Horner Homes, reveal that many residents are refusing to relocate. Their refusals reflect the fear that locations to which they are being moved are less safe than the ones in which they currently reside. Although residents are being relocated only three blocks away, culturally and symbolically the distance is a world apart; in fact, it is a nation apart. To elaborate, there are five different active gangs under two different gang nations in the Henry Horner Homes: the Folk Nation and the People Nation. The problem is that the new town homes are located in an area that is under the control of the People Nation, while the high-rises are within the control of the Folk Nation. These gang boundaries have been in place for many years and provide a rigid map for residents' movements. Thus, despite the fact that the CHA and other nonresidents of the Henry Horner Homes regard this public housing development as one neighborhood, residents recognize it as two separate and distinct neighborhoods.

Can social organization theory explain why there has been resistance and violence in a public housing development that is undergoing redevelopment? Social disorganization theory is most simply defined by Sampson and Groves as "the inability of a community structure to realize the common values of its residents and maintain effective social controls."[11] Shaw and McKay developed the theory of social disorganization in *Juvenile Delinquency and Urban Areas,* which connects neighborhood characteristics with rates of crime.[12] The authors contend that three structural factors lead to community social disorganization, resulting in crime and delinquency: low economic status; ethnic heterogeneity; and residential mobility. Shaw and McKay's social disorganization theory has withstood the test of time. Sixty years after their landmark publication, social disorganization theory is still considered valid and widely used. Yet, despite the substantial influence of Shaw and McKay's research on crime, there has been little direct testing of the way community organization is achieved.[13]

Here, I demonstrate how an expanded version of social organization theory, which includes cognitive maps, provides a more thorough explanation of impediments to the redevelopment of the Henry Horner Homes. Incorporating cognitive maps into social organization theory requires a nuanced examination of space that demonstrates how it operates as a mechanism of social organization and social control. The present research is unique both in describing the dominant mechanisms of social control and in analyzing how they are affected by federal policies that threaten to eradicate important systems of relationships. Hence, the permanent or ephemeral nature of cognitive maps is documented as an outside force, namely CHA's Plan for Transformation, threatens them. As a result, social organization is viewed not as static but as a process that is perpetually negotiated and performed. Through the lens of social organization theory, we are able to observe how the Henry Horner community developed a vital mechanism of social control, which is not easily altered by outside forces. The clear lesson points to the strength of cognitive maps as mechanisms of social control. They are deeply embedded in the community and not quickly altered by restructuring the physical surroundings.

Methodology

Data for this research are from three sources: participant observation in the Henry Horner Homes between 1999 and 2003; in-depth interviews with residents; and census data from 1990 and 2000. The intensive participant observation and in-depth interviews generated hypotheses for designing and undertaking additional shorter interviews at the end of the research period. Expanding the interviews in this way enabled me to verify the broader applicability of the stories and allowed more residents' voices to be heard.

The Setting

The Horner Homes are situated on the Near West Side of Chicago. This neighborhood has a long history of immigration, poverty, and transitory residence. These characteristics are the ones that Shaw and McKay viewed as causing social disorganization. This area absorbed most of Chicago's early immigrants and was one of the original locations of African American settlement. Accommodating almost 10 percent of all of Chicago housing project residents, the Near West Side has one of the highest concentrations of public housing in the city.[14] In 1990, more than 20 percent of the adult labor force was unemployed, median family income was among the lowest in the city, and more than half of all families reported incomes below the poverty line. According to 2000 census reports, 37.5 percent of the population in the Near West Side lives below the poverty line, and 52.9 percent of the population is African American.

In 2000, the Horner Homes housed approximately eighty-one hundred residents and the median household income was $10,895. Horner residents are almost 100 percent African American, and less than half of the adult residents have completed high school. Fifty percent reported that their 1997 household income was below $5,000, and only 8 percent reported an income over $20,000.[15] Eighty-two percent reported receiving welfare at some time in their lives, and 55 percent of Horner adults say they have received welfare for more than five years, which is the new federally mandated cutoff period for most recipients.[16] The immediate areas surrounding the Horner development have similar demographic characteristics, with 100 percent of the population being African American and at least 74 percent having an income below the poverty line.[17]

Horner has long been one of the CHA's most dilapidated and dangerous developments,[18] which is especially notable given that Chicago's public housing is considered the worst in the nation. By the 1990s, Horner was so decrepit that former CHA director and chairman Vincent Lane claimed that CHA officials saw no value in rehabilitation. Currently, Horner is undergoing one of the "largest and most ambitious attempts in the nation to revitalize a severely distressed public housing development and convert it into a healthy, mixed income community"[19] with the assistance of an $18 million Hope VI grant.

The Henry Horner Homes were developed in 1954 and consist of three sections: the Horner Homes, the Horner Extension, and the Horner Annex. The Horner Homes were built in 1954 and are the oldest and largest section of the development. They consist of a mix of 15-story high-rise and 7-story mid-rise buildings. The Horner Extension opened in 1961 and consists of four 13-story high-rises and three 8-story mid-rises. The Horner Homes and the Horner Extension are approximately one mile long and two blocks wide, and they make up the majority of the development. The Horner Annex is slightly separated from the Horner Homes and the Horner Extension. It is located a few blocks south of the Horner Homes on Warren Street and sits directly across the street from the United Center, home of the Chicago Bulls basketball team and the Blackhawks hockey team.

Once construction of the Horner Homes was completed, residents began to form an identity based on where they lived within this 7-block public housing development. People who lived east of Damen Avenue would be called "the Henry Horners," those west of Damen would be called "the reds" because the color of these buildings had a red hue. Individuals who lived in two of the buildings west of Damen Avenue had an additional identity—"the turnstiles." These two buildings had a large turnstile that acted as the entryway. Families living south of the Horner Homes in the Henry Horner Annex were known as the "the valleys." In the following passage, a 47-year-old woman reflects on how the buildings in Horner have always been divided into "us and them" territories.

> *Trisha:* You know, the girls, when we was little, they used to chase us, but it wasn't no gang bangin'. They just use to say, there go the Henry Horner girls.
> *Wenona:* Now, if they would call you the Henry Horner girls, what would they call the people on the other side of Damen that was still Horner?
> *Trisha:* The reds.
> *Wenona:* The reds, okay.
> *Trisha:* You know they'd say, oh the reds.
> *Wenona:* Yeah, the reds, the turnstiles, the valleys.
> *Trisha:* There were the turnstile girls, yeah. [laughing]

As arbitrary and simplistic as it may seem for people to form identity and oppositional identities based on the color of public housing high-rises, Suttles noted this same phenomenon in 1972 in *The Social Construction of Communities*. While the color and type of building initially determined territories within this neighborhood, gangs and gang boundaries currently divide and shape residents' views of space in the neighborhood. Gangs and violence have been epidemic in this public housing development as well as in other developments throughout Chicago.[20] These communities have been described as abandoned by police, industry, and the Chicago Housing Authority. Yet, people live there, and many people call it home.

Two conditions in Horner gave rise to the opportunity for gangs to form, dominate social space, and perpetuate the recognized spatial boundaries within the housing development. First, community identity and spatial boundaries were already established in Horner on the basis of the location and construction at different times of high-rise buildings. The result was cognitive maps composed of defended neighborhoods.[21] Friends and foes were already established before gangs formed within the Horner Homes, and one was well aware of the spatial boundaries that contained friends and foes.

Rival gang boundaries developed along these established social and spatial boundaries. As Figure 16.1 illustrates, both gang nations are situated within the Henry Horner Homes, setting the stage for gang problems within these housing units. Gangs rival each other for "control" of each of the housing developments. Typically, one or two gangs are found in particular CHA developments. A unique feature of the Henry Horner Homes is the large number of different gangs that live within its boundaries. As noted, there are five gangs in Horner vying for control. Three of these gangs are members of the People Nation and two are members of the Folk Nation (see Figure 16.2). Where these invisible borders meet is where most of the gang warfare occurs.

The formation of gangs in Horner was also facilitated by the absence of formal social control agents, such as the police. Urban sociologists and anthropologists have devoted much attention to the ways that poor minority communities attempt to circumvent macrostructural domination,

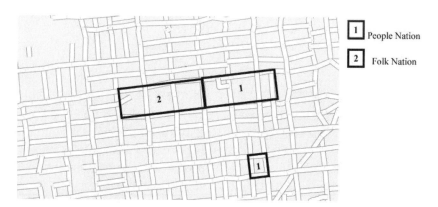

Fig. 16.1. Gang Nations

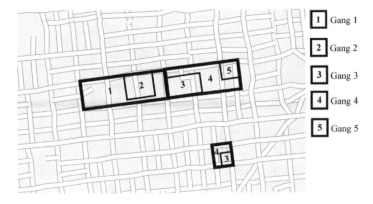

Fig. 16.2. Gang Territories

neglect, and discrimination, in the process establishing their own social order and organization.[22]

Cognitive Maps of Residents of the Henry Horner Homes

My research on the Henry Horner Homes demonstrates that residents have a clear sense of safe and dangerous areas and use these perceptions to shape their cognitive maps. Residents collectively recognize specific streets or intersections as dangerous. Damen Avenue, where most of the fights and violence occur, is such a street in Horner. This street divides the two rival gang nations in the public housing development. Serena, an on-and-off-again resident of the Henry Horner Homes, discusses the area west of Damen Avenue:

> When they was the projects [meaning high-rise buildings rather than town homes west of Damen Avenue], I used to be scared of them too. I, my sister, you know, that stay here, she used to stay down there. I refuse to go see her.

Regardless of the physical landscape of the area just west of Damen Avenue, Serena remembers always being afraid of this area. Her perception of the area as dangerous did not decrease when the high-rises were demolished and replaced with town homes. Serena's cognitive mapping of dangerous areas guided her decisions not to visit family members and informed her of safe locations where she is willing to reside.

Another location within the Near West Side that Horner residents collectively acknowledge as perilous is a public housing development located approximately one mile from Horner. My questions on safety near this housing development often elicited terse and annoyed responses. For example, I asked Serena to identify the area that she considered the most dangerous on a map of the Near West Side. She quickly responded, "Rockwell [name of the nearby public housing development], everybody know that. . . . That was a question that I even, I know you know that!"

Despite the fact that Serena was homeless and had been on the wait list for a public housing apartment for over a year, her perception of Rockwell as being unsafe influenced her decision not to relocate to that area regardless of the fact that being selective would probably increase her wait time and homeless status.

> But if they woulda sent me to another, another CHA property, I woulda said I—I—I wouldn't do Rockwell though, I'm scared of those buildings. . . . I'm scared of that building, I am really scared of that building.

When asked by a Chicago Housing Authority employee to list her housing preferences, Serena declared that she did not want to relocate to another public housing development or to receive a Section 8 voucher. The only place that she agreed to was a Henry Horner apartment east of Damen Avenue, an area controlled by gangs associated with the People Nation.

As of mid-2004, public housing high-rises have been demolished on both sides of Damen Avenue. However, new buildings have only been built on the west side of Damen Avenue. This means that some of the displaced families from both the west side of Damen and the east side of Damen have the option of moving into newly constructed town homes, but only on the west side. However, this option is often refused because individuals from the east side believe that the lives of family members will be put in jeopardy if they move across this symbolic border.

Below is an interview excerpt from a woman who was offered a five-bedroom town home west of Damen Avenue in 2001 because her high-rise public housing building east of Damen was scheduled for demolition. She refused to be relocated to the new town home because it was in a rival gang territory. Patricia explains,

I didn't want to be down there [west of Damen] because I knew how it was down there. They moved people from the buildings that was surrounding me down there. But I knew that there was going be a lot of commotion and I didn't wanta be in the middle of it. I know a lot of people that has stayed down there that has put in for transfers because of the stuff that goes on down there. I mean as far as I'm concerned it's just as bad as it was before they knocked the buildings down. Cause now it's like, I said, all these people down there in different gangs.

Yolanda echoes Patricia's concerns. She claims, "Worse over there than it is here." When I asked Yolanda if she would move from her high-rise apartment east of Damen Avenue to a new town home west of Damen Avenue, she responded, "They shoot too much down there! I know this ain't perfect but it's more perfect than living down there. They shoot you, they'll shoot, they'll shoot you up down there if you ain't in the hood right with them over there." Yolanda currently lives in a high-rise in Henry Horner and is resisting relocation until town homes are constructed east of Damen Avenue. I asked Yolanda if she had informed a CHA employee of the reason for her unwillingness to be relocated west of Damen Avenue. Her reply shows her concern, which her sons share:

I told them I ain't movin' down there! Is you all crazy? I have too many sons. They'll [gang members west of Damen Avenue] never jump on my sons with knives, when they don't do nothin'. Can't walk through. But my sons don't wanna move down there. No way. They don't wanna move over there.

This quotation highlights four significant themes of my research. First, it illuminates the fact that Yolanda possesses a cognitive map of safe and dangerous areas. Second, it emphasizes the collective aspect of her cognitive map in that her sons share it. Third, it corresponds with the collective cognitive maps of other individuals that I have interviewed because it identifies the same streets as unsafe. Finally, the quotation emphasizes the particular dangers that men have with crossing into territories marked as unsafe.

At the time of my observation (1999–2003), some high-rises east of Damen had been demolished to make room for construction of town homes, but construction had not yet begun. Residents did not expect to move

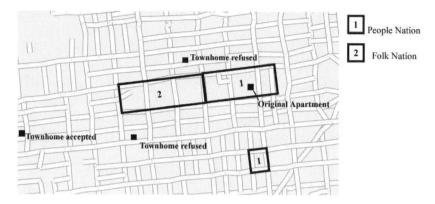

Fig. 16.3. Location of Town Home Offers

until 2004, but they were willing to wait in their dilapidated high-rises until then. By the end of 2004, town homes were built east of Damen, and some residents who were waiting for an apartment were relocated.

I did not expect another woman I interviewed, Shandra, to have the same views as Yolanda and Patricia because she and her disabled son lived on the seventh floor of a high-rise in Horner with an elevator that was frequently out of order. When the elevator was broken, Shandra had to carry her son and his wheelchair up seven flights of stairs. She currently lives in a scattered-site town home west of Damen, despite the fact that the high-rise that she lived in was east of Damen. In trying to interview a wide range of residents of the Henry Horner Homes, I chose Shandra because I thought her desperate situation might make her willing to take any relocation option offered to her. However, she also refused to be relocated to several town homes because they were located in rival gang territory. Figure 16.3 indicates the location of homes that were refused by Shandra. Shandra discussed with me her experience and interactions with Chicago Housing Authority officials:

> *Shandra:* So, in the meantime Melvin caught rheumatic fever. And by me staying on the seventh floor with a wheelchair, they really had to move me. So, they showed me quite a few apartments. I turned three down.
> *Wenona:* What were the addresses and why?
> *Shandra:* One of them was across Damen in the new housing. In the turnstile, that's what they called them, turnstile. Because it's two different sides. Or two different gangs. And I had teenagers. I had boys and I can't

move my boys somewhere where they can't go. By us being across Damen, they didn't like our people or our kids to come across there. If you
did, then they jump on you. No matter what. So I didn't feel like moving
my kids down there cause I know I gonna jeopardize my sons' life. So, I
turned that one down.

Wenona: Did you tell CHA why?

Shandra: Yeah. They knew. They knew I wasn't going anywhere my kids did-
n't feel safe. So they showed me another one. 12345 W. Warren. You know
the house. They showed me that one, which was a four bedroom. I told
them no because that still in the same area. I have boys! I'm trying to
bring my boys up somewhere where they can come home safe, that they
didn't have a problem. . . . So that means, she [woman who works for
the CHA] said "well, the apartment I show you, you only get three [op-
tions]." They offer you three places that you choose. You don't have to
take them, you could take them. The third one. She said "well, we don't
have any more right now, any four bedroom, you gonna have to wait
until 2004." . . . So I say, ok. I wait. I didn't care because I wasn't moving
down there, Wenona! And then Tyrell come home he get shot up or
Johnny come home he dead. Down there they would have killed my kids.
I couldn't take it. So.

Despite the fact that Shandra had a disabled son and was struggling
carrying him up and down seven flights of stairs, she still found the high-
rise option better than being relocated into a town home west of Damen
Avenue. Eventually the CHA found her a town home where she was willing to move her family. This town home is west of Damen Avenue, but it is
about a mile and a half away from the Henry Horner Homes. After turning down two apartments that the CHA offered her, she found a town
home in which she thought she and her family would be safe. Shandra
describes her experience of finding a suitable home to be relocated to:

So she [CHA employee] said "ok, go to housing and tell them I sent you
down there to get the keys and take you to look inside." Oh Wenona, when I
came in. Oh god. It was gorgeous. I got to redo my house. It was gorgeous.
I'm like, "I take it! I take it! No more questions, I take it. I want it." And I'm
here.

Although the town home that she moved into is located in a rival gang
territory from where she used to live, she claims,

Yes, still where the Disciples at. It's not like it's in the projects. Because they [gangs in the projects] don't have nothing else to do. These people over here they work. And then if their kids do try to do gang, it different than the project.

She further explains the difference between the gangs in the projects and the gangs in her new location: "And over here they do gang bang, it's like four of five of them. From the Horner's you looking at sixty and seventy boys. That's a totally different thing." Although all the new town homes built so far are located in rival gang areas, there are locations that have more gang activity than others. Patricia also eventually settled on a scattered-site town home in a location where she believed the rival gang was less active than in the area just west of Damen Avenue.

Trisha, Serena, Patricia, Yolanda, and Shandra all know of people who originally lived east of Damen, then took a town home just west of Damen, and have had numerous problems stemming from residing in a rival gang's territory. All three of the women know families that have requested to be transferred out of this area because they feel unsafe. Trisha knew several "kids" who were killed after being moved into the area just west of Damen Avenue. Trisha explains,

> *Trisha:* Yeah, a lot of people got killed. A lot of my girlfriends' kids. One of them came out of the door, getting ready to go outside; they shot him in the head three times. Bam, bam, bam. A lot of them got killed standing on the corner. Bam. In the head. Dead.
>
> *Wenona:* And this is someone that was moved over [from across Damen Avenue]?
>
> *Trisha:* Yeah.
>
> *Wenona:* And it was gang related?
>
> *Trisha:* Yeah. A lot of them shot up and paralyzed in wheelchairs. That's bad. I wish I wouldn't walk out my door and see one of my kids get shot. You know that mess you up for life? It damage the whole family.

Trisha also told me that she knows a few people who were enticed into moving out of the high-rises and into their own town home, and each of these families has been victimized to varying degrees. Many have requested to be transferred out of their town homes because of their experiences. In one situation, a young man was shot and killed right in front of his mother's town home. This woman continues to live there, but Trisha refuses to be lured into moving to this neighborhood. According to her, "I not taking nothing. Ok, it might be good for me, but I have kids. And when you have kids you don't live for you no more. You live for your kids."

Yolanda also feels that the new town homes being offered are "real nice" and some people are enticed into accepting them despite the fact that the neighborhood is hostile towards them. While many residents of high-rises east of Damen Avenue have refused to relocate west of Damen for fear of living in rival gang territory, there are individuals willing to take the risk because they are tempted by the ability to live in their own town home. Yolanda's niece is one such individual. Unfortunately, her desire to live in a newly constructed town home was aborted due to "shootin' too much," which led her to request a transfer. Yolanda also told me about two other unsuccessful relocations of people from the east side of Damen to the west side of Damen. In both of these situations, Yolanda's explanation for why the relocation was unsuccessful had to do with violations of gang boundaries dividing the housing development into two separate neighborhoods. In the first case, "They shot through this lady window down there." In the second unsuccessful relocation, gang members raided a "girl and her momma's" home: "They [the gang bangers] raid they home, they throw out their clothes, their beds, everything. They ran them up out of the house. The gang bangers ran them up out of they house!" The "girl" never came back to her home and never retrieved any of her belongings.

Conclusion

The Plan for Transformation is not the first time that attempts to spatially relocate people to better living conditions has backfired in Chicago. The CHA considered the original construction of public housing a well intentioned policy to provide decent housing to the working and nonworking poor. During urban renewal in the 1950s, slum areas were cleared and replaced with the now maligned high-rise public housing developments. During this period, high-rise developments such as the Henry Horner Homes were considered improvements in the lives of the urban poor. Many unintended and negative consequences occurred, most notably racial and economic segregation and high levels of violence. Less than fifty years later, one hundred thousand units, or 10 percent of all public housing built during urban renewal, have been slated for demolition at a staggering cost of $2.5 billion dollars to the federal government. Data gathered and analyzed on cognitive maps and social control in Henry Horner demonstrate that the $18 million dedicated to the redevelopment of Horner may be poorly spent because policymakers lack an understanding of "local culture."

The Henry Horner Homes is one of the most impoverished and dangerous communities in the United States; nonetheless, there is a discernible social organization. Order exists in the Henry Horner Homes, despite nonresidents' perception of disorganization. In fact, this perception is an underlying assumption of public housing policies throughout the nation. Unfortunately, the Plan for Transformation is not just dismantling physical structures but is also dismantling a community. Some call the new physical structures built in place of the high-rises "architectures of normalcy," which implies that there is a clear sense of normal and abnormal, and that what they are replacing is abnormal.[23] My research suggests that social control built on gang boundaries provides a sense of normalcy for residents of what appears to others as disorganized environments. This is, of course, an unusual neighborhood system, but not "abnormal" under conditions of dysfunctional and ineffective policing.

As demonstrated above, residents of the Henry Horner Homes have developed a collective cognitive map, which divides the development into two separate neighborhoods peopled by two distinct gang nations who direct violence at each other. Due to violence and resistance caused by relocating individuals from one neighborhood into the other, it would behoove housing authorities to redevelop areas in such a way as to allow individuals the option of remaining in parts of neighborhoods where they feel and may be safe. LaKeisha, a Henry Horner resident, makes this seemingly simple recommendation:

> I mean, if you gonna move a person, move them somewhere they gonna feel comfortable and safe. Then they put in a transfer because someone threaten them or their family. . . . Everyone deserves to live in peace. Shouldn't nobody feel threaten where they live at. You kids should be able to play without there being any problem."

Recognizing cognitive mapping as a mechanism of social control has significant policy implications. In Horner, this goal could be realized by assessing community conflicts and demolishing and redeveloping equally and at approximately the same time on both sides of Damen Avenue. Although violence has been a consequence of redevelopment for the past four years, it is possible that this is a temporary response to the mixing of individuals from different neighborhoods. Perhaps gang boundaries and cognitive maps will shift over time. Though the gang boundaries have remained for the first four years of redevelopment, this does not mean they will persist indefinitely.

This chapter has taken an important step in identifying a central mechanism of social organization for disadvantaged minority communities. In taking this step, I have demonstrated how the use of cognitive maps, as a conceptual tool, works in protecting individuals and families from victimization in a particular setting. Lessons from the data collected at the Henry Horner Homes suggest that it is imperative that policies not be enacted in disadvantaged communities without recognition of the organizational structure and tools of the community itself.

This research raises several questions for future analysts. While it is well documented that poor minority communities devise informal mechanisms of social control due to having a different relationship to law enforcement and the legal system more broadly, we do not understand fully the ways in which this occurs. Nor do we fully understand the ways in which social organization can be threatened or altered by policies that restructure communities. Additional qualitative research similar to that presented here should provide answers to these questions and explicate the mechanisms linking race and crime.

In this chapter, I assumed that there is nothing particularly unique about the African American experience. However, further research is needed on the organizational structures of a variety of race/ethnic and class communities to determine whether and to what extent cognitive mapping is of particular significance to varied disadvantaged communities. Possibly the heightened level of racial and economic segregation, as well as the widespread poverty and gang problems experienced by Horner residents, provide the unique conditions for particular mechanisms of social control. Future research on the prevalence and use of cognitive maps as a mechanism of social control may lead to informative comparisons with different neighborhoods and racial and ethnic groups.

NOTES

1. The individuals interviewed have been given pseudonyms and their addresses have been changed in order to protect their anonymity.

2. Sampson and Wilson 1995:47.

3. Anderson 1999; Carr 2003; Janowitz 1975; Kasarda and Janowitz 1974; Pattillo-McCoy 1999; Sampson, Raudenbush, and Earls 1997; Venkatesh 1997.

4. Jacobs 1962; Sampson et al. 1997; Shaw and McKay 1942.

5. Bourgois 1995:18.

6. Janowitz 1967; Merry 1981; Suttles 1972.

7. Suttles 1972.

8. Ibid.:22.

9. Grossman 2003.

10. Kamin 1998.

11. Sampson and Groves 1989:777.

12. Shaw and McKay 1942.

13. Sampson and Groves 1989.

14. *Local Community Fact Book* 1990.

15. Abt 1998:x.

16. Ibid.:xiv.

17. U.S. Bureau of the Census 1991.

18. Abt 1998.

19. Ibid.:I.

20. Garbarino, Kostelny, and Dubrow 1991.

21. Suttles 1972.

22. Anderson 1978, 1999; Bourgois 1995; Gans 1962; Granovetter 1973; Liebow 1967; Merry 1981; Stack 1974; Suttles 1968, 1972.

23. Kamin 1998.

Chapter 17

Toward a Developmental and Comparative Conflict Theory of Race, Ethnicity, and Perceptions of Criminal Injustice

Carla Shedd and John Hagan

The perception of criminal injustice is common among disadvantaged American racial and ethnic minority groups. This perception of injustice is especially common for highly educated and socially and economically successful African Americans. It is also well established that encounters between citizens and the police play an important part in such perceptions of racial injustice. Yet, there is much about these perceptions that remains unknown. For example, perceptions of injustice can be more acute among more, rather than less, advantaged minority group members. This is a conundrum that poses important explanatory and methodological challenges. We believe that a comparative conflict theory of crime and punishment can help to address this puzzle.

We first elaborate a comparative conflict theory by discussing the age structure and relative racial and ethnic gradients of perceptions of criminal injustice. We then examine the nature of police contacts that influence the development of these perceptions and the strategies of minority citizens for responding to their contacts with the police. Finally, we speculate about the broader developmental, comparative, and societal implications of minority perceptions of criminal injustice for racial and ethnic relations in America more generally. Our goal is to outline the foundations for a developmental and comparative conflict theory that can inform research and policy within, as well as beyond, the field of crime and punishment.

Foundations of a Comparative Conflict Theory

Conflict theory historically has stressed the roles of group threat, hierarchical subordination, and economic powerlessness in explaining crime and the way it is controlled in America.[1] While economic forces dominated early and influential formulations of conflict theory,[2] subsequent specifications and elaborations have emphasized the salience of race, above that of class or status, in grounding social relationships.[3] Much early empirical work assessing conflict theory revolved around the degree to which official decisions about punishment for crime are racially motivated and biased.[4]

Despite an ensuing debate about the role of outright prejudice as a specific source of racial disparity in crime and punishment in America,[5] there is certainty about disproportionality by race in rates of arrest, imprisonment, and capital punishment.[6] For example, African Americans make up over half of the more than two million imprisoned in the United States.[7] African Americans regard this disproportionate imprisonment as unjustified,[8] and some social scientists argue that imprisonment represents a new form of ghettoization, if not enslavement.[9]

Large numbers of African American youth come into conflict with the criminal law and perceive it as unjust. Yet, we know little about how this conflict is socially structured, or how a sense of injustice may extend to other ethnic groups and governmental sectors. There is growing concern that perceived injustice itself causes criminal behavior.[10] This adds urgency to the need to better understand the micro- and macrolevel mechanisms leading to racial and ethnic differences in perceptions of criminal injustice.

Race, Economic Disadvantage, and Perceived Injustice

The processes involved in perceptions of injustice may have broad and generic features that encompass a wide range of American institutions. For example, African Americans perceive inequality and discrimination in areas as diverse as education, employment, health care, and housing.[11] While the majority of Whites may believe that African American economic inequality results from motivational weaknesses, most African Americans believe that inequality is the result of White racism and other structural barriers.[12]

These beliefs about racial inequality are deeply and historically corrosive forces in American society. Orlando Patterson observes that "centuries of public dishonor and ritualized humiliation by Euro-Americans were . . . certain to engender deep distrust."[13] Yet Patterson also argues that the American racial divide is even more complicated than this. We argue, consequently, that a developmental and comparative conflict theory must encompass this complexity in order for it to meet our explanatory and policy needs.

Race is considerably more important than social class in explaining variation in urban American arrest rates.[14] Empirical evidence supports the importance attached to race in a renewed comparative conflict theory of crime. Still, there are suggestions that micro- and macrolevel economic disadvantages can be further root causes of perceived criminal injustice. For example, using a national sample, Hagan and Albonetti found that unemployed members of the "surplus population," as well as African Americans, perceive higher levels of criminal injustice than do Americans of higher class position.[15] Sampson and Bartusch found that individual-level socioeconomic status is positively linked to satisfaction with the police; concentrated neighborhood disadvantage increases dissatisfaction with the police; and the concentration of poverty further accounts for racial differences in dissatisfaction at the individual level.[16]

Sampson and colleagues make several noteworthy contributions to research on perceived injustice. First, in moving beyond the individual level to contextualize issues of racial disparity, Sampson and Bartusch suggest that we further conceptualize differences in racial orientations in terms of perceived macrolevel "cognitive landscapes" of neighborhood and community.[17] Second, Sampson and Lauritsen observe that it is potentially misleading to think of socially organized differences in cognitive orientations as neatly divided in binary, Black-White terms.[18] They emphasize that "recent immigration from Mexico and Cuba in particular is reshaping the landscape of many American cities. Hence, future criminal justice processing may be closely tied to the experiences of race or ethnic groups that have heretofore been neglected by mainstream criminological research."[19]

Meanwhile, Collins and Cose each provide compelling accounts of feelings of discontent and distrust among middle-class African American professionals in the workplace and beyond.[20] Affluent and better educated African Americans view disadvantaged African Americans as much worse off than poor Whites.[21] Middle-class African Americans are also the most impatient with the progress on civil rights in America.[22] This pattern is further reflected in widespread suspicions that economically and educationally advantaged African Americans have about the American legal system.[23]

Studies of perceived criminal injustice that separate respondents by race often yield marked contrasting evidence. Some studies indicate that income reduces perceived injustice among African Americans, while others report that class position increases the sense of injustice among members of this group.[24] Still other research finds no income effects, regardless of race.[25] The possibility that more, rather than less, well off African Americans perceive greater injustice is an *apparent* exception to the conflict theory prediction that economic *disadvantage* should heighten perceptions of injustice. Variation in findings suggests that something beyond absolute economic deprivation is involved in racial perceptions of criminal injustice. We argue that this involves variation in frames of reference and comparison, which a more nuanced developmental and comparative conflict theory can elucidate.

Developmental and Comparative Processes in Socio-Legal Conflict Theory

Leading conflict criminologists have traditionally framed their hypotheses in class terms.[26] More recently, however, Chambliss has emphasized that "the intensive surveillance of Black neighborhoods, the corresponding looseness of surveillance of white neighborhoods, and differences in punishments for white and Black offenders reinforce the belief that the system is not only inherently racist but is designed to oppress . . . black people."[27] Bobo and Johnson also note that "a number of scholars see in changing U.S. criminal justice policy a deliberate, if loosely coordinated, effort to reassert control and dominance over African Americans."[28]

There is continuing debate in life course research about when, or whether, such politically sensitive beliefs ever fully crystallize. Nonetheless, there is agreement that adolescence is a critical formative period for such development.[29] Bobo and Johnson emphasize that "political and social values are developed early in life and are rather stable,"[30] and then conclude that "views on the criminal justice system are rather rigid and resistant to change."[31] Early and middle adolescence is the time when minority youth are likely to first regularly encounter the police.[32] During this period, youth begin to range further away from home for longer periods of time.[33] They are also undergoing changes in their physical and social development, through which they begin to be perceived as threatening by other members of the community.[34] A developmental and comparative conflict theory of perceptions of criminal injustice must therefore focus first—if not foremost—on these formative teenage years.

Adolescence is also a developmental period in which youth begin to form "reflected appraisals" of themselves vis-à-vis others.[35] For disadvantaged minority youth, these reflected appraisals have an important comparative dimension involving a growing awareness of the abstract consequences of racial hierarchy and subordination.[36] More importantly, adolescence is often a period for minority youth of a more specific and connected awareness of a police presence in their social lives.[37]

Davis observes that when a deprived person contrasts himself or herself with a nondeprived person, the resulting attitude may be "relative subordination,"[38] whereby "people's attitudes, aspirations and grievances largely depend on the frame of reference within which they are conceived."[39] Race is, of course, a sensitive point of reference in American society, and a reference point that can become acute for minority youth during early to middle adolescence.

Portes and Rumbaut highlight the racial framing of this issue, noting that "in America, race is a paramount criterion of social acceptance that can overwhelm the influence of class background, religion, or language."[40] They add that a "racial gradient continues to exist in U.S. culture so that the darker a person's skin, the greater is the social distance from dominant groups and the more difficult it is to make his or her personal qualifications count."[41] We argue, similarly, that skin tone is a visible marker that can create inequality—a social fact that gives meaning to the concept of *visible* minority group status.

For conflict criminologists, visible social dissimilarity and distance are especially likely to be associated with powerlessness and threat.[42] African Americans are seen by dominant groups as less powerful and more threatening to Whites than Latino Americans, who nonetheless form a growing comparative presence and point of reference in contemporary American society.[43] This sense of differential threat may further derive from the longer history involving slavery of African Americans in the United States, as contrasted with the more recent and increasing presence of Latinos in many American cities.

The implication for a comparative conflict theory of crime is that Latino Americans occupy a disadvantaged middle ground. Latinos are subject to a less comprehensive and less intensive focus of criminalization efforts than African Americans, but they are still much more at risk than

Whites. Comparative conflict theory, therefore, predicts a racial gradient in adolescent perceptions of criminal injustice, with more visible and vulnerable African American youth perceiving greater injustice than Latino American youth, who are more likely to perceive injustice than White youth. The few surveys that have considered Latino views yield some evidence that this is the case.[44] Thus, a comparative conflict theory of perceptions of criminal injustice will increasingly require attention to Latino and African American adolescent experiences.

Police attention to African American youth is frequent and increasingly examined in empirical studies.[45] Relatively little is known about how Latino youth respond to experiences with the police. A study sampling Latino Americans of various ages reports that "in general . . . attitudes toward the police are good until [the respondent] has experience with the police,"[46] but "as contact with the police increases . . . expectations for the police decrease."[47] As the Latino population grows in U.S. cities, this group will become more visible. Resulting encounters with police may become more problematic. Differences, as well as similarities, in Latino and African American experiences with the police will need to be taken into account in assessments of perceptions of criminal injustice for minority populations. Taking such differences into account may, ironically, prove to be a key to uncovering more fundamental commonalities between groups.

Further Elaborating the Racial Dimension in Comparative Conflict Theory

Neighborhood, school, and workplace experiences provide additional contexts of racial and ethnic subordination. These are public settings where hierarchical relationships are enacted, and these contexts further influence comparative perceptions of criminal injustice. Brooks uses a contextualized comparative perspective to explain the unexpected outrage about discrimination that we have noted among more advantaged African Americans.[48]

He observes that in contrast to advantaged Blacks, "low-income African Americans may be more inclined to restrict the frame of reference to their immediate community when evaluating their outcomes."[49] The concentrated separateness of the African American ghetto experience may actually make the experience of police harassment so familiar that it becomes an "experience of the expected" and produces less outrage than would otherwise be predicted.

By contrast, "successful blacks develop multiple reference groups, which allow them to compare more easily their outcomes to whites and other racial groups," so that "despite achieving good individual outcomes, they continue to feel deprived as long as blacks as a whole fare poorly."[50] Brooks argues that being aware of the possibility of improved outcomes may lead one to perceive familiar and even expected experiences (e.g., police contact) as more outrageous. In a parallel way, when less advantaged groups gain exposure to more advantaged groups in a surrounding neighborhood, at work, or in school, they may evince feelings of deprivation.[51]

Brooks places the general linear relationship between opportunity and grievance within the quantifiable context of residential and occupational segregation. He suggests that middle-class African Americans who move more widely in the mainstream of American life may be caught off guard when their status does not protect them from police harassment, while their peers living and working in measurably more homogeneous racial environments may be conditioned to expect less. The latter conditioning can result in the "experience of the expected" we noted earlier.

Alternatively, Brooks suggests, "African Americans in integrated (or mostly white) residential or workplace settings may have more occasions to observe racial bias."[52] He further notes that this may "place middle-class and upper-class blacks in a constant state of alert with respect to differential treatment."[53] This observation is consistent with Patterson's point that when Afro- and Euro-Americans "meet more and more, the possibility for conflict is bound to increase."[54]

For adolescents, schools provide an appropriate comparative developmental context in which they initially form observations and perceptions as part of the educational process and on their own. "The subversive potentialities of knowledge derive from its capacity to act as an independent influence on reference groups and thereby create relative deprivations where they did not exist before."[55] The experience of integration with Whites in schools may be a key macrolevel mechanism that unexpectedly drives perceived injustice. Yet, there may be more to this hypothesis than a simple linear, Black-and-White formulation implies.

Brooks notes that "scholars speculate that better-off blacks are more concerned about the status of blacks compared to other groups as opposed to maintaining a strictly black reference group."[56] This pluralization of reference groups invites an extension of the concept of a macrolevel racial gradient into our comparative conflict theory. Specifically, it implies that the racial gradient of racial/ethnic effects on perceived adolescent criminal injustice results in African American youth being comparatively more affected than Latino youth by the proportion of White youth in their schools.

In assessing this hypothesis, it is important to take into account differences in responses to police contacts. It may be the novelty of the reduction in separateness and isolation that is as salient as the familiar problem of police harassment.

In framing our model, we must also take into account the possibility of a curvilinear limit to the perceived injustices we are examining.[57] An optimistic hope is that the impact of integration on perceived injustice eventually can reach a point where inclusion with the majority group begins to become more benign for perceptions of injustice. We cannot estimate in advance what this tipping point might be, and there is the further concern that the public schools' general failure to prevent White flight, and to be meaningfully integrated, places an upper bound on the possibilities of reaching such a tipping point. Nonetheless, if such a tipping point can be established, it would have obvious policy relevance vis-à-vis the ordeal of integration. Patterson's commitment to the ideal of integration implies his belief that such a tipping or turning point exists.[58]

The Chicago Public Schools Study

It may be useful to illustrate some of what we have been suggesting in the context of the Chicago public schools. School segregation has been increasing in the United States since the 1980s.[59] Chicago continues to be one of the nation's most segregated cities.[60] The proportion of White students in Chicago public schools has decreased from 19 percent in 1980 to 10 percent in 2000. During this same period the proportion of African American students has decreased from just over 60 percent to about 50 percent; because of immigration and a higher birth rate, the proportion of Latino American students is now more than one-third.[61]

The conflicts accompanying changes in educational and residential segregation in Chicago are played out through the lives of young people and prominently feature encounters with the law, often in ways that link the schools with the police and the justice system. Nearly every Chicago public school has one or more police officers stationed in and patrolling its hallways.[62] In 1992, the Chicago City Council passed a "gang loitering" law, which permitted police to arrest anyone suspected of being a gang member for congregating with no apparent legal purpose.[63] The crackdown resulted in more than forty-two thousand arrests before a string of court decisions ruled the law unconstitutional.[64] The sheer volume of these arrests attests to the familiarity of the "experience of the expected" noted above.

In 1997, Chicago enacted a "reciprocal records agreement" that requires the city police department to release to each school's administrators on a daily basis the names of youth arrested off-campus.[65] These arrests can be used to justify school suspension and expulsion decisions, thus suggesting an interconnection beginning in adolescence of the child's school and justice system experiences.

By the 1960s, Gerald Suttles was writing about the racially and ethnically segmented neighborhoods of Chicago and the resulting conflicts between groups of youth as well as with the police.[66] One notorious practice in White neighborhoods involved the police picking up African American youth whom they suspected of, but could not charge with, crimes.[67] The police dropped these youth off in locations where they knew they were likely to be beaten by local residents. A quarter-century later this practice again came to light when the Chicago Police Board fired two officers who left two African American youth in a predominantly White south side neighborhood (formerly a part of the "Back of the Yards" area), where they were assaulted by a gang of White youth.[68] Such incidents persist as familiar topics of discussion in Chicago public schools.[69]

Data we have analyzed from a Chicago Consortium sample of ninth- and tenth-grade students parallels and adds insight to the above account.[70] The sample contains 18,251 students.[71] African American students make up nearly half of the sample, Latino/Hispanic youth form more than a third, White adolescents just over 10 percent, and Asian American and Native American students constitute the remainder.

The survey included five measures of perceived criminal injustice. Using a four-point Likert scale ranging from "strongly disagree" to "strongly agree," respondents were asked their reactions to the following statements: "people from my racial group are more likely to be unfairly stopped and questioned by the police"; "police treat young people worse than old people"; "police treat rich people better than poor people"; "police treat people from my racial group worse than people from other racial groups"; and "police treat males worse than females."[72] With strong agreement assigned the highest value and the scale scores ranging from five to twenty, ninth- and tenth-grade Chicago youth scored an average of 14.16 on this scale. Specifically, the results confirmed the predicted racial/ethnic gradient, with African American youth at 14.94, Latino youth at 14.20, White youth at 12.74, and Asian youth at 12.58.

We also found evidence of a substantial increase between ninth and tenth grades in African American and Latino American perceptions of criminal injustice. Both before and especially after this shift, African American youth perceive more criminal injustice than Latinos. As expected, both groups react very negatively to their contacts with the police during this period.

Interestingly, while African American youth are exposed more frequently to police contacts, Latinos are actually more sensitive to police contacts when subjected to them. We believe that Latino youth, who are less familiar with police harassment, may fear that their contacts with the police place them in a similar risk status as Black youth.[73] Regardless of the level of police contacts, both groups are more likely to perceive more criminal injustice than White youth.[74]

The comparative perceptions of Latino and African American youth are shaped by the frames of reference that result from their daily experiences in school. As we noted, segregated residential and educational settings restrict the perceptions of ghettoized African American and Latino youth.[75] Meanwhile, more integrated institutional experiences increase contacts and comparisons across groups, heightening their relative sensitivity and placing them on intensified alert for differential treatment.[76]

As this comparative *racial* frame of reference expands to include an awareness of the relative and group-specific risks of exposure to mistreatment, minority youth who feel uniquely targeted by the police and courts become increasingly sensitive to the perception of injustice. The familiar "experience of the expected" is newly perceived as outrageous.[77] This is the empirical confirmation of the "outrage of liberation."[78] We found this pattern in Chicago among both Latino and African American youth who become more sensitive to perceptions of injustice as they are exposed to increasing contact with White students in their public school experiences.[79] This pattern parallels, and is probably a foundation for, the more skeptical attitudes toward criminal justice among more advantaged and more highly educated African American adults. Further, there may be a part of this story of comparative conflict that begins in adolescence and involves the minor nature of the contacts with police that often engender strong feelings of injustice among minority youth.

Police Contacts and the Development of Perceptions of Criminal Injustice

Thus far we have discussed variation in the perceptions of criminal injustice between and among minority and majority group youth without giving much attention to the seriousness and frequency of the contacts these youth have with the police. There are indications that the minor nature but high frequency of these contacts heavily impact the perceptions of minority youth. It is important to first get a sense of youth encounters with the police in Chicago.

Low Visibility Policing of Visibly Minority Youth

The Chicago Consortium research reveals that adolescent contact with the police—ranging from the low-visibility experience of being "told off" and to "move on" through the official and, therefore, more visible contact of being arrested—is quite substantial.[80] At the lower visibility level, 45 percent of White students, 49 percent of African American students, and 43 percent of Latino students were "told off" or told to "move on" by police.[81] At the officially more visible and severe level of sanctioning, arrests of African Americans were greater than for other racial groups: 12 percent of White youth and 14 percent of Latino youth were arrested at least once, while 19 percent of African American youth had been arrested. Even more notable are the ways in which youth in Chicago and elsewhere respond to police contacts.

Friedman and Hott reported that young African American and Latino men believe that they are singled out and unjustifiably harassed by police in police interrogations.[82] They found that 71 percent of students reported having been stopped by the police, with 62 percent of African American students who were stopped feeling that the police had been disrespectful.

A survey of Cincinnati residents found that nearly half (46.6 percent) of African Americans said that they have been personally "hassled" by the police, compared with only 9.6 percent of Whites.[83] "Hassled" was defined as being "stopped or watched closely by a police officer, even when you had done nothing wrong."[84] Furthermore, police harassment of suspects produced a vicarious effect that differed by race: 66 percent of African Americans reported feeling vicariously hassled, compared to only 13 percent of White respondents.

This collection of studies makes a point that Brockett has provocatively summarized: "the idea of being considered a suspect is incarcerating. It is a form of punishment. This punishment . . . places African Americans in a state of conceptual incarceration."[85] Thus, even low-visibility police contacts involving verbal exchanges have highly negative impacts on the perceptions of minority youth, who feel, as a result, highly visible and vulnerable to the police.

This point became particularly apparent in analyses of the Chicago school data. We expected perceptions of criminal injustice to rise as the visibility and severity of the police contacts increased.[86] Instead, low-visibility contacts were perceived as most unjust, and the perception of injustice declined rather than increased with official visibility and severity.

The gradient of unstandardized regression coefficients summarizing the relationship between type of police contact and perceptions of criminal injustice ranged from 1.0 for being told off or told to move on, 0.8 for being stopped, and 0.7 for being searched to 0.2 for being arrested.[87] Thus, there is an inverse, rather than direct, relationship between the visibility and severity of the sanction and the level of perceived injustice. This relationship is very probably part of the reason why minority youth in more integrated school settings, as well as more educationally and economically successful minority adults, perceive higher levels of criminal injustice. In spite of being advantaged in other ways, the latter group continues to be highly susceptible to low-visibility police contacts.

Code-Switching and Police Contacts

Anderson further delineates and demystifies the attitudes and behavior of minority youth in response to the police and the criminal justice system, and adds an additional dimension to a comparative conflict theory of perceived injustice.[88] He distinguishes two urban minority attitude sets: "decent" and "street" orientations. These categories are not fixed. Rather, individuals can oscillate between them. Anderson refers to this oscillation as "code-switching."

Anderson asserts that an inner-city urban environment produces a "code of the street," a set of informal rules governing interpersonal public behavior, including violence. According to Anderson, "At the heart of the code is a set of . . . informal rules of behavior organized around a desperate search for respect."[89]

The "code of the street" is viewed as a cultural adaptation to a profound lack of faith in the police and the judicial system. The police present a special problem for minority youth by insisting on deference and respect that, in effect, demands their observance of an asymmetric status norm in which the police return less respect than they receive from youth.[90] Minority youth have the further problem of perceiving these encounters in terms that devalue their racial status as well as their youth.[91]

Code-switching is common among minority youth, as well as some minority adults, who must shift between inner-city street contacts and contacts with the larger world of police, teachers, employers, and other agents of conventional authority. Anderson further explains the mechanisms of this concept:

> [A] person may behave according to either set of rules, depending on the situation. Decent people, especially young people, often put a premium on the ability to code-switch. They share many of the middle-class values of the wider white society but know that the open display of such values carries little weight on the street: it doesn't provide the emblems that say, "I can take care of myself." . . . Those strongly associated with the street, who have less exposure to the wider society, may have difficulty code-switching; imbued with the code of the street, they either don't know the rules for decent behavior or may see little value in displaying such knowledge.[92]

Anderson's concept can be easily connected to the growing body of theory and research in which the importance of one's appearance and demeanor in interactions with authority is emphasized.[93] Vrij and Winkel present evidence that when Black citizens exhibit nonverbal "White" behaviors, police tend to treat them with more respect.[94] "This observation may be an indicator of the class differential that causes nonverbal behavior to be interpreted differently based on race."[95] From Brockett's viewpoint, respectful behavior by police, a kind of reverse code-switching, often can result in reciprocity of respect between citizen and police.

Nonetheless, Walker, Spohn, and DeLone report that African Americans have much less favorable attitudes toward the police than other groups.[96] Further, many African American parents make special efforts "to teach their children to be very respectful when confronted by a police officer, out of fear that their children (and particularly their sons) might be beaten or shot if they displayed any disrespect."[97] We suggest that this is a parent-induced form of code-switching that is designed to protect African American youth.[98]

In essence, code-switching is a device for changing one's "public identity" (i.e. race, presumed class, etc.) to elicit a more favorable outcome in an otherwise threatening situation. There is a class component to code-switching among peers-of-color who are sometimes referred to as "acting white": this device may play a key role when the situation involves the police.[99] Anderson has observed that social out-group members may relish conflicts with police, while more advantaged members of the same groups will more often seek to avoid conflict with police because they have more to lose.[100] Thus code-switching in encounters with the police may occur more often among "middle-class" minorities, or among those with expanded frameworks of comparative experience.[101] There is considerable evidence for Anderson's claims and, therefore, for adding code-switching as a dimension of our larger developmental and comparative conflict framework.

Code-switching requires a competency from minority youth that is neither a part of any formal educational curriculum nor demanded of majority-group youth. It is instead an added burden assumed by otherwise disadvantaged youth. It should not be surprising if this informal obligation increases the cynicism of minority youth and exacerbates their perceptions of criminal injustice. Understanding this aspect of police contacts with minority youth is another avenue that can be usefully developed with a conflict theory of perceived criminal injustice.

Cognitive Landscapes of Criminal Injustice

Sampson and Bartusch suggest the metaphor of "cognitive landscapes" to describe the demographic and ecological structuring of troubled American settings where "crime and deviance are more or less expected and institutions of criminal justice are mistrusted."[102] Some of the contours of these landscapes are becoming clear as the surveys reviewed in this paper attend to the multiple groupings and age-graded settings in which citizens and law enforcement officials come into contact. We focus on young persons in secondary schools because perceptions of justice and political institutions are formed at relatively young ages and remain persistent through adulthood. Our Chicago research reveals that perceptions of criminal justice become more negative in middle adolescence among Latino and African American youth, but not among White youth of the same ages.[103]

Mental maps of distrust have both generic and differentiated features, including, on the one hand, African American skepticism of a range of governmental institutions in addition to criminal justice agencies and, on the other hand, distinctive Latino American and African American perceptions of the justice system. These mental maps vary along dimensions that a developmental and comparative conflict theory can help to identify and explain.

In American cities where Latinos and African Americans live, work, and attend school in varying degrees of proximity to one another as well as to Whites, there is an implicit racial gradient of relative subordination that corresponds to the variable skin tones and racial visibility of minority groups. Comparative conflict theory acknowledges that, in the aggregate, African American youth are most visible and therefore at heightened comparative risk of justice-system sanctioning relative to Latino Americans, who, in turn, are at greater risk than Whites. These differential risks probably lead African American youth to collectively perceive more criminal injustice than Latino youth. Latino youth nonetheless react strongly to police contacts and, in turn, when stopped by the police, may perceive more criminal injustice than their White or African American counterparts.

This type of theory also emphasizes the impact among visible minority-group adolescents of exposure to White youth at school. Survey results indicate that as Latino American and African American youth encounter White youth in increasing numbers in school, they also become more skeptical about their criminal justice encounters. Brooks anticipated this finding,[104] and Patterson described it as an effect of intergroup contact, which he considered as an initial phase of the ordeal of integration and a preliminary source of resulting outrage that accompanies liberation from some of the constraints of segregation.[105]

This outrage intensifies in early to middle adolescence, when youth begin to confront the police in increasingly charged public encounters. Thus, this response to the criminal justice system is probably a precursor of a wider skepticism among visible minorities about a range of governmental institutions responsible for employment, housing, health care, voting, and other aspects of adolescent and adult life. That is, criminal justice contacts and perceptions formed in early to middle adolescence are of wider developmental significance in later phases of the adolescent and adult life course.

Code-switching may be a crucial part of the comparative developmental process that merits further study. Code-switching is uniquely required of visible minority youth who often must anticipate and manage low-visibility unofficial police contacts, as well as official and higher-visibility contacts and conflicts with the justice system, both of which can occur while upwardly mobile minority youth are coincidentally achieving improved positions of advantage and distinction in school. Such youth are required to manage dual identities that straddle the demands of school, work, and everyday living in minority and majority group settings. There may be notable social-psychological costs to managing the demands of these dual identities, with one cost being a skepticism that generalizes from the police and the criminal justice system to other authority-based governmental institutions.

Conclusion

In sum, we have argued that the structure of a developmental conflict theory of perceptions of criminal injustice will need to take into account a multiplicity of visible minority groups and police contacts in the developmental context of early and middle adolescence. Comparative conflict theory also will need to consider the comparative meanings, especially of injustice, that these encounters assume among visible minority youth who experience a widening range of contacts with White youth, and who consequently often become outraged by feelings of unjustifiable subordination. Finally, we have argued that a developmental and comparative conflict theory needs to explore how code-switching may be especially frustrating to these youth, who must manage dual identities in successfully moving between the inner-city and mobility contexts that extend well beyond the borders of their segregated communities. A broader sociological benefit of developing a conflict theory of perceptions of criminal injustice along the lines we have outlined may be the insights this theory can provide into a wider range of later adolescent and adult perceptions extending well beyond the justice system.

New Directions in Empirical Work on Race and Crime

Along with the theoretical developments discussed in detail above, we suggest that our ideas have significant implications for empirical advancements that are also required. Criminological analysis must take a new direction to explore the meaning of race and crime and the corresponding relationship of race and punishment, particularly in the context of urban youth. Although stops, searches, and arrests by the police are often used as proxies for delinquency, these same measures may also indicate bias in punishment or policing. This distinction must be addressed theoretically, methodologically, and analytically.

We have much to consider in understanding both the frequency and the substance of youth contact with police. Markowitz contends that research studying the nexus between race and crime must do more than simply attempt to "define the motivation of the individual offender. . . . It must also center on the interplay between individual and community and the extent to which such interactions are affected by race and produce criminality in various contexts."[106] The key is to focus on a *dynamic* portrayal of the processes involved, thus avoiding the static tendency that has dominated much research on race and crime. This will require a change in the research orientation of those who study crime. Markowitz views the long-held commitment of social scientists to quantitative methodologies as useful in assembling only part of the puzzle. He continues, "If we are to understand the role of race in crime in a unique way, then we must commit the time and energies necessary to measure this phenomenon in all its complexity."[107] We argue that ethnographic studies, participant analyses, and longitudinal designs must be incorporated into this research tradition to explore the subtle dimensions of the social impact of race on crime.

The approach we are advocating emphasizes the use of both quantitative and qualitative methods. Sunshine and Tyler stress the need for tests of causal sequence (longitudinal data) and context (qualitative methods) to best assess their procedural, justice-based model of legitimacy and compliance with the law. They warn, "It is always possible that compliance leads to legitimacy and perceptions of procedural justice."[108] Laub and Sampson advocate integrative strategies for bridging quantitative and qualitative data. Their quantitative reanalysis of Sheldon and Eleanor Glueck's data on delinquent nondelinquent youth were used as a source for their age-graded theory of crime. Their book, *Crime in the Making*, has been quite influential in shaping understanding of the life-course trajectory of crime.[109] Further insight was gained from their quantitative analyses that examined life-course persistence in or desistance from crime, as predicted by various structural and process variables (employment, marriage, etc.). However, in addition to a traditional quantitative *variables-oriented* approach, they adopted a *person-oriented* strategy to achieve understanding of the complex processes of criminal offending over the life course. This plan entailed the identification of a random subset of cases for intensive qualitative analysis identified by cross-classification of key social dimensions (e.g., employment, marriage, and crime). Consistent with the goal of merging quantitative and qualitative methods, they used the results from the quantitative analyses as a means of identifying their cases (persons) for in-depth qualitative analysis.[110] In particular, they conducted deeper analyses of sampled cases that were consistent with their hypotheses (high employment, less crime) and those that were clearly inconsistent (high employment, high crime) with their expectations.

We believe this approach may also be used to critically assess the complex (and hypothesized) reciprocal relationship between youth contact with police and perceptions of injustice. It is imperative that researchers of race and crime gain more in-depth information on youths' reactions to police contact, particularly at the lower levels when discrimination by police is more likely to be perceived. Further examination of the attitudes of students with low-level or no police contact will allow an opportunity for researchers to explore when, why, and how these perceptions have been shaped vicariously.

NOTES

1. For example, Quinney 1970; Turk 1969.

2. For example, Chambliss and Seidman 1971.

3. Hawkins 1987; Liska, Chamlin, and Reed 1985; Mitchell and Sidanius 1995; Walker, Spohn, and DeLone 2000.

4. For example, Tittle 1994.

5. For general discussions, see Chambliss 1999; Mann 1993; Wilbanks 1987.

6. Blumstein 1982; Kennedy 1997; Mauer 1999; Tonry 1995.

7. Western and Beckett 1999.

8. Bobo and Johnson 2004; Brooks 2000; Brooks and Jeon-Slaughter 2001; Wortley, Hagan, and Macmillan 1997. Also, for a study on African Americans' heightened perception of criminal injustice, see Hagan and Albonetti 1982. For work demonstrating that the African American middle-class neighborhood holds a unique perception of police-citizen relations to minorities, see Weitzer 2000a.

9. Wacquant 2000.

10. LaFree 1998; Mann 1993; Russell 1998; Tyler 1990.

11. For discussions of the frustrations and negativity middle-class African Americans feel towards persistent discrimination, see Feagin and Sikes 1994;

Hochschild 1995; and Schuman et al. 1997. For a general discussion on African American self-perception and political behavior, see Dawson 1994.

12. For a general discussion on the progression of White racial attitudes despite the persistence of structural barriers to racial equality, see Bobo, Kluegel, and Smith 1997.

13. Patterson 1997:15.

14. Liska et al. 1985.

15. Hagan and Albonetti 1982.

16. Sampson and Bartusch 1998.

17. Sampson, Raudenbush, and Earls 1997:918.

18. Sampson and Lauritsen 1997.

19. Ibid.:364.

20. Collins 1997; Cose 1993.

21. For a comparative study of affluent and poor African American perspectives about American society, see Hochschild 1995.

22. Schuman et al. 1997.

23. Brooks and Jeon-Slaughter 2001; Peek, Lowe, and Alston 1981. For a discussion on a possible role class plays with respect to African American attitudes toward criminal justice systems, see Weitzer and Tuch 1999.

24. Brooks 2000; Wortley et al. 1997.

25. See Hagan and Albonetti 1982; Henderson and Cullen 1997; Tuch and Weitzer 1997.

26. For example, Chambliss and Seidman 1971.

27. Chambliss 1999:75.

28. Bobo and Johnson 2004:152.

29. Flanagan and Sherrod 1998; Niemi and Hepburn 1995.

30. Bobo and Johnson 2004:155.

31. Ibid.

32. See Piliavin and Briar 1964; Taylor et al. 2001.

33. Sullivan 1989.

34. Anderson 1999.

35. Matsueda 1992; Matsueda and Heimer 1987.

36. Heimer and Matsueda 1994.

37. Ibid.

38. Davis 1959.

39. Merton and Rossi 1957; Runciman 1966.

40. Portes and Rumbaut 2001:47.

41. Ibid.

42. Hawkins 1987.

43. Portes and Rumbaut 2001.

44. Brooks and Jeon-Slaughter 2001.

45. Young 2004.

46. Carter 1985:498.
47. Ibid. See also Skogan et al. 2002.
48. Brooks 2000.
49. Ibid.:1255.
50. Ibid.:1256.
51. See also Patterson 1997.
52. Brooks 2000:1256.
53. Ibid.:1256–57.
54. Patterson 1997:51.
55. Runciman 1966:25.
56. Brooks 2000:1256.
57. Runciman 1966:19.
58. Patterson 1997:52.
59. Frankenberg and Lee 2002; Frankenberg, Lee, and Orfield 2003.
60. Orfield and Lee 2004.
61. Frankenberg et al. 2003:54, 57.
62. Hirschfield 2003.
63. *City of Chicago v. Morales,* 527 US 41:45–47 (1999).
64. Ibid.:49.
65. Martinez 1998.
66. Suttles 1968.
67. Casey and Fornek 1992.
68. Ibid.
69. Hagan, Hirschfield, and Shedd 2002.
70. Consortium on Chicago School Research 2001; See also Hagan, Shedd, and Payne 2005.
71. Hagan et al. 2005.
72. The measures and results described here are from Hagan et al. 2005.
73. Carter 1985; Mindiola, Niemann, and Rodriguez 2002.
74. Mindiola et al. 2002:36.
75. Patterson 1997; Brooks 2000.
76. Brooks 2000.
77. Hagan et al. 2005.
78. Patterson 1997.
79. Hagan et al. 2005.
80. Ibid.
81. Shedd and Hagan 2005.
82. Cited in Walker et al. 2000:117.
83. Browning et al. 1994.
84. Ibid.:4.
85. Brockett 2000:116–17. For an analysis of racial stigma, see Loury 2002.
86 Shedd and Hagan 2005.

87. Hagan et al. 2005.
88. Anderson 1999.
89. Ibid.:9.
90. Sykes and Clark 1975.
91. Ibid.:589–90.
92. Anderson 1999:36.
93. See Piliavin and Briar 1964 for an early influential work on these issues.
94. Vrij and Winkel 1992.
95. Brockett 2000:120.
96. Walker et al. 2000:90–91.
97. Walker et al. 2000:100.
98. Shedd and Hagan 2005:30.
99. Ibid.
100. Anderson 1978.
101. Shedd and Hagan 2005:29–30.
102. Sampson and Bartusch 1998:800.
103. Hagan et al. 2005.
104. Brooks 2000.
105. Patterson 1997.
106. Markowitz 2000:12.
107. Ibid.
108. Sunshine and Tyler 2003:519.
109. Sampson and Laub 1993.
110. Laub and Sampson 2004:85–86.

Chapter 18

Race and Neighborhood Codes of Violence

Ross L. Matsueda, Kevin Drakulich,
and Charis E. Kubrin

Research on violence suggests that disadvantaged inner-city neighborhoods spawn violent subcultures, in which social status—denied in the conventional realm of schools and jobs—is attained through acts of violence and intimidation, shows of nerve and courage, and displays of manhood and honor. Such social systems are governed by codes of violence—rules or norms that help define social status on the streets, bring order, predictability, and structure to violent acts, and thereby allow members to use the system for their own instrumental needs—whether to acquire respect on the streets, gain protection from violence, or avoid humiliating situations of status degradation.

Codes of violence are norms with sanctions that regulate violent acts. Classic criminological studies have identified criminal codes in a variety of realms. Thrasher, for example, found that a gang code exerted group control over members: "we are not allowed to fight among ourselves," "if you get caught, don't squeal on the other guys," "be loyal to the officers," "defend ladies and girls in trouble," "do not lie to each other."[1] Sutherland found that professional thieves adhered to occupational rules such as "profits are shared equally," "fall dough is used for anyone who is pinched," "thieves deal honestly with one another," and "show class and high status," which functioned to reduce conflict, increase cooperation, and decrease risk of punishment.[2] Cressey identified a Mafia code—consisting of the tenets "be loyal to the organization," "don't squeal," "be rational," "be a man of honor," "respect women and elders," "don't sell out," "be a stand-up guy by showing courage and heart"—which functioned to control the behavior of members of organized crime families.[3] Such codes foreshadow, in form and function, contemporary neighborhood codes of violence.

In this chapter, we examine the concept of neighborhood codes of violence. We proceed in four steps. First, we provide a brief historical review of the criminological literature on structural opportunities, violent subcultures, and codes of violence. We emphasize the most influential of this work, Elijah Anderson's "code of the streets." Second, we develop key theoretical implications from this work with an eye toward applying it systematically, using social-scientific methods. Third, using recent data collected on Seattle neighborhoods, we explore whether such codes can be measured accurately with survey instruments. Fourth, we test a model in which neighborhood codes of violence vary by structural characteristics of neighborhoods, such as race and concentrated poverty.

Structure, Culture, and Neighborhood Codes of Violence

Classic Criminological Studies of Structure and Culture

A long history of criminological theory and ethnographic research has discussed the interplay between social structure and culture in producing violence.[4] A prominent role is played by the spatial organization of culture and structure across neighborhoods, which can be traced to work by Shaw and McKay.[5] They argued that high rates of delinquency in inner-city neighborhoods are explained by social disorganization (weak local institutions, such as families and schools, undermine control over youth who congregate on the street) and cultural transmission (a tradition of delinquent values and pressures transmitted across generations of gangs).

Sutherland combined the two processes in his concept of differential social organization: weak organization against crime included social disorganization, whereas strong organization in favor of crime included cultural transmission, and the crime rate was determined by the relative strength of the conflicting processes.[6] Applied to the neighborhood, Sutherland's theory predicts that violence will be high when conventional organization against violence is weak, including the dissemination of definitions or codes against violence, and organization in favor of violence is strong, including the dissemination of definitions or codes favoring violence.[7]

Later, Cohen and Cloward and Ohlin developed structural theories of delinquent subcultures, and identified their content.[8] Each argued that illicit subcultures were an adaptation to barriers to attaining success, respect, and self-esteem in conventional society. For Cohen, lower-class boys, unlikely to measure up to middle-class standards in school, face failure and status anxiety.[9] In response, they collectively innovate an oppositional subculture, which turns middle-class values on its head: malicious, seemingly irrational acts of theft and vandalism, which flout capitalist values of rationality and the sanctity of private property, become normative within the subculture. Miller argued that lower-class culture consists of focal concerns (trouble, toughness, smartness, fate, and autonomy) causing lower-class males to be preoccupied with displaying toughness and physical prowess, getting into trouble with drugs, alcohol, and sex, seeking thrills, demanding autonomy, showing street smarts, and being fatalistic.[10]

Cloward and Ohlin argued that structural barriers to conventional success cause lower-class males to experience frustration and alienation.[11] When such youth attribute the source of their failure to the illegitimacy of the system, they tend to withdraw their allegiance to society and innovate an alternate system of gaining status. While theft subcultures—comprised of pecuniary illicit acts that lead to success as conventionally defined—arise in organized slums consisting of stable organization between older and younger criminals, and between criminals and conventional elements (the fence, fix, and bail bondsman), violent subcultures arise in disorganized neighborhoods. Lacking tangible resources, youth in disorganized communities resort to their own physical prowess to attain status and success. Here, turf gangs dominate the neighborhood. Status is attained through acts of violence:

> The principal prerequisites for success are "guts" and the capacity to endure pain. One doesn't need "connections," "pull," or elaborate technical skills in order to achieve "rep." The essence of the warrior adjustment is an expressed feeling-state: "heart." The acquisition of status is not simply a consequence of skill in the use of violence or of physical strength but depends, rather, on one's willingness to risk injury or death in the search for "rep."[12]

Short and Strodbeck extended this thesis to show that, within gangs, leaders attained status through shows of heart, toughness, and daring.[13] In deciding to join a gang fight, they often weigh their subjective expectation of a definite loss of immediate group status against the distant and unlikely event of being punished.

Contemporary Ethnographic Studies of Cultural Codes

More recently, Ruth Horowitz examined culture and identity in a Latino neighborhood and posited two cultural codes that structure an inner-city neighborhood.[14] The instrumental code of the American Dream, organized around economic success, is espoused by community members, but conflicts with the reality of negative experiences in lower-class schools and available jobs, each of which fail to link residents to the broader culture. The code of honor, organized around respect, manhood, and deference, is espoused by young men on the streets; violations of the code can lead to violence.

In an honor-bound subculture that emphasizes manhood and defines violations of interpersonal etiquette in an adversarial manner, any action that challenges a person's right to deferential treatment in *public*— whether derogating a person, offering a favor that may be difficult to return, or demonstrating lack of respect for a female relative's sexual purity —can be interpreted as an insult and a potential threat to manhood. Honor demands that a man be able physically to back his claim to dominance and independence.[15]

The street identities of young men are shaped by their responses to insult, negotiations of threats to manhood, and ability to maintain honor. For Horowitz, Latino youth must balance the instrumental code of the American Dream, which requires being "decent" from the standpoint of the larger community, against the honor code of the streets.

In his ethnography of an inner-city African American neighborhood in Philadelphia, Elijah Anderson provided perhaps the most vivid description of codes of violence.[16] Anderson argues that the code of the streets is rooted in the local circumstances of ghetto poverty as described by Wilson's underclass thesis.[17] Structural conditions of concentrated poverty, joblessness, racial stigma, and drug use lead to alienation and a sense of hopelessness in the inner city, which, in turn, spawn an oppositional culture consisting of norms "often consciously opposed to those of mainstream society."[18]

But what explains the content of such oppositional norms? We can identify three intersecting processes. First, Anderson argues that structural disadvantage hampers inner-city impoverished African American youth from gaining respect and esteem from school and work, which puts them at risk of embracing street culture. Second, he suggests that alienated African—American youth come to distrust conventional institutions—

particularly the police and legal system—for resolving their local disputes and problems, which puts them at risk of pursuing illicit dispute resolution. Third, Anderson observes that structural disadvantage disproportionately affects males, which leads to an emphasis on "manhood" for resolving disputes and gaining status.

The conjunction of these processes produces the "code of the streets." Distrustful of police, inner-city youth must rely on their own resources for addressing interpersonal problems. Lacking material resources, they have little recourse other than resorting to violence and aggression to resolve disputes.[19] Violence becomes institutionalized within this social system on the streets, which serves the twin functions of resolving disputes and allocating status outside of conventional society. This system is governed by specific norms about violence, which comprise the street code, the content of which echoes that described by earlier subcultural theorists. The multiplicity of underlying norms gives the code multiple dimensions or domains of meaning.

The most fundamental norm is "never back down from a fight." Backing down will not only result in a loss of street credibility and status but also increase the likelihood of being preyed upon in the future:

> To run away would likely leave one's self esteem in tatters, while inviting further disrespect. Therefore, people often feel constrained not only to stand up and at least attempt to resist during an assault but also to "pay back"—to seek revenge—after a successful assault on their person. Revenge may include going to get a weapon or even getting relatives and friends involved. Their very identity, their self-respect, and their honor are often intricately tied up with the way they perform on the street during and after such encounters. And it is this identity, including credible reputation for payback, or vengeance, which is strongly believed to deter future assaults.[20]

This quotation illustrates an underlying norm of reciprocity, in which one is expected to respond in kind when disrespected by name calling, challenges, assaults, etc. This is consistent with Luckenbill's classic study showing that homicide is often a dynamic "character contest," in which victim and offender, while trying to save face by responding in kind to insults and threats, commit—sometimes unwittingly—to a murderous definition of the situation.[21] The norms of reciprocity and never backing down apply to peers, gangs, and family members. When a peer is threatened or assaulted, other group members must never run or "punk out." The phrase "I got your back" illustrates this norm of peers standing up for each other, which frees members to aggress against others with impunity.

Status on the street is achieved by developing a reputation as a "man," or "badass." Manhood is associated with having "nerve": a willingness to express disrespect for other males—for example, by getting in their face, throwing the first punch, pulling the trigger, messing with their woman—and thereby risking retaliation. Katz argues that "badasses" demonstrate a "superiority of their being" by dominating and forcing their will on others, and showing that they "mean it."[22]

Moreover, street youth recognize this status system and manipulate it instrumentally to increase their status, or "juice," by "campaigning for respect"—challenging or assaulting others and disrespecting them by stealing their material possessions or girlfriends.[23] They start a fight or "force a humiliating show of deference" by accidentally bumping another male, or challenging them with eye contact and the opening line, "Whatchulookin-at?"[24] These are self-image promoters.[25] At times, status is allocated on the basis of violent acts against outsiders in the neighborhood, such as members of other racial groups, which simultaneously increase the offender's status as well as the neighborhood's, as in the "defended communities" thesis.[26]

The proliferation of guns on the streets has raised the stakes: guns not only provide a quick and often final resolution to a dispute but also level the playing field, allowing less physical youth to compete for status if they are willing to "pull the trigger." Guns can instantly transform a minor dispute over a stare, bump, or swear word into a deadly act. Guns become a valued commodity, infused with symbols of toughness, power, and dominance, and thereby an indication of repute and esteem.[27]

Once established, the code regulates and organizes violence on the streets. As an institutional feature of street life, it produces a strong incentive to acquire knowledge of its tenets not only for "street" but "decent" youth as well (to use Anderson's ideal types). Those familiar with the code will know how to project a self-image as "not to be messed with," how to prevent confrontations by avoiding eye contact with others, how to talk one's way out of a dispute without violence or loss of respect. Naïve youth ignorant of the code will unwittingly invite confrontations, appear to be easy prey, and be unable to escape altercations unharmed. They risk victimization by violence. Thus, knowledge of the code serves a protective function for all youth, regardless of whether they participate in the street culture.

This is perhaps Anderson's most novel observation, and from it we can derive an important theoretical proposition: the "code of the streets" is an objective property of the neighborhood, rather than merely a subjective property of the individuals inhabiting the neighborhood. This proposition, in turn, has implications for the causes of violence. Violent behavior within the neighborhood is not merely an individual process in which a youth internalizes the code and thereby becomes motivated to attack others. There is also a contextual—in this case a neighborhood—effect due to the status system governed by the code. For example, an individual may not espouse the code, but in a neighborhood dominated by the code, be educed into violence through confrontations by status enhancers. Even those young males who reject the code, and its prescription for violence as a way of resolving disputes, may have difficulty turning the other cheek when challenged in public. In other words, on the streets, within confrontational situations, the result of interactions is not merely the sum of the biographical histories individuals bring to the setting but also an emergent property in which the "doing" of the code (in the ethnomethodological sense) results in a novel adjustment to the code. This emergence is illustrated by the character contest described by Luckenbill, in which actors exercise agency to adjust their responses in light of another's aggression, the code, and their own threatened identities. Emergence arises from the situation and thus, the *spatial* context within which it is embedded.

Youth who are ignorant of the code may be at greater risk of violence. Indeed, it might be that a mixed neighborhood dominated by the code but, at the same time, populated by many naïve youth ignorant of the code, will have the highest rates of violence. The volatile mix of potential violent offenders (motivated by the prospect of enhancing their status) and vulnerable youth victims (whose ignorance of the code makes them attractive targets) may spark explosive violence in the neighborhood.

Race, Structure, and Neighborhood Codes of Violence

Race, Structural Opportunity, and Disadvantage

Research on the spatial configuration of disadvantage in urban areas shows that inequality in the labor market, coupled with residential segregation, produces inner-city neighborhoods characterized by high rates of poverty, residential instability, racial minorities, drug use, and violence.

These configurations are generated, in part, by a sorting process in which individuals at a competitive disadvantage in the labor market sort into disadvantaged and undesirable neighborhoods through preferences, or more likely because they either lack financial resources or face racial discrimination in the housing market.[28]

Over time, these sorting patterns become institutionalized and feed back to reinforce residential instability, poverty, and the like. Instability, poverty, and political powerlessness, in turn, undermine local institutions, such as families and schools, which undercut social control and supervision over youth. Such youth—having experienced violence in the home, failure in school, and early alienation—find themselves on the street joining other similarly situated youth, in the market for a sense of identity and self-worth. They are at risk of developing and participating in a system of neighborhood codes. As Shaw and McKay observed, such processes persist over generations of street youth through cultural transmission, so that spatial arrangements of neighborhood codes of violence remain stable over time.[29] The key to the diffusion of codes within and across neighborhoods is the distribution of communication networks. Concentrations of individual characteristics that increase interaction on the streets will increase the likelihood of codes diffusing within a neighborhood. For example, the intersection of concentrations of racial minorities and poverty should spawn a code of violence within a neighborhood. And if neighborhoods with similar race-class compositions are spatially contiguous, increasing communication, codes may diffuse across neighborhoods.

Local Neighborhoods as Social Systems and Codes of Violence

In general, the principles underlying codes of violence are available in American culture and known to most members of society, regardless of social class or neighborhood. As noted by Anderson, principles such as avenging a violent act perpetrated on a family member or never backing down from a fight can be traced to earlier historical periods such as the American Wild West and Japanese Samurai era. While cognizant of these codes, most members of society live their lives unencumbered by the codes' consequences. Thus, we disagree with Anderson, who implies that such codes are known only to inner-city residents. Indeed, toughness, aggression, and violence have been central to the concept of masculinity throughout American life, causing young males to connect masculinity-power-aggression-violence as part of their own developing male identities.[30] We agree, however, that such codes become institutionalized as part of a social group's culture only when interacting members face structural barriers to conventional roles and a positive sense of self. For example, adolescents face barriers to full participation in adult roles and are, therefore, at risk of participating in the code to gain status.

The process by which individuals are allocated to housing creates neighborhoods with distinct socioeconomic characteristics, access to resources, and cultural complexions. Such neighborhood attributes facilitate or impede local solidarity and consensus, collective efficacy, and organization against crime. Affluent, homogenous, stable neighborhoods are able to create consensus and use political, cultural, and social capital to organize against crime. Codes of violence may be known to residents but are not relevant for everyday life. Affluent youth may be exposed to such codes on the playground, but fail to internalize them (as their parents counter the codes' violent themes), and instead find more attractive conventional ways of attaining self-worth.

In contrast, heterogeneous neighborhoods with high rates of instability, poverty, African Americans, and immigrants are less likely to achieve consensus, organize against violence, and provide the capital necessary for their children to develop positive self-images within conventional institutions. Indeed, as Anderson observed, parents themselves may be from "street" backgrounds, and socialize their children, sometimes consciously, sometimes unconsciously, into the tenets of violent codes: "Don't come in here crying that somebody beat you up; you better get back out there and whup his ass. If you don't whup his ass, I'll whup your ass when you come home."[31] In these neighborhoods, not only are violent codes known, but they become an organizing principle around which status is allocated. The code is perhaps most institutionalized when it organizes violent turf gangs in the neighborhood.[32]

Systematic Variation and Measurement

From our discussion so far, we conclude that subcultural theories and ethnographic studies suggest that something like the code of the streets within inner-city, impoverished, African American neighborhoods plays a key role in their high rates of violence. From a social-scientific standpoint, however, the limitations of ethnographic methods suggest the need for a more systematic examination of the street code thesis. Therefore, in this chapter, we explore four preliminary questions that are fundamental to the viability of the thesis. First, can we use social-scientific measuring instruments to determine whether neighborhood codes of violence exist? Second, assuming they can be measured reliably, are neighborhood codes distributed spatially in ways implied by ethnographic observations and predicted by subcultural theory? Ethnographic research has identified codes of the street in the inner-city, impoverished, African American neighborhoods studied, but have only assumed, rather than demonstrated, that such codes are absent in other neighborhoods. An important question is whether these codes are the exclusive property of the neighborhoods studied or are equally present in more affluent White neighborhoods. Third, can we conceive of codes of violence as an objective property of neighborhoods, rather than a subjective property of individuals? Here we cannot resolve the ontological question of objective existence, but instead can provide a scientific, evidence-based answer derived from the measurement properties of neighborhood codes and their distribution across areas. Fourth, are codes related to neighborhood violence, as expected?

Data and Methods

We examine these questions using survey data on Seattle neighborhoods collected in 2002–2003. Seattle provides an instructive case, given that most research on codes of violence has been carried out in large cities, such as Philadelphia and New York, which are racially segregated and have high rates of violence. In contrast, Seattle has a moderate level of residential segregation, a small but growing minority population, moderate levels of concentrated disadvantage, and relatively little violence. Thus, we might expect difficulty in identifying neighborhood codes of violence in Seattle, and consequently, empirical support for such codes would constitute very strong evidence.

The Seattle "Neighborhoods and Crime Survey"

We use data from the "Seattle Neighborhoods and Crime Survey," a multilevel survey of nearly five thousand households within 123 census tracts in Seattle. The survey combined three sampling designs. First, a stratified cluster sample randomly selected two block groups for each census tract, and eight households per block group. Second, an ethnic oversample randomly selected two households within each of the two blocks (with the highest rates of minorities) for each of 141 block groups with the highest proportions of minorities. Third, a replication sample randomly selected two households in each of six street segments selected in the earlier Seattle Criminal Victimization Survey of one hundred census tracts.[33] A telephone survey of one adult per household yielded a response rate of approximately 50 percent. Comparisons with census data suggest that our sample contains more highly educated, White, and affluent respondents than are found in the city as a whole. We therefore control for these characteristics in our analyses.

We asked respondents about their households, crime victimization, neighborhoods, and ties to the community. We also asked a series of questions designed to measure individual, as well as neighborhood, codes of violence. Neighborhoods are defined by census tracts. Empirical research, as well as local knowledge of neighborhoods, suggests that census tracts are fairly good approximations of neighborhoods in Seattle.

Statistical Methods

We begin our analysis by examining reliability and other measurement properties of our indicators of neighborhood and individual codes of violence. That is, we determine whether they hang together, or covary, in ways consistent with ethnographic research, using confirmatory factor analysis on ordinal measures.[34] We then examine whether our neighborhood codes of violence are related to neighborhood characteristics using a three-level hierarchical linear model.[35] The first (measurement) level incorporates our confirmatory factor model of five indicators. The second (individual) level adjusts our neighborhood-level estimates of neighborhood codes for response bias due to differences in the demographic composition of neighborhood residents (informants)—and their own personal beliefs in violent codes. The third (neighborhood) level examines whether our neighborhood codes of violence correlate with neighborhood characteristics (e.g., racial composition, poverty, stability), as predicted.

Modeling Neighborhood Codes of Violence

There are two ways of measuring neighborhood codes of violence. In the most straightforward method, we could measure the degree to which individuals espouse the code and then aggregate their responses to the neighborhood level. This method has three weaknesses: (1) measures of individual codes may be fraught with social desirability effects; (2) youth participating in street codes in one neighborhood may reside in another; and (3) youth espousing the code will be rare, difficult to sample, and least likely to respond to surveys.

Alternatively, under the assumption that neighborhood codes of violence are objective properties of neighborhoods, we could use residents as "informants" about codes in their neighborhoods. This would avoid the difficulties with measuring individual codes. It does assume, however, that residents are aware of codes within their neighborhood. However, this assumption should hold because all residents have an incentive to know the code, either to protect themselves or to gain status.

Measures of Neighborhood Codes of Violence

To measure neighborhood codes of violence, we use our samples of residents as informants, who report on the existence of codes within their neighborhood. Because violent codes have multiple dimensions, we use five measures, each designed to tap into a different domain. Each question was prefaced by, "Do people in your neighborhood agree that . . ." The first item gets at the heart of the code, which entails gaining respect through violence: "In this neighborhood, for young people to gain respect among their peers, they sometimes have to be willing to fight." The second item captures the socialization process, in which "street" parents teach their kids to fight back: "In this neighborhood, parents teach their kids to fight back if they are insulted or threatened." The third item taps the concept of reciprocity, and specifically the notions of "payback" and "disrespect": "In this neighborhood, if a loved one is disrespected, people retaliate even if it means resorting to violence." The fourth item captures Anderson's observation that knowledge of the code can serve a protective function: "In this neighborhood, young men often project a tough or violent image to avoid being threatened with violence." The fifth item reflects the street status that accrues to possession of guns: "In this neighborhood, young men who own guns are often looked up to and respected." These five items capture the major dimensions of codes, and collectively should differentiate those neighborhoods in which the code is a key feature of social life, organizing status and violence, from those in which the code is irrelevant, nonexistent, or rejected.

Measures of Individual Codes of Violence

We could be wrong to assume that neighborhood codes of violence are an objective property of neighborhoods, but instead are merely the subjective properties of the individuals who inhabit a neighborhood. To address this issue, we collected five measures of *individual* violence codes, which asked residents about their own subjective views of violence. These measures resemble the neighborhood items, but use the stem, "Do you agree with the following?" The first item captures the core notion of respect from being tough: "It is important for young men to have a reputation as someone who is tough and not to be messed with." The second item taps the norm of never backing down: "If someone insults you or threatens you, you should turn the other cheek." The third item captures the protective function of knowing the code: "Out in public, it is important to avoid confrontations with strangers to avoid violence." The fourth item taps the socialization process by which parents, in this case, *discourage* the tenets of the code: "If your child were insulted and physically threatened by other children, you'd want them to talk their way out of it, rather than fight." The fifth item captures a general negative attitude about violence: "Violence is never justified under any circumstances."

Measurement Models

As a first step in assessing the accuracy of our neighborhood and individual indicators of violence codes, we examine their reliability by modeling covariation across the individual items. We estimate a confirmatory factor model, which posits, for each respondent, that the neighborhood (individual) codes are each linear functions of the true neighborhood (individual) codes plus a random measurement error term. A poor or unreliable measure of a concept will not covary with the other measures, and this will result in large measurement errors and low reliabilities.

Figure 18.1 presents the models' standardized loadings, which are the correlations between the "true score" and the indicator.[36] Higher loadings indicate greater reliability. The loadings for the neighborhood code items are uniformly high (about .80) and nearly identical. The loadings for the individual codes vary, ranging from highly reliable ("talk their way out") to moderately reliable ("turn the other cheek," "avoid confrontations," and "violence never justified").[37] Thus, we have some evidence that our neighborhood code measures hang together better than do our individual

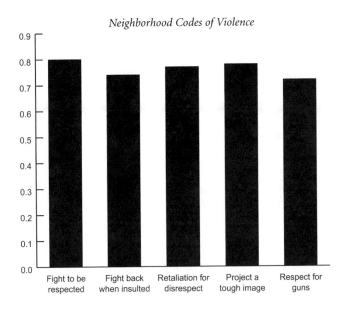

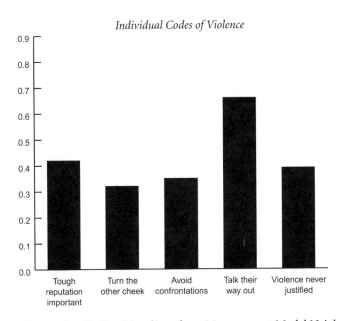

Fig. 18.1. Standardized Loadings from Measurement Model Neighborhood Codes of Violence

measures. Of more importance is whether they vary across neighborhoods and correlate with neighborhood variables as expected.

Multilevel Models of Neighborhood Codes

We test a substantive model in which codes of violence are structured by the neighborhood composition of race, class, violence, and residential mobility. Before estimating this model, however, we need to obtain unbiased estimates of neighborhood codes from our survey measures. We do this using a three-level hierarchical linear model. The first level models between-item, within-individual variation in neighborhood codes, and controls for random measurement error in each item.[38] The standardized loading estimate (.77) is about the average of the individual loadings from our confirmatory factor analysis.

The second level models within-neighborhood, between-respondent variation in neighborhood codes. Here we address the issue of measurement bias. Given that we use our respondents as informants about their neighborhood's true codes, we need to adjust our neighborhood-level estimates of codes for individual characteristics that might bias those estimates. For example, suppose older White respondents tend to underestimate their neighborhood's codes of violence. Then, if our neighborhood sample has a disproportionate number of older White respondents, our estimates of neighborhood codes might be underestimated relative to other neighborhood samples with fewer older White respondents. Our individual-level model uses covariates that may influence a respondent's estimates of neighborhood codes: sex, age, education, income, race, length of residence, and victim of violence. We also adjust our neighborhood estimates for our respondents' individual subjective belief in codes. We hypothesize that those who believe in violent codes will tend to think other residents are like themselves, and overestimate the true neighborhood codes; conversely, those who reject the codes will tend to underestimate the true level. The key to this approach to measuring neighborhood codes is the assumption that most residents—decent or street—have an incentive to know the codes, either to gain status or to protect themselves from violence. Consequently, the average resident will know whether objective codes of violence exist in the neighborhood or not.

We can also test the competing assumption that codes of violence are actually subjective properties of individuals, rather than objective properties of neighborhoods. Under this assumption, once we control for indi-

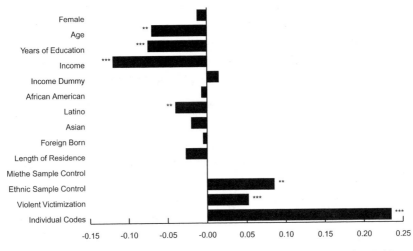

Fig. 18.2. Standardized Person-Level Coefficients from Regression of Neighborhood Codes of Violence. * p < .05, ** p < .01, *** p < .001

vidual codes—now, the "true" codes of violence—our informant reports of neighborhood codes will have little variance, which is randomly distributed across neighborhoods. Therefore, neighborhood codes will not be related to neighborhood structural characteristics in our substantive models, once we control for individual codes at the individual level. Regardless of which assumption is correct, our estimates of neighborhood variation in codes will be conservative, given that individual codes could partly tap "true" codes.

Figure 18.2 depicts our individual-level coefficients. We find, as expected, that neighborhood codes are underestimated by respondents who are older, are more educated, and earn more income. Thus, it appears that respondents isolated from the streets—more affluent and older respondents—tend to underestimate the presence of neighborhood codes. Being female has no effect, perhaps because females are aware of what goes on in the streets through their husbands, boyfriends, and brothers. Surprisingly, among our race (dummy) variables, only the coefficient for Latino is significant: relative to Whites—the omitted category—Hispanics tend to underestimate neighborhood codes. The coefficients for Blacks and Asians are nonsignificant. We do find that net of race, members of our ethnic oversample tend to overestimate neighborhood codes. As hypothesized, those who have been victimized by violence overestimate neighborhood codes. Finally, as expected, those respondents who espouse individual codes themselves tend to overestimate the existence of neighborhood codes. This is the largest effect in the model. Once we purge respondents' estimates of neighborhood codes of the biasing effects of respondent characteristics, we can model the effects of neighborhood composition on neighborhood codes.

The third level models effects of neighborhood characteristics—race, poverty, affluence, and residential stability—on neighborhood codes of violence. Our demographic attributes of neighborhoods derive from the 2000 census. Our measures of race/ethnicity consist of the percentage of African Americans and Hispanics in a census tract. We discovered, however, that percent Asian and percent immigrants are nearly perfectly correlated due to the high percentage of Asian immigrants living in the same neighborhood. We therefore construct an index combining the two into Asian/Immigrant.

To measure concentrated affluence and poverty, we use Massey's index of concentration at the extremes (ICE), which can be computed for a given neighborhood by first subtracting the number of poor families from the number of affluent families, and then dividing the result by the total number of families.[39] ICE provides a measure of the imbalance of affluence versus poverty in a neighborhood on a scale that ranges from +1 (all families are poor) to –1 (all families are affluent), with values of 0 indicating an equal balance of poor and affluent families. We measure residential stability with an index of two census items: average length of residence and percent homeowners.

Figure 18.3 depicts coefficients for our model of neighborhood codes of violence. The bivariate relationship reveals that neighborhood codes are disproportionately present in extremely impoverished neighborhoods: the ICE coefficient is negative and significant, indicating that neighborhood codes diminish in balanced neighborhoods, and diminish even more in affluent neighborhoods. However, controlling for race, the ICE coefficient diminishes in size and becomes nonsignificant. Moreover, as expected, neighborhood codes are disproportionately present in neighborhoods with more African Americans. This coefficient, the largest of the model, supports ethnographic research that suggests that street codes are characteristic of inner-city neighborhoods with higher proportions of Blacks.

Similarly, we find that neighborhood codes are more prevalent in neighborhoods with higher percentages of Latinos, again consistent with

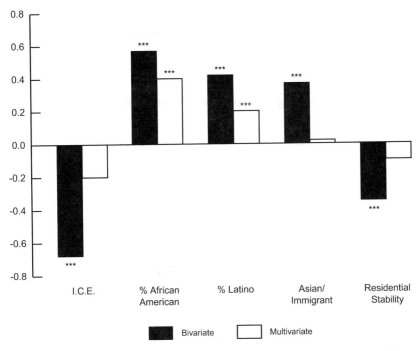

Fig. 18.3. Standardized Bivariate and Multivariate Contextual Effects on Neighborhood Codes of Violence. * p < .05, ** p < .01, *** p < .001

ethnographic research. The bivariate effects of Asian/immigrant and residential stability are significant and in the expected direction, but disappear in our multivariate models. Finally, we examined the crucial hypothesis that neighborhood codes are associated with neighborhood violence. From our multilevel model, we computed predicted neighborhood scores for violence codes adjusted for response error (first level) and bias due to individual covariates (second level), and computed a correlation with violent crime rates (years 2002–2004) by census tracts.[40] We find a strong, statistically significant correlation (.56), which is depicted in Figure 18.4.[41] We see that the violent crime rate is low in the northern half of the city and high in the southern half, and neighborhood codes follow a similar pattern. Neighborhood codes are concentrated in the inner city (Central District) and surrounding neighborhoods, and remain high as one moves southward down the Rainier Valley. Rates of violence are highest in the Central District, and are somewhat higher down the Rainier Valley. These

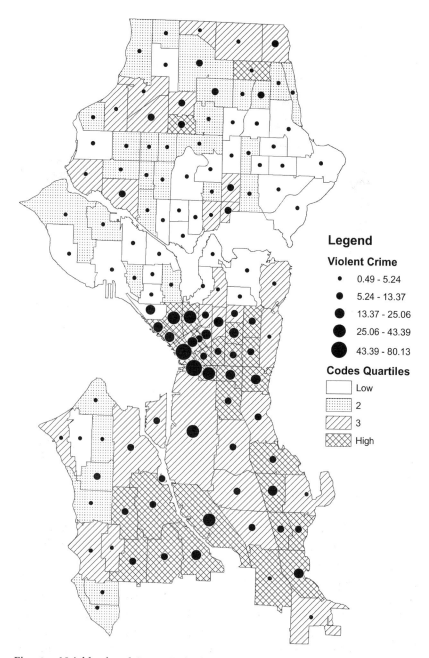

Fig. 18.4. Neighborhood Street Codes by 2002–2004 Average Yearly Violent Crime Rate, Seattle

patterns generate the high correlation between neighborhood codes and violence, supporting our key proposition.

Discussion

This chapter draws on a long history of ethnographic research on race, social structure, and neighborhood codes of violence to subject the findings to systematic empirical test. This is important because critics often argue that ethnographic findings do not meet conventional social science standards of evidence. According to this argument, ethnographers do not show that the street codes are disproportionately represented in violent inner-city neighborhoods, but merely observe examples in a single inner-city neighborhood, infer they are widespread there, and assume they are absent elsewhere. Furthermore, critics argue that concepts such as "code of the streets" cannot be measured using scientific instruments, and therefore, we cannot determine their distribution in violent inner-city neighborhoods versus others.

Our research tackles this challenge, takes the ethnographic evidence seriously, and translates concepts discovered through careful ethnographic research into quantitative survey measures. The content of our measures captures dimensions of "never back down from a fight," "violence gains respect," "got your back," "retaliate when one's crew is disrespected," "project a tough image to avoid being punked." We find their measurement properties acceptable, and in models of neighborhood variation in codes, we find support for theoretical expectations: neighborhood codes are disproportionately found in Black and Hispanic neighborhoods, as well as neighborhoods with high rates of violence. Thus, contrary to critics, we find support for the basic propositions of ethnographic research on codes of violence.

Our findings also raise new research questions about the dynamics of neighborhood codes. We noted that ethnographic research suggests that Black males from inner-city impoverished neighborhoods distrust the police and legal system, and therefore turn to their own devices, using violence to resolve their disputes. Research is needed to examine this proposition empirically: Do inner-city residents in fact distrust the police and does that foster the formation of codes of violence to resolve disputes and gain status?

Shaw and McKay's social-disorganization and cultural-transmission theories suggest that neighborhood disorganization leads to loss of social control over youth, which in turn spawns a delinquent cultural tradition and high rates of delinquency. Recent research on social disorganization emphasizes neighborhood collective efficacy as a key aspect of informal social control. Our research suggests that neighborhood codes of violence constitute an important aspect of a delinquent cultural tradition. This raises the question of whether collective efficacy and neighborhood codes are related, as suggested by Shaw and McKay: Disorganized neighborhoods undermine collective efficacy, which spawns neighborhood street codes, and consequently criminal violence.

Our perspective is consistent with social learning theories, such as differential association, in presuming that codes of violence diffuse spatially across households and neighborhoods. Such diffusion is related to communication networks, which may explain why race has stronger effects than social class, given racial barriers to social interaction. Future research is needed to model potential spatial diffusion effects across geographic units. Do contiguous neighborhoods share similar codes, and do we observe diffusion over time?

We found a strong correlation between neighborhood codes and violent crime rates. Additional research, however, is needed to model this relationship explicitly, controlling for other covariates of neighborhood violence. Furthermore, does the effect of neighborhood codes on violence rates persist even when researchers control for spatial autoregressive effects?

Finally, although we carefully operationalized the multiple dimensions of violent codes on the basis of a close reading of the ethnographic literature, there remains the question of how such codes operate in concrete situations—a question that qualitative research is better suited to answer. Research is needed in which analysts go into key neighborhoods and gather qualitative data. Such data can explore the nuances by which neighborhood codes are used to negotiate confrontations, achieve a sense of respectability while maintaining safety, and innovate new twists on the codes' themes—in short, to accomplish a sense of the neighborhood code of violence in everyday street settings. Moreover, by sampling on and off the regression lines of our models, we may gain further insights into the operation and nonoperation of codes.[42] In particular, by sampling neighborhood outliers, and exploring local processes of social control, we may gain new theoretical insights beyond our principal findings supporting neighborhood codes of violence.

NOTES

1. Thrasher 1927:287.
2. Sutherland 1937:35–38.
3. Cressey 1969.
4. Cloward and Ohlin 1960; Sampson and Wilson 1995; Wolfgang and Ferracuti 1967.
5. Shaw and McKay 1942.
6. Sutherland 1947.
7. Matsueda 1988; Sutherland and Cressey 1978.
8. Cloward and Ohlin 1960; Cohen 1955.
9. Cohen 1955.
10. Miller 1958.
11. Cloward and Ohlin 1960.
12. Ibid.:175.
13. Short and Strodbeck 1965.
14. Horowitz 1983.
15. Ibid.:81.
16. Anderson 1999.
17. Wilson 1987.
18. Anderson 1999:81.
19. See also Kubrin and Weitzer 2003.
20. Anderson 1999:76.
21. Luckenbill 1977.
22. Katz 1988:81.
23. Anderson 1999.
24. Katz 1988:110.
25. Toch 1969.
26. Green, Strolovitch, and Wong 1998; Pinderhughes 1997:134.
27. Fagan and Wilkinson 1998.
28. Massey and Denton 1993.
29. Shaw and McKay 1942.
30. Messerschmidt 1986:56.
31. Anderson 1999:70–71.
32. For example, see Decker and Van Winkle 1996.
33. Miethe and Meier 1994.
34. Jöreskog and Sörbom 1996–2001.
35. Raudenbush and Bryk 2002.
36. Because our measures used ordinal (Likert) scales, we used polychoric correlations, a weight matrix indexing departures from normality, and weighted least squares estimation using Jöreskog and Sörbom's LISREL approach.

37. We also find that neighborhood, but not individual, codes approximate parallel measures (equal slopes and measurement error variances).

38. Here we incorporate our confirmatory factor model, but assume parallel measures. This measurement model corrects for attenuation in our substantive regression coefficients due to unreliability in each item.

39. Massey 1996.

40. Our measure of the violent crime rate is based on reported violence by census tract from the Seattle Police Department.

41. Details of statistical models and full tables are available upon request.

42. Pearce 2002.

Conclusion

A Deeper Understanding of Race, Ethnicity, Crime, and Criminal Justice

Ruth D. Peterson, Lauren J. Krivo, and John Hagan

One summer evening a few years ago, a group of criminologists, including many of the contributors to this book, were in St. Augustine, Florida, sitting on the sunny veranda of a neighborhood restaurant sharing a relaxing moment. We might have been consuming a beverage or two. The group was colorful (a mixture of African Americans, Hispanics, and Whites, males and females), and had gathered for an academic meeting of researchers who all study crime and violence. Everyone had engaged strenuously in the work of the day. Now it was time to kick back. We waited for our food, talked, laughed, and were generally enjoying the reflected good feelings of a peaceful collective moment. Suddenly, we heard what could have been a gun shot followed by the high-pitched scream of sirens. The reactions were diverse. Some took little notice, others glanced briefly in the direction of the nearby street and surrounding neighborhood, while a few of us shifted abruptly into a heightened and nervous state of alertness, perhaps even alarm. Bob broke the brittle tension of our brief uncertain silence with his typically wry comment, "Notice, the 'brothers' took cover!"

The group met again the following year. But this time we were joined by a group of juniors and seniors from Morehouse and Spelman Colleges. We brought this new group of young scholars to the table hoping to excite them and us by making them a part of our discussions about crime and violence. Maybe we could even stimulate some to ultimately become a part of the research community through future graduate study, and eventual teaching and research of their own. The setting for this meeting was beautiful and serene: a beach resort on the gulf coast of Florida.

Discussions had been good, but it was time for a break. A group of the students took off for what they expected to be a pleasant walk along the beach and through the nearby town. When they returned, we learned that the walk was not as pleasant as they had hoped. As they strolled along enjoying the serenity, they were stopped by the police and questioned regarding their doings and whereabouts. The students returned chagrined and somewhat despondent.

These two stories reflect both the ultimate irony and the stark reality of the topics of discussion that were taking place in the academic meetings. Here were highly educated, poised groups of African Americans reacting almost unconsciously to their fear of being in an unpleasant encounter, or indeed being singled out, by criminal justice authorities, in this case the police. For many considering these two incidents, interpretations/explanations might seem easy. "African Americans are sensitive and tend to unnecessarily overreact to or attribute racial causes to encounters with the police." "Police, or other agents of criminal justice, are racist or unquestioningly carry out racist policies." But the discussions that ensued after we witnessed these events, and told stories about many other such incidents, beg for more complex explanations of how and why crime and justice are meted out and perceived so inequitably in the United States. How and why do people of different races, ethnicities, classes, genders, and intersecting combinations of these experience and think about crime and the justice system in such dramatically varying ways? On the two days described above it seemed that we had only slim and simplistic answers to these broad questions. As a result, over the last few years, we have talked, pondered, gathered, and analyzed data (together and separately) in an attempt to raise more complex questions and begin to find more complicated answers.

The results are presented in this volume. The most general theme that we hope has come through is that race and ethnicity in relationship to crime are not simply concepts. Rather, these constructs must be considered as structural factors that are part of the way society is organized that, in turn, shape crime and criminal justice processes and outcomes. Beyond this general observation, the book highlights the limitations of current approaches, presents new ideas and findings, and suggests future (and we believe cutting-edge) directions for research so that we can move forward in a fruitful fashion.

Chief among the limitations that we have noted is the narrowness of the central concepts that currently drive research, and consequently our understanding, of the interrelationships among race, ethnicity, crime, and criminal justice. Most notably, conceptual and operational definitions of race and ethnicity have too often meant a limited consideration of Blacks, Whites, and sometimes Latinos, with no regard for other groups and their potentially unique relations to crime and justice. Equally, if not more, important is that criminological research considers racial and ethnic groups in a static manner, ignoring the fluid and contextualized (historically, geographically, and socially) and interactive (by gender, class, and the like) nature of the meaning of race/ethnicity as it affects processes and outcomes.

Similarly, definitions of crime are limited mainly to a focus on the activities that are the disproportionate purview of subordinate populations, i.e., property and violent street offenses. In a sense, limiting our focus to these crimes places scholars in the position of stereotyping and reifying the very processes and relationships that they seek to understand regarding race and crime. The activities of African Americans and other minorities become synonymous with crime. In contrast, the illegal activities of Whites (as well as white-collar, corporate, and other forms of nonstreet crime) become invisible regardless of the harms incurred.

Undoubtedly, each reader's journey through the individual chapters opened his or her eyes to particular new ideas and findings. Thus, we do not attempt here to review all of the unique insights generated in the chapters. Rather, and at the risk of doing some injustice to the complexity of the findings discovered, we step back to remind the reader of the questions the chapters tackled and the general types of answers provided. One set of questions alerts us to misleading assumptions about the patterning of crime and criminal justice by considering heretofore unexamined populations and intersectionalities. A number of chapters offer findings that bear on this issue. The answers they provide are intriguing, and as we anticipated, make it clear that the race/ethnicity–crime/criminal justice relationships are indeed complex; it is not possible to draw simple conclusions about any racial group, or to offer explanations of differential patterns of crime and criminal justice, that are valid across broad categories of race or ethnicity. For example, Blacks and other subordinate racial and ethnic populations are not a single undifferentiated group, even when they reside in similarly disadvantaged areas. Note Martinez and Nielsen's finding that Haitians, although Black and poor, experience crime levels that are more similar to those of other immigrants who are White than to their poor African American counterparts. Other chapters highlight this same point when they show how risks of crime or victimization for members of some subordinate groups vary depending on location of residence (Krivo et al.; Vazsonyi and Trejos-Castillo), gender dynamics (Miller and Like), neighborhood context (Like and Miller; Crutchfield et al.), and connections to political and economic elites (Vélez).

The book also raises questions about how differential settings shape the nature and levels of crime, perceptions about crime, consequences of incarceration, and other outcomes. This type of question is not unique to this book, of course. What is different about the approach taken here is that all the analyses are guided by the premise that race and ethnicity are themselves embedded within the historical and social context of crime, criminal justice, and other closely related outcomes. The chapters also often rely on unique databases that allow the authors to expand the race/ethnic groups analyzed (e.g., Crutchfield et al.; Matsueda et al.), the kinds of outcomes under consideration (Piquero et al.), and/or the types of race/ethnic-by-class comparisons that can be made (Krivo et al.; Piquero et al.). Such innovations are necessary to provide tests of critical arguments, and in general to broaden our understanding of race and crime issues. One important "take home" point from studies of how context matters for the race/ethnicity–crime/criminal justice link is what they reveal regarding the stark reality of the benefits of being White (and the combination of White race and middle-class status) in U.S. urban society. Two examples suffice to illustrate this point. First, a key finding that emerges in Piquero et al.'s analysis is the exceedingly low incarceration rate for Whites absolutely, and in comparison to Latinos and Blacks even when they live in the same neighborhoods. Further, White incarceration does not have negative consequences for neighborhood well-being among Whites. Second, Krivo et al. show that residents of a White middle-class area are privileged in feeling the most safe and perceiving the least crime compared to residents in any other area. And this perception of enhanced safety exceeds that which would be warranted by their class status alone (i.e., they feel safer than middle-class Blacks). Further, such perceptions appear to be a response to the internal social conditions of the White middle-class community (physical disorder and social cohesion), while perceptions in the middle-class African American area are not tied to this internal character.

An increasingly important concern for scholars trying to develop more comprehensive explanations of social relationships is what unique mechanisms and processes account for racial and ethnic differences in patterns of crime and criminal justice. Several chapters in this book attend to this issue. They provide an array of different answers, but there are a few main themes. Several chapters document how the structure of laws and official policies provide de jure mechanisms that produce the appearance of differential patterns of criminality or criminal justice outcomes along race and ethnic lines (Provine; Rymond-Richmond; Valdez). Such racialized legislative and policing policies are particularly important in generating differential patterns of drug crimes and sentences. Several other chapters point to cultural codes as central mechanisms for avoiding violent victimization and as a source of criminal offending (Matsueda et al.; Rymond-Richmond; Sampson and Bean). These codes take various forms: e.g., cognitive maps that residents use to guide their daily activities and thereby protect themselves and family members from violent encounters in unsafe neighborhoods (Rymond-Richmond); and, *neighborhood* codes that prescribe the use of violence under particular circumstances (Matsueda et al.). One chapter documents differences in perceptions of criminal injustice across youth from various race and ethnic groups, and demonstrates how such perceptions are an important intervening link between race/ethnicity and criminal outcomes (Shedd and Hagan). These obviously will not be the only mechanisms that account for the racial and ethnic patterning of crime and criminal justice. But the chapters in this volume go a long way toward documenting these dynamic processes, thereby setting the stage for additional analyses that will expand on these insights.

Having come to this point, we hope that, along with the authors, you as readers will not only have learned from the chapters but also see them as stimuli for further in-depth theoretical and empirical analyses of race, ethnicity, crime, and criminal justice. Indeed this book is intended only as the beginning of a longer journey toward comprehension of the inequalities that pervade the structure of crime and justice in subtle and complex ways. To that end, we end this stage of the journey by suggesting types of new efforts that we think might usefully be undertaken. The first three recommendations propose broad endeavors, while the remaining ones call for detailed and in-depth consideration of specific substantive issues.

- *Go beyond the Black-White divide through comparative analyses across combinations of various racial, ethnic (immigrant and nonimmigrant), gender, and class populations and communities.* Like and Miller's work suggests that the violence and sexual victimization experiences of girls in a poor African American community are rooted in the race, class, and gender dynamics of their area. Yet, comparisons to other racial, ethnic, class, and gender groups and communities will be needed to fully explicate how these factors play out. Krivo et al. make comparisons across race and class lines but study only a few neighborhoods and examine only Whites and African Americans. A number of the other chapters go beyond Blacks and Whites to examine broad pan-ethnic groups such as Asian Americans or Latinos, but they do not consider the diversity of groups within these categories. (Martinez and Nielsen, and Valdez are exceptions, but they each study just one more specific group.) A concerted effort to collect data and conduct analyses across many groups along intersecting dimensions must be a critical next step in verifying and extending conclusions offered in this volume.

- *Comparative analyses across nations.* All of the research reported in this book focuses on racial and ethnic dynamics as they relate to crime and criminal justice in the United States. However, disparities in victimization as well as involvement in crime and criminal justice systems across racial, ethnic, class, and gender lines is a concern of comparable, and sometimes graver, consequence in other nations around the world. The massive crimes against humanity perpetrated on Africans in Rwanda and Darfur are current and egregious examples of neglect and denial, by criminologists as well as citizens. Thus, we implore researchers to take up the challenge of extending and applying perspectives set forth here to studies around the globe.

- *The application of multiple methods of data collection and analysis.* The empirical chapters in this volume are based on qualitative or quantitative approaches. The quantitative studies allow for comparisons across a wide range of observed characteristics and permit statistical tests of generalizability. By contrast, the qualitative studies present rich and in-depth pictures of the way crime and justice are connected with people's lives, communities, and/or the decisions of the powerful, but do so for a single area or relatively few cases. Even more will be gained by conducting studies of race, ethnicity, crime, and criminal justice that incorporate both qualitative and quantitative components that are specifically designed to complement one another (i.e., to assess the full range of characteristics while also probing the meaning of observed patterns through thick descriptions offered by those involved). For example, surveys of youths' perceptions of justice across a national sample of schools that include diverse racial and ethnic populations could be paired with observations and in-depth interviews of girls and boys in a set of schools in various cities critically chosen to vary along race, ethnic, and class lines.

- *Studying a broader set of crime types.* The overemphasis on official reported street crime in analyses of race, ethnicity, crime, and criminal justice must be rectified. A necessary first step (as Young argues in this volume) is to conceptualize crime more broadly and in ways that can be incorporated into empirical analyses. This conceptualization should then be applied in new data collection efforts that reflect the full range of criminal activities. Moving in this direction is critical for eliminating stereotypic images of the *criminalblackman* (or similar stereotypes associated with other groups) from research and the public eye, and ultimately for providing a more accurate picture of crime and the interrelationships among race, ethnicity, crime, and criminal justice.

- *New explorations of culture and the interactions between culture and structure in creating and reproducing intergroup inequalities in crime and criminal justice.* Matsueda et al. demonstrate the fruitfulness of examining cultural codes of violence as a community construct that is differentially embedded within various neighborhoods of color in ways that affect criminal victimization. But this is the first systematic analysis of its type. Sampson and Bean suggest an alternative approach to incorporating culture in studies of race and crime drawing on new advances in the sociology of culture. They advocate viewing "culture in action" as a property that is relational and dynamic rather than as a constant static force that can be juxtaposed to the impact of structure. Empirical studies that evaluate and build on both Matsueda et al.'s and Sampson and Bean's new approaches are sorely needed.

- *Research on the role of criminal justice organizations and workers in the application of justice.* Although there is considerable research on criminal justice processing, Ward's chapter points toward a need to look carefully and critically at the way in which the occupational hierarchy of criminal justice professions and the characteristics of those working in these professions could affect the equitable or inequitable application of justice. It is widely assumed that the criminal justice system will operate more fairly when persons of color are workers. But the differential distribution of groups across the professional hierarchy may lead to more complex or even counterintuitive outcomes by race and ethnicity. This is an area of research that is clearly important but has been virtually unexplored.

- *Critical studies of the interrelationships among perceptions of justice, experiences with the criminal justice system, and criminal behaviors of diverse populations.* The gulf between African Americans and Whites in perceptions and experiences with the criminal justice system is wide. Yet, we know little about how these patterns extend to other populations of color. Further, the implications of intergroup perceptual divisions for actions are unclear. For example, does greater distrust in the criminal justice system among African Americans or other racial/ethnic minorities actually affect levels of criminal involvement and reactions to police and other authorities, thereby reproducing or increasing inequalities in crime and justice? The answer to this critical question is not well understood and deserves significant attention in the future.

- *Expanded attention to research on the origins and consequences of policies, legislation, and actions of authoritative agencies.* The official decisions implemented by legislative bodies and government policymakers can serve to enhance (or diminish) inequalities in crime and safety by race, ethnicity, class, and gender. They can also serve to recreate such inequalities within families, jobs, communities, and the like. Provine's analysis of crack cocaine sentencing legislation makes clear that government decisions may be profoundly affected by racial bias, and Rymond-Richmond shows that policies that disregard the cultural organization that exists in communities of color can have deleterious rather than advantageous outcomes. Studies are needed to help us understand the array of government laws and policies that increase racial and ethnic inequality in crime, safety, and the operation of criminal justice. Furthermore, we need to understand whether and how such laws and policies operate to enhance inequality beyond the sphere of crime and justice in other arenas such as the labor market, family, and education.

As far back as 1899, W. E. B. Du Bois analyzed patterns of crime among "Negros," pointing to their overrepresentation in arrest, court, and prison statistics.[1] He attempted to interpret these statistics in the context of the times, which were far more overtly discriminatory than today, and the social circumstances that defined urban Black life. What is most insightful to us is that Du Bois was seeking to identify the *deeper social roots* of the patterns he described. Although his tools were less sophisticated than those available today, his goals were much the same as those articulated in this book. Our final hope for the volume is that it truly does push us all to think and work seriously in ways that provide the deeper understanding that Du Bois called for, so that in another hundred years scholars are not yet again making this same plea.

NOTE

1. Du Bois 1899.

Bibliography

Abt Associates, Inc. 1998. *Gauging the Effects of Public Housing Redesign: Final Report on the Early Stages of the Horner Revitalization Initiative.* Report prepared for the MacArthur Foundation and the Department of Housing and Urban Developments.

Aguirre, Ana. 2004. "Arguments for a Diverse Workforce." *Corrections Magazine* 66:72–75.

Alabama State Department of Education. 2003. "School Reports." Available at http://www.alsde.edu/html/home.asp.

Alba, Richard D. and John R. Logan. 1993. "Minority Proximity to Whites in Suburbs: An Individual-Level Analysis of Segregation." *American Journal of Sociology* 98:1388–1427.

Albonetti, Celesta. 1997. "Sentencing under the Federal Sentencing Guidelines: Effects of Defendant Characteristics, Guilty Pleas, and Departures on Sentencing Outcomes for Drug Offenses, 1991–1992." *Law and Society Review* 31:789–822.

Alex, Nicholas. 1969. *Black in Blue: A Study of the Negro Policeman.* New York: Appleton-Century Crofts.

Alexander, Harry T. 1974. "The Black Judge as Change Agent." Pp. 23–37 in *The Administration of Criminal Justice: A View from Black America,* edited by L. P. Brown. Washington, DC: Institute for Urban Affairs and Research, Howard University.

Anderson, Elijah. 1978. *A Place on the Corner.* Chicago: University of Chicago Press.

———. 1999. *Code of the Street: Decency, Violence, and the Moral life of the Inner City.* New York: Norton.

Anderson, Margaret L. and Patricia Hill Collins (editors). 2001. *Race, Class, and Gender: An Anthology.* 2nd ed. Belmont CA: Wadsworth.

Anderson, Robert N. 2002. *Deaths: Leading Causes for 2000.* Hyattsville, MD: National Center for Health Statistics.

Andrisani, Paul J. 1973. *An Empirical Analysis of the Dual Labor Market Theory.* Ph.D. Dissertation, Department of Business Administration, Ohio State University, Columbus, OH.

Armistead, Lisa, Rex Forehand, Gene H. Brody, and Shira Maguen. 2002. "Parenting and Child Psychological Adjustment in Single-Parent African American Families: Is Community Context Important?" *Behavior Therapy* 33:361–375.

Associated Press. 2005. "Tribes Give State $9.9 Million in Gaming Revenue." *Arizona Republic*, January 28. Available at http://www.azcentral.com/news/articles/0128GamingRev28-ON.html.

Austin, Regina. 1992. "'The Black Community': Its Lawbreakers, and a Politics of Identification." *Southern California Law Review* 65:1769–1817.

Baca Zinn, Maxine and Bonnie Thornton Dill. 1994. "Difference and Domination." Pp. 3–12 in *Women of Color in U.S. Society*, edited by M. B. Zinn and B. T. Dill. Philadelphia: Temple University Press.

Bachman, Ronet. 1992. *Death and Violence on the Reservation: Homicide, Family Violence, and Suicide in American Indian Populations*. New York: Auburn House.

Bachman, Ronet, Alexander Alvarez, and Craig Perkins. 1996. "Discriminatory Imposition of the Law: Does It Affect Sentencing Outcomes for American Indians?" Pp. 197–202 in *Native Americans, Crime, and Justice*, edited by M. O. Nielsen and R. A. Silverman. New York: Westview Press.

Balbus, Isaac D. 1973. *The Dialectics of Legal Repression: Black Rebels before the American Criminal Courts*. New Brunswick, NJ: Transaction Books.

Ball, John C. 1965. "Two Patterns of Narcotic Drug Addiction in the United States." *Journal of Criminal Law, Criminology and Police Science* 56:203–211.

Bass, Sandra. 2001. "Policing Space, Policing Race: Social Control Imperatives and Police Discretionary Decisions." *Social Justice* 28:156–175.

Baumer, Eric. 2002. "Neighborhood Disadvantage and Police Notification by Victims of Violence." *Criminology* 40:579–616.

Baumer, Eric, Janet L. Lauritsen, Richard Rosenfeld, and Richard Wright. 1998. "The Influence of Crack Cocaine on Robbery, Burglary, and Homicide Rates: A Cross-city, Longitudinal Analysis." *Journal of Research in Crime and Delinquency* 35:316–340.

Bayley, David H. 1994. *Police for the Future*. New York: Oxford University Press.

Becker, Gary S. 1991. *A Treatise on the Family*. Enlarged ed. Cambridge, MA: Harvard University Press.

Beckett, Katherine. 1997. *Making Crime Pay: Law and Order in Contemporary Politics*. New York: Oxford.

Beckett, Katherine and Theodore Sasson. 2000. *The Politics of Injustice: Crime and Punishment in America*. Thousand Oaks, CA: Pine Forge Press.

Belenko, Steven R. 1993. *Crack and the Evolution of Anti-Drug Policy*. Westport, CT: Greenwood.

Belknap, Joanne. 2001. *The Invisible Woman: Gender, Crime, and Justice*. 2nd ed. Belmont, CA: Wadsworth.

Bell, Daniel. 1960. *The End of Ideology: On the Exhaustion of Political Ideas in the Fifties*. Glencoe, IL: Free Press.

Bellair, Paul E., Vincent J. Roscigno, and Thomas L. McNulty. 2003. "Linking Local Labor Market Opportunity to Violent Adolescent Delinquency." *Journal of Research in Crime and Delinquency* 40:6–33.

Bendick, Marc, Jr., Charles W. Jackson, and Victor A. Reinoso. 1997. "Measuring Employment Discrimination through Controlled Experiments." Pp. 77–100 in *African Americans and Post-Industrial Labor Markets,* edited by J. B. Stewart. New Brunswick, NJ: Transaction.

Bennett, Katherine J. and W. Westley Johnson. 2000. "African American Wardens: Managerial Perspectives and Attitudes." *Corrections Management Quarterly* 4: 52–63.

Benson, Michael L., Greer L. Fox, Alfred DeMaris, and Judy Van Wyk. 2003. "Neighborhood Disadvantage, Individual Economic Distress, and Violence against Women in Intimate Relationships." *Journal of Quantitative Criminology* 19:207–235.

Berger, Peter. 1967. *The Sacred Canopy: Elements of a Sociological Theory of Religion.* Garden City, NY: Doubleday.

Berger, Peter and Thomas Luckmann. 1967. *The Social Construction of Reality: A Treatise in the Sociology of Knowledge.* Garden City, NY: Doubleday.

Biskup, Peter. 1973. *Not Slaves, Not Citizens: The Aboriginal Problem in Western Australia, 1898–1954.* St. Lucia, NY: University of Queensland Press.

Blau, Judith R. and Peter M. Blau. 1982. "The Cost of Inequality: Metropolitan Structure and Violent Crime." *American Sociological Review* 47:114–129.

Blauner, Bob. 1972. *Racial Oppression in America.* New York: Harper and Row.

Block, Carolyn Rebecca, Richard L. Block, and the Illinois Criminal Justice Information Authority. 1998. "Homicides in Chicago, 1965–1995" [Computer file]. 4th ICPSR version. Chicago, IL: Illinois Criminal Justice Information Authority [producer], Ann Arbor, MI: Inter-University Consortium for Political and Social Research [distributor].

Bluestone, Barry. 1970. "The Tripartite Economy: Labor Markets and the Working Poor." *Poverty and Human Resources* 5:15–35.

Blumstein, Alfred. 1982. "On the Racial Disproportionality of United States' Prison Populations." *Journal of Criminal Law and Criminology* 73:1259–1270.

Blumstein, Alfred, Jacqueline Cohen, and Richard Rosenfeld. 1991. "Trend and Deviation in Crime Rates: A Comparison of UCR and NCS Data for Burglary and Robbery." *Criminology* 29:237–263.

Bobo, Jacqueline, Cynthia Hudley, and Claudine Michel (editors). 2004. *The Black Studies Reader.* New York: Routledge.

Bobo, Lawrence and Devon Johnson. 2004. "A Taste for Punishment: Black and White Americans' Views on the Death Penalty and the War on Drugs." *Du Bois Review* 1:151–180.

Bobo, Lawrence, James R. Kluegel, and Ryan A. Smith. 1997. "Laissez-Faire Racism: The Crystallization of a Kinder, Gentler, Antiblack Ideology." Pp. 15–42 in

Racial Attitudes in the 1990s: Continuity and Change, edited by S. A. Tuch and J. K. Martin. Westport, CT: Praeger.

Bobo, Lawrence and Michael Massagli. 2001. "Stereotyping and Urban Inequality." Pp. 89–162 in *Urban Inequality: Evidence from Four Cities,* edited by A. O'Connor, C. Tilly, and L. Bobo. New York: Russell Sage.

Bobo, Lawrence D. and Camille L. Zubrinsky. 1996. "Attitudes on Residential Integration: Perceived Status Differences, Mere In-Group Preference, or Racial Prejudice." *Social Forces* 74:883–909.

Bolton, Kenneth and Joe R. Feagin. 2004. *Black in Blue: African-American Police Officers and Racism.* New York: Routledge.

Bosanquet, Nicholas and Peter B. Doeringer. 1973. "Is There a Dual Labor Market in Great Britain?" *Economic Journal* 83:421–435.

Bourdieu, Pierre. 1984. *Distinction: A Social Critique of the Judgement of Taste.* London: Routledge.

Bourdieu, Pierre and Loïc Wacquant. 1992. *Towards a Reflexive Sociology.* Oxford: Polity.

Bourgois, Philippe. 1995. *In Search of Respect: Selling Crack in El Barrio.* Cambridge: Cambridge University Press.

———. 1996. "In Search of Masculinity: Violence, Respect, and Sexuality among Puerto Rican Crack Dealers in East Harlem." *British Journal of Criminology.* 36:412–427.

Bowser, David. 2003. *West of the Creek: Murder, Mayhem, and Vice in Old San Antonio.* San Antonio, TX: Maverick.

Bradshaw, Benjamin, David R. Johnson, Derral Cheatwood, and Stephen Blanchard. 1998. "A Historical Geographical Study of Lethal Violence in San Antonio." *Social Science Quarterly* 79:863–878.

Bridges, George and Sara Steen. 1998. "Racial Disparities in Official Assessments of Juvenile Offenders: Attributional Stereotypes as Mediating Mechanisms." *American Sociological Review* 63:554–570.

Brischetto, Robert. 2000. *Making Connections on San Antonio's West Side: The Neighborhood Transformation/Family Development Project.* Baltimore, MD: Annie E. Casey Foundation.

Britt, Chester. 2000. "Social Context and Racial Disparities in Punishment Decisions." *Justice Quarterly* 17:707–732.

Britton, Dana M. 2003. *At Work in the Iron Cage: The Prison as Gendered Organization.* New York: New York University Press.

Broadhurst, Roderic. 1997. "Aborigines and Crime in Australia." Pp. 407–468 in *Ethnicity, Crime, and Immigration,* edited by Michael H. Tonry. Chicago: University of Chicago Press.

Brockett, Ramona. 2000. "Conceptual Incarceration: A Thirteenth-Amendment Look at African Americans and Policing." Pp. 109–124 in *The System in Black and White: Exploring the Connections between Race, Crime, and Justice,* edited by M. W. Markowitz and D. D. Jones-Brown. Westport, CT: Praeger.

Brody, Gene H., Velma McBride Murry, Su Yeong Kim, and Anita C. Brown. 2002. "Longitudinal Pathways to Competence and Psychological Adjustment among African American Children Living in Rural Single-parent Households." *Child Development* 73:1505–1516.

Brogden, Mike and Clifford Shearing. 1993. *Policing for a New South Africa.* London: Routledge.

Brooks, Richard R. W. 2000. "Fear and Fairness in the City: Criminal Enforcement and Perceptions of Fairness in Minority Communities." *Southern California Law Review* 73:1219–1273.

Brooks, Richard R. W. and Haekyung Jeon-Slaughter. 2001. "Race, Income, and Perceptions of the U.S. Court System." *Behavioral Sciences and the Law* 19:249–264.

Brown, Craig and Barbara D. Warner. 1992. "Immigrants, Urban Politics, and Policing in 1900." *American Sociological Review* 57:293–305.

Browning, Christopher R., Seth L. Feinberg, and Robert D. Dietz. 2004. "The Paradox of Social Organization: Networks, Collective Efficacy, and Violent Crime in Urban Neighborhoods." *Social Forces* 83:503–534.

Browning, Rufus P., Dale Rogers Marshall, and David Tabb. 1984. *Protest Is Not Enough: The Struggle for Blacks and Hispanics for Equality in Urban Politics.* Berkeley: University of California Press.

Browning, Sandra Lee, Frank T. Cullen, Liqun Cao, Renee Kopache, and Thomas J. Stevenson. 1994. "Race and Getting Hassled by the Police: A Research Note." *Police Studies* 17:1–11.

Brownsberger, William N. 2000. "Race Matters: Disproportionality of Incarceration for Drug Dealing in Massachusetts." *Journal of Drug Issues* 30:345–374.

Buckner, John C. 1988. "The Development of an Instrument to Measure Neighborhood Cohesion." *American Journal of Community Psychology* 16:771–791.

Bullington, Bruce. 1977. *Heroin Use in the Barrio.* Lexington, MA: Lexington Books.

Bureau of Justice Statistics. 2004. *Homicide Trends in the U.S.: Age, Gender, and Race Trends.* Washington, DC: Bureau of Justice Statistics. Available at http://www.ojp.usdoj.gov/bjs/homicide/tables/oarstab.htm.

Burgess, Ernest W. 1967. "The Growth of the City: An Introduction to a Research Project." Pp. 47–62 in *The City,* edited by R. E. Park, E. W. Burgess, and R. McKenzie. Chicago: University of Chicago Press.

Bursik, Robert J., Jr., and Harold G. Grasmick. 1993. *Neighborhoods and Crime.* New York: Lexington.

Burt, Martha R., Lisa C. Newmark, Krista K. Olson, Laudan Y. Aron, and Adele V. Harrell. 1997. *1997 Report: Evaluation of the STOP Formula Grants under the Violence against Women Act of 1994.* Washington, DC: Urban Institute.

Byers, Mark. 2002. "Correctional Initiatives for Maori in New Zealand." *Corrections Today* 64:25–29.

Bynum, Timothy S. and Raymond Paternoster. 1984. "Discrimination Revisited: An Exploration of Frontstage and Backstage Criminal Justice Decision Making." *Sociology and Social Research* 69:90–108.

Camerer, Colin F. 2003. *Behavioral Game Theory.* New York: Russell Sage Foundation: Princeton, NJ: Princeton University Press.

Campbell, Anne. 1984. *The Girls in the Gang.* New York: Basil Blackwell.

Cantor, David and James P. Lynch. 2000. "Self-Report Surveys as Measures of Crime and Victimization." Pp. 85–138 in *Measurement and Analysis of Crime and Justice*, Vol. 4, edited by D. Duffee, D. McDowall, B. Ostrom, R. D. Crutchfield, S. D. Mastrofski, and L. G. Mazerolle. Washington, DC: National Institute of Justice.

Capaldi, Deborah M., Mike Stoolmiller, Sara Clark, and Lee D. Owen. 2002. "Heterosexual Risk Behaviors in At-Risk Young Men from Early Adolescence to Young Adulthood: Prevalence, Prediction, and Association with STD Contraction." *Developmental Psychology* 38:394–406.

Carr, Patrick J. 2003. "The New Parochialism: The Implications of the Beltway Case for Arguments concerning Informal Social Control." *American Journal of Sociology* 108:1249–1291.

Carter, David L. 1985. "Hispanic Perception of Police Performance: An Empirical Assessment." *Journal of Criminal Justice* 13:487–500.

Carter, Prudence. 2005. *Keepin' It Real: School Success beyond Black and White.* New York: Oxford University Press.

Casavantes, Edward J. 1976. *El Tecato: Cultural and Sociologic Factors Affecting Drug Use among Chicanos.* Revised ed. Washington, DC: National Coalition of Spanish-Speaking Mental Health Organizations.

Case, Patricia and Dais Fasenfest. 2004. "Expectations for Opportunities Following Prison Education: A Discussion of Race and Gender." *Journal of Correctional Education* 55:24–39.

Casey, Jim and Scott Fornek. 1992. "Police Fire Two Officers over Incident with Teens." *Chicago Sun-Times* March 21, 5.

Cashmore, Ernest and Eugene McLaughlin. 1991. *Out of Order? Policing Black People.* New York: Routledge.

Ceballo, Rosario and Vonnie C. McLoyd. 2002. "Social Support and Parenting in Poor, Dangerous Neighborhoods." *Child Development* 73:1310–1321.

Chambliss, William. 1969. *Crime and the Legal Process.* New York: McGraw Hill.

———. 1973. "The Saints and the Roughnecks." *Society* 11:24–31.

———. 1999. *Power, Politics, and Crime.* Boulder, CO: Westview.

Chambliss, William and Robert Seidman. 1971. *Law, Order, and Power.* Reading, MA: Addison-Wesley.

Champion, Dean J. 1994. *Measuring Offender Risk: A Criminal Justice Sourcebook.* Westport, CT: Greenwood.

Chapman, Arthur. 1912. "The Red Police: The Faithful Service of the Red Men Who Maintain the Peace on the Reservation, Often at Risk of Life and Dishonor among Their Own People." *Harper's Weekly* 56:13–16.

Charles, Camille Zubrinsky. 2003. "The Dynamics of Racial Residential Segregation." *Annual Review of Sociology* 29:167–207.

Chesney-Lind, Meda. 1988. "Doing Feminist Criminology." *The Criminologist* 13:1.

Chinchilla, Norma, Nora Hamilton, and James Loucky. 1993. "Central Americans in Los Angeles: An Immigrant Community in Transition." Pp. 51–78 in *In the Barrios: Latinos and the Underclass Debate,* edited by J. Moore and R. Pinderhughes. New York: Russell Sage.

Chiricos, Ted and Charles Crawford. 1995. "Race and Imprisonment: A Contextual Assessment of the Evidence." Pp. 281–309 in *Ethnicity, Race, and Crime,* edited by D. F. Hawkins. Albany, NY: State University of New York Press.

Chiricos, Ted, Michael Hogan, and Marc Gertz. 1997. "Racial Composition of Neighborhoods and Fear of Crime." *Criminology* 35:107–131.

Chiricos, Ted, Ranee McEntire, and Marc Gertz. 2001. "Perceived Racial and Ethnic Composition of Neighborhood and Perceived Risk of Crime." *Social Problems* 48:322–340.

City of Chicago. 1991. *Index to the Journal of the Proceedings of the City Council of the City of Chicago for the Council Year of 1991–1992.* Chicago: City Clerk of Chicago.

City of Chicago v. Morales et al. 1999. Supreme Court of the United States. 527 U.S. 41–115.

Clark, William A. V. and Sarah A. Blue. 2004. "Race, Class, and Segregation Patterns in U.S. Immigrant Gateway Cities." *Urban Affairs Review* 39:667–688.

Clear, Todd R. and David Karp. 1999. *The Community Justice Ideal.* Boulder, CO: Westview.

Clear, Todd R., Dina R. Rose, and Judith A. Ryder. 2001. "Incarceration and the Community: The Problem of Removing and Returning Offenders." *Crime and Delinquency* 47:335–351.

Clear, Todd R., Dina R. Rose, Elin Waring, and Kristen Scully. 2003. "Coercive Mobility and Crime: A Preliminary Examination of Concentrated Incarceration and Social Disorganization." *Justice Quarterly* 20:33–64.

Cloward, Richard A and Lloyd E. Ohlin. 1960. *Delinquency and Opportunity: A Theory of Delinquent Gangs.* Glencoe, IL: Free Press.

Cochran, Johnnie L. and David Fisher. 2002. *A Lawyer's Life.* New York: St. Martin's Press.

Cohen, Albert K. 1955. *Delinquent Boys.* New York: Free Press.

Cohen, Lawrence and Marcus Felson. 1979. "Social Changes and Crime Rate Trends: A Routine Activity Approach." *American Sociological Review* 44:588–608.

Cohen, Stanley. 2002. *Folk Devils and Moral Panics: The Creation of the Mods and Rockers.* 3rd ed. London: Routledge.

Collins, Patricia Hill. 1989. "The Social Construction of Black Feminist Thought." *Signs* 14:745–773.

———. 1990. *Black Feminist Thought: Knowledge, Consciousness, and the Politics of Empowerment.* New York: Routledge.

———. 2004. *Black Sexual Politics.* New York: Routledge.

Collins, Sharon M. 1997. *Black Corporate Executives: The Making and Breaking of a Black Middle Class.* Philadelphia: Temple University Press.

Collison, Mike. 1996. "In Search of the High Life: Drugs, Crime, Masculinities, and Consumption." *British Journal of Criminology* 36:428–445.

Connell, R. W. 1987. *Gender and Power: Society, the Person, and Sexual Politics.* Stanford, CA: Stanford University Press.

———. 1990. "The State of Gender and Sexual Politics: Theory and Appraisal." *Theory and Society* 19:507–544.

———. 2000. *The Men and the Boys.* Berkeley: University of California Press.

Consortium on Chicago School Research, Public Use Data Set: User's Manual. 2001. Available at http://www.consortium-chicago.org/surveys/pdfs/2001%20User%27s%20Manual.pdf.

Conyers, John and Jerrold Nadler. 2003. Letter to Honorable Glenn Klein, Inspector General. November, 3. Available at http://www.house.gov/judiciary_democrats/dojigdiversityltr11303.pdf.

Cook, Philip J. and John H. Laub. 2002. "After the Epidemic: Recent Trends in Youth Violence in the United States." *Crime and Justice* 29:1–37.

Copes, Heith and Andy Hochstetler. 2003. "Situational Construction of Masculinity among Male Street Thieves." *Journal of Contemporary Ethnography* 32:279–304.

Cose, Ellis. 1993. *The Rage of a Privileged Class.* New York: HarperCollins.

Covington, Jeanette and Ralph B. Taylor. 1991. "Fear of Crime in Urban Residential Neighborhoods: Implications of Between- and Within-Neighborhood Sources for Current Models." *The Sociological Quarterly* 32:231–249.

Crawford, Charles. 2000. "Gender, Race, and Habitual Offender Sentencing in Florida." *Criminology* 38:263–280.

Crenshaw, Kimberlé. 1989a. "Demarginalizing the Intersection of Race and Sex: A Black Feminist Critique of Anti-Discrimination Doctrine, Feminist Theory, and Anti-Racist Politics." *University of Chicago Legal Forum* 1989:139–167.

———. 1989b. "Forward: Toward a Race-Conscious Pedagogy in Legal Education." *National Black Law Journal* 11:1.

Cressey, Donald R. 1969. *Theft of the Nation.* New York: Harper and Row.

Cross, Harry, Genevieve Kenney, Jane Mell, and Wendy Zimmerman. 1990. *Employer Hiring Practices: Differential Treatment of Hispanic and Anglo Job Seekers.* Washington, DC: Urban Institute Press.

Crouch, Ben M. and Geoffrey P. Alpert. 1980. "Prison Guards' Attitudes toward Components of the Criminal Justice System." *Criminology* 18:227–236.

Crutchfield, Robert D. 1989. "Labor Stratification and Violent Crime." *Social Forces* 68:489–512.

Crutchfield, Robert D., Ann Glusker, and George S. Bridges, 1999. "A Tale of Three Cities: Labor Markets and Homicide." *Sociological Focus* 32:65–83.

Crutchfield, Robert D. and Susan R. Pitchford. 1997. "Work and Crime: The Effects of Labor Stratification." *Social Forces* 76:93–118.

Cullen, Francis T., Edward J. Latessa, Jr., Velmer S. Burton, and Lucien X. Lombardo. 1993. "The Correctional Orientation of Prison Wardens: Is the Rehabilitative Ideal Supported?" *Criminology* 31:69–92.

Curtis, Ric. 1998. "The Improbable Transformation of Inner-City Neighborhoods: Crime, Violence, Drugs, and Youth in the 1990s." *Journal of Criminal Law and Criminology* 88:1233–1276.

———. 2003. "The Negligible Role of Gangs in Drug Distribution in New York City in the 1990s." Pp. 41–61 in *Gangs and Society: Alternative Perspectives,* edited by L. Kontos, D. C. Brotherton, and L. Barrios. New York: Columbia University Press.

D'Alessio, Stewart and Lisa Stolzenberg. 2003. "Race and the Probability of Arrest." *Social Forces* 81:1381–1397.

Daly, Kathleen. 1993. "Class-Race-Gender: Sloganeering in Search of Meaning." *Social Justice* 20:56–71.

———. 1997. "Different Ways of Conceptualizing Sex/Gender in Feminist Theory and Their Implications for Criminology." *Theoretical Criminology* 1:25–51.

———. 1998. "Gender, Crime, and Criminology." Pp. 85–110 in *The Handbook of Crime and Justice,* edited by M. Tonry. Oxford: Oxford University Press.

Daly, Kathleen and Meda Chesney-Lind. 1988. "Feminism and Criminology." *Justice Quarterly* 5:101–143.

Davis, Angela Y. 2003. *Are Prisons Obsolete?* New York: Seven Stories.

Davis, James A. 1959. "A Formal Interpretation of the Theory of Relative Deprivation." *Sociometry* 22:280–296.

Dawley, David. 1992. *A Nation of Lords: The Autobiography of the Vice Lords.* Prospect Heights, IL: Waveland.

Dawson, Michael C. 1994. *Behind the Mule: Race and Class in African-American Politics.* Princeton, NJ: Princeton University Press.

Day, David. 2001. *Claiming a Continent: A New History of Australia.* Sydney, NSW: HarperCollins.

Decker, Scott H., and Barrick Van Winkle. 1996. *Life in the Gang: Family, Friends, and Violence.* New York: Cambridge University Press.

Deloria, Vine and Clifford M. Lytle. 1983. *American Indians, American Justice.* Austin: University of Texas Press.

Demetriou, Demetrakis Z. 2001. "Connell's Concept of Hegemonic Masculinity: A Critique." *Theory and Society* 30:337–361.

Demuth, Stephen. 2002. "The Effect of Citizenship Status on Sentencing Outcomes in Drug Cases." *Federal Sentencing Reporter* 14:271–275.

———. 2003. "Racial and Ethnic Differences in Pretrial Release Decisions and Outcomes: A Comparison of Hispanic, Black, and White Felony Arrestees." *Criminology* 41:873–908.

Desmond, David P. and James F. Maddux. 1984. "Mexican-American Heroin Addicts." *American Journal of Drug and Alcohol Abuse* 10:317–346.

Drug Trafficking on the Southwest Border. 2001. Available at http://www.house.gov/judiciary/72144.pdf.

Du Bois, W. E. B. 1899. *The Philadelphia Negro: A Social Study.* Philadelphia: University of Pennsylvania.

Dugan, Laura. 1999. "The Effect of Criminal Victimization on a Household's Decision to Move." *Criminology* 37:903–930.

Dugan, Laura and Robert Apel. 2003. "An Exploratory Study of the Violent Victimization of Women: Race/Ethnicity and Situational Context." *Criminology* 41:959–979.

Dulaney, W. Marvin. 1996. *Black Police in America.* Bloomington: Indiana University Press.

Dunn, Marvin. 1997. *Black Miami in the Twentieth Century.* Gainesville: University Press of Florida.

Edsall, Thomas Byrne and Mary D. Edsall. 1991. *Chain Reaction: The Impact of Race, Rights, and Taxes on American Politics.* New York: Norton.

Edwards, G. Franklin. 1982 (1959). *The Negro Professional Class.* Westport, CT: Greenwood Press.

Eliasoph, Nina. 1998. *Avoiding Politics: How Americans Produce Apathy in Everyday Life.* New York: Cambridge University Press.

Elliott, Delbert S., Kirk R. Williams, and Beatrix Hamburg. 1998. "An Integrated Approach to Violence Prevention." Pp. 379–386 in *Violence in American Schools: A New Perspective,* edited by D. S. Elliott, B. Hamburg, and K. R. Williams. Cambridge, UK: Cambridge University Press.

Elwood, William N. 1994. *Rhetoric in the War on Drugs: The Triumphs and Tragedies of Public Relations.* Westport, CT: Praeger.

Emirbayer, Mustafa and Ann Mische. 1998. "What Is Agency?" *American Journal of Sociology* 103:962–1023.

Enders, Walter. 1995. *Applied Econometric Time Series.* New York: John Wiley.

Epstein, Cynthia F. 1993. *Women in Law.* Urbana: University of Illinois Press.

Escobar, Edward J. 1999. *Race, Police, and the Making of a Political Identity: Mexican Americans and the Los Angeles Police Department, 1900–1945.* Berkeley: University of California Press.

Fagan, Jeffrey and Garth Davies. 2002. *Substance Abuse Policy Research Program,*

Robert Wood Johnson Foundation: The Effects of Drug Enforcement on the Rise and Fall of Homicides in New York City, 1985–95. Final Report. New York: Columbia University.

Fagan, Jeffrey and Richard B. Freeman. 1999. "Crime and Work." *Crime and Justice* 25:113–178.

Fagan, Jeffrey and Tracey Meares. 2000. "Punishment, Deterrence, and Social Control: The Paradox of Punishment in Minority Communities." Public Law and Legal Theory Working Paper Program, Legal Scholarship Network. Available at http://papers.ssrn.com/paper.taf?abstract_id=223148.

Fagan, Jeffrey, Valerie West, and Jan Holland. 2003. "Reciprocal Effects of Crime and Incarceration in New York City Neighborhoods." *Fordham Urban Law Journal* 30:1551–1602.

Fagan, Jeffrey and Deanna Wilkinson. 1998. "Guns, Youth Violence, and Social Identity in Inner-Cities." *Crime and Justice* 24:105–188.

Fagan, Jeffrey and Franklin E. Zimring. 2000. *The Changing Borders of Juvenile Justice: Transfer of Adolescents to the Criminal Court.* Chicago: University of Chicago Press.

Farley, Reynolds. 1977. "Trends in Racial Inequalities: Have the Gains of the 1960s Disappeared in the 1970s?" *American Sociological Review* 42:189–208.

———. 1984. *Blacks and Whites: Narrowing the Gap?* Cambridge, MA: Harvard University Press.

———. 1996. *The New American Reality: Who We Are, How We Got Here, Where We Are Going.* New York: Russell Sage Foundation.

Farley, Reynolds, Charlotte Steeh, Maria Krysan, Tara Jackson, and Keith Reeves. 1994. "Stereotypes and Segregation: Neighborhoods in the Detroit Area." *American Journal of Sociology* 100:750–789.

Feagin Joe R. and Melvin P. Sikes. 1994. *Living with Racism: The Black Middle-Class Experience.* Boston: Beacon.

Federal Bureau of Investigation. 2004. *Uniform Crime Reports: Crime in the United States—2003.* Available at http://www.fbi.gov/ucr/03cius.htm.

Federal Financial Institutions Examination Council. 2001. *Home Mortgage Disclosure Act Raw Data 2000.* Washington, DC: Federal Reserve System.

Feld, Barry C. 1999. *Bad Kids: Race and the Transformation of the Juvenile Court.* New York: Oxford University Press.

Feliner, Jamie and Marc Mauer. 1998. *Losing the Vote: The Impact of Felony Disenfranchisement Laws in the United States.* Washington, DC: Human Rights Watch and the Sentencing Project.

Fels, Marie H. 1988. *Good Men and True: The Aboriginal Police of the Port Phillip District, 1837–1853.* Carlton: Melbourne University Press.

Ferrante, Joan and Prince Browne, Jr. (editors). 2001. *The Social Construction of Race and Ethnicity in the United States.* 2nd ed. Upper Saddle River, NJ: Prentice Hall.

Fischer, Claude S., Gretchen Stockmayer, Jon Stiles, and Michael Hout. 2004. "Distinguishing the Geographic Levels and Social Dimensions of U.S. Metropolitan Segregation, 1960–2000." *Demography* 41:37–59.

Fischer, Mary. 2003. "The Relative Importance of Income and Race in Determining Residential Outcomes in U.S. Urban Areas, 1970–2000." *Urban Affairs Review* 38:669–696.

Fisher-Giorlando, Marianne and Shanhe Jiang. 2000. "Race and Disciplinary Reports: An Empirical Study of Correctional Officers." *Sociological Spectrum* 20: 169–194.

Fishman, Laura T. 1988. "Vice Queens: An Ethnographic Study of Black Female Gang Behavior." Pp. 83–92 in *The Modern Gang Reader*, edited by M. W. Klein, C. L. Maxson, and J. Miller. Los Angeles: Roxbury.

Flanagan, Constance A. and Lonnie R. Sherrod. 1998. "Youth Political Development: An Introduction." *Journal of Social Issues* 54:447–456.

Flannery, Daniel J. and C. Ronald Huff. 1999. "Implications for Prevention, Intervention, and Social Policy with Violent Youth." Pp. 293–306 in *Youth Violence: Prevention, Intervention, and Social Policy*, edited by D. J. Flannery and C. R. Huff. Washington, DC: American Psychiatric Press.

Forehand, Rex, Gene H. Brody, Lisa Armistead, Shannon Dorsey, Edward Morse, Patricia Simon Morse, and Mary Stock. 2000. "The Role of Community Risks and Resources in the Psychosocial Adjustment of At-Risk Children: An Examination across Two Community Contexts and Two Informants." *Behavior Therapy* 31:395–414.

Forehand, Rex, Kim S. Miller, Robin Dutra, and Meridith Watts Chance. 1997. "Role of Parenting in Adolescent Deviant Behavior: Replication across and within Two Ethnic Groups." *Journal of Counseling and Clinical Psychology* 65: 1036–1041.

Fox, James A. and Marianne W. Zawitz. 2003. *Homicide Trends in the United States: 2000 Update*. Washington, DC: Bureau of Justice Statistics.

Frankenberg, Erica and Chungmei Lee. 2002. *Race in American Public Schools: Rapidly Resegregating School Districts*. Harvard Civil Rights Project. Available at http://www.civilrightsproject.harvard.edu/research/deseg/Race_in_American_Public_Schools1.pdf.

Frankenberg, Erica, Chungmei Lee, and Gary Orfield. 2003. *A Multiracial Society with Segregated Schools: Are We Losing the Dream?* Harvard Civil Rights Project. Available at http://www.civilrightsproject.harvard.edu/research/reseg03/AreWeLosingtheDream.pdf.

Franklin II, Clyde W. 1984. *The Changing Definition of Masculinity*. New York: Plenum Press.

Freeman, Richard B. 1976. *Black Elite: The New Market for Highly Educated Black Americans*. New York: McGraw-Hill.

———. 1996. "Why Do So Many Young American Men Commit Crimes and What Might We Do about It?" *Journal of Economic Perspectives* 10:25–42.

Freeman, Richard B. and Harry J. Holzer (editors). 1996. *The Black Youth Unemployment Crisis*. Chicago: University of Chicago Press.

Fridell, Lorie, Robert Lunney, Drew Diamond, and Bruce Kubu. 2001. *Racially Biased Policing: A Principled Response*. Washington, DC: Police Executive Research Forum.

Fuguitt, Glenn V. and David L. Brown. 1990. "Residential Preferences and Population Redistribution: 1972–1988." *Demography* 27:589–600.

Gaarder, Emily, Nancy Rodriguez, and Marjorie S. Zatz. 2004. "Criers, Liars, and Manipulators: Probation Officers' Views of Girls." *Justice Quarterly* 21:547–578.

Gans, Herbert J. 1962. *The Urban Villagers: Group and Class in the Life of Italian-Americans*. New York: Free Press.

Garbarino, James, Kathleen Kostelny, and Nancy Dubrow. 1991. *No Place to Be a Child: Growing Up in a War Zone*. Lexington, MA: Lexington Books.

Garcia, Mario T. 1989. *Mexican Americans: Leadership, Ideology, and Identity, 1930–1960*. New Haven, CT: Yale University Press.

Garland, David. 2001. *The Culture of Control: Crime and Social Order in Contemporary Society*. Chicago: University of Chicago Press.

Gest, Ted. 2001. *Crime and Politics: Big Government's Erratic Campaign for Law and Order*. New York: Oxford.

Glenn, Evelyn Nakano. 1999. "The Social Construction and Institutionalization of Gender and Race: An Integrative Framework." Pp. 3–43 in *Revisioning Gender*, edited by M. M. Ferree, J. Lorber, and B. B. Hess. Thousand Oaks, CA: Sage.

Goffman, Erving. 1956. *The Presentation of Self in Everyday Life*. Edinburgh: University of Edinburgh: Social Sciences Research Centre.

———. 1974. *Frame Analysis: An Essay on the Organization of Experience*. Cambridge, MA: Harvard University Press.

Goode, Erich. 1990. "The American Drug Panic of the 1980s: Social Construction or Objective Threat?" *International Journal of Addictions* 25:1083–1098.

Goodey, Jo. 1997. "Biographical Lessons for Criminology." *Theoretical Criminology* 4:473–498.

Gorman-Smith, Deborah, Patrick H. Tolan, and David Henry. 1999. "The Relation of Community and Family to Risk among Urban-Poor Adolescents." Pp. 349–367 in *Historical and Geographical Influences on Psychopathology*, edited by P. Cohen, C. Slomkowski, and L. N. Robins. Mahwah, NJ: Lawrence Erlbaum.

Gottschall, Jon. 1983. "Carter's Judicial Appointments: The Influence of Affirmative Action and Merit Selection on Voting on the U.S. Court of Appeals." *Judicature* 67:165–173.

Gould, Mark. 1999. "Race and Theory: Culture, Poverty, and Adaptation to Discrimination in Wilson and Ogbu." *Sociological Theory* 17:171–200.

Gould, Peter. 2002. "Changing Face of Justice." Available at http://news.bbc.co.uk/hi/english/static/in_depth/uk/2002/race/changing_face_of_justice.stm.

Gould, Roger. 2000. "Revenge as Sanction and Solidarity Display: An Analysis of Vendettas in Nineteenth-Century Corsica." *American Sociological Review* 65: 682–704.

Gove, Walter R., Michael Hughes, and Michael Geerken. 1985. "Are Uniform Crime Reports a Valid Indicator of the Index Crimes? An Affirmative Answer with Minor Qualifications." *Criminology* 23:451–502.

Granovetter, Mark S. 1973. "The Strength of Weak Ties." *American Journal of Sociology* 78:360–380.

———. 1974. *Getting a Job: A Study of Contacts and Careers.* Chicago: University of Chicago Press.

Gray, Mike. 1998. *Drug Crazy: How We Got into This Mess and How We Can Get Out.* New York: Routledge.

Green, Donald P., Dara Z. Strolovitch, and Janelle S. Wong. 1998. "Defended Neighborhoods, Integration, and Racially Motivated Crime." *American Journal of Sociology* 104:372–403.

Greene, Helen T. 2000. "Black Females in Law Enforcement." *Journal of Contemporary Criminal Justice* 16:230–239.

Greene, Helen T. and Shaun L. Gabbidon. 2000. *African American Criminological Thought.* Albany: State University of New York Press.

Grieco, Elizabeth M. and Rachel C. Cassidy. 2001. *Overview of Race and Hispanic Origin: 2000.* Washington, DC: U.S. Census Bureau.

Grogger, Jeffrey. 1995. "The Effects of Arrests on the Employment and Earnings of Young Men." *Quarterly Journal of Economics* 51:61–66.

Grossman, Kate N. 2003. "CHA Breaks Ground on Near West Side." *Chicago Sun-Times.* January 10.

Guinier, Lani and Gerald Torres. 2002. *The Miner's Canary: Enlisting Race, Resisting Power, Transforming Democracy.* Cambridge, MA: Harvard University Press.

Gusfield, Joseph R. 1986. *Symbolic Crusade: Status Politics and the American Temperance Movement.* Urbana: University of Illinois Press.

Hagan, John. 1993. "The Social Embeddedness of Crime and Unemployment." *Criminology* 31:465–491.

———. 1995. "Rethinking Crime Theory and Policy: The New Sociology of Crime and Disrepute." Pp. 29–42 in *Crime and Public Policy: Putting Theory to Work,* edited by H. D. Barlow. Boulder, CO: Westview.

Hagan, John and Celesta Albonetti. 1982. "Race, Class, and the Perception of Criminal Injustice in America." *American Journal of Sociology* 88:329–355.

Hagan, John and Ronit Dinovitzer. 1999. "Collateral Consequences of Imprisonment for Children, Communities, and Prisoners." Pp. 121–162 in *Prisons: Crime and Justice,* Vol. 26, edited by M. Tonry and J. Petersilia. Chicago: University of Chicago Press.

Hagan, John, Paul Hirschfield, and Carla Shedd. 2002. "First and Last Words: Apprehending the Social and Legal Facts of an Urban High School Shooting." *Sociological Methods and Research* 31:218–254.

Hagan, John and Alberto Palloni. 1990. "The Social Reproduction of a Criminal Class in Working-Class London, circa 1950–1980." *American Journal of Sociology* 96:265–299.

———. 1999. "Sociological Criminology and the Mythology of Hispanic Immigration and Crime." *Social Problems* 46:617–632.

Hagan, John, Carla Shedd, and Monique Payne. 2005. "Race, Ethnicity, and Perceptions of Criminal Injustice: Toward a Comparative Conflict Theory of Similarity and Difference." *American Sociological Review* 70:381–407.

Hagedorn, John M. 1998. *The Business of Drug Dealing in Milwaukee.* Report. Thiensville: Wisconsin Policy Research Institute.

Hall, Steve. 2002. "Daubing the Drudges of Fury: Men, Violence, and the Piety of the 'Hegemonic Masculinity' Thesis." *Theoretical Criminology* 6:35–62.

Hamid, Ansley. 1990. "The Political Economy of Crack-Related Violence." *Contemporary Drug Problems* 17:31–78.

Hamilton, James D. 1994. *Time Series Analysis.* Princeton, NJ: Princeton University Press.

Hannon, Lance, Peter Knapp, and Robert DeFina. 2005. "Racial Similarity in the Relationship between Poverty and Homicide Rates: Comparing Transformed Coefficients. *Social Science Research* 34:893–914.

Hansson, Desirée and Dirk van Zyl Smit. 1990. *Towards Justice? Crime and State Control in South Africa.* Cape Town: Oxford University Press.

Harer, Miles D. and Darrell J. Steffensmeier. 1992. "The Differing Effects of Economic Inequality on Black and White Rates of Violence." *Social Forces* 70:1035–1054.

Harper, Sara. 1991. "The Judicial Council of the National Bar Association, 1971–1991." Pp. 3–4 in *Elected and Appointed Black Judges in the United States, 1991.* Washington, DC: Joint Center for Political and Economic Studies and the Judicial Council of the National Bar Association.

Harris, Angela. 1990. "Race and Essentialism in Feminist Legal Theory." *Stanford Law Review* 42:581–616.

Harris, Mary G. 1988. *Cholas: Latino Girls and Gangs.* New York: AMS.

Harrison, Paige M. and Allen J. Beck. 2003. *Prisoners in 2002.* NCJ 200248. Washington, DC: U.S. Department of Justice.

Hawdon, James E. 2001. "The Role of Presidential Rhetoric in the Creation of a Moral Panic: Reagan, Bush, and the War on Drugs." *Deviant Behavior* 22:419–445.

Hawkins, Darnell F. 1987. "Beyond Anomalies: Rethinking the Conflict Perspective on Race and Criminal Punishment." *Social Forces* 65:719–745.

———. (editor). 1995. *Ethnicity, Race, and Crime: Perspectives across Time and Place.* Albany: State University of New York Press.

———. 2003. "Editor's Introduction." Pp. xiii–xxv in *Violent Crime: Assessing Race and Ethnic Differences.* New York: Cambridge University Press.

Hawkins, Darnell F., Samuel L. Myers, Jr., and Randolph N. Stone (editors). 2003. *Crime Control and Social Justice: The Delicate Balance.* Westport, CT: Greenwood.

Hays, Sharon. 1994. "Structure and Agency and the Sticky Problem of Culture." *Sociological Theory* 12:57–72.

Heimer, Karen. 1995. "Gender, Race, and Pathways to Delinquency: An Interactionist Analysis." Pp. 140–173 in *Crime and Inequality,* edited by J. Hagan and R. D. Peterson. Palo Alto, CA: Stanford University Press.

———. 1996. "Gender, Interaction, and Delinquency: Testing a Theory of Differential Social Control." *Social Psychology Quarterly* 59:39–61.

———. 1997. "Socioeconomic Status, Subcultural Definitions, and Violent Delinquency." *Social Forces* 75:799–833.

Heimer, Karen and Stacy De Coster. 1999. "The Gendering of Violent Delinquency." *Criminology* 37:277–317.

Heimer, Karen and Ross L. Matsueda. 1994. "Role-Taking, Role Commitment, and Delinquency: A Theory of Differential Social Control." *American Sociological Review* 59:365–390.

Henderson, Martha L. and Francis T. Cullen. 1997. "The Impact of Race on Perceptions of Criminal Justice." *Journal of Criminal Justice* 25:447–462.

Herbert, Steve. 1997. *Policing Space: Territoriality and the Los Angeles Police Department.* Minneapolis: University of Minnesota Press.

Herman, Madelynn M. 2002. *Race and Ethnic Bias Trends in 2002: Diversity in the Courts.* Williamsburg, VA: National Center for State Courts Knowledge and Information Services Office.

Hero, Rodney E. and Caroline J. Tolbert. 1995. "Latinos and Substantive Representation in the U.S. House of Representatives: Direct, Indirect, Nonexistent?" *American Journal of Political Science* 39:640–652.

Higginbotham, A. Leon. 1992. "The Case of the Missing Black Judges." *New York Times,* July 29, A21.

Hindelang, Michael J. 1981. "Variations in Sex-Race-Age-Specific Incident Rates of Offending." *American Sociological Review* 46:461–474.

Hirschfield, Paul. 2003. "Preparing for Prison? The Impact of Legal Sanctions on Educational Performance." Ph.D. Dissertation, Department of Sociology, Northwestern University.

Hochschild, Jennifer L. 1995. *Facing Up to the American Dream: Race, Class, and the Soul of the Nation.* Princeton, NJ: Princeton University Press.

Holdaway, Simon. 1996. *The Racialisation of British Policing.* New York: Macmillan.
———. 1997. "Some Recent Approaches to the Study of Race in Criminological Research: Race as Social Process." *British Journal of Criminology* 37:383–400.
Holdaway, Simon and Anne-Marie Barron. 1997. *Resigners? The Experience of Black and Asian Police Officers.* Hampshire: Macmillan.
Holmes, Malcolm D. 1998. "Perceptions of Abusive Police Practices in a U.S.–Mexico Border Community." *Social Science Journal* 11:107–118.
Holmes, Malcolm D., Harmon M. Hosch, Howard C. Daudistel, Dolores A. Perez, and Joseph B. Graves. 1993. "Judges' Ethnicity and Minority Sentencing: Evidence Concerning Hispanics." *Social Science Quarterly* 74:496–506.
hooks, bell. 1981. *Ain't I a Woman: Black Women and Feminism.* Boston, MA: South End.
Horowitz, Ruth. 1983. *Honor and the American Dream: Culture and Identity in a Chicano Community.* New Brunswick, NJ: Rutgers University Press.
———. 1987. "Community-Tolerance of Gang Violence." *Social Problems* 34:437–449.
Howell, James C. and Debra K. Gleason. 1999. "Youth Gang Drug Trafficking." *Juvenile Justice Bulletin,* December 1–11.
Hughes, Langston. 1932. *Scottsboro Limited: Four Poems and a Play in Verse.* New York: Golden Stair.
Irwin, John. 1980. *Prisons in Turmoil.* Boston: Little, Brown.
Jackson, Jerome E. and Sue Ammen. 1996. "Race and Correctional Officers' Punitive Attitudes toward Treatment Programs for Inmates." *Journal of Criminal Justice* 24:153–166.
Jackson, John. 2001. *Harlemworld: Doing Race and Class in Contemporary Black America.* Chicago: University of Chicago Press.
Jackson, Kenneth T. (Introduction) and John B. Manbeck (Editor). 1998. *The Neighborhoods of Brooklyn.* New Haven, CT: Yale University Press.
Jacobs, James B. and Jay Cohen. 1978. "The Impact of Racial Integration on the Police." *Journal of Police Science and Administration* 6:168–183.
Jacobs, James B. and Lawrence J. Kraft. 1978. "Integrating the Keepers: A Comparison of Black and White Prison Guards in Illinois." *Social Problems* 25:304–318.
Jacobs, Jane. 1962. *The Death and Life of Great American Cities.* New York: Vintage.
Jankowski, Martin Sanchez. 1991. *Islands in the Street: Gangs and American Urban Society.* Berkeley: University of California Press.
Janowitz, Morris. 1967. *The Community Press in an Urban Setting: The Social Elements of Urbanism.* 2nd ed. Chicago: University of Chicago Press.
———. 1975. "Sociological Theory and Social Control." *American Journal of Sociology* 81:82–108.
Jargowsky, Paul A. 1996. "Take the Money and Run: Economic Segregation in U.S. Metropolitan Areas." *American Sociological Review* 61:984–998.

Jargowsky, Paul A. 1997. *Poverty and Place: Ghettos, Barrios, and the American City.* New York: Russell Sage Foundation.

Jasinski, Jana L., Nancy L. Asdigian, and Glenda Kaufman Kantor. 1997. "Ethnic Adaptations to Occupational Strain: Work-Related Stress, Drinking, and Wife Assault among Anglo and Hispanic Husbands." *Journal of Interpersonal Violence* 12:814–831.

Jensen, Eric L. and Jurg Gerber. 1998. "The Social Construction of Drug Problems: An Historical Overview." Pp. 1–23 in *The New War on Drugs: Symbolic Politics and Criminal Justice Policy,* edited by E. L. Jensen and J. Gerber. Cincinnati: Anderson Publishing.

Joe, Karen A. and Meda Chesney-Lind. 1995. "Just Every Mother's Angel: An Analysis of Gender and Ethnic Variations in Youth Gang Membership." *Gender and Society* 9:408–430.

Jöreskog, Karl G. and Dag Sörbom. 1996–2001. *LISREL 8: User's Reference Guide.* Lincolnwood, IL: Scientific Software International.

Jurik, Nancy C. 1985. "Individual and Organizational Determinants of Correctional Officer Attitudes toward Inmates." *Criminology* 23:523–539.

Kalleberg, Arne L. and Aage B. Sørenson. 1979. "The Sociology of Labor Markets." *Annual Review of Sociology* 5:351–379.

Kamin, Blair. 1998. "Out of Housing, into Homes." *Chicago Tribune,* March 31.

Kanan, James W. and Matthew V. Pruitt. 2002. "Modeling Fear of Crime and Perceived Victimization Risk: The (In)Significance of Neighborhood Integration." *Sociological Inquiry* 72:527–548.

Karmen, Andrew. 2000. *New York Murder Mystery.* New York: New York University Press.

———. 2004. "Zero Tolerance in New York City: Hard Questions for a Get-Tough Policy." Pp. 23–39 in *From Hard Cop, Soft Cop: Dilemmas and Debates in Contemporary Policing,* edited by R. H. Burke. Portland, OR: Willan.

Kasarda, John D. 1985. "The Severely Distressed in Economically Transformed Cities." Pp. 45–98 in *Drugs, Crime, and Social Isolation: Barriers to Urban Opportunity,* edited by A. V. Harrell and G. E. Peterson. Washington, DC: Urban Institute.

———. 1989. "Urban Industrial Transition and the Underclass." *Annals of the American Academy of Political and Social Science* 501:26–47.

Kasarda, John D. and Morris Janowitz. 1974. "Community Attachment in Mass Society." *American Sociological Review* 39:328–339.

Katz, Jack. 1988. *Seductions of Crime: Moral and Sensual Attractions in Doing Evil.* New York: Basic Books.

Kennedy, Randall. 1997. *Race, Crime, and the Law.* New York: Pantheon.

Kenway, Jane and Anna Kraack. 2004. "Reordering Work and Destabilizing Masculinity." Pp. 95–109 in *Learning to Labor in New Times,* edited by N. Dolby and G. Dimitriadis (with P. Willis). New York: Routledge.

Kim, Sunwoong. 2000. "Race and Home Price Appreciation in Urban Neighborhoods: Evidence from Milwaukee, Wisconsin." *Review of Black Political Economy* 28:9–28.

Kimmel, Michael. 1996. *Manhood in America: A Cultural History.* New York: Free Press.

Kituai, August I. K. 1998. *My Gun, My Brother: The World of the Papua New Guinea Colonial Police, 1920–1960.* Honolulu: University of Hawaii Press.

Kleck, Gary. 1981. "Racial Discrimination in Criminal Sentencing: A Critical Evaluation of the Evidence with Additional Evidence on the Death Penalty." *American Sociological Review* 46:783–805.

Klein, Dorie and June Kress. 1976. "Any Woman's Blues: A Critical Overview of Women, Crime, and the Criminal Justice System." *Crime and Social Justice* 5: 34–49.

Klein, Malcolm W. 1971. *Street Gangs and Street Workers.* Englewood Cliffs, NJ: Prentice Hall.

———. 1995. *The American Street Gang: Its Nature, Prevalence, and Control.* New York: Oxford University Press.

Kornblum, William. 1993. "Drug Legalization and the Minority Poor." Pp. 115–135 in *Confronting Drug Policy: Illicit Drugs in a Free Society,* edited by R. Bayer and G. M. Oppenhiemer. New York: Cambridge University Press.

Kornhauser, Ruth Rosner. 1978. *Social Sources of Delinquency: An Appraisal of Analytic Models.* Chicago: University of Chicago Press.

Koss, Mary P., Christine A. Gidycz, and Nadine Wisniewski. 1987. "The Scope of Rape: Incidence and Prevalence of Sexual Aggression and Victimization in a National Sample of Higher Education Students." *Journal of Consulting and Clinical Psychology* 55:162–170.

Krivo, Lauren J. and Ruth D. Peterson. 1996. "Extremely Disadvantaged Neighborhoods and Urban Crime." *Social Forces* 75:619–650.

———. 2000. "The Structural Context of Homicide: Accounting for Racial Differences in Process." *American Sociological Review* 65:547–559.

Kubrin, Charis E. and Ronald Weitzer. 2003. "Retaliatory Homicide: Concentrated Disadvantage and Neighborhood Culture." *Social Problems* 50:157–180.

LaFree, Gary D. 1989. *Rape and Criminal Justice: The Social Construction of Sexual Assault.* Belmont, CA: Wadsworth.

———. 1995. "Race and Crime Trends in the United States, 1946–1990." Pp. 169–193 in *Ethnicity, Race, and Crime: Perspectives across Time and Place,* edited by D. F. Hawkins. Albany: State University of New York Press.

———. 1998. *Losing Legitimacy: Street Crime and the Decline of Social Institutions in America.* Boulder, CO: Westview.

———. 2005. "Evidence for Elite Convergence in Cross-National Homicide Victimization Trends, 1956 to 2000." *Sociological Quarterly* 46:191–211.

LaFree, Gary D. and Kris A. Drass. 1996. "The Effect of Changes in Interracial

Income Inequality and Educational Attainment on Changes in Arrest Rates for African Americans and Whites, 1957 to 1990." *American Sociological Review* 61: 614–634.

LaFree, Gary D. and Kris A. Drass. 2002. "Counting Crime Booms among Nations: Evidence for Homicide Victimization Rates, 1956–1998." *Criminology* 40:769–800.

LaFree, Gary D., Kris A. Drass, and Patrick O'Day. 1992. "Race and Crime in Postwar America: Determinants of African-American and White Rates, 1957–1988." *Criminology* 30:157–188.

LaFree, Gary D. and Gwen Hunnicutt. 2005. "Examining Female and Male Homicide Victimization Trends in 35 Nations, 1950 to 2001." Pp. 195–229 in *Gender and Crime: Patterns in Victimization and Offending*, edited by Karen Heimer and Candace Kruttschnitt. New York: New York University Press.

Laidler, Karen Joe. 2002. "'Senator, Sir, Meet Susie Wong and the Inscrutable Fu Manchu.'" Pp. 37–44 in *Images of Color, Images of Crime*, edited by C. R. Mann and M. S. Zatz. 2nd ed. Los Angeles: Roxbury.

Laidler, Karen A. Joe and Geoffrey Hunt. 1997. "Violence and Social Organization in Female Gangs." *Social Justice* 24:148–169.

Lamont, Michèle. 2000. *The Dignity of Working Men: Morality and the Boundaries of Race, Class, and Immigration*. Cambridge, MA: Harvard University Press and Russell Sage Foundation.

Lamont, Michèle and Virág Molnár. 2002. "The Study of Boundaries in the Social Sciences." *Annual Review of Sociology* 28:167–195.

Land, Kenneth C., Patricia L. McCall, and Lawrence E. Cohen. 1990. "Structural Covariates of Homicide Rates: Are There Any Invariances across Time and Social Space?" *American Journal of Sociology* 95:922–963.

Laub, John H. 2004. "The Life Course of Criminology in the United States: The American Society of Criminology 2003 Presidential Address." *Criminology* 42: 1–26.

Laub, John H. and Robert J. Sampson. 2004. "Strategies for Bridging the Quantitative and Qualitative Divide: Studying Crime over the Life Course." *Research in Human Development* 1:81–99.

Lauderback, David, Joy Hansen, and Dan Waldorf. 1992. "Sisters are Doin' It for Themselves: A Black Female Gang in San Francisco." *Gang Journal* 1:57–70.

Lauderdale, Pat and James Inverarity. 1984. "Rationalization of Economy and Bureaucracy: The Regulation of Opiates." *Journal of Drug Issues* 14:567–578.

Lauritsen, Janet L. 2001. "The Social Ecology of Violent Victimization: Individual and Contextual Effects in the NCVS." *Journal of Quantitative Criminology* 17:3–32.

———. 2003. *How Families and Communities Influence Youth Victimization*. Washington, DC: U.S. Department of Justice, Office of Juvenile Justice and Delinquency Prevention.

Lauritsen, Janet L., Robert J. Sampson, and John H. Laub. 1991. "The Link between Offending and Victimization among Adolescents." *Criminology* 29:265–292.

Lauritsen, Janet L. and Robin J. Shaum. 2004. "The Social Ecology of Violence against Women." *Criminology* 42:323–357.

Lauritsen, Janet L. and Norman A. White. 2001. "Putting Violence in Its Place: The Influence of Race, Ethnicity, Gender and Place on the Risk for Violence." *Criminology and Public Policy* 1:37–59.

LeBlanc, Adrian Nicole. 2003. *Random Family: Love, Drugs, Trouble, and Coming of Age in the Bronx.* New York: Scribner.

Lee, Matthew T. and Ramiro Martinez, Jr. 2002. "Social Disorganization Revisited: Mapping the Recent Immigration and Black Homicide Relationship in Northern Miami." *Sociological Focus* 35:363–380.

Lee, Matthew T., Ramiro Martinez, Jr., and Richard Rosenfeld. 2001. "Does Immigration Increase Homicide Rates?: Negative Evidence from Three Border Cities." *Sociological Quarterly* 42:559–580.

Leiber, Michael J. 1994. "Comparison of Juvenile Court Outcomes for Native Americans, African Americans, and Whites." *Justice Quarterly* 11:257–279.

Leonard, Eileen. 1982. *Women, Crime, and Society: A Critique of Theoretical Criminology.* New York: Longman.

Levy, Jerold, Stephen Kunitz, and Michael Everett. 1969. "Navajo Criminal Homicide." *Southwestern Journal of Anthropology* 25:124–152.

Liebow, Elliot. 1967. *Tally's Corner.* Boston: Little, Brown.

Lindquist, Christine, Jennifer Hardison, and Pamela K. Lattimore. 2004. "Reentry Court Initiative: Court-Based Strategies for Managing Released Prisoners." *Justice Research and Policy* 6:93–118.

Liska, Allen E., Mitchell B. Chamlin, and Mark D. Reed. 1985. "Testing the Economic Production and Conflict Models of Crime Control." *Social Forces* 64:119–138.

Liska, Allen E., Joseph J. Lawrence, and Andrew Sanchirico. 1982. "Fear of Crime as a Social Fact." *Social Forces* 60:760–770.

Local Community Fact Book: Chicago Metropolitan Area. 1990. Community Renewal Program Study. Chicago: Chicago Review Press.

Logan, John R. and Glenn Deane. 2003. *Black Diversity in Metropolitan America.* Albany, NY: Lewis Mumford Center for Comparative Urban and Regional Research.

Logan, John R. and Steven F. Messner. 1987. "Racial Residential Segregation and Suburban Violent Crime." *Social Science Quarterly* 68:528–538.

Logan, John R. and John Mollenkopf. 2004. "People and Politics in America's Big Cities." Available at http://mumford.albany.edu/census/report.html.

Logan, John R., Brian J. Stults, and Reynolds Farley. 2004. "Segregation of Minorities in the Metropolis: Two Decades of Change." *Demography* 41:1–22.

Lombroso, Cesare and Guglielmo Ferrero. 2004. *Criminal Woman, the Prostitute, and the Normal Woman* (translated and with a new introduction by N. H. Rafter and M. Gibson). Durham, NC: Duke University Press.

Lopez, Ian Haney. 1996. *White by Law: The Legal Construction of Race.* New York: New York University Press.

Loury, Glenn C. 2002. *The Anatomy of Racial Inequality.* Cambridge, MA: Harvard University Press.

Luckenbill, David F. 1977. "Homicide as a Situated Transaction." *Social Problems* 25: 176–186.

Lujan, Carol Chiago. 1995. "Women Warriors: American Indian Women, Crime, and Alcohol." *Women and Criminal Justice* 7:9–33.

Luna-Firebaugh, Eileen M. 2003. "Incarcerating Ourselves: Tribal Jails and Corrections." *Prison Journal* 83:51–66.

Lundman, Richard and Robert L. Kaufman. 2003. "Driving While Black: Effects of Race, Ethnicity, and Gender on Citizen Self-Reports of Traffic Stops and Police Actions." *Criminology* 41:195–220.

Lusane, Clarence. 1991. *Pipe Dream Blues: Racism and the War on Drugs.* Boston: South End Press.

Lynch, James P. and William J. Sabol. 2004. "Assessing the Effects of Mass Incarceration on Informal Social Control in Communities." *Criminology and Public Policy* 3:267–294.

Mac an Ghaill, Mairtin. 1994. *The Making of Men: Masculinities, Sexualities, and Schooling.* Buckingham, PA: Open University Press.

Maddux, James F. and David P. Desmond. 1981. *Careers of Opioid Users.* New York: Praeger.

Madriz, Esther. 1997. *Nothing Bad Happens to Good Girls: Fear of Crime in Women's Lives.* Berkeley: University of California Press.

Maher, Lisa. 1997. *Sexed Work: Gender, Race, and Resistance in a Brooklyn Drug Market.* Oxford: Clarendon Press.

Majors, Richard and Janet Mancini Billson. 1992. *Cool Pose: The Dilemmas of Black Manhood in America.* New York: Macmillan.

Maltz, Michael D. 1998. "Which Homicides Decreased? Why?" *Journal of Criminal Law and Criminology* 88:1479–1486.

———. 1999. *Bridging Gaps in Police Crime Data.* (NCJ Report 177615.) Bureau of Justice Statistics, Washington, DC. Available at http://www.ojp.usdoj.gov/bjs/pub/pdf/bgpcd.pdf.

Mann, Coramae Richey. 1993. *Unequal Justice: A Question of Color.* Bloomington: Indiana University Press.

Mann, Coramae Richey and Marjorie S. Zatz (editors). 2002. *Images of Color, Images of Crime.* 2nd ed. Los Angeles: Roxbury.

Markowitz, Michael W. 2000. "Theoretical Explanations of the Nexus between Race and Crime." Pp. 3–14 in *The System in Black and White: Exploring the*

Connections between Race, Crime, and Justice, edited by M. W. Markowitz and D. D. Jones-Brown. Westport, CT: Praeger.

Marshall, Thurgood. 1993. "Foreword." In *Emancipation: The Making of the Black Lawyer, 1844–1944,* edited by J. C. Smith. Philadelphia: University of Pennsylvania Press.

Martinez, Michael. 1998. "Chicago Schools, Police Target Violent Juveniles: Records of Arrests, Offenses to Be Shared." *Chicago Tribune Metro,* January 8.

Martinez, Ramiro, Jr. 2000. "Immigration and Urban Violence: The Link between Immigrant Latinos and Types of Homicide." *Social Science Quarterly* 81:363–374.

———. 2002. *Latino Homicide: Immigration, Violence, and Community.* New York: Routledge.

Martinez, Ramiro, Jr., and Matthew T. Lee. 2000a. "Comparing the Context of Immigrant Homicides in Miami: Haitians, Jamaicans, and Mariels." *International Migration Review* 34:794–812.

———. 2000b. "On Immigration and Crime." Pp. 485–524 in *The Nature of Crime: Continuity and Change, Criminal Justice 2000,* Vol. 1, edited by G. LaFree, R. J. Bursik, Jr., J. F. Short, Jr., and R. B. Taylor. Washington, DC: National Institute of Justice.

Martinez, Ramiro, Jr., Matthew T. Lee, and Amie L. Nielsen. 2004. "Segmented Assimilation, Local Context, and Determinants of Drug Violence in Miami and San Diego: Does Ethnicity and Immigration Matter?" *International Migration Review* 38:131–157.

Massey, Douglas S. 1995. "Getting Away with Murder: Segregation and Violent Crime in Urban America." *University of Pennsylvania Law Review* 143:1203–1232.

———. 1996. "The Age of Extremes: Concentrated Affluence and Poverty in the Twenty-First Century." *Demography* 33:395–412.

———. 2001. "Segregation and Violent Crime in Urban America." Pp. 317–344 in *Problem of the Century: Racial Stratification in the United States,* edited by E. Anderson and D. S. Massey. New York: Russell Sage Foundation.

Massey, Douglas S. and Nancy Denton. 1993. *American Apartheid: Segregation and the Making of the Underclass.* Cambridge, MA: Harvard University Press.

Mastrofski, Stephen, Michael Reisig, and John McCluskey. 2002. "Police Disrespect toward the Public: An Encounter-Based Analysis." *Criminology* 40:519–552.

Matsuda, Mari. 1992. "When the First Quail Calls: Multiple Consciousness as Jurisprudential Method." *Women's Rights Law Report* 14:297–300.

Matsueda, Ross L. 1988. "The Current State of Differential Association Theory." *Crime and Delinquency* 34:277–306.

———. 1992. "Reflected Appraisals, Parental Labeling, and Delinquency: Specifying a Symbolic Interactionist Theory." *American Journal of Sociology* 97:1577–1611.

Matsueda, Ross L. and Karen Heimer. 1987. "Race, Family Structure, and Delinquency: A Test of Differential Association and Social Control Theories." *American Sociological Review* 52:826–840.

———. 1997. "A Symbolic Interactionist Theory of Role-Transitions, Role-Commitments, and Delinquency." Pp. 163–213 in *Developmental Theories of Crime and Delinquency*, edited by T. P. Thornberry. New Brunswick, NJ: Transaction.

Mauer, Marc. 1999. *Race to Incarcerate*. New York: New Press.

Mauer, Marc and Meda Chesney-Lind. 2002. *Invisible Punishment: The Collateral Consequences of Mass Imprisonment*. New York: New Press.

McCall, George J. and J. L. Simmons. 1978. *Identities and Interaction*. New York: Free Press.

McGahey, Richard M. 1986. "Economic Conditions, Neighborhood Organization, and Urban Crime." Pp. 231–270 in *Communities and Crime*, edited by A. J. Reiss, Jr., and M. Tonry. Chicago: University of Chicago Press.

McGillivray, Anne and Brenda Comaskey. 1999. *Black Eyes All of the Time: Intimate Violence, Aboriginal Women, and the Justice System*. Toronto: University of Toronto Press.

McLanahan, Sara and Larry Bumpass. 1998. "Intergenerational Consequences of Family Disruption." *American Journal of Sociology* 94:130–152.

McLanahan, Sara and Gary Sandefur. 1994. *Growing Up with a Single Parent: What Hurts, What Helps*. Cambridge, MA: Harvard University Press.

McLloyd, Vonnie C. 1997. "The Impact of Poverty and Low Socioeconomic Status on the Socioemotional Functioning of African-American Children and Adolescents: Mediating Effects." Pp. 7–34 in *Social and Emotional Adjustment and Family Relations in Ethnic Minority Families*, edited by R. D. Taylor and M. C. Wang. Mahwah, NJ: Erlbaum.

McNulty, Thomas L. 1999. "The Residential Process and the Ecological Concentration of Race, Poverty, and Violent Crime in New York City." *Sociological Focus* 32:25–42.

———. 2001. "Assessing the Race-Violence Relationship at the Macro Level: The Assumption of Racial Invariance and the Problem of Restricted Distributions." *Criminology* 467–490.

McNulty, Thomas L. and Paul E. Bellair. 2003a. "Explaining Racial and Ethnic Differences in Adolescent Violence: Structural Disadvantage, Family Well-Being, and Social Capital." *Justice Quarterly* 20:201–231.

———. 2003b. "Explaining Racial and Ethnic Differences in Serious Adolescent Violent Behavior." *Criminology* 41:709–748.

McNulty, Thomas L. and Steven R. Holloway. 2000. "Race, Crime, and Public Housing in Atlanta: Testing a Conditional Effect Hypothesis." *Social Forces* 79: 707–729.

McRobbie, Angela. 1980. "Settling Accounts with Subcultures: A Feminist Critique." *Screen Education* 34:37–49.

Mead, George. 1934. *Mind, Self, and Society.* Chicago: University of Chicago Press.

Meehan, Albert J. and Michael C. Ponder. 2002. "Race and Place: The Ecology of Racial Profiling African American Motorists." *Justice Quarterly* 19:399–430.

Melton, Ada Pecos. 2002. "Images of Crime and Punishment: Traditional and Contemporary Tribal Justice." Pp. 164–176 in *Images of Color, Images of Crime,* edited by C. R. Mann and M. S. Zatz. 2nd ed. Los Angeles: Roxbury.

Merry, Sally Engle. 1981. *Urban Danger: Life in a Neighborhood of Strangers.* Philadelphia: Temple University Press.

Merton, Robert. 1938. "Social Structure and Anomie." *American Sociological Review* 3:672–682.

———. 1957. *Social Theory and Social Structure.* New York: Free Press of Glencoe.

Merton, Robert K. (with Alice Rossi). 1957. "Contributions to the Theory of Reference Group Behavior." Pp. 225–280 in *Social Theory and Social Structure,* by R. K. Merton. New York: Free Press of Glencoe.

Messerschmidt, James W. 1986. *Capitalism, Patriarchy, and Crime: Toward a Socialist Feminist Criminology.* Totowa, NJ: Rowman and Littlefield.

———. 1993. *Masculinities and Crime.* Lanham, MD: Rowman and Littlefield.

———. 1995. "From Patriarchy to Gender: Feminist Theory, Criminology, and the Challenge of Diversity." Pp. 167–188 in *International Feminist Perspectives in Criminology: Engendering a Discipline,* edited by N. H. Rafter and F. Heidensohn. Philadelphia: Open University Press.

———. 1997. *Crime as Structured Action: Gender, Race, Class, and Crime in the Making.* Thousand Oaks, CA: Sage.

———. 2000. *Nine Lives: Adolescent Masculinities, the Body, and Violence.* Boulder, CO: Westview.

Messner, Michael A. 1996. *Politics of Masculinities: Men in Movements.* Thousand Oaks, CA: Sage.

Messner, Steven and Robert J. Sampson. 1991. "The Sex Ratio, Family Disruption, and Rates of Violent Crime: The Paradox of Demographic Structure." *Social Forces* 69:693–713.

Miethe, Terance D. and Robert F. Meier. 1994. *Crime and Its Social Context.* Albany: State University New York.

Miller, Jerome. 1996. *Search and Destroy: African-American Males in the Criminal Justice System.* New York: Cambridge University Press.

Miller, Jody. 1998. "Up It Up: Gender and the Accomplishment of Street Robbery." *Criminology* 36:37–65.

———. 2001. *One of the Guys: Girls, Gangs, and Gender.* New York: Oxford University Press.

———. 2002. "The Strengths and Limits of 'Doing Gender' for Understanding Street Crime." *Theoretical Criminology* 6:433–460.

Miller, Jody and Rod K. Brunson. 2000. "Gender Dynamics in Youth Gangs: A Comparison of Males' and Females' Accounts." *Justice Quarterly* 17:419–448.

Miller, Jody and Barry Glassner. 2004. "The 'Inside' and the 'Outside': Finding Realities in Interviews." Pp. 125–139 in *Qualitative Research,* 2nd ed., edited by David Silverman. London: Sage.

Miller, Jody and Christopher W. Mullins. 2005. "The Gendered Context of Young Women's Violence." Pp. 41–66 in *Gender and Crime: Patterns of Victimization and Offending,* edited by Karen Heimer and Candace Kruttschnitt. New York: New York University Press.

Miller, Jody and Norman A. White. 2003. "Gender and Adolescent Relationship Violence: A Contextual Examination." *Criminology* 41:1501–1541.

Miller, Walter B. 1958. "Lower-Class Culture as a Generating Milieu of Gang Delinquency." *Journal of Social Issues* 14:5–19.

———. 1975. *Violence by Youth Gangs and Youth Groups as a Crime Problem in Major American Cities.* Report to the National Institute for Juvenile Justice and Delinquency Prevention. Washington, DC: Department of Justice.

Mindiola, Tatcho, Jr., Yolanda Flores Niemann, and Nestor Rodriguez. 2002. *Black-Brown Relations and Stereotypes.* Austin: University of Texas Press.

The Minnesota Daily. 2003. "School Shootings Will Not Be Stopped by Legislation." Available at www.mndaily.com/articles/2003/09/26/6698. September 26, 2003.

Miranda, Rowan A. and Ittipone Tunyavong. 1994. "Patterned Inequality? Reexamining the Role of Distributive Politics in Urban Service Delivery." *Urban Affairs Quarterly* 29:509–534.

Mirande, Alfredo. 1997. *Hombres y Machos: Masculinity and Latino Culture.* Boulder, CO: Westview.

Mitchell, Michael and Jim Sidanius. 1995. "Social Hierarchy and the Death Penalty: A Social Dominance Perspective." *Political Psychology* 16:591–619.

Moeller, Gertrude L. 1989. "Fear of Criminal Victimization: The Effect of Neighborhood Racial Composition." *Sociological Inquiry* 2:209–221.

Montejano, David. 1987. *Anglos and Mexicans in the Making of Texas, 1836–1986.* Austin: University of Texas Press.

Montoya, Margaret. 1994. "Mascaras, Trenzas y Grenas: Un/masking the Self While Un/braiding Latina Stories and Legal Discourse." *Chicano-Latino Law Review* 15:1–37.

Moore, Joan W. 1978. *Homeboys: Gangs, Drugs, and Prison in the Barrios of Los Angeles.* Philadelphia: Temple University Press.

———. 1989. "Is There a Hispanic Underclass?" *Social Science Quarterly* 70:265–284.

Moore, Joan W. and Raquel Pinderhughes (editors). 1993. *In the Barrios: Latinos and the Underclass Debate.* New York: Russell Sage Foundation.

Morenoff, Jeffrey D. 2003. "Neighborhood Mechanisms and the Spatial Dynamics of Birth Weight." *American Journal of Sociology* 108:976–1017.

———. 2005. "Racial and Ethnic Disparities in Crime and Delinquency in the

U.S." Pp. 139–173 in *Ethnicity and Causal Mechanisms,* edited by M. Tienda and M. Rutter. New York: Cambridge University Press.

Morenoff, Jeffrey D., Robert J. Sampson, and Stephen W. Raudenbush. 2001. "Neighborhood Inequality, Collective Efficacy, and the Spatial Dynamics of Urban Violence." *Criminology* 39:517–559.

Morrill, Calvin. 1995. *The Executive Way: Conflict Management in Corporations.* Chicago: University of Chicago Press.

Morrill, Calvin, Christine Yalda, Madelaine Adelman, Michael Musheno, and Cindy Bejarano. 2000. "Telling Tales in School: Youth Culture and Conflict Narratives." *Law and Society Review* 24:521–565.

Morrison, Toni (editor). 1992. *Race-ing Justice, En-Gendering Power: Essays on Anita Hill, Clarence Thomas, and the Construction of Social Reality.* New York: Pantheon Books.

Moyer, Imogene. 2001. *Criminological Theories: Traditional and Nontraditional Voices and Themes.* Thousand Oaks, CA: Sage.

Moynihan, Daniel P. 1972. "Address to Entering Class at Harvard College." *Commentary* 54:55–60.

Mullins, Christopher W., Richard Wright, and Bruce A. Jacobs. 2004. "Gender, Streetlife, and Criminal Retaliation." *Criminology* 42:911–940.

Musto, David F. 1987. *The American Disease: Origins of Narcotic Control.* London: Oxford University Press.

———. 1999. *The American Disease: Origins of Narcotic Control.* 3rd ed. New York: Oxford University Press.

Myers, Laura B., Myrna Cintron, and Kathryn Scarborough. 2000. "Latinos: The Conceptualization of Race." Pp. 151–180 in *Multicultural Perspectives in Criminal Justice and Criminology,* 2nd ed., edited by J. E. Hendricks and B. D. Byers. Springfield, IL: Charles C. Thomas.

Myers, Martha A. and Susette Talarico. 1987. *The Social Contexts of Criminal Sentencing.* New York: Springer-Verlag.

Myers, Samuel L., Jr. 2000. "Unintended Impacts of Sentencing Reforms." Paper presented at the American Sociological Association Annual Meetings. Washington, DC.

Napolitano, Janet. 2001. *Report on Racial Profiling.* Phoenix: Office of the Arizona Attorney General.

National Advisory Commission on Civil Disorders. 1968. *U.S. Riot Commission Report.* New York: Bantam.

National Center for Education Statistics. 2003. *Common Core of Data (CCD).* Available at http://nces.ed.gov/ccd/schoolsearch/.

National Institute of Justice. 1996. *1995 Drug Use Forecasting: Annual Report on Adult and Juvenile Arrestees.* Research Report. Rockville, MD: Office of Justice Programs.

Neaigus, Alan. 1998. "The Network Approach and Intervention to Prevent HIV among Injection Drug Users." *Public Health Reports* 113:140–150.

Nelson, Charles R. and Charles I. Plosser. 1982. "Trends and Random Walks in Macroeconomic Time Series." *Journal of Monetary Economics* 10:139–162.

Newman, Kathy. 1999. *No Shame in My Game: The Working Poor in the Inner City.* New York: Knopf.

New York City Department of Planning. 2003. *Community District Profiles.* Available at http://www.ci.nyc.ny.us/html/dcp/html/lucds/cdstart.html.

Nielsen, Amie L., Ramiro Martinez, Jr., and Matthew T. Lee. 2005. "Alcohol, Ethnicity, and Violence: The Role of Alcohol Availability and Other Community Factors for Group-Specific Non-Lethal Violence." *Sociological Quarterly* 46:477–500.

Niemi, Richard G. and Mary A. Hepburn. 1995. "The Rebirth of Political Socialization." *Perspectives* 24:7–16.

Nisbett, Richard E. and Dov Cohen. 1996. *Culture of Honor: The Psychology of Violence in the South.* Boulder, CO: Westview.

Oboler, Suzanne. 1995. *Ethnic Labels, Latino Lives: Identity and the Politics of (Re)presentation in the United States.* Minneapolis: University of Minnesota Press.

O'Brien, Robert M. 1985. *Crime and Victimization Data.* Beverly Hills, CA: Sage.

———. 1996. "Police Productivity and Crime Rates: 1973–1992." *Criminology* 34: 183–207.

———. 1999. "Measuring the Convergence/Divergence of Serious Crime Arrest Rates for Males and Females: 1960–1995." *Journal of Quantitative Criminology* 15:97–114.

———. 2003. "UCR Violent Crime Rates, 1958–2000: Recorded and Offender-Generated Trends." *Social Science Research* 32:499–518.

O'Donnell, John A. and Judith P. Jones. 1968. "Diffusion of the Intravenous Technique among Narcotic Addicts in the United States." *Journal of Health and Social Behavior* 9:120–130.

Office of National Drug Control Policy. 2003. Southwest Border HIDTA. Available at http://www.whitehousedrugpolicy.gov/hidta/noframes/southwest.html.

Office of the Inspector General. 2004. *A Review of the Response by the Department of Justice to Freedom of Information Act Requests for the Workplace Diversity Report.* Washington, DC: Department of Justice.

Oliver, William. 1994. *The Violent Social World of Black Men.* New York: Lexington Books.

Omi, Michael and Howard Winant. 1994. *Racial Formation in the United States.* 2nd ed. New York: Routledge.

Orfield, Gary and Chungmei Lee. 2004. "Brown at 50: King's Dream or Plessy's Nightmare?" Harvard Civil Rights Project. Available at http://www.civilrights project.harvard.edu/research/reseg04/brown50.pdf.

Osgood, D. Wayne and Jeff M. Chambers. 2000. "Social Disorganization outside the Metropolis: An Analysis of Rural Youth Violence." *Criminology* 38:81–115.

Ousey, Graham C. 1999. "Homicide, Structural Factors, and the Racial Invariance Assumption." *Criminology* 37:405–425.

Pager, Devah. 2003. "The Mark of a Criminal Record." *American Journal of Sociology* 108:937–975.

Parker, Karen F. and Patricia L. McCall. 1999. "Structural Conditions and Racial Homicide Patterns: A Look at the Multiple Disadvantages in Urban Areas." *Criminology* 37:447–478.

Patterson, Orlando. 1997. *The Ordeal of Integration: Progress and Resentment in America's "Racial" Crisis.* Washington, DC: Basic.

Pattillo-McCoy, Mary E. 1999. *Black Picket Fences: Privilege and Peril among the Black Middle Class.* Chicago: University of Chicago Press.

Paugram, Serge. 1991. *La Disqualification Sociale: Essai Sur La Nouvelle Pauvreté.* Paris: Presses Universitaires de France.

Pearce, Lisa D. 2002. "Integrating Survey and Ethnographic Methods for Systematic Anomalous Case Analysis." *Sociological Methodology* 32:103–132.

Peek, Charles W., George D. Lowe, and Jon P. Alston. 1981. "Race and Attitudes toward Local Police: Another Look." *Journal of Black Studies* 11:361–374.

Peeples, Faith and Rolf Loeber. 1994. "Do Individual Factors and Neighborhood Context Explain Ethnic Differences in Juvenile Delinquency?" *Journal of Quantitative Criminology* 10:141–157.

Perkins, Douglas D. and Ralph B. Taylor. 1996. "Ecological Assessments of Community Disorder: Their Relationship to Fear of Crime and Theoretical Implications." *American Journal of Community Psychology* 24:63–107.

Peterson, Ruth D. and Lauren J. Krivo. 1993. "Racial Segregation and Black Urban Homicide." *Social Forces* 71:1001–1026.

———. 1999. "Racial Segregation, the Concentration of Disadvantage, and Black and White Homicide Victimization." *Sociological Forum* 14:465–493.

———. 2005. "Macrostructural Analyses of Race, Ethnicity, and Violent Crime: Recent Lessons and New Directions for Research." *Annual Review of Sociology* 31:331–356.

Peterson, Ruth D., Lauren J. Krivo, and Mark A. Harris. 2000. "Disadvantage and Neighborhood Violent Crime: Do Local Institutions Matter?" *Journal of Research in Crime and Delinquency* 37:31–63.

Pettit, Becky, and Bruce Western. 2004. "Mass Imprisonment and the Life Course: Race and Class Inequality in U.S. Incarceration." *American Sociological Review* 69:151–169.

Philliber, Susan. 1987. "Thy Brother's Keeper: A Review of the Literature on Correctional Officers." *Justice Quarterly* 4:9–37.

Phillips, Coretta and Benjamin Bowling. 2003. "Racism, Ethnicity and Criminology: Developing Minority Perspectives." *British Journal of Criminology* 43:269–290.

Phillips, Julie A. 2002. "White, Black, and Latino Homicide Rates: Why the Difference?" *Social Problems* 49:349–373.

Piliavin, Irving and Scott Briar. 1964. "Police Encounters with Juveniles." *American Journal of Sociology* 70:206–214.

Pinderhughes, Ellen E., Robert Nix, E. Michael Foster, and Damon Jones. 2001. "Parenting in Context: Impact of Neighborhood Poverty, Residential Stability, Public Services, Social Networks, and Danger on Parental Behaviors." *Journal of Marriage and the Family* 63:941–953.

Pinderhughes, Howard. 1997. *Race in the Hood*. Minneapolis: University of Minnesota.

Piore, Michael J. 1970. "The Dual Labor Market: Theory and Implications." Pp. 55–59 in *The State and the Poor,* edited by S. H. Beer and R. E. Barringer. Cambridge, MA: Winthrop.

———. 1975. "Notes for a Theory of Labor Market Stratification." Pp. 125–150 in *Labor Market Segmentation,* edited by R. C. Edwards, M. Reich, and D. M. Gordon. New York: Heath.

Pittman, Laura D. and P. Lindsay Chase-Lansdale. 2001. "African American Adolescent Girls in Impoverished Communities: Parenting Style and Adolescent Outcomes." *Journal of Research on Adolescence* 112:199–224.

Pope, Carl E. and Rick Lovell. 2000. *Synthesis of Disproportionate Minority Confinement (DMC) Literature*. Washington, DC: U.S. Department of Justice.

Pope, Carl E. and Howard N. Snyder. 2003. *Race as a Factor in Juvenile Arrests*. Washington, DC: U.S. Department of Justice, Office of Juvenile Justice and Delinquency Prevention.

Portes, Alejandro and Robert L. Bach. 1985. *Latin Journey: Cuban and Mexican Immigrants in the United States*. Berkeley: University of California Press.

Portes, Alejandro and Leif Jensen. 1989. "The Enclave and the Entrants: Patterns of Ethnic Enterprise in Miami before and after Mariel." *American Sociological Review* 54:929–949.

Portes, Alejandro and Ruben G. Rumbaut. 2001. *Legacies: The Story of the Immigrant Second Generation*. Berkeley: University of California Press; New York: Russell Sage.

Portes, Alejandro and Alex Stepick. 1993. *City on the Edge: The Transformation of Miami*. Berkeley: University of California Press.

Portillos, Edwardo L. 1999. "Women, Men, and Gangs: The Social Construction of Gender in the Barrio." Pp. 232–244 in *Female Gangs in America: Essays on Girls, Gangs, and Gender,* edited by M. Chesney-Lind and J. Hagedorn. Chicago: Lake View.

———. 2002. "Latinos, Gangs, and Drugs." Pp. 192–200 in *Images of Color, Images of Crime,* 2nd ed., edited by C. R. Mann and M. S. Zatz. Los Angeles: Roxbury.

————. 2004. *Race-ing to Control and Negotiate Space: Community and Police Relations in a Latino/a Barrio.* Ph.D. Dissertation, School of Justice Studies, Arizona State University, Tempe AZ.

Powers, Ron. 2002. "The Apocalypse of Adolescence." *Atlantic Monthly* March, 3.

Pratt, Travis and Frances Cullen. 2005. "Assessing Macro-Level Predictors and Theories of Crime: A Meta-Analysis." Pp. 373–450 in *Crime and Justice: A Review of Research,* edited by M. Tonry. Chicago: University of Chicago Press.

President's Commission on Law Enforcement and Administration of Justice. 1967. *Crime and Its Impact: An Assessment.* Washington, DC: U.S. Government Printing Office.

Provine, Doris Marie. 2003. "Race in America's First War on Drugs." Paper presented at the Annual Meeting of the Law and Society Association, Vancouver, Canada.

Quillian, Lincoln. 1999. "Migration Patterns and the Growth of High-Poverty Neighborhoods." *American Journal of Sociology* 105:1–37.

Quillian, Lincoln and Devah Pager. 2001. "Black Neighbors, Higher Crime? The Role of Racial Stereotypes in Evaluations of Neighborhood Crime." *American Journal of Sociology* 107:717–767.

Quinney, Richard. 1970. *The Social Reality of Crime.* Boston: Little, Brown.

Quintero, Gilbert A. and Antonio L. Estrada. 1998. "Cultural Models of Masculinity and Drug Use: 'Machismo,' Heroin, and Street Survival on the U.S.–Mexico Border." *Contemporary Drug Problems* 25:147–168.

————. 2000. "'Machismo,' Heroin, and Street Survival on the U.S.–Mexico Border." *Free Inquiry in Creative Sociology* 28:57–64.

Rabrenovic, Gordana. 1996. *Community Builders: A Tale of Neighborhood Mobilization in Two Cities.* Philadelphia: Temple University Press.

Rafter, Nicole Hahn. 2004a. "Ernest A. Hooten and the Biological Tradition in American Criminology." *Criminology* 42:735–771.

————. 2004b. "The Unrepentant Horse-Slasher: Moral Insanity and the Origins of Criminological Thought." *Criminology* 42:979–1008.

Raganella, Anthony and Michael White. 2004. "Race, Gender, and Motivation for Becoming a Police Officer: Implications for Building a Representative Police Department." *Journal of Criminal Justice* 32:501–513.

Ramirez, Roberto R. 2004. *We the People: Hispanics in the United States: CENSR-18.* Washington, DC: U.S. Census Bureau.

Ramirez, Roberto R. and G. Patricia de la Cruz. 2002. "The Hispanic Population in the United States: March 2002." *Current Population Reports, P20-545.* Washington, DC: U.S. Census Bureau.

Ramos, Reyes. 1995. *An Ethnographic Study of Heroin Abuse by Mexican Americans in San Antonio, Texas.* Austin: Texas Commission on Alcohol and Drug Abuse.

Ramsland, Katherine. 2004. *School Killers.* Available at http://www.crimelibrary.com/serial_killers/weird/kids1/index_1.html.

Rand, Michael R., James P. Lynch, and David Cantor. 1997. *Criminal Victimization, 1973–95.* Washington, DC: Bureau of Justice Statistics, Office of Justice Programs.

Raudenbush, Stephen W. and Anthony S. Bryk. 2002. *Hierarchical Linear Models.* 2nd ed. Thousand Oaks, CA: Sage.

Razack, Sherene. 1994. "What Is to Be Gained by Looking White People in the Eye? Culture, Race, and Gender in Cases of Sexual Violence." *Signs* 19:894–923.

Redlinger, Lawrence J. and Jerry B. Michel. 1970. "Ecological Variations in Heroin Abuse." *Sociological Quarterly* 11:219–229.

Reeves, Jimmie L. and Richard Campbell. 1994. *Cracked Coverage: Television News, the Anti-Cocaine Crusade, and the Reagan Legacy.* Durham, NC: Duke University Press.

Reiman, Jeffrey. 2001. *The Rich Get Richer and the Poor Get Prison: Ideology, Class, and Criminal Justice.* Boston: Allyn and Bacon.

Reinarman, Craig and Ceres Duskin. 2002. "The Culture's Drug Addict Imagery." Pp. 32–41 in *Deviance: The Interactionist Perspective,* 8th ed., edited by E. Rubington and M. S. Weinberg. Boston: Allyn and Bacon.

Reinarman, Craig and Harry G. Levine. 1988. "The Politics of America's Latest Drug Scare." Pp. 251–258 in *Freedom at Risk: Secrecy, Censorship, and Repression in the 1980s,* edited by R. O. Curry. Philadelphia: Temple University Press.

———. 1997. "The Crack Attack: Politics and the Media in the Crack Scare." Pp. 18–56 in *Crack in America: Demon Drugs and Social Justice,* edited by C. Reinarman and H. G. Levine. Berkeley: University of California Press.

Reisig, Michael D. and Roger B. Parks. 2004. "Can Community Policing Help the Truly Disadvantaged?" *Crime and Delinquency* 50:139–167.

Reynolds, Henry. 1998. *This Whispering in Our Hearts.* St. Leonards, NSW: Allen and Unwin.

Richie, Beth. 1996. *Compelled to Crime: The Gender Entrapment of Battered Black Women.* New York: Routledge.

Riedel, Marc. 1999. "Sources of Homicide Data: A Review and Comparison." Pp. 75–95 in *Homicide: A Sourcebook of Social Research,* edited by M. D. Smith and M. A. Zahn. London: Sage.

Robbins, Susan P. 1984. "Anglo Concepts and Indian Reality: A Study of Juvenile Delinquency." *Journal of Contemporary Social Work* 85:235–241.

Roberts, Dorothy. 2004. "The Social and Moral Costs of Mass Incarceration in African-American Communities." *Stanford Law Review* 56:1271–1305.

Rodriguez, Nancy. 2005. "Restorative Justice, Communities, and Delinquency: Whom Do We Reintegrate?" *Criminology and Public Policy* 4:103–130.

Rose, Dina R. and Todd R. Clear. 1998. "Incarceration, Social Capital, and Crime: Implications for Social Disorganization Theory." *Criminology* 36:441–480.

Rosenfeld, Richard and Scott H. Decker. 1999. "Are Arrest Statistics a Valid Measure of Illicit Drug Use? The Relationship between Criminal Justice and Public Health Indicators of Cocaine, Heroin, and Marijuana Use." *Justice Quarterly* 16: 685–700.

Ross, Stephen and John Yinger. 2002. *The Color of Credit: Mortgage Discrimination, Research Methodology, and Fair-Lending Enforcement.* Cambridge, MA: MIT Press.

Rountree, Pamela W. and Kenneth C. Land. 1996. "Burglary Victimization, Perceptions of Crime Risk, and Routine Activities: A Multilevel Analysis across Seattle Neighborhoods and Census Tracts." *Journal of Research in Crime and Delinquency* 33:147–180.

Rudwick, Elliott M. 1961a. "Negro Police Employment in the Urban South." *Journal of Negro Education* 30:102–108.

———. 1961b. "The Southern Negro Policeman and the White Offender." *Journal of Negro Education* 30:426–431.

Rumbaut, Rubèn and Alejandro Portes. 2001. "Introduction-Ethnogenesis: Coming of Age in Immigrant America." Pp. 1–20 in *Ethnicities: Children of Immigrants in America.* Berkeley: University of California Press; New York: Russell Sage.

Runciman, W. G. 1966. *Relative Deprivation and Social Justice: A Study of Attitudes to Social Inequality in Twentieth-Century England.* Berkeley: University of California Press.

Russell, Katheryn. 1992. "Development of a Black Criminology and the Role of the Black Criminologist." *Justice Quarterly* 9:667–683.

———. 1998. *The Color of Crime: Racial Hoaxes, White Fear, Black Protectionism, Police Harassment, and Other Microaggressions.* New York: New York University Press.

Russell-Brown, Katheryn. 2004. *Underground Codes: Race, Crime, and Related Fires.* New York: New York University Press.

Sabol, William J., Claudia Coulton, and Jill E. Korbin. 2004. "Building Community Capacity for Violence Prevention." *Journal of Interpersonal Violence* 19:322–340.

Sabol, William J. and James P. Lynch. 2003. "Assessing the Longer-Run Consequences of Incarceration." Pp. 3–26 in *Crime Control and Social Justice: The Delicate Balance,* edited by D. F. Hawkins, S. Myers, and R. Stone. Westport, CT: Greenwood Press.

Sachs, Albie. 1973. *Justice in South Africa.* Berkeley: University of California Press.

Saenz, Rogelio. 2004. "Latinos and the Changing Face of America." New York: Russell Sage Foundation; Washington, DC: Population Reference Bureau.

Saltzman Chafetz, Janet. 1997. "Feminist Theory and Sociology: Underutilized Conceptions for Mainstream Theory." *Annual Review of Sociology* 23:97–120.

Sampson, Robert J. 1987. "Urban Black Violence: The Effect of Male Joblessness and Family Disruption." *American Journal of Sociology* 93:348–382.

Sampson, Robert J. and Dawn Jeglum Bartusch. 1998. "Legal Cynicism and (Subcultural?) Tolerance of Deviance: The Neighborhood Context of Racial Differences." *Law and Society Review* 32:777–804.

Sampson, Robert J. and W. Byron Groves. 1989. "Community Structure and Crime: Testing Social Disorganization Theory." *American Journal of Sociology* 94:774–802.

Sampson, Robert J. and John H. Laub. 1990. "Crime and Deviance over the Life Course: The Salience of Adult Social Bonds." *American Sociological Review* 55: 609–627.

———. 1993. *Crime in the Making: Pathways and Turning Points through Life.* Cambridge, MA: Harvard University Press.

Sampson, Robert J. and Janet L. Lauritsen. 1997. "Racial and Ethnic Disparities in Crime and Criminal Justice in the United States." *Ethnicity, Crime, and Immigration* 21:311–374.

Sampson, Robert J., Jeffrey D. Morenoff, and Felton Earls. 1999. "Beyond Social Capital: Spatial Dynamics of Collective Efficacy for Children." *American Sociological Review* 64:633–660.

Sampson, Robert J., Jeffrey D. Morenoff, and Thomas Gannon-Rowley. 2002. "Assessing Neighborhood Effects: Social Processes and New Directions in Research." *Annual Review of Sociology* 28:443–478.

Sampson, Robert J., Jeffrey D. Morenoff, and Stephen W. Raudenbush. 2005. "Social Anatomy of Racial and Ethnic Disparities in Violence." *American Journal of Public Health* 95:224–232.

Sampson Robert J. and Stephen W. Raudenbush. 1999. "Systematic Social Observation of Public Spaces: A New Look at Disorder in Urban Neighborhood." *American Journal of Sociology* 105:603–651.

———. 2004. "Seeing Disorder: Neighborhood Stigma and the Social Construction of Broken Windows." *Social Psychology Quarterly* 67:319–342.

Sampson, Robert J., Stephen W. Raudenbush, and Felton Earls. 1997. "Neighborhoods and Violent Crime: A Multilevel Study of Collective Efficacy." *Science* 227:918–924.

Sampson, Robert J. and William Julius Wilson. 1995. "Toward a Theory of Race, Crime, and Urban Inequality." Pp. 37–54 in *Crime and Inequality,* edited by J. Hagan and R. D. Peterson. Stanford, CA: Stanford University Press.

Sanders, William B. 1994. *Gangbangs and Drive-Bys: Grounded Culture and Juvenile Gang Violence.* Chicago, IL: Aldine.

Sanders, Jimy M. and Victor Nee. 1996. "Immigrant Self-Employment: The Family as Social Capital and the Value of Human Capital." *American Sociological Review* 61:231–249.

Schuman, Howard, Charlotte Steeh, Lawrence Bobo, and Maria Krysan. 1997. *Racial Attitudes in America: Trends and Interpretations.* Cambridge, MA: Harvard University Press.

Scully, Diana. 1990. *Understanding Sexual Violence*. Boston: Unwin Hyman.

Sellin, Thorsten. 1928. "The Negro Criminal: A Statistical Note." *The Annals of the American Academy of Political and Social Science* 140:52–64.

Sellin, Thorsten and Marvin E. Wolfgang. 1964. *The Measurement of Delinquency*. New York: Wiley.

Serrano, José E. 2003. *Letter to Attorney General John Ashcroft*. Available at http://www.house.gov/serrano/pressarchive/031031_ashcroftletter.html.

Sewell, William H. 1992. "A Theory of Structure: Duality, Agency, and Transformation." *American Journal of Sociology* 98:1–29.

Shaw, Clifford R. and Henry D. McKay. 1942. *Juvenile Delinquency and Urban Areas*. Chicago: University of Chicago Press.

———. 1949. "Rejoinder." *American Sociological Review* 14:614–617.

———. 1969 (1942). *Juvenile Delinquency and Urban Areas*. Rev. ed. Chicago: University of Chicago Press.

Shedd, Carla and John Hagan. 2005. "Defiance and Compliance: A Critical Assessment of Race, Crime, and Perceptions of Criminal Injustice." Unpublished manuscript. Evanston, IL: Department of Sociology, Northwestern University.

Shibutani, Tamotsu and Kian M. Kwan. 1965. *Ethnic Stratification: A Comparative Approach*. New York: Macmillan.

Shihadeh, Edward S., and Nicole Flynn. 1996. "Segregation and Crime: The Effect of Black Social Isolation and the Rates of Black Urban Violence." *Social Forces* 74:1325–1352.

Shihadeh, Edward S. and Wesley M. Shrum. 2004. "Serious Crime in Urban Neighborhoods: Is There a Race Effect?" *Sociological Spectrum* 24:507–533.

Shlay, Anne B. 1988. "Not in That Neighborhood: The Effects of Housing and Population on the Distribution of Mortgage Finance within the Chicago SMSA from 1980–1983." *Social Science Research* 17:137–163.

Short, James F. and Fred L. Strodtbeck. 1965. *Group Process and Gang Delinquency*. Chicago: University of Chicago Press.

Silver, Eric and Lisa L. Miller. 2002. "A Cautionary Note on the Use of Actuarial Risk Assessment Tools for Social Control." *Crime and Delinquency* 48:138–161.

Simon, Jonathan. 1997. "Governing through Crime." Pp. 171–190 in *The Crime Conundrum: Essays on Criminal Justice*, edited by L. M. Friedman and G. Fisher. Boulder, CO: Westview Press.

Simons, Ronald, YiFu Chen, Eric Steward, and Gene Brody. 2003. "Incidents of Discrimination and Risk for Delinquency: A Longitudinal Test of Strain Theory with an African American Sample." *Justice Quarterly* 20:827–854.

Simpson, Sally S. 1991. "Caste, Class, and Violent Crime: Explaining Difference in Female Offending." *Criminology* 29:115–135.

Simpson, Sally S. and Lori Elis. 1995. "Doing Gender: Sorting out the Caste and Crime Conundrum." *Criminology* 33:47–81.

Simpson, Sally S. and Carole Gibbs. 2005. "Making Sense of Intersections." Pp.

269–302 in *Gender and Crime: Patterns of Victimization and Offending,* edited by Karen Heimer and Candace Kruttschnitt. New York: New York University Press.

Skogan, Wesley G. 1990. *Disorder and Decline: Crime and the Spiral of Decay in American Neighborhoods.* Berkeley: University of California Press.

————. 1995. "Crime and the Racial Fears of White Americans." *Annals of the American Academy of Political and Social Science* 539:59–71.

Skogan, Wesley G., Lynn Steiner, Jill DuBois, J. Erik Gudell, and Aimee Fagan. 2002. *Community Policing and "the New Immigrants": Latinos in Chicago.* Washington, DC: National Institute of Justice.

Smart, Carol. 1984. *Women, Crime, and Criminology: A Feminist Critique.* London: Routledge and Kegan Paul.

Smetana, Judith G., Hugh F. Crean, and Christopher Daddis. 2002. "Family Processes and Problem Behaviors in Middle-Class African American Adolescents." *Journal of Research on Adolescence* 122:275–304.

Smith, Brent L. and C. Ronald Huff. 1982. "Crime in the Country: The Vulnerability and Victimization of Rural Citizens." *Journal of Criminal Justice* 10:271–282.

Smith, J. Clay, Jr. 1993. *Emancipation: The Making of the Black Lawyer, 1844–1944.* Philadelphia: University of Pennsylvania Press.

————. 1998. *Rebels in Law: Voices in History of Black Women Lawyers.* Ann Arbor: University of Michigan Press.

Smith, James P. and Finis R. Welch. 1977. "Black-White Male Wage Ratios: 1960–70." *American Economic Review* 67:323–338.

Smith, Michael D. 1983. *Race versus Robe: The Dilemma of Black Judges.* Port Washington, NY: Associated Faculty Press.

Snow, David A. and Leon Anderson. 1987. "Identity Work among the Homeless: The Verbal Construction and Avowal of Personal Identities." *American Journal of Sociology* 92:1336–1371.

Snyder-Joy, Zoann K. 1995. "Self-Determination and American Indian Justice." Pp. 310–322 in *Ethnicity, Race, and Crime,* edited by D. F. Hawkins. Albany: State University of New York Press.

"Sojourner Truth's Speech to the Akron Convention, 1851." 1998 (1851). In the Appendices of *A History of the American Suffragist Movement* by D. Weatherford. Santa Barbara, CA: ABC-CLIO.

Sokoloff, Natalie J. 1992. *Black Women and White Women in the Professions: Occupational Segregation by Race and Gender, 1960–1980.* New York: Routledge.

Sparks, Richard F. 1981. "Surveys of Victimization: An Optimistic Assessment." Pp. 1–60 in *Crime and Justice: An Annual Review of Research,* Vol. 3, edited by M. Tonry and N. Morris. Chicago: University of Chicago Press.

Spelman, Elizabeth V. 1989. *Inessential Woman.* Boston: Unwin Hyman.

Spelman, William. 2000. "The Limited Importance of Prison Expansion." Pp. 97–

129 in *The Crime Drop in America,* edited by A. Blumstein and J. Wallman. New York: Cambridge University Press.

Spohn, Cassia. 1990a. "Decision Making in Sexual Assault Cases: Do Black and Female Judges Make a Difference?" *Women and Criminal Justice* 2:83–105.

———. 1990b. "The Sentencing Decisions of Black and White Judges: Expected and Unexpected Similarities." *Law and Society Review* 24:1197–1216.

Spohn, Cassia and David Holleran. 2000. "Imprisonment Penalty Paid by Young, Unemployed Black and Hispanic Male Offenders." *Criminology* 38:281–306.

Squires, Gregory D., Larry Bennett, Kathleen McCourt, and Philip Nyden. 1987. *Chicago: Race, Class, and the Response to Urban Decline.* Philadelphia: Temple University Press.

Squires, Gregory D. and Sally O'Connor. 2001. *Color and Money: Politics and Prospects for Community Reinvestment in Urban America.* Albany: State University of New York Press.

Stack, Carol B. 1974. *All Our Kin: Strategies for Survival in a Black Community.* New York: Harper and Row.

St. John, Craig. 2002. "The Concentration of Affluence in the United States, 1990." *Urban Affairs Review* 37:500–520.

Steffensmeier, Darrell and Stephen Demuth. 2000. "Ethnicity and Sentencing Outcomes in U.S. Federal Courts: Who Is Punished More Harshly?" *American Sociological Review* 65:705–729.

Steffensmeier, Darrell, Jeffery Ulmer, and John Kramer. 1998. "The Interaction of Race, Gender, and Age in Criminal Sentencing: The Punishment Cost of Being Young, Black, and Male." *Criminology* 36:763–797.

Stenson, Kevin and Adam Edwards. 2004. "Policy Transfer in Local Crime Control: Beyond Naive Emulation." Pp. 209–233 in *Criminal Justice and Political Cultures: National and International Dimensions of Crime Control,* edited by T. Newburn and R. Sparks. Cullumpton, UK: Willan Publishing.

Stepick, Alex. 1998. *Pride against Prejudice: Haitians in the United States.* Boston: Allyn and Bacon.

Stepick, Alex, Guillermo Grenier, Max Castro, and Marvin Dunn. 2003. *This Land Is Our Land: Immigrants and Power in Miami.* Berkeley: University of California Press.

Stepick, Alex, Carole Dutton Stepick, Emmanuel Eugene, Deborah Teed, and Yves Labissere. 2001. "Shifting Identities and Intergenerational Conflict: Growing up Haitian in Miami." Pp. 229–266 in *Ethnicities: Children of Immigrants in America.* Berkeley: University of California Press; New York: Russell Sage Foundation.

Stolzenberg, Lisa, Stewart D'Alessio, and David Eitle. 2004. "Multilevel Test of Racial Threat Theory." *Criminology* 42:673–698.

Stryker, Sheldon. 1980. *Symbolic Interactionism: A Social Structural Version.* Menlo Park, CA: Benjamin/Cummings.

Styles, Fitzhugh L. 1934. *The Negro Lawyers' Contribution to Seventy-One Years of Our Progress.* Philadelphia: Summer.

Sudbury, Julia. 2004. *Global Lockdown: Race, Gender, and the Prison-Industrial Complex.* New York: Routledge.

Sullivan, Mercer L. 1989. *"Getting Paid": Youth, Crime, and Work in the Inner City.* Ithaca, NY: Cornell University Press.

Sun, Ivan Y. and Brian K. Payne. 2004. "Racial Differences in Resolving Conflicts: A Comparison of Black and White Police Officers." *Crime and Delinquency* 50:516–541.

Sunshine, Jason and Tom R. Tyler. 2003. "The Role of Procedural Justice and Legitimacy in Shaping Public Support for Policing." *Law and Society Review* 37:513–547.

Sutherland, Edwin H. 1937. *The Professional Thief.* Chicago: University of Chicago Press.

———. 1947. Principles of Criminology. 4th ed. Philadelphia: Lippincott.

Sutherland, Edwin and Donald R. Cressey. 1978. *Principles of Criminology.* 10th ed. Philadelphia: Lippincott.

Suttles, Gerald D. 1968. *The Social Order of the Slum: Ethnicity and Territory in the Inner City.* Chicago: University of Chicago Press.

———. 1972. *The Social Construction of Communities.* Chicago: University of Chicago Press.

Swain, Carol M. 1995. *Black Faces, Black Interests: The Representation of African Americans in Congress.* Cambridge, MA: Harvard University Press.

Swidler, Ann. 1986. "Culture in Action." *American Sociological Review* 51:273–286.

Sykes, Richard E. and John P. Clark. 1975. "A Theory of Deference Exchange in Police-Civilian Encounters." *American Journal of Sociology* 81:584–600.

Takagi, Paul and Tony Platt. 1978. "Behind the Gilded Ghetto: An Analysis of Race, Class, and Crime in Chinatown." *Crime and Social Justice* 9:2–25.

Tang, Eric, Khatharya Um, and Karen Umemoto. 2001. *Asian/Pacific Islander Communities: An Agenda for Positive Action.* Washington, DC: U.S. National Council on Crime and Delinquency.

Tatum, Becky L. 2000. *Crime, Violence, and Minority Youths.* Aldershot: Ashgate.

Taylor, Carl S. 1990. *Dangerous Society.* East Lansing: Michigan State University Press.

Taylor, Terrance J., K. B. Turner, Finn-Aage Esbensen, and L. Thomas Winfree. 2001. "'Coppin' an Attitude: Attitudinal Differences among Juveniles toward Police." *Journal of Criminal Justice* 29:295–305.

Thomas, David A. and Robin J. Ely. 2001. "Cultural Diversity at Work: The Effects of Diversity Perspectives on Work Group Processes and Outcomes." *Administrative Science Quarterly* 46:229–262.

Thompson, Mark E. 2002. "Don't Do the Crime If You Ever Intend to Vote Again:

Challenging the Disenfranchisement of Ex-Felons as Cruel and Unusual Punishment." *Seton Hall Law Review* 33:167–205.

Thornberry, Terence P., and Marvin D. Krohn. 2002. "Comparison of Self-Report and Official Data for Measuring Crime." Pp. 43–94 in *Measurement Problems in Criminal Justice Research: Workshop Summary,* edited by J. Pepper and C. Petrie. Washington, DC: National Academies Press.

Thornton, Timothy N., Carole A. Craft, Linda L. Dahlberg, Barbara S. Lynch, and Katie Baer (editors). 2000. *Best Practices of Youth Violence Prevention: A Sourcebook of Community Action.* Atlanta: Centers for Disease Control and Prevention.

Thrasher, Frederic M. 1927. *The Gang.* Chicago: University of Chicago.

Tilly, Charles. 2004. "Social Boundary Mechanisms." *Philosophy of the Social Sciences* 34:211–326.

Tittle, Charles R. 1994. "The Theoretical Bases for Inequality in Formal Social Control." Pp. 32–44 in *Inequality, Crime, and Social Control,* edited by G. S. Bridges and M. Myers. Boulder, CO: Westview.

Toch, Hans. 1969. *Violent Men.* Chicago: Aldine.

Tonry, Michael. 1995. *Malign Neglect.* New York: Oxford University Press.

———. 2004. *Thinking about Crime: Sense and Sensibility in American Penal Culture.* New York: Oxford.

Travis, Jeremy. 2002. "Invisible Punishment: An Instrument of Social Exclusion." Pp. 15–36 in *Invisible Punishment: The Collateral Consequences of Mass Imprisonment,* edited by M. Mauer and M. Chesney-Lind. New York: New Press.

Travis, Jeremy and Sarah Lawrence. 2002. *Beyond the Prison Gates: The State of Parole in America.* Washington, DC: Urban Institute.

Tuch, Steven A. and Ronald Weitzer. 1997. "The Polls—Trends: Racial Differences in Attitudes toward the Police." *Public Opinion Quarterly* 61:642–663.

Turk, Austin. 1969. *Criminality and Legal Order.* Chicago: University of Chicago Press.

Turner, Margery, Michael Fix, and Raymond Struyk. 1991. *Opportunities Denied, Opportunities Diminished: Racial Discrimination in Hiring.* Washington, DC: Urban Institute Press.

Tyler, Tom. 1990. *Why People Obey the Law.* New Haven, CT: Yale University Press.

Uggen, Christopher. 2000. "The Socioeconomic Determinants of Ill-Gotten Gains: Within-Person Changes in Drug Use and Illegal Earnings." *American Journal of Sociology* 109:146–185.

Uggen, Christopher and Jeff Manza. 2002. "Democratic Contraction? Political Consequences of Felon Disenfranchisement in the United States." *American Sociological Review* 67:777–803.

Uhlman, Thomas M. 1978. "Black Elite Decision Making: The Case of Trial Judges." *American Journal of Political Science* 22:884–895.

Uhlman, Thomas M. 1979. *Racial Justice: Black Judges and Defendants in an Urban Trial Court.* Lexington, MA: Lexington Books.

Ulmer, Jeffrey T. and Brian Johnson. 2004. "Sentencing in Context: A Multilevel Analysis." *Criminology* 42:137–177.

U.S. Bureau of the Census. 1990. *Special Equal Employment Opportunity (EEO) Tabulation, 1990,* generated by author using Census EEO Data Tool. Available at http://censtats.census.gov/eeo/eeo.shtml.

———. 1991. *Census of Population and Housing, 1990: Summary Tape File 3A.* Washington, DC: Bureau of the Census.

———. 2000a. *Census of Population and Housing, 2000.* Washington, DC: Bureau of the Census.

———. 2000b. *Quick Tables: QT-PL. Race, Hispanic or Latino, and Age: 2000 for San Antonio City, Texas.* Available at http://factfinder.census.gov.

———. 2000c. *Special Equal Employment Opportunity (EEO) Tabulation, 2000,* generated by author using Census EEO Data Tool. Available at http://www.census.gov/eeo2000/.

———. 2000d. *Two or More Races: The Geography of U.S. Diversity.* Available at http://www.montagediversity.com/docs/Two%20or%20more%20races.pdf.

———. 2001. *Annual Demographic Survey: March Supplement.* Table 2. Age, Sex, Household Relationship, Race and Hispanic Origin by Ratio of Income to Poverty Level: 2001. Available at http://ferret.bls.census.gov/macro/032002/pov/new02_001.htm.

———. 2002a. *Census 2000: Summary File 3.* Washington, DC: U.S. Bureau of the Census.

———. 2002b. *Poverty in the United States: 2001, Current Population Reports.* Available at http://www.census.gov/prod/2002pubs/p60-219.pdf.

———. 2003a. *Profile of Selected Economic Characteristics: 2000.* Available at http://factfinder.census.gov/bf/_lang=en_vt_name=DEC_2000_SF3_U_DP3_geo_id=05000US01011.html.

———. 2003b. *State and County Quick Facts.* Available at http://quickfacts.census.gov/qfd/states/01/01011.html.

———. 2004. *U.S. Interim Projections by Age, Sex, Race, and Hispanic Origin.* Table 1a. Washington, DC: Bureau of the Census.

U.S. Department of Health and Human Services. 2001. *Youth Violence: A Report of the Surgeon General.* Rockville, MD: U.S. Department of Health and Human Services, Centers for Disease Control and Prevention; National Center for Injury Prevention and Control; Substance Abuse and Mental Health Services Administration, Center for Mental Health Services; and National Institutes of Health, National Institute of Mental Health.

U.S. Department of Justice. 2002. "Analysis of Diversity in the Attorney Workforce: Final Report." Washington, DC: KPMG Consulting.

————. 2003. "Justice Department Initiates New Diversity Program: Press Release (03-070)." Washington, DC.

————. 2005. "Criminal Offenders Statistics." Washington, DC. Office of Justice Programs, Bureau of Justice Statistics.

U.S. Sentencing Commission. 1995. *Special Report to Congress: Cocaine and Federal Sentencing Policy.* Washington, DC: U.S. Sentencing Commission.

Valdez, Avelardo. 1993. "Persistent Poverty, Crime, and Drugs: U.S.–Mexican Border Region." Pp. 173–194 in *In the Barrios: Latinos and the Underclass Debate,* edited by J. Moore and R. Pinderhughes. New York: Russell Sage Foundation.

Valdez, Avelardo, Alice Cepeda, Charles D. Kaplan, and Zenong Yin. 1998. "The Legal Importation of Prescription Drugs into the United States from Mexico: A Study of Customs Declaration Forms." *Substance Use and Misuse* 33:2485–2497.

Valdez, Avelardo and Charles D. Kaplan. 1999. "Reducing Selection Bias in the Use of Focus Groups to Investigate Hidden Populations: The Case of Mexican American Gang Members from South Texas." *Drugs and Society* 14:209–224.

Valdez, Avelardo, Charles D. Kaplan, and Alice Cepeda. 2000. "The Process of Paradoxical Autonomy and Survival in the Heroin Careers of Mexican American Women." *Contemporary Drug Problems* 27:189–212.

Valdez, Avelardo, Charles D. Kaplan, and Edward A. Codina. 2000. "Psychopathy among Mexican American Gang Members: A Comparative Study." *International Journal of Offender Therapy and Comparative Criminology* 44:46–58.

Valdez, Avelardo, Alberto G. Mata, Jr., G. Edward Codina, Katrina Kubicek, and Stephanie Tovar. 2001. *Childhood Trauma, Family Stress, and Depression among Mexican American Gang Non-Injecting Heroin Users: An Exploratory Study.* San Antonio: Final Report to the Hogg Foundation Submitted by the Center for Drug and Social Policy Research, University of Texas at San Antonio.

Valdez, Avelardo and Stephen J. Sifaneck. 2004. " 'Getting High and Getting By': Dimensions of Drug Selling Behaviors among U.S. Mexican Gang Members in South Texas." *Journal of Research in Crime and Delinquency* 41:82–105.

Vazsonyi, Alexander T. and Jennifer M. Crosswhite. 2004. "A Test of Gottfredson and Hirschi's General Theory of Crime in African American Adolescents." *Journal of Research in Crime and Delinquency* 41:407–432.

Vazsonyi, Alexander T., Jeffrey R. Hibbert, and J. Blake Snider. 2003. "Exotic Enterprise No More? Adolescent Reports of Family and Parenting Process in Youth from Four Countries." *Journal of Research on Adolescence* 132:129–160.

Vazsonyi, Alexander T. and Lloyd E. Pickering. 2003. "The Importance of Family and School Domains in Adolescent Deviance: African-American and Caucasian Youth." *Journal of Youth and Adolescence* 322:115–128.

Vazsonyi, Alexander T., Lloyd E. Pickering, Marianne Junger, and Dick Hessing. 2001. "An Empirical Test of a General Theory of Crime: A Four-Nation Comparative Study of Self-Control and the Prediction of Deviance." *Journal of Research in Crime and Delinquency* 382:91–131.

Vélez, María B. 2001. "The Role of Public Social Control in Urban Neighborhoods: A Multilevel Analysis of Victimization Risk." *Criminology* 39:837–864.

Venkatesh, Sudhir Allad. 1997. *The Social Organization of Street Gang Activity in an Urban Ghetto.* Chicago: University of Chicago Press.

———. 1998. "Gender and Outlaw Capitalism: A Historical Account of the Black Sisters United 'Girl Gang.'" *Signs* 23:683–709.

———. 2000. *American Project: The Rise and Fall of a Modern Ghetto.* Cambridge, MA: Harvard University Press.

Visher, Christy A. and Jeremy Travis. 2003. "Transitions from Prisons to Community: Understanding Individual Pathways." *Annual Review of Sociology* 29:89–113.

Vrij, Aldert and Frans Willem Winkel. 1992. "Crosscultural Police-Citizen Interactions: The Influence of Race, Beliefs, and Nonverbal Communications on Impression Formation." *Journal of Applied Social Psychology* 22:1546–1559.

Wacquant, Loic. 1998. "Inside the Zone: The Social Art of the Hustler in the Black American Ghetto." *Theory, Culture, and Society* 15:1–36.

———. 2000. "The New 'Peculiar Institution': On the Prison as a Surrogate Ghetto." *Theoretical Criminology* 4:377–389.

———. 2001. "Deadly Symbiosis: When Ghetto and Prison Meet and Merge." *Punishment and Society* 3:95–134.

———. 2002. "Scrutinizing the Street: Poverty, Morality, and the Pitfalls of Urban Ethnography." *American Journal of Sociology* 107:1468–1532.

Walker, Samuel. 1980. *Popular Justice: A History of American Criminal Justice.* New York: Oxford University Press.

———. 1998. *Popular Justice: A History of American Criminal Justice.* 2nd ed. New York: Oxford University Press.

Walker, Samuel, Cassia Spohn, and Miriam DeLone. 2000. *The Color of Justice: Race, Ethnicity, and Crime in America.* Belmont, CA: Wadsworth.

———. 2004. *The Color of Justice: Race, Ethnicity, and Crime in America.* 3rd ed. Belmont, CA: Wadsworth/Thomson Learning.

Walker, Thomas and Deborah Barrow. 1985. "The Diversification of the Federal Bench: Policy and Process Ramifications." *Journal of Politics* 47:596–617.

Washington, Linn. 1994. *Black Judges on Justice: Perspectives from the Bench.* New York: New Press.

Washington, Michele. 1972. "Black Judges in White America." *Black Law Journal* 1: 241–245.

Wattenberg, Ben J. and Richard M. Scammon. 1973. "Black Progress and Liberal Rhetoric." *Commentary* 55:35–44.

Weitzer, Ronald. 1995. *Policing under Fire: Ethnic Conflict and Police-Community Relations in Northern Ireland.* Albany: State University of New York Press.

———. 1999. "Citizen's Perceptions of Police Misconduct: Race and Neighborhood Context." *Justice Quarterly* 16: 819–846.

———. 2000a. "Racialized Policing: Residents' Perceptions in Three Neighborhoods." *Law and Society Review* 34:129–155.

———. 2000b. "White, Black, or Blue Cops?" *Journal of Criminal Justice* 28:313–324.

Weitzer, Ronald and Steven A. Tuch. 1999. "Race, Class, and Perceptions of Discrimination by Police." *Crime and Delinquency* 45:494–507.

———. 2002. "Perceptions of Racial Profiling: Race, Class, and Personal Experience." *Criminology* 40:435–456.

———. 2004. "Reforming the Police: Racial Differences in Public Support for Change." *Criminology* 42:391–416.

Welch, Susan. 1990. "The Impact of At-Large Elections on the Representation of Blacks and Hispanics." *Journal of Politics* 52:1050–1076.

Welch, Susan, Michael Combs, and John Gruhl. 1988. "Do Black Judges Make a Difference?" *American Journal of Political Science* 32:126–136.

Wendel, Travis and Richard Curtis. 2000. "The Heraldry of Heroin: 'Dope Stamps' and the Dynamics of Drug Markets in New York City." *Journal of Drug Issues* 302:225–260.

West, Candace and Sarah Fenstermaker. 1995. "Doing Difference." *Gender and Society* 9:8–37.

West, Candace and Don H. Zimmerman. 1987. "Doing Gender." *Gender and Society* 1:124–151.

Western, Bruce D. 2002. "The Impact of Incarceration on Wage Mobility and Inequality." *American Sociological Review* 64:526–546.

Western, Bruce D. and Katherine Beckett. 1999. "How Unregulated Is the U.S. Labor Market? The Penal System as a Labor Market Institution." *American Journal of Sociology* 104:1030–1060.

Western, Bruce D., Jeffrey R. Kling, and David F. Weiman. 2001. "The Labor Market Consequences of Incarceration." *Crime and Delinquency* 47:410–427.

Wikström, Per-Olof and Robert J. Sampson. 2003. "Social Mechanisms of Community Influences on Crime and Pathways in Criminality." Pp. 118–148 in *Causes of Conduct Disorder and Serious Juvenile Delinquency*, edited by B. Lahey, T. Moffitt, and A. Caspi. New York: Guilford Press.

Wilbanks, William. 1987. *The Myth of a Racist Criminal Justice System.* Monterey, CA: Brooks/Cole.

Wilkes, Rima and John Iceland. 2004. "Hypersegregation in the Twenty-First Century." *Demography* 41:23–36.

Wilkins, David B. 2004. "From 'Separate Is Inherently Unequal' to 'Diversity Is Good for Business': The Rise of Market-Based Diversity Arguments and the Fate of the Black Corporate Bar." *Harvard Law Review* 117:1548–1615.

Wilkinson, Deanna. 2001. "Violent Events and Social Identity: Specifying the Relationship between Respect and Masculinity in Inner-City Violent Youth." *Sociological Studies of Children and Youth* 8:235–269.

Williams, Patricia J. 1991. *The Alchemy of Race and Rights.* Cambridge, MA: Harvard University Press.

Williams, Terry M. 1989. *The Cocaine Kids: The Inside Story of a Teenage Drug Ring.* Reading, MA: Addison Wesley.

Willis, Paul E. 1977. *Learning to Labor: How Working-Class Kids Get Working-Class Jobs.* New York: Columbia University Press.

Wilson, William Julius. 1978. *The Declining Significance of Race: Blacks and Changing American Institutions.* Chicago: University of Chicago Press.

———. 1987. *The Truly Disadvantaged: The Inner City, the Underclass, and Public Policy.* Chicago: University of Chicago Press.

———. 1996. *When Work Disappears: The World of the New Urban Poor.* New York: Random House.

Wimberley, Ronald C. and Libby V. Morris. 1997. *The Southern Black Belt: A National Perspective.* Lexington, KY: TVA Rural Studios, University of Kentucky.

Wing, Adrien Katherine (editor). 1997. *Critical Race Feminism: A Reader.* New York: New York University Press.

Wolfgang, Marvin and Franco Ferracuti. 1967. *The Subculture of Violence.* London: Tavistock.

Wooldredge, John and Amy Thistlethwaite. 2004. "Bilevel Disparities in Court Dispositions for Intimate Assault." *Criminology* 42:417–456.

World Policy Institute. 2004. *Islam and Elections. Report of the Dialogues: Islamic World—U.S.—The West Workshop* (Amman, Jordan, March 6–8, 2004). New York: New School University.

Wortley, Scot, John Hagan and Ross Macmillan. 1997. "Just Des(s)erts? The Racial Polarization of Perceptions of Criminal Justice." *Law and Society Review* 31: 637–676.

Wright, Bruce M. 1973. "A Black Brood on Judges." *Judicature* 57:22–23.

———. 1984. "A View from the Bench." Pp. 205–218 in *The Criminal Justice System and Blacks,* edited by D. E. Georges-Abeyie. New York: Clark Boardman.

———. 1987. *Black Robes, White Justice.* Secaucus, NJ: L. Stuart.

Wright, Erik Olin and Rachel E. Dwyer. 2003. "The Patterns of Job Expansions in the USA: A Comparison of the 1960s and 1990s." *Socio-Economic Review* 1:289–325.

Yablonsky, Lewis. 1962. *The Violent Gang.* New York: Macmillan.

Yin, Zenong, Avelardo Valdez, Alberto G. Mata, Jr., and Charles D. Kaplan. 1996. "Developing a Field-Intensive Methodology for Generating a Randomized Sample for Gang Research." *Free Inquiry in Creative Sociology* 242:195–204.

Yinger, John. 1995. *Closed Doors, Opportunities Lost: The Continuing Cost of Housing Discrimination.* New York: Russell Sage.

Yoshioka, Marianne R., Jennifer DiNoia, and Komal Ullah. 2001. "Attitudes toward Marital Violence: An Examination of Four Asian Communities." *Violence against Women* 7:900–926.

Young, Alford A., Jr. 1999. "The (Non) Accumulation of Capital: Explicating the Relationship of Structure and Agency in the Lives of Poor Black Men." *Sociological Theory* 17:201–227.

———. 2004. *The Minds of Marginalized Black Men: Making Sense of Mobility, Opportunity, and Future Life Chances.* Princeton, NJ: Princeton University Press.

Young, Iris M. 1990. *Justice and the Politics of Difference.* Princeton, NJ: Princeton University Press.

Young, Thomas J. 1990. "Native American Crime and Criminal Justice Require Criminologists' Attention." *Journal of Criminal Justice Education* 1:111–116.

Young, Vernetta and Helen Taylor Greene. 1995. "Pedagogical Reconstruction: Incorporating African-American Perspectives into the Curriculum." *Journal of Criminal Justice Education* 6:85–104.

Zatz, Marjorie S. 1987. "The Changing Forms of Racial/Ethnic Biases in Sentencing." *Journal of Research in Crime and Delinquency* 24:69–92.

———. 2000. "The Convergence of Race, Ethnicity, Gender, and Class on Court Decision Making: Looking toward the Twenty-First Century." Pp. 503–552 in *Policies, Processes, and Decisions of the Criminal Justice System: Criminal Justice 2000*, Vol. 3, edited by J. Horney, J. Martin, D. L. MacKenzie, R. D. Peterson, and D. Rosenbaum. Washington, DC: National Institute of Justice.

Zatz, Marjorie S., Carol Chiago Lujan, and Zoann K. Snyder-Joy. 1991. "American Indians and Criminal Justice: Some Conceptual and Methodological Considerations." Pp. 100–112 in *Race and Criminal Justice*, edited by M. J. Lynch and E. B. Patterson. New York: Harrow and Heston.

Zimring, Franklin and Gordon Hawkins. 1992. *The Search for Rational Drug Control.* New York: Cambridge University Press.

Zule, William A. and David P. Desmond. 1999. "An Ethnographic Comparison of HIV Risk Behaviors among Heroin and Methamphetamine Injectors." *American Journal of Drug and Alcohol Abuse* 25:1–23.

Contributors

Eric Baumer is Associate Professor of Criminology and Criminal Justice, University of Missouri–St. Louis. He is a recipient of the American Society of Criminology's Ruth Shonle Cavan Young Scholar Award.

Lydia Bean is a Ph.D. candidate in the Department of Sociology at Harvard University. Her research focuses on the cultural models of citizenship that street-level bureaucrats use to make sense of their work.

Robert D. Crutchfield is Professor of Sociology at the University of Washington and past Vice-President of the American Society of Criminology. His research focuses on labor market patterns and criminal behavior.

Stacy De Coster is Assistant Professor of Sociology at North Carolina State University. She conducts research on gender and delinquency, adolescent mental health, and sexual harassment in the workplace.

Kevin Drakulich is a Ph.D. candidate in the Department of Sociology at the University of Washington. His research focuses on criminal victimization, and neighborhood and community processes.

Jeffrey Fagan is Professor of Law and Public Health at Columbia University. He is a Soros Senior Fellow, and a Fellow of the American Society of Criminology. He conducts research on capital punishment, mass incarceration, criminal violence, and legal socialization of adolescents. He is coeditor of *Changing Borders of Juvenile Justice.*

John Hagan is John D. MacArthur Professor of Sociology and Law at Northwestern University and Senior Research Fellow at the American Bar Foundation. He is author of *Mean Streets: Youth Crime and Homelessness* (with Bill McCarthy) and *Northern Passage: American Vietnam War Resisters in Canada.* He is the series editor for New Perspectives in Crime, Deviance, and Law published by New York University Press.

Karen Heimer is Associate Professor of Sociology at the University of Iowa. She is coeditor (with Candace Kruttschnitt) of *Gender and Crime: Patterns of Victimization and Offending,* published by NYU Press.

Jan Holland is a Research Associate for the Center for Violence Research and Prevention in the Mailman School of Public Health at Columbia University. She studies the impact of incarceration on neighborhoods.

Diana L. Karafin is a Ph.D. candidate in the Department of Sociology at Ohio State University. Her work focuses on racial-ethnic inequality, housing discrimination, and crime and community.

Lauren J. Krivo is Professor of Sociology and Associate Director of the Criminal Justice Research Center at Ohio State University. Her research focuses on racial and ethnic inequality in patterns of crime and housing.

Charis Kubrin is Assistant Professor of Sociology at George Washington University. She studies neighborhoods, culture, race, and violence. She is a recipient of the American Society of Criminology's Ruth Shonle Cavan Young Scholar Award.

Gary LaFree is Director of the National Center for the Study of Terrorism and Responses to Terrorism and Professor of Criminology and Criminal Justice at the University of Maryland. He is the author of *Losing Legitimacy: Street Crime and the Decline of Social Institutions in America.* He is the current president of the American Society of Criminology.

Toya Like is a Ph.D. candidate in the Department of Criminology and Criminal Justice at the University of Missouri–St. Louis. Her research focuses on victimization, especially among minority and economically disadvantaged groups.

Ramiro Martinez, Jr., is Associate Professor of Criminal Justice and Public Health at Florida International University. He is the author of *Latino Homicide: Immigration, Violence, and Community.*

Ross L. Matsueda is Professor of Sociology at the University of Washington. His research examines social disorganization, collective efficacy and codes of violence in Seattle neighborhoods, and life course trajectories of substance use and crime. He is a Fellow of the American Society of Criminology and a member of the Sociological Research Association.

Jody Miller is Associate Professor of Criminology and Criminal Justice at the University of Missouri–St. Louis. Her research focuses on gender, crime and victimization. She is the author of *One of the Guys: Girls, Gangs, and Gender,* and a recipient of the American Society of Criminology's Ruth Shonle Cavan Young Scholar Award.

Amie L. Nielsen is Associate Professor of Sociology at the University of Miami. She conducts research on racial/ethnic differences in alcohol use and criminal behavior.

Robert O'Brien is Professor and Head of the Department of Sociology at the University of Oregon. He conducts research on crime trends, age and cohort patterns of crime, police violence, and quantitative methods.

Ruth D. Peterson is Professor of Sociology and Director of the Criminal Justice Research Center at Ohio State University. She is coeditor (with John Hagan) of *Crime and Inequality.* She is a Fellow and former Vice-President of the American Society of Criminology (ASC) and former Co-Chair of ASC's Division on People of Color and Crime.

Alex R. Piquero is Professor of Criminology, Law, and Society and 2005 Magid Term Professor at the University of Florida. He is a member of the MacArthur Foundation's Research Network on Adolescent Development and a recipient of the American Society of Criminology's Ruth Shonle Cavan Young Scholar Award.

Doris Marie Provine is Professor and Director of the School of Justice and Social Inquiry at Arizona State University. She was a Program Officer for the Law and Social Sciences Program at the National Science Foundation. She is the author of *Judging Credentials: Non-lawyer Judges and the Politics of Professionalism.*

Nancy Rodriguez is Associate Professor of Criminal Justice and Criminology at Arizona State University at West Campus. Her research focuses on the role of race/ethnicity and gender in sentencing polices, juvenile court processes, and substance abuse prevention. She is coeditor of *Images of Color, Images of Crime.*

Wenona Rymond-Richmond is a Ph.D. candidate in the Department of Sociology at Northwestern University. She is conducting qualitative longitudinal research on public housing, geographic space, and violent victimization and offending.

Robert J. Sampson is Henry Ford II Professor of the Social Sciences and Chair of Sociology at Harvard University. He is Scientific Director of the Project on Human Development in Chicago Neighborhoods, and a recipient of the American Society of Criminology's Edwin H. Sutherland Award. He is the author of *Crime in the Making: Pathways and Turning Points Through Life* (with John Laub) and *Shared Beginnings, Divergent Lives: Delinquent Boys to Age 70* (with John Laub).

Carla Shedd is a Ph.D. candidate in the Department of Sociology at Northwestern University. Her research seeks to uncover the impact of interactions and experiences with authorities in different social contexts on youth's perceptions of injustice and involvement in crime.

Elizabeth Trejos-Castillo is a Ph.D. student in the Department of Human Development and Family Studies at Auburn University. Her research focuses on the role of family characteristics and immigration in the etiology of adolescent crime and deviance.

Avelardo Valdez is Professor of Social Work and Director of the Office for Drug and Social Policy Research at the University of Houston. His research focuses on substance use and its consequences for Mexican Americans in South Texas and on the U.S.–Mexico border.

Alexander T. Vazsonyi is Professor of Human Development and Family Studies at Auburn University. His research uses a systematic comparative approach to the study of human development. He is the editor of the *Journal of Early Adolescence* and one of the editors of the forthcoming *Cambridge Handbook of Violent Behavior.*

María B. Vélez is Assistant Professor of Sociology at the University of Iowa. Her research examines the relationship between political processes and neighborhood crime for Latino, African American, and White communities.

Geoff K. Ward is Assistant Professor of Criminal Justice at Northeastern University. He studies the scope and significance of racial and ethnic group representation in justice occupations. He was an Andrew W. Mellon Postdoctoral Fellow at the Vera Institute, and served as coordinator of the Africana Criminal Justice Project at Columbia University.

Valerie West is a Research Scientist in the Law School and the Mailman School of Public Health at Columbia University. Her research examines judicial review, capital punishment, and comparative rates of imprisonment in U.S. states.

Vernetta Young is Associate Professor of Administration of Justice in the Department of Sociology and Anthropology at Howard University. She is a coeditor of *African American Classics in Criminology and Criminal Justice,* and coauthor (with Rebecca Reviere) of *Women Behind Bars: Gender and Race in U.S. Prisons.*

Marjorie S. Zatz is Professor of Justice and Social Inquiry and Vice-Provost at Arizona State University. She conducts research on comparative legal systems, and the ways in which race, ethnicity, and gender impact juvenile and criminal court processing and sanctioning. She is author of *Producing Legality: Law and Socialism in Cuba* and coeditor of *Images of Color, Images of Crime* and *Making Law: The State, the Law, and Structural Contradictions.*

Index

Abuse. *See* Victimization; Violence

Action. *See* Agency; Culture-in-action

Adaptations, 22, 111, 119–20, 233; cultural, 8, 16, 29, 223, 241

Addiction/addicts, 227, 230–31, 233, 235, 283–84; among drug sellers, 223, 287, 289

Adjustment, 124–25

Adolescents. *See* Youth

Advantage, 241, 250–51. *See also* Disadvantage

Affective cognition, 25–26

African-Americans. *See* Blacks

Afro-Caribbeans, 45, 95, 108–21

Age, 41, 51, 170, 213, 244, 255n15, 326

Agency, 2, 6, 28, 29, 82, 144, 151, 340

Aggression, 141, 146, 149, 153, 341

Alabama, 123, 127, 135

Albonetti, Celesta, 315

Alcohol: abuse of, 44, 227, 336; prohibition of, 290; rape involving, 164, 167–69, 171

Alienation, 31, 120n14, 336–37, 341

American Indians, 52n19, 120n1; crime rates for, 108; in criminal justice workforce, 78–80; culture of, 40, 43–44, 48, 50; violence among, 41, 174n11; youth, 321

Anderson, Elijah, 23, 30, 142–43, 159, 218, 324–26, 335, 337–41, 345

Anslinger, Harry, 290

Anti-Drug Abuse Act(s), 222, 283–89

Apartheid, 72, 75, 182

Arizona tribes, 51, 52n19

Arrests: drug-related, 262, 264–68, 278; for misdemeanors, 265; racial disparities in, 46–48, 73, 179–98, 314–15, 361–62. *See also* Blacks, arrest rates for; Whites, arrest rates for

Asian Pacific Islanders, 49, 50

Asians, 120n1, 219; crime rates for, 5–6, 108, 204, 207, 213, 215, 217; in criminal justice workforce, 78–80; culture of, 43, 46; heterogeneity of, 200, 362; social disorder among, 214; violence among, 5–6, 41, 217–19; youth, 321

Assaults, 131–32, 133fig.7.1; aggravated, 4, 47, 55, 110, 114–19, 138, 195–97, 207; arrest rates for, 180, 184–87, 189fig.10.1, 190, 192fig.10.2, 193–94; sexual, 144, 159–71

Assimilation: negative, 118; perspective of, 180–81, 183, 194–96; racial/ethnic, 5, 59, 202; segmented, 110–13, 119–20

Atlanta, Georgia, 93–94

Authorities. *See* Courts; Law enforcement; Police

Baca Zinn, 139

Bad girl femininities, 146–47, 149

Barriers: to adaptation, 120; economic, 180; to equality, 331n12; of language, 43–45, 48–51, 109; racial, 354; structural, 8, 223, 314, 336, 342. *See also* Constraints

Barrios, 43, 221–22, 225–27, 232–34. *See also* Ghettos

Bartusch, Dawn Jeglum, 315, 326

Battering. *See* Victimization; Violence

Baumer, Eric, 5, 179

Bean, Lydia, 3, 8, 361, 363

Beckett, Katherine, 282

Behavior, 25–26, 152; anti-social, 126, 182, 233; criminal, 195, 364; gender-related, 146–47; public, 324–25; spatial, 297; standards of, 16; violent, 340

Bellair, Paul E., 14

Bennett, William, 281

Benson, Michael L., 172

Berger, Peter, 27

Biases, urban, 122–23. *See also* Police, biases of